READING CANADIAN WO

Inspired by the question of "what's next?" in the field of Canadian women's and gender history, this broadly historiographical volume represents a conversation among established and emerging scholars who share a commitment to understanding the past from intersectional feminist perspectives. It includes original essays on Quebecois, Indigenous, Black, and immigrant women's histories and tackles such diverse topics as colonialism, religion, labour, warfare, sexuality, and reproductive labour and justice. Intended as a regenerative retrospective of a critically important field, this collection both engages analytically with the current state of women's and gender historiography in Canada and draws on its rich past to generate new knowledge and areas for inquiry.

(Studies in Gender and History)

NANCY JANOVICEK is an associate professor of History at the University of Calgary.

CARMEN NIELSON is an associate professor of History at Mount Royal University.

STUDIES IN GENDER AND HISTORY

General Editors: Franca Iacovetta and Karen Dubinsky

Reading Canadian Women's and Gender History

EDITED BY
NANCY JANOVICEK AND CARMEN NIELSON

UNIVERSITY OF TORONTO PRESS
Toronto Buffalo London

ISBN 978-1-4426-2970-7 (cloth)   ISBN 978-1-4426-2971-4 (paper)

Library and Archives Canada Cataloguing in Publication

Title: Reading Canadian women's and gender history / edited by Nancy Janovicek
and Carmen Nielson.
Names: Janoviček, Nancy, 1968– editor. | Nielson, Carmen J., 1972– editor. Series:
Studies in gender and history.
Description: Series statement: Studies in gender and history | Includes
bibliographical references and index.
Identifiers: Canadiana 20189065834 | ISBN 9781442629707 (hardcover) | ISBN
9781442629714 (softcover)
Subjects: LCSH: Women – Canada – History. | LCSH: Feminism – Canada –
History. | LCSH: Women – Canada – Social conditions. | LCSH: Women's
studies – Canada – History.
Classification: LCC HQ1453 .R43 2019 | DDC 305.40971—dc23

University of Toronto Press acknowledges the financial assistance to its publishing
program of the Canada Council for the Arts and the Ontario Arts Council, an
agency of the Government of Ontario.

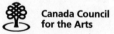

Canada Council   Conseil des Arts
for the Arts   du Canada

ONTARIO ARTS COUNCIL
CONSEIL DES ARTS DE L'ONTARIO
an Ontario government agency
un organisme du gouvernement de l'Ontario

Funded by the   Financé par le
Government   gouvernement
of Canada   du Canada

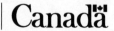

MIX
Paper from
responsible sources
FSC® C016245

Contents

Acknowledgments

It is an honour to belong to the community of feminist scholars reading and writing Canadian women's and gender history. Working on this volume has given us the opportunity to collaborate with some of the women who inspired us to become historians and who taught us that knowing the past strengthens feminist activism. It's given us the chance to have new conversations about feminism and history with friends who were there with us in grad school and at the early stages of our careers. And we have continued to learn from the emerging scholars whose work as PhD students excited us when we first met them at conferences. To support future feminist historians, we are donating our royalties to the CCWH-CCHF Marta Danylewycz Memorial Fund, which supports a scholarship for doctoral students working on women's and gender history from a feminist perspective.

Our first thank you is to the contributors, whose professionalism, collegiality, and dedication to the project made our jobs that much easier. Mike Schubert gave us permission to use the beautiful work of his late wife, Joane Cardinal Schubert, an award-winning Kainaiwa artist. We live and work on the homelands of the Niitsitapi (the Siksika, Piikani, and Kainai), the Îyârhe Nakoda, and Tsuut'ina Nations. The Métis Nation of Alberta, Region III also have strong relationships to these territories. It was important for us to acknowledge our respect for and indebtedness to these nations with the work of an Indigenous artist from this land. Cardinal Shubert's artistic practice engaged with Indigenous sovereignty, politics, history, and the environment. She also mentored emerging Indigenous artists in Alberta and Canada. For us, *Monarch Resting* symbolizes not only the potential for transformation but also the connectedness of all things – land and spirit, past and present, individual and community.

We would also like to thank Len Husband, our acquisitions editor at University of Toronto Press, and the Studies in Gender and History series editors, Franca Iacovetta and Karen Dubinsky, who encouraged us and believed in and supported this project from the beginning. Christine Robertson, the managing editor at UTP, was a great help and managed to keep us on schedule throughout the final stages. Siusan Moffat is responsible for the index; we extend our thanks for her timely assistance.

Mount Royal University's Deans of Arts, Jeffrey Keshen and Jennifer Pettit, and the University of Calgary Dean of Arts, Richard Sigurdson, provided funding for our 2014 workshop in Ottawa and assisted with the book's production costs. We thank them for their support of feminist scholarship.

A lot of our work happened at a Ramsay dining room and Martin L'Heureux made sure we were fed and watered on these writing and production days. He also helped us work through tricky translations in Baillargeon's chapter. He's probably learned more about feminist historiography than he wanted to. But Nancy likes to think that this informs his efforts to make spaces to ensure that women are heard and thrive in his male-dominated profession.

Working on collaborative projects can make or break a friendship. We are happy to report that theoretical debates, difficult conversations, and celebrations at various stages of production have made ours stronger.

READING CANADIAN WOMEN'S AND GENDER HISTORY

1 Introduction:
Feminist Conversations

NANCY JANOVICEK AND CARMEN NIELSON

This collection began as a conversation between the co-editors about middle age. In reflecting on our own experiences, we made connections between our lives and the life course of women's and gender history in Canada. We, like the field, were born in the late 1960s and early 1970s and could be perceived as both young and old, depending on one's perspective. As our conversation drifted from the personal to the professional, we agreed that while Canadian women's and gender history as a field was not as long-lived or well-established as national political history, for example, it is often talked about as if it were much more immature and fragmentary than it really is. Although several excellent essays that assessed the contours of women's and gender history in northern North America have been written for international audiences, these unintentionally amplify the impression of a small field that can be apprehended in 10,000 words or less.[1] We knew that Canadian women's and gender history could sustain, and merited, a broadly historiographical volume of its own. And, as middle age inspires self-reflection, stock-taking, and contemplation of "what next?," a collection of essays that coped with the field's past and future seemed like an idea that's time had come. We envisioned a book that captured the field's continuities and identified discontinuities; offered a platform for established, mid-career, and emerging scholars to reflect on reading and writing Canadian women's and gender history; and brought together the themes, issues, and questions that had animated the field over the long term. We also wanted to show the field's maturity, extensiveness, variety, sophistication, and connectedness to international literature and theoretical perspectives.

Our call for chapters prompted contributors to critically examine Canadian women's and gender history from its first texts to its most recent contributions with the aim of generating new connections, vantage points, and knowledge about the field. The proposals we received exceeded our expectations, and we were inspired by the diverse ways the authors approached our questions. Most were co-authored, demonstrating that feminist history continues to be a collaborative scholarly endeavour. Since we wanted to preserve the contributors' unique interpretations of their projects, we encouraged them to chart their own paths through the literature according to their particular interests and experience. Our objective as editors was to create an open platform for contributors to offer their critiques, judgments, and evaluations according to their own perspectives. What follows are not conventional historiographies.

At the 2015 annual meeting of the Canadian Historical Association (CHA) in Ottawa, we hosted a one-day workshop for the contributors to share drafts, give each other feedback, and discuss the volume's key themes. In this way, the book became a continuation of our initial conversation that extended to include the contributors. Those who could not be present videoconferenced into the discussion. We talked about how various streams of women's and gender history have informed each other, how to deepen the field by privileging diverse and marginalized voices, the ongoing disconnection between English and French historiography, and the potential for new directions.[2] Our introduction to this collection is organized according to some of the themes arising out of our conversations that day: representation and meaningful inclusion in academe and in historical consciousness; the interconnections between feminist politics and the development of the field; and "recovery" history as an ongoing political project. A touchstone question guided our discussions: How can putting past and present historiography into dialogue with each other help us address the field's ongoing silences and absences?

Although the following chapters cover many of the major themes in Canadian women's and gender history, there are some important areas of scholarship that have been left out. Politics, the law, family and domesticity, medicine, and education, for instance, have been topics of interest to women's and gender historians since the field's beginnings, but due to considerations of space or in the absence of viable proposals, these have not received sustained analysis here.[3] There are also new topics and themes that have emerged relatively recently as distinct subfields – such as healthism and disability, body history, and the histories of affect and emotion – which are not represented but are acknowledged by several contributors as offering important theoretical and methodological insights that will shape future research. The impossibility of achieving anything approaching complete coverage in one volume offers only more evidence of the field's breadth and extent.

Feminist Theory and History

We entered graduate school at the height of the divisive debates about whether or not the turn to gender history strengthened or threatened the feminist project of women's history. Joan Wallach Scott's influential 1986 *American Historical Review* article on gender as a category of historical analysis was a synthesis and critique of Marxist and psychoanalytic feminist debates about how to think beyond essentialist theorizations of women as subordinated subjects. Scott criticized these theories because they rested on biological differences between men and women and presented a definition of gender that encouraged historians to examine how perceived gender binaries appeared to be constant while they were in fact various and contingent on historical context. Unpacking the linguistic constructions of how the perceived differences between men and women were crucial to power relations, Scott argued, would bring women's history from the periphery to the centre of all historical analysis and would allow for a deeper interrogation of the differences between women's and men's experiences.[4]

Response to Scott's article divided feminist historians. Proponents of Scott's appeal to linguistic analysis argued that understanding how subjectivity was constructed within discourses of power could transform how race, sexuality, class, and ethnicity intersected with variable ideas about masculinity and femininity across time and space. They agreed with Scott that this approach had more political potential for understanding the inequalities that women faced, and would generate strategies for change that would not deepen these inequalities among women. Many scholars remained staunch supporters of materialist feminist approaches, arguing that advocates of the linguistic turn had oversimplified complex analyses of race, sexuality, and the relationship between women and men in women's history.[5] The chapters here show that while Canadian women's and gender history has found and continues to find value in focusing on the lived experience of gender, attention to the cultural production of gender identities, as well as the material conditions in which these discourses were produced, naturalized, and resisted, has added significantly to our understanding of the Canadian past. Pasolli and Smith's chapter, for instance, traces the development of two central themes in Canadian women's history – women's participation in the paid labour force and the construction of gendered discourses about mothering, caregiving, and unpaid "labours of love." Bringing these two bodies of literature into conversation demonstrates that Marxist feminism's focus on social relations and post-structuralism's consideration of cultural meanings have both made significant contributions to historians' understanding of women's relationships to caregiving work in particular. In her chapter, Stanley rereads key texts in Canadian women's and gender history to explore the tension and conflict inherent in discursive constructions of sexualized bodies and material, embodied experiences. She argues that this discordance belies national mythologies about idealized citizen bodies and offers an important challenge to nationalist investments in normative sexual identities.

Early women's historians' identification with a feminist project committed to challenging "malestream" history quite predictably forestalled enthusiasm for (re)centring men's experiences. The gender turn has nonetheless compelled many women's historians to confront the question of how power is unevenly distributed between the sexes, which necessarily entails evaluating how men are also implicated in the gender system. Excellent scholarship has been produced in Canada since the 1990s,[6] some of which informs the chapters to follow. Katherine M.J. McKenna makes particular note of masculinity studies' underdevelopment and provides an important discussion of masculine norms in early British North America. She uses Kossuth and Walmsley's notion of "bush" and "gentry" masculinity to illustrate the importance of social position to defining manliness in colonial Canada, and she considers the effects of an emerging liberal order on masculine (and feminine) norms and privileges. Brookfield and Glassford's chapter also points to the underdevelopment of masculinity studies and notes that its enormous potential for re-conceptualizing military history remains largely unrealized in Canada. The authors argue that the liberation/transformation paradigm that has dominated women's history perspectives on twentieth-century war since Ruth Roach Pierson's field-defining monograph, *"They're Still Women after All,"* is no longer viable when men's experiences are considered alongside those of women. By integrating analyses of men's gendered experience, as well as the experiences of gender-nonconforming men and women, a new war studies perspective promises to dramatically reconfigure the history of violence and conflict in Canada.

Diverse scholarship in feminist, queer, and trans studies has recently generated important theoretical challenges to the gender binary. Judith Butler's argument about gender – that the notion that humans are either male or female is not a biological fact but, rather, is an effect of interpellations into normative cultural systems that constitute sexed bodies as intelligible and liveable only when they conform to the male/female binary – presents an opportunity for historians to reconsider a two-gender analytical framework.[7] Critics like Anna Krylova argue that post-structural analyses like Joan Scott's, while succeeding in historicizing the gender binary, fail to escape the binarism inherent in the analytical framework of gender. Gender historians have provided a multitude of examples of how, in different times and places, the dualism man/woman was given meaning by differentially valuing these two categories. An assumption that the latter is ascribed less value than the former is at the essence of the gender binary, which Krylova suggests theorists and historians have, in fact, reified rather than challenged. These analyses, she explains, propose that because this valuation is historical and cultural – and not based in biology – then the possibility of escaping the binary exists somewhere in the future. What Krylova argues is that even writing about gender "transgressions" wherein heteronormative scripts are temporarily challenged or discarded, the gender transgressor has nowhere to return to but the confines of the gender binary. In contrast, Krylova proposes historians engage with the notion of a gender *dichotomy*, which she frames as an acknowledgment of difference that does not imply greater/lesser. She challenges historians to consider gender dichotomy as an analytical category and as an experience that is both historical and possible in the now. Krylova poses the question: What have gender historians occluded and suppressed about non-gender-normative experience by using gender as their primary analytical category? Studying these experiences not as transgressions against the gender binary but rather as legitimate experiences outside the gender binary opens up fascinating new avenues of inquiry.[8]

Trans scholars are coming out and are introducing another significant theoretical re-evaluation of the field. Their interventions also offer compelling arguments against the gender binary. A. Finn Enke explains that the power of trans perspectives lies in their recognition of the expectation that all bodies must conform to a stable gender identity while simultaneously understanding that this perceived stability is impossible without the "ubiquity of gender variation."[9] The few histories about transgender experiences in Canada examine trans women's work in strip clubs and paid sex work, analysing how marginal economies created spaces where they could support themselves and form community.[10] Histories of activism emphasize the long struggle to gain trans rights and the limitations of rights frameworks to extend to gender variance.[11] An important part of that struggle has been intense opposition from some feminists who sought to protect women-only spaces by insisting that only "women-born-women" should have access; Kimberly Nixon's 1995 human rights complaint against Vancouver Rape Relief is perhaps the most well-known Canadian example. Bobby Noble, a trans activist and scholar who worked in rape crisis centres, sex workers advocacy groups, and organized Take Back the Night marches, explains, "*Trans* entities have always been present inside feminist spaces; to make a claim to the contrary would be to fly in the face of at least thirty years of writing and debate about the presence of *trans-bodies* 'on the front line.'"[12] Bringing trans lives into mainstream academic history will require that women's and gender historians begin from the premise that transgender people have always been everywhere. Finding these histories is only more evidence that recovery history is a vital, ongoing political project.

Community, Politics, and Recovery History

Community activists are often the first to recognize the political importance of recovering their history and preserving their past. Their importance also tends to be ignored by academic and professional historians. One example is historian Gwendolyn Robinson, mother of five and founder of the W.I.S.H. Centre in Chatham, Ontario, a community-based organization dedicated to preserving the history of Chatham-Kent's Black community. A descendant of the Shadd and Robbins families, Robinson's passion for preserving her community's past began when her son could not find a book in the local library about Black history. She organized a group of community volunteers to collect records on the history of the Underground Railroad and Black community leaders. The archive they created is now housed in the Black Mecca Museum, organized by the Chatham-Kent Black Historical Society, and has become an important resource for scholars and community-based researchers. Despite her central role in preserving "a portion of history which is conspicuous by its absence from most of today's history books," few people know and acknowledge her important contributions to preserving and writing history.[13] She did, however, receive the Sovereign's Medal for Volunteer Work, awarded by the Office of the Governor General, in September 2017. Flynn and Aladejebi argue, in this collection, that women like Robinson are vital resources for Black women's history, but the work that they produce is too often dismissed as celebratory history that does not meet formal academic criteria. They insist that academics' tendency to dismiss the contributions of local histories undermines the political work of women who are the guardians of their community history and know that their pasts mattered.[14]

These community-based historians belong to a long tradition of politically engaged women interested in history whose work was marginalized as "amateur" as the field professionalized.[15] This tradition has continued alongside the development of the professional discipline. Much of this work is done by volunteers committed to representing women's pasts in local museums and archives or by activists to ensure that their history does not disappear. Grassroots feminists preserved the documents of their activism by founding the Canadian Women's Movement Archives in 1982.[16] While this grassroots initiative has moved to an institution, the Canadian Lesbian and Gay Archives, founded in 1973, continues to operate as an independent, volunteer-run organization.[17] Sangster takes seriously the work of "second wave" activists who wrote women's history – often derided in academic journals as slapdash and substandard – in her chapter. These activists understood the transformative potential of recovering women's history, too, though their work tends not to be cited in historiographical discussions of 1970s feminist mobilizations.

Several authors demonstrate that the kind of recovery work that motivated the earliest women's historians is still useful and necessary, particularly to access racialized women's histories. The contributors use various and creative approaches to reflect on historiography and propose methodological, epistemological, and theoretical approaches that would speak to the ongoing absences in the literature. Flynn and Aladejebi make this point most forcefully, arguing that the "rootedness" narrative in early Black women's histories was politically important but also served to obscure the transnational lives of many Black families. Many of the stories of Black communities are migration histories, as discussed in Epp and Iacovetta's chapter. Their reflection on their roles in the development of the history of immigrant communities and migration histories illustrates that recovery history remains an important political project due to changing Canadian immigration patterns. The diasporic frame, they argue, is more effective to tease out the complex gendered experiences and identities of immigrant and refugee women than the multicultural framework that focused on incorporating these stories into a national history. McKenna's chapter points to the particular challenges faced by historians who attempt to recover the lives of colonial-era women: sources about elite women's experiences are relatively rare, and those that capture the lives of subaltern and racialized women are even scarcer. She argues that creative approaches to source material like church records, petitions, newspapers, and even colonial government records and oral histories can nonetheless yield important new discoveries about gendered identities and experiences in the colonial past.

McCallum and Hill's chapter also addresses methodological questions about recovery. They write back to the historiography on Indigenous peoples that begins from the premise that the impact of university-trained Indigenous scholars is a recent development. Historians of Indigenous peoples have been collaborating with elders for a long time and acknowledge their role in the development of the field. While the authors are critical of the underrepresentation of Indigenous scholars in the profession, they challenge the assumption of the absence of Indigenous contributions to historical knowledge by bringing Indigenous intellectual traditions, histories, and epistemologies to the foreground.

Indigenous peoples have always valued stories, ceremony, and song as ways to transmit historical knowledge. The oral tradition is rooted in specific cultural contexts that connect Indigenous nations to the land and the protocols for passing knowledge from one generation to the next. Gaining access and learning to listen to elders and traditional knowledge-keepers requires a deep understanding of Indigenous epistemology and historical consciousness. Researchers accept the obligation to follow protocol and maintain reciprocal relationships with Indigenous communities.[18] McCallum and Hill explain that traditional oral sources also provide context for the archival records, which do have a great deal of information about Indigenous women. Read carefully alongside community archives, family records, and knowledge preserved through oral sources, state documents provide an institutional framework that is required to understand lived experiences.

The challenges and opportunities described by McCallum and Hill compel us to continue to interrogate and resist the disciplinary powers of the archive. Flynn and Aladejebi also argue that writing Black women's history compels us to question what counts as a source because Black women appear sporadically in the archival record, thus making it difficult to follow them through their life course. Nancy Forestell begins her chapter on first wave feminism discussing a picture and petition by Catherine Hay, a Jamaican woman, to Lady Ishbel Aberdeen protesting unfair treatment from the YWCA. Finding the document in the archive compelled Forestell to rethink racialized women's participation in early twentieth-century feminist mobilizations. Her unsuccessful search for more records about the women who petitioned for equal treatment illustrates the necessity of thinking beyond the archive to find sources to write these histories.

For historians of the more recent past, oral sources have filled gaps in the archival record. The Indigenous oral tradition is distinct from oral history methodologies and theories developed with the emergence of social history in the 1960s, though both recognize that relationship-building is the foundation of a meaningful conversation. Oral historians and narrators collaborate to produce a new source with the goal of allowing narrators to guide the interview. When it first emerged as a field, practitioners argued that oral history would empower people by giving them a role in redefining research questions, agendas, and thus historical narratives. Feminist oral historians were among the first to question the power relationships between university-based researchers and narrators and to develop self-reflexive research strategies to address the power imbalance.[19]

Epp and Iacovetta demonstrate that oral interviews have always been an important source for immigrant women's history. In their chapter, they trace the significant theoretical shifts that have shaped the interpretation of oral sources. They also remind us that interviews are often the only source available to understand immigrant and refugee women's lives, especially those from communities that have not attracted scholarly attention. It is uncommon today for historians to question the reliability of oral history. Informed by gender theory, memory studies, and oral history theory, oral historians see strength in the incompleteness and fallibility of oral histories. Understanding how people interpret their lives in relation to grand political narratives and intimate personal experiences is a powerful way to make sense of women's lives, even if we don't know exactly what happened. Theoretical robustness has enriched the field, but we should not ignore the power of simply telling one's life story. Community-based oral history projects – such as Calgary's Gay History Project, the Archives of Lesbian Oral Testimony (ALOT), and the Montreal Life Stories Project – demonstrate that at the grassroots and community level, recovering the stories of past generations of activists remains a vital political project. A key strength of these projects is that they take direction from community members to ensure that they have broad appeal.[20]

Public history initiatives draw larger audiences than academic publications. Yet, despite increasing emphasis on community outreach as a pillar of university strategic plans, the academic discipline of history tends to rank public history as inferior to academic work; curating an exhibition, for example, is less prestigious than publishing a scholarly article, even though both require rigorous scholarly work. Academics often deride museum exhibitions for creating romantic depictions of the past but have little appreciation for how political controversy, budget cuts to heritage projects, and the nature of the collections at museums inform the work of feminist historians working in these institutions.[21] Feminist historians taking positions in museums continue to work to change practices to ensure that diverse women's voices are in collections.

Despite the efforts of feminist public historians to integrate meaningful gender analysis into museum exhibitions, the dominance of narratives that emphasize masculine achievements, such as military victories and founding the nation, thwarts attempts to present a more diverse past in public spaces. There is, however, a grassroots concern about the lack of women commemorated in public spaces. One recent example is the #CompletingTheStory campaign. Paula Kirman, one of the organizers of the 2017 Edmonton Women's March, launched the project to draw attention to how few women are commemorated in public spaces. She argues that the focus on men as leaders ignores women's contributions to social and economic development: "When people are underrepresented, when they're invisible, that's a form of marginalization."[22] Kirman makes a compelling argument about the impact of the lack of representation of women in public spaces on girls' sense of possibility; this is an important consideration at a time when misogynist attacks on women politicians in social media are easier and more frequent and when women's representation in government is decreasing. Some activists and academics have questioned the value of commemoration as a way to relate the complexity of the past, dismissing it as heroine worship; the ongoing debate about the Famous Five monuments on Parliament Hill and in Calgary is perhaps the best-known Canadian example. But people want to see women represented in public history and spaces. Collaborations among academics, public historians, and community groups interested in commemorating women's experiences could produce projects that commemorate women whose contributions have been forgotten while at the same time initiating public and community-based discussions that critically analyse whose stories remain untold.

Who Is Still at the Margins?

When we initiated this project we were convinced that the field of women's and gender history has made vital historiographical contributions that have changed how we think about the past. When women began to pursue graduate degrees in history and take up tenure-track positions in history departments in the 1970s, they introduced feminist perspectives to historical scholarship. Postwar government investment in the expansion of post-secondary education made a university education accessible to working-class youth; some of these students were the first generation of rural, working-class, and immigrant families to attend university, which also brought diverse experiences to historical practice. Most of these women were, nevertheless, white.[23] Despite political alliances with Indigenous scholars and racialized women in community and academe to advance diversity, history departments in Canada remain predominantly white. There are, however, important exceptions, and these scholars are making epistemological and methodological interventions that demonstrate how the exclusionary politics at the foundation of history as an academic profession maintain the systemic barriers that exclude scholars from marginalized communities.

The persistent problem of white bias in the field is raised in many of following chapters. Several authors point explicitly to the distortions created by foregrounding white – but also Anglo, middle-class, and Christian – women's experiences. McCallum and Hill and Flynn and Aladejebi each comment on the profound effect that colonization and racism have had on Canadian history writing, in general, and women's and gender history in Canada, specifically, evinced by an absenting and silencing of racialized experiences and perspectives.

Several chapters demonstrate how interpretative frameworks that have privileged white women's experiences become untenable when racialized or otherwise marginalized women are moved to the centre of analysis. Forestell, for example, recentres Indigenous feminisms to challenge the Canadian women's movement's "origin story," which has focused almost exclusively on white, middle-class suffragists in the late Victorian and Edwardian periods. She also foregrounds the feminism of Black women activists, like Mary Ann Shadd Cary, and others who organized self-education and abolitionist initiatives, which predated white women's activism by decades.[24] Robertson argues in her chapter that feminist narratives about agency are blinkered by a specific kind of liberal, Western, white, feminist politics that assumes that "autonomous and rational self-direction must be the uniform desire and sole option of every woman throughout history." By divesting from this politics, Canadian historians could accommodate more women's historical experiences and, in the process, "remake our theories."[25] Brookfield and Glassford also argue that integrating racialized women's experiences will not simply add to existing narratives but will radically alter our understandings of war and conflict in northern North America. They note that while research on Black and Japanese women written in the 1990s offered some important challenges to these narratives, there is a great deal of work to be done, particularly on Indigenous and francophone women.

Informed by Arundhati Roy's assertion that the "voiceless" are women who we have chosen not to hear,[26] Stettner, Burnett, and Chambers also challenge white scholars to examine their biases about knowledge, credible sources, and research questions. The authors explain that the effects of these biases on the history of reproductive justice in Canada has been, for instance, to focus on white middle-class women's fight for the right to limit their fertility, and to ignore the criminalization of motherhood for Indigenous women through the residential school system, forced or coerced sterilization, and the Sixties Scoop. These chapters show that decentring white narratives is no less transformative than decentring masculine narratives, which was the central goal of the first women's histories that sought to "rethink Canada."

In the case of Quebec, the work of challenging masculinist national historiographies is ongoing. Francophone historians engage with a nationalist historiographical tradition that distinguishes itself from the Canadian one. Baillargeon's chapter on Quebec critiques nationalist histories that seek to foster a Quebecois identity rooted in language, the Quebec state, and religion. The integrity of those narratives, she argues, relies on the exclusion of women's and gender history. These schools of Quebec historiography, which grew out of the sovereigntist movement, marginalized the social histories of Indigenous peoples, immigrant groups, and racial, ethnic, and religious minorities because they disrupted the notion of one cohesive Quebecois identity and culture. Baillargeon's challenge to integrate alternative narratives threatens the mythology of a homogeneous Quebecois nation. An intervention like Baillargeon's is essential to shifting historical paradigms to accommodate the intersectional approaches that are already influencing the work of Quebecois women's and gender historians.

Several chapters rely on an intersectional framework to demonstrate the imperative to write histories that racialize white women and consider the simultaneity of multiple vectors of identity in addition to race, class, and gender. Kimberlé Crenshaw introduced the term "intersectionality" in her important intervention into critical race theory in legal studies. Her critique was directed at discrimination laws that operated on one vector of identity at a time, such as discrimination on the basis of sex *or* of race. These single-issue laws could not, for example, protect Black women, for whom these two modes of discrimination were experienced simultaneously. Crenshaw used the example of *DeGraffenreid v. General Motors* wherein African American women sued the company on the basis that they were denied access to better jobs. Federal courts dismissed their case, citing that access to better jobs was available to African American men (thus no racism) and to white women (thus no sexism). The law could not account for employment discrimination particularly against women who were Black.[27]

In her examination of three Canadian feminist newspapers, Sangster argues that intersectionality has been implicit in the work of socialist-feminist historians for a very long time. Like Sangster, Linda Gordon has argued that intersectional thinking is not new to feminism. Gordon points out that "the basic concept – that multiple forms of domination interact and even fuse into new forms – has a long history in Left feminism and anti-racist, anti-nationalist and anti-colonial discourse." She also corrects the myth that the women's liberation movement in the United States "consisted exclusively of white, educated, middle-class, young women" by pointing out that it was "*mainly* white and middle class."[28] She goes on to note that "to mark it as exclusively that serves to obliterate influential African American feminist groups, actions and writings."[29] For Sangster, casting second wave feminism as a white, middle-class project marginalizes these and other voices in the Canadian narrative as well. It is perhaps because white, middle-class women have become the dominant voices in academe that this narrative has become entrenched.

Challenging systemic racism in academe remains one of the most important political issues in the field of women's and gender history – and history more broadly – in Canada. Innovation requires serious reflection about who gets jobs in history departments, who determines the research agenda, and whose historical scholarship is recognized as making a significant contribution to Canadian history beyond the field of gender and women's history. The indisputable whiteness of academic history and the discipline's role in perpetuating colonialist narratives and practices forestalls real systemic changes to women's and gender history's practices and perspectives. But decolonization and reversing invisibilization cannot be achieved by white academics writing race into capital-H history; these processes must begin with creating meaningful inclusion for Indigenous people and people of colour both within and outside the academy. As Stettner, Burnett, and Chambers argue here, "marginalized peoples must be in academe to tell their own stories."

Mary Jane Logan McCallum's critique suggests that the ontological structures of the discipline will need to be undone for real, systemic change to occur. From the perspective of an Indigenous scholar, McCallum points out that "historians actively produced histories that served to protect the boundaries of the historical profession in ways that eliminated not just the presence of Indian intellectuals, but also even the possibility of that presence."[30] In recent years, more Indigenous people have pursued graduate degrees in history and are working in universities, yet almost all of them find positions in Indigenous studies programs or other disciplines, not history departments.[31] In response to the calls to action by the Truth and Reconciliation Commission, more university administrations are committing to "indigenize the academy" and hiring Indigenous scholars is central to these strategies. A key concern that Indigenous scholars raise at consultations about the indigenization of the academy is the emphasis on hurried publication because it ignores the slow process of following protocols to build meaningful research relationships. Moreover, Indigenous scholars have responsibilities to collaborate with their communities to write research reports that advance political rights, publications that tend to be considered less valuable in evaluations and as relevant publications for promotion because they are not considered peer-reviewed work. This is especially pertinent in the field of history, which values the single-authored monograph more than collaborative work.[32]

Change will not happen without a critical mass of racialized women in academe. In the early stages of the profession, feminist scholars developed professional organizations to overcome isolation in their departments and advance feminist politics in their profession. The foundation of the Canadian Committee on Women's History / Comité canadien de l'histoire des femmes (CCWH/CCHF) in 1975 to promote teaching and research in women's history provided a national, bilingual organization for the new field within the CHA and a place where the first generation of women's historians could discuss the challenge of integrating women's pasts as core to all fields of history. It has traditionally been one of the largest subcommittees of the CHA and has played an important role in mentoring subsequent generations of feminist historians.[33] Over the years, the structure of the CCWH/CCHF has been modified to reflect changing political concerns about how best to represent the membership and to address systemic racism in academe. As the membership changes, we anticipate an ongoing discussion about how to be more inclusive to all people engaged in women's and gender history and to ensure the best representation of the diversity in the field within its governance model.[34] These conversations about how to advance racial and gender equity in the profession demonstrate that the politics of grassroots activism continue to direct the development of the professoriate.

Canadian women's and gender historians have risen to the top of the field; they have won major national awards for their research, served as presidents of the CHA, and received prestigious research endowments and chairs. As the editors of the seventh edition of *Rethinking Canada: The Promise of Women's History* state, "it would be pessimistic and simply incorrect to conclude that women remain huddled at the margins of historical scholarship as either authors or subjects."[35] It is nonetheless notable that since its inception in 1927 only two women have won the R.B. Tyrrell Historical Medal, awarded biennially to members of the Fellowship of the Royal Society of Canada for outstanding contributions to Canadian history (Joy Parr in 2000 and Veronica Strong-Boag in 2010). And recently, some have raised concerns about the ghettoization of women's and feminist history in the field, as well as the effects of institutionalized impediments to women's career trajectories in academe. These problems are particularly acute for female-identified academics further marginalized by race, sexual and gender identity, and class.[36]

Since women's history was founded over forty years ago, social justice movements have guided feminist historians' research questions to address silences and absences in the field. The contributors to this volume continue to do so. Their recommendations for future directions in their areas of expertise are also reflections on current politics. We are writing in a different political and cultural context than the scholars who wrote the first women's histories. There was a sense of optimism among feminists organizing in the 1970s that once government and society became aware of the systemic oppressions that women faced, they would develop policy, based on women's experiences, that would end gender inequality. The United Nations Decade of Women (1976–85) perhaps best exemplified the belief that with a global plan for action, coupled with activists at the local level, achieving women's equality would be possible in ten years.[37] Feminist historians engaged in these debates by researching the history of issues – such as violence against women and pay inequities between women and men and among women – argued that directions forward would benefit from knowledge of the past.

While we were working on this volume, we wrote with deep awareness about the global resurgence of racist and misogynist political discourses. Renewed mobilizations of social justice movements, however, have been organized to resist these politics of exclusion. Grassroots Indigenous movements with strong female leadership continue the work of previous generations who have sought to unsettle colonialist narratives. Idle No More makes connections between extinguishment narratives, the appropriation of Indigenous lands, the disproportionate levels of violence against women in Indigenous communities, and women's political marginalization.[38] The 2017 and 2018 Women's Marches that mobilized people around the world were an act of solidarity with women in the United States, but they generated large crowds in Canada and elsewhere because of the very real threats to women's rights closer to home. These are just two examples of movements that demonstrate the continuing strength and necessity of feminist activism. We are encouraged by the intergenerational participation in these events and our students' excitement about their involvement in acts of resistance. Yet we also worry that one day we'll be the elderly women marching with placards that read, "I cannot believe I still have to protest this shit."

Pundits have for decades questioned the usefulness of history degrees, especially in fields such as women's and gender history, that challenge the unifying narrative of nation-building and progress. More recent events have compelled historians to demonstrate that historical knowledge is crucial to engaged citizenship. Like the scholars who founded the field, we remain convinced that "thinking with history" helps us understand the connections between the past and the present in order to envision the future we want.[39] The next generation of women's and gender historians will know best what questions to ask that will contribute most effectively to the political debates and issues of their time.

NOTES

1 See as examples Ruth Roach Pierson, "Experience, Difference, Dominance, and Voice in the Writing of Canadian Women's History," in *Writing Women's History: International Perspectives*, ed. Karen Offen, Ruth Roach Pierson, and Jane Rendall (London: Macmillan, 1991), 76–106; Franca Iacovetta, "Gendering Trans/National Historiographies: Feminists Rewriting Canadian History," *Journal of Women's History* 19, 1 (2007): 206–13; Linda Kealey, "North America from North of the 49th Parallel," in *A Companion to Gender History*, ed. Teresa A. Meade and Merry E. Wiesner-Hanks (Oxford: Blackwell, 2006), 492–510. The 25th anniversary issue of *Atlantis* also has good essays on the state of the field, although these are now more than twenty years old: Margaret Conrad and Linda Kealey, eds, "Special Issue: Feminism and Canadian History (25th anniversary volume part I)," *Atlantis* 25, 1 (2000).

2 Some of the papers were presented at a roundtable entitled "Rethinking Gender and Women's History: Reflections on Interdisciplinary Approaches" at the 2015 CHA annual general meeting. How the authors planned to incorporate francophone and Quebec literature was a question raised during the discussion. Many, but not all, of the chapters in this book engage with the Quebec historiography. We advised contributors who have not engaged with Quebec historiography to provide an explanation in their chapter. We thank Nicole Neatby for this recommendation.

3 A few notable and influential texts include (politics) Carol Lee Bacchi, *Liberation Deferred? The Ideas of the English-Canadian Suffragists, 1877–1918* (Toronto: University of Toronto Press, 1983); Linda Kealey and Joan Sangster, eds, *Beyond the Vote: Canadian Women and Politics* (Toronto: University of Toronto Press, 1989); Joan Sangster, *Dreams of Equality: Women on the Canadian Left, 1920–1950* (Toronto: University of Toronto Press, 1989); Mariana Valverde, *The Age of Light, Soap, and Water: Moral Reform in English Canada, 1885–1920* (Toronto: McClelland and Stewart, 1991); (law) Constance Backhouse, *Petticoats and Prejudice: Women and the Law in Nineteenth-Century Canada* (Toronto: The Osgoode Society by Women's Press, 1991); Karen Dubinsky, *Improper Advances: Rape and Heterosexual Conflict in Ontario, 1880–1929* (Chicago: University of Chicago Press, 1993); Joan Sangster, *Regulating Girls and Women: Sexuality, Family, and the Law in Ontario, 1920–1960* (Toronto: Oxford University Press, 2001); (family and domesticity) Bettina Bradbury, *Working Families: Age, Gender, and Daily Survival in Industrializing Montreal* (Toronto: McClelland and Stewart, 1993); Andrée Lévesque, *Making and Breaking the Rules: Women in Quebec, 1919–1939*, trans. Yvonne M. Klein (Toronto: McClelland and Stewart, 1994); Katherine McKenna, *A Life of Propriety: Anne Murray Powell and Her Family, 1755–1849* (Kingston: McGill-Queen's University Press, 1994); Denyse Baillargeon, *Making Do: Women, Family, and Home in Montreal during the Great Depression*, trans. Yvonne Klein (Waterloo: Wilfrid Laurier University Press, 1999); (medicine) Wendy Mitchinson, *The Nature of Their Bodies: Women and Their Doctors in Victorian Canada* (Toronto: University of Toronto Press, 1991); Wendy Mitchinson, *Giving Birth in Canada, 1900–1950* (Toronto: University of Toronto Press, 2002); Denyse Baillargeon, *Babies for the Nation: The Medicalization of Motherhood in Quebec 1910–1970*, trans. W. Donald Wilson (Waterloo: Wilfrid Laurier University Press, 2009); (education) Susan Houston and Alison Prentice, *Schooling and Scholars in Nineteenth-Century Ontario* (Toronto: University of Toronto Press, 1988); Mary Kinnear, *In Subordination: Professional Women, 1870–1970* (McGill-Queen's University Press, 1995); Mona Gleason, *Normalizing the Ideal: Psychology, Schooling, and the Family in Post-War Canada* (Toronto: University of Toronto Press, 1999).

4 Joan Wallach Scott, "Gender: A Useful Category of Historical Analysis," *American Historical Review* 91, 5 (December 1986): 1053–105.

5 See Joan Sangster, "Beyond Dichotomies: Re-assessing Gender History and Women's History in Canada," *Left History* 3, 1 (1995): 109–21; Karen Dubinsky and Lynne Marks, "Beyond Purity: A Response to Sangster," *Left History* 3, 2/1 (1995): 205–20; Franca Iacovetta and Linda Kealey, "Women's History, Gender History, and Debating Dichotomies," *Left History* 3, 2/1 (1995): 221–37.

6 Notable monographs include Joy Parr, *The Gender of Breadwinners: Women, Men, and Change in Two Industrial Towns, 1880–1950* (Toronto: University of Toronto

Press, 1990); Pamela Sugiman, *Labour's Dilemma: The Gender Politics of Auto Workers in Canada, 1937–1979* (Toronto: University of Toronto Press, 1994); Cecilia Morgan, *Public Men and Virtuous Women: The Gendered Languages of Religion and Politics in Upper Canada, 1791–1850* (Toronto: University of Toronto Press, 1996); Gillian Creese, *Contracting Masculinity: Gender, Class, and Race in a White-Collar Union, 1944–1994* (Toronto: University of Toronto Press, 1999); Mark Moss, *Manliness and Militarism: Educating Young Boys in Ontario for War* (Don Mills: Oxford University Press, 2001); Mary-Ellen Kelm, *A Wilder West: Rodeo in Western Canada* (Vancouver: UBC Press, 2011); Christopher Dummitt, *The Manly Modern: Masculinity in Postwar Canada* (Vancouver: UBC Press, 2007); Paul Jackson, *One of the Boys: Homosexuality in the Military during World War II* (Montreal: McGill-Queen's University Press, 2010); Jeffrey Vacante, *National Manhood and the Creation of Modern Quebec* (Vancouver: UBC Press, 2017).

7   Judith Butler, *Bodies That Matter: On the Discursive Limits of "Sex"* (New York: Routledge, 1993).

8   Anna Krylova, "Gender Binary and the Limits of Poststructuralist Method," *Gender and History* 28, 2 (2016): 307–23, and *Soviet Women in Combat: A History of Violence on the Eastern Front* (Cambridge: Cambridge University Press, 2010).

9   A. Finn Enke, "Introduction: Transfeminist Perspectives," in *Transfeminist Perspectives in and beyond Transgender and Gender Studies*, ed. Anne (now Finn) Enke (Philadelphia: Temple University Press, 2015), 5.

10 Viviane K. Namaste, *C'était un spéctacle: Les histoires des artistes transsexuales à Montréal, 1955–1985* (Montreal: McGill-Queen's University Press, 2005); Becki Ross, "Outdoor Brothel Culture: The Un/Making of the Transsexual Stroll in Vancouver's West End, 1975–1984," *Journal of Historical Sociology* 25, 1 (2012): 126–50.

11 Dan Irving and Rupert Raj, eds, *Trans Activism in Canada: A Reader* (Toronto: Canadian Scholars Press, 2014). See also Patrizia Gentile, Gary Kinsman, and L. Pauline Rankin, *We Still Demand: Redefining Resistance in Sex and Gender Struggles* (Vancouver: UBC Press, 2017).

12 Bobby Noble, "Trans. Panic. Some Thoughts toward a Theory of Feminist Fundamentalism," in *Transgender Perspectives in and beyond Transgender and Gender Studies*, ed. Anne (now Finn) Enke (Philadelphia: Temple University Press, 2012), 51. See also Finn Enke, "Collective Memory and the Transfeminist 1970s: Toward a Less Plausible History," *TSQ: Transgender Studies Quarterly* 5, 1 (February 2018): 9–29.

13 The quotation is from the foreword to her book, *Seek the Truth,* cited in "Robinson, Gwendolyn Susan (1932–)," *Heritage Resources,* Municipality of Chatham-Kent, https://www.chatham-kent.ca/HeritageResources/Pages/RobinsonGwendolynSusan.aspx. See also the Black Mecca Museum, https://ckbhs.org/about/. Nancy Janovicek thanks Dennis Makowetsky for bringing Robinson's contributions to her attention.

14 We borrow this phrase from the Calgary Gay History Project's slogan: "Our pasts matter." Founded by Kevin Allen, this volunteer initiative is building an archive, interviewing elders from Calgary's LGBTQ community, and conducting regular public history talks and tours. https://calgaryqueerhistory.ca/. See also Kevin Allen, *Our Pasts Matter: Stories of Gay Calgary* (Calgary: ASPublishing, 2018).

15 Donald Wright, "Gender and the Professionalization of History in English Canada before 1960," *Canadian Historical Review* 81, 1 (2006): 29–66; Donald Wright, *The Professionalization of History in English Canada* (Toronto: University of Toronto Press, 2005).

16 The archives are now housed in the University of Ottawa Special Collections: https://biblio.uottawa.ca/en/archives-and-special-collections/womens-archives. Activists have recently launched "Rise Up: Digital Archive of Feminist Activism": http://riseupfeministarchive.ca/.

17 Canadian Lesbian and Gay Archives, http://clga.ca/. See also the Transgender Archives housed at the University of Victoria: http://www.uvic.ca/transgenderarchives/.

18 Julie Cruikshank, "Oral Tradition and Oral History: Reviewing Some Issues," *Canadian Historical Review* 75, 3 (1994): 403–18; Brian Caillou, "Methodology for Recording Oral Histories in the Aboriginal Community," in *The Canadian Oral History Reader*, ed. Kristina R. Llewellyn, Alexander Freund, and Nolan Reilly (Montreal: McGill-Queen's University Press, 2015), 25–52; Wendy C. Wickwire, "To See Ourselves as the Other's Other: Nlaka'pamux Contact Narratives," *Canadian Historical Review* 75, 1 (1994): 1–20. Attempts to codify these protocols in the Tri-Council Policy Statement conflated the distinction between Indigenous oral traditions and oral history. This made it difficult for researchers to speak to women who had lost connection to their communities. As a result of engagement, the revised TCPS2 has a more robust discussion of scholarly engagement with Aboriginal communities that recognizes marginalization within these communities and the need to develop research projects to ensure that their voices are heard. See Nancy Janovicek, "Oral History and Ethics Practice after *TCPS2*," in *The Canadian Oral History Reader*, ed. Kristina R. Llewellyn, Alexander Freund, and Nolan Reilley (Montreal: McGill-Queen's University Press, 2015), 73–97.

19 Joan Sangster, "Telling Our Stories: Feminist Debates and the Use of Oral History," *Women's History Review* 3, 1 (1994): 5–28; Sherna Berger Gluck and Daphne Patai, eds, *Women's Words: The Feminist Practice of Oral History* (New York: Routledge, 1991).

20 ALOT is available at http://alotarchives.org/content/elise-chenier, accessed 14 July 2017. Montreal Life Stories is available at http://storytelling.concordia.ca/projects/montreal-life-stories, accessed 14 July 2017.

21 It should also be noted that the most influential positions are held by men, who have final say on how women and other marginalized communities will be represented in

exhibition narratives. Krista Cooke, "Representing Women at Canada's Public History Sites," in *Women and Social Movements in America, 1600–2000* (2009), http://asp6new.alexanderstreet.com.ezproxy.lib.ucalgary.ca/wam2/wam2.object.details.aspx?dorpid=1002869393, accessed 13 July 2017 (membership required). Rhonda Hinther, "From the Edges to the Centre: The Challenge and Promise of Feminist Public History," CCWH Keynote Address presented at the 2013 Canadian Historical Association Meeting, University of Victoria, 4 June 2013.

22 Omar Mosle, "'For Young Girls, Who Are Their Role Models?' Campaign Pushes for More Female Faces in Public Spaces," *Metro,* 15 June 2017, http://www.metronews.ca/news/edmonton/2017/06/15/campaign-pushes-for-more-female-faces-in-public-spaces-.html, accessed 6 July 2017 (no longer available).

23 See the "Life in History" series in *Canadian Historical Review [CHR]*: Veronica Strong-Boag, "From There to Here: The Making of a Feminist Historian," *CHR* 95, 2 (2014): 242–65; Wendy Mitchinson, "No One Becomes a Feminist to Be Appreciated," *CHR* 94, 3 (2013): 436–58; Micheline Dumont, "Insérer les femmes dans l'histoire: Le parcours d'une vie," *CHR* 93, 4 (2012): 641–64; Alison Prentice, "Winding Trails: My Life in History," *CHR* 93, 4 (2012): 611–40; Margaret Conrad, "It Was All about Me: Making History Relevant," *CHR* 92, 4 (2011): 694–721.

24 See also the UBC Press Women's Suffrage and Social Democracy series edited by Veronica Strong-Boag: Joan Sangster, *One Hundred Years of Struggle: The History of Women and the Vote in Canada*, 2018; Tarah Brookfield, *Our Voices Must Be Heard: Women and the Vote in Ontario*, 2018; Denyse Baillargeon, *To Be Equals in Our Own Country: Women and the Vote in Quebec*, forthcoming 2019; Sarah Carter, *Ours by Every Law of Right and Justice: Women and the Vote in the Prairie Provinces*, forthcoming 2019; Lara Campbell, *A Great Revolutionary Wave: Women and the Vote in British Columbia*, forthcoming; Heidi MacDonald, *We Shall Persist: Women and the Vote in the Atlantic Provinces*, forthcoming; and Lianne Leddy, *Working Tirelessly for Change: Indigenous Women and the Vote in Canada*, forthcoming.

25 Robertson, chapter 6 in this volume.

26 Arundhati Roy, "The 2004 Sydney Peace Prize Lecture: Peace and the New Corporate Liberation Theology," *University of Sydney News Blog*, 4 November 2004, http://sydney.edu.au/news/84.html?newsstoryid=279.

27 Kimberlé Williams Crenshaw, "Race, Reform, and Retrenchment: Transformation and Legitimation in Antidiscrimination Law," *Harvard Law Review* 101, 7 (1988): 1331–87.

28 Linda Gordon, "'Intersectionality,' Socialist Feminism and Contemporary Activism: Musings by a Second-Wave Socialist Feminist," *Gender and History* 28, 2 (2016): 342.

29 Gordon, "Intersectionality," 343.

30 Mary Jane Logan McCallum, *Indigenous Women, Work, and History, 1940–1980* (Winnipeg: University of Manitoba Press, 2014), 234.

31 Mary Jane Logan McCallum, "Indigenous Labor and Indigenous History," *American Indian Quarterly* 33, 4 (2009): 523–44.

32 We acknowledge Heather Devine, Cora Voyageur, and Daniel Voth for these insights.

33 Deborah Gorham, "Making History: Women's History in Canadian Universities in the 1970s," in *Creating Historical Memory: English-Canadian Women and the Work of History*, ed. Beverly Boutilier and Alison Prentice (Vancouver: UBC Press, 1997), 273–97.

34 Most recently, the 2016–17 Executive struck an Ad Hoc Committee on Representation to survey members on how best to expand the community and to structure the organization to represent diversity among members. See "Please complete our survey (June 15th) – Veuillez completer notre sondage (le 15 juin)," CCWH – CCHF Blog/Blogue, 5 June 2017, http://chashcacommittees-comitesa. ca/ccwh-cchf/2017/06/05/please-complete-our-survey-june-15th-veuillez-completer-notre-sondage-le-15-juin/.

35 Adele Perry, Tamara Myers, and Lara Campbell, eds, *Rethinking Canada: The Promise of Women's History*, 7th ed. (Toronto: Oxford University Press, 2016), 5.

36 Elise Chenier, Lori Chambers, and Anne Frances Toews, "Still Working in the Shadow of Men? An Analysis of Sex Distribution in Publications and Prizes in Canadian History," *Journal of the Canadian Historical Association* 26, 1 (2015): 291–318.

37 Arvonne Fraser, "UN Decade for Women: The Power of Words and Organizations," in *Women and Social Movements, International, 1840 to Present*, ed. Kathryn Kish Sklar and Thomas Dublin, https://search.alexanderstreet.com/ preview/work/bibliographic_entity%7Cbibliographic_details%7C2476931#search/ Arvonne+Fraser, accessed 12 July 2017 (membership required).

38 See the "Calls for Change" on the Idle No More website, http://www.idlenomore. ca/calls_for_change, accessed 13 July 2017.

39 John Tosh, *Why History Matters* (New York: Palgrave Macmillan, 2008).

2 Our Historiographical Moment: A Conversation about Indigenous Women's History in Canada in the Early Twenty-First Century

MARY JANE LOGAN MCCALLUM AND SUSAN M. HILL

Introduction

Accounts on the writing of Indigenous women's history often begin with the contributions of non-Indigenous historians who wrote in the 1960s and 1970s and end with recent contributions by historians who are Indigenous. While this trend reflects an old and continuing pattern of under-representation of Indigenous scholars in our discipline, it gives the false impressions that the work of the former led to and resulted in the latter in a linear way and that our historiography must necessarily begin in our absence. In this contribution, we examine our own historiographical moment including how we came to study Indigenous women's history, what kind of work we do and read, our experiences of teaching, and our broader sense of the state of the field. Our method was to record a four-hour discussion we had in which we asked each other four types of questions about our work and our field. Though grounded in our own specializations (which tend to focus on central and south-eastern Canada and the northern United States and on English-language histories), we hope there will be a variety of entry points for thinking about other work as well.

We want to remark on the pattern in the location of Indigenous history, especially in the context of edited collections of Canadian history. Indigenous history chapters are often put at either the beginning or the end of an edited collection, reflecting two important and problematic patterns in the ways that Indigenous history is framed in the Canadian context. While acknowledging their much greater length of history in Canada, placing Indigenous people's history early in a book can inadvertently also depict Indigenous people, unlike the others in the volume, as only historic. By placing Indigenous chapters at the end of an edited collection, this can inadvertently depict Indigenous history as a "recent" phenomenon without having a long and enduring importance.

One other trend in Canadian history and historiography collections such as this one is to isolate Indigenous chapters (and chapters on the histories of people of colour) as specific, unique examples of difference and diversity. Framed this way, these chapters come to represent distinctions of ethnography, language, or a politics of "race"; however, they tend to be otherwise disconnected from or peripheral to the central trajectory of the book. This organizational pattern inadvertently often isolates Indigenous chapters from those that focus on more analytical or methodological themes. Because of this emphasis on difference or uniqueness, these chapters rarely speak to one another – separating for example Quebec history, Black history, and Indigenous history. This is a problem in that it presents Indigenous historical scholarship as one-dimensional and not factoring in the central questions of historical methodology and analysis. Indigenous historiographies, like all histories, are not written in a vacuum or in outer space; rather, they draw on and impact the world around us in important ways. One way that edited collections that follow this pattern can avoid these unintended and implied conclusions is to ensure that Indigenous history is engaged with throughout. We hope that you will read this chapter and think about it alongside the rest of the chapters in this volume.

We also wanted to comment on the style of the essay – which is undertaken as a conversation between two scholars and two friends. This format was chosen purely pragmatically; we found writing collaboratively very difficult and most of our greatest insights came out of conversations we were having, rather than our writing. We want to ensure that our using a dialogue did not imply that Indigenous history is merely "story," or that Indigenous people inherently distrust the written word and are less able to communicate their true or authentic concepts in writing – an assumption that has in fact led to the justification of the avoidance of scholarly consideration of Indigenous peoples' history by historians and has, until recently, enabled historians not to take Indigenous people who are historians seriously. This was a pragmatic design that fit both our multiple demands and genuine interest and investment in women's history in the place now known as Canada.

Part One: Coming to Study Indigenous Women's History in Canada

How did you come to be a historian?

> Susan: I don't think I ever had a plan to be a historian, but I've always loved history, so it just kind of happened. It was funny, as I always wanted to be an architect; that's what I went to university for in the first place. As I was heading towards

the prep courses in architecture, I found that all the electives I wanted to take had an emphasis on histories of Indigenous people. My school didn't have a Native studies program in any formal way – rather, I took Indigenous-themed courses in American culture, English, anthropology, music, social science, and other courses that had a historical component to them. In fact, the history department at my university had some Indigenous history courses on the books but they were not taught at the time. When I found that I was taking everything except electives related to architecture, I realized that maybe I didn't want to be an architect. As I was finishing my degree in history, my mentor suggested that I go to the State University of New York at Buffalo to continue my studies in their Native American studies program, which was in the American studies department. I wanted to continue research I started as an undergraduate on Seneca land history and that's what I ended up doing. And from there, I had a professional career in higher education but realized that I still had this desire for research, and that's how I ended up going on to get the doctorate. It was never a plan to be a professional historian.

Mary Jane: That's so interesting. I came to Indigenous women's history through a very different route, although I, too, was deeply interested in history. Learning history was always important to my parents – different aspects of our family's past and the history of the area we lived: Simcoe County, Ontario, but also beyond, to other areas of Canada and the United States as well as Great Britain and Ireland. I took history in university as a major in my undergraduate years, but to learn about Indigenous people's history, I took a Native studies course as our history department did not offer courses in Indigenous history. Looking back, it is ironic that it was much easier for me to study medieval European history than Indigenous history even though I was studying at a Canadian university. I don't think that it should be either/or; however, I am glad to see that this is changing now at some universities. After my undergraduate years, I went to England, France, Spain, and the Netherlands to travel and work and to see some of the churches and monasteries I had studied. I had a great time seeing that part of the world on my own; however, I recall getting frustrated with the great wealth of the churches and cathedrals I visited. My suspicion was that much of that wealth was connected in important but concealed ways to our history in North America. When I returned I decided that I wanted to study more about Indigenous history. Like you, I never planned to do this, but I was fortunate that some of my close friends at school wanted to pursue graduate school so I learned more about this option by watching them. In my honours year, I was given a reading by Dr John Milloy[2] that explained federal Indian policy in a way I had never considered before. I wrote to him and then went to see him at Trent when I returned from Europe. Working on an MA with him meant moving out of history and into Native studies.

How did you come to study Indigenous women's histories in particular?

Susan: The teachings that I have received from my community around gender
relationships taught me that there should always be balance. And that is certainly
not how the historical record has been reflected. The historical record has rarely
been constructed by Indigenous people. We have a historical record, but it
rarely makes it into the canon of History – with a capital H. So my interest in
improving History is in trying to integrate the Indigenous historical record and
to bring balance overall, and a central process to bringing balance is to study
what has been left out. And that is almost always about women, it's almost
always about children, and it's almost always about the natural world. Because
it's not all about the humans – it's about the territories that we come from. In
our cultural teachings, we are taught that you are a product of the land that
you come from and you are part of that land. Humans aren't necessarily the
most important part though. Those pieces almost always get left out. Even in
environmental history, where we clearly have something important to say, Native
people are often presented only as backdrop. My approach to Native women's
history is integrated into the entire picture of Indigenous history, but certainly
trying to find the information that can be shared and to bring light to those areas
that haven't been discussed in the mainstream historical presentation is always a
challenge.

Mary Jane: I went to Trent with an idea that I might study one of two topics.
I thought I would look at my own First Nations community history or look into
a topic that connected my interest in medieval European history with my interest
in Indigenous history – such as medical history and early missionaries. My
knowledge of both was very slim, and I spent a lot of time without a particular
research plan in mind, but just reading, both archives and secondary sources.
At one point Dr Milloy sent me to the Anglican archives in Toronto, and while
I was there I saw a very compelling image of Inuit from around the 1950s at
a residential school in Aklavik, in the Northwest Territories. The girls in the
photo were wearing a uniform I was very familiar with – I too had been a Girl
Guide and my mom was a leader in the organization. I showed it to Dr Milloy,
who was also interested. He suggested that I do my thesis on the history of
the organization and its place in Indian residential schools in Canada. My first
reaction was "You can't do a thesis on Girl Guides in residential schools! That's
not a real topic of history! History is old – well, older than the 1950s – and it
is about important people, not schoolchildren – girls, no less!" Or so I thought
at the time. I really hadn't considered that things I myself could relate to on a
personal level count as "real" scholarly history. And yet I was just so interested

in the photo and wanted to go back and see if there were more photos like it. For several months I had this back and forth until finally I just ended up being so interested that I couldn't help but do more research on it. And once I started looking for this history, I found it literally everywhere. There was evidence of residential school Girl Guide groups in the National Archives, the Girl Guides archives, church archives, and newspapers across the country. The sources I found said a lot about women and their roles in settling and populating the British Empire. They discussed Canadian women's organizations and their philanthropic work with Native girls. The sources also spoke about Native people, assimilation, and authenticity. I think it was those early months of struggling with what I thought university history was supposed to be and especially the primary research and secondary readings that I did for that thesis that brought me to the field of Indigenous women's history.

What readings about Indigenous women's history did you appreciate the most while you were at graduate school?

Susan: I would say that the pieces of literature that I found the most telling of Indigenous women's history were often those problematic texts that were focused on ethnography. Because even though the ethnographer was most often a man who didn't understand the communities or Nations that they were talking about, there are still gems of information in there, and when you are able to process that written material in the context of community life, that's when it comes together for me. Like Hewitt's[3] different versions of the Haudenosaunee creation story. I even find some great information in the *Jesuit Relations* – but that's a source where you have to have a lot of patience and an ability to sift through religious zeal in order to "read" between the lines and discern some really great information about Indigenous women.[4] There are many texts that focus on the Haudenosaunee Great Law that also contain amazing information. One of my favourite examples of the linguistic ethnographic studies completed at the turn of the twentieth century (for a decidedly non-Native audience) was re-translated and contextualized in a 1992 publication, *Concerning the League*.[5] That's a narrative in the Onondaga language that has been translated, including by some native speakers who became an active part of the translation process. So that text was really important to understand what the epic teachings of the Haudenosaunee say about gender relationships and about the mutual responsibilities between men and women and then being able to use that as a lens to process other written material.

In Six Nations, we actually do have a fairly long legacy of written history, even written by our own people. But it's always by men, for different reasons.

Sometimes they were put into those roles internally and sometimes externally. And sometimes both. You have, for example, John Brant, who is a really complicated historical figure. Most people know him as the son of Joseph Brant. But actually, from a Haudenosaunee view, John Brant was born into leadership via his mother's family. He became a traditional chief because his mother's family line carried those responsibilities. We certainly do acknowledge our father's relatives, but you cannot claim leadership descent in that way. And most mainstream historians miss that piece. Even though they know the Haudenosaunee are matrilineal, they don't always apply that. The bulk of people who have written histories about the Grand River community have almost always been anthropological in their training. Men and women scholars alike tend to follow a paternal lineage in their work. For example, Seth Newhouse was Onondaga, because his mother was Onondaga, but he spoke Mohawk. Anthropologist Sally Weaver misrepresented Newhouse as being "as much Mohawk as he was Onondaga."[6] From our traditional standpoint, that is not possible. Most scholars never get to that level of understanding. Much of it is not written in a way that those who are not immersed into the culture can understand. If you lack training in kinship, especially Haudenosaunee kindship, you won't understand that. Even our own scholars sometimes miss it.[7]

You asked about key texts that influenced me. For me, several key influential texts came from Deborah Doxtator, whose family came from Tyendinaga. Most notable of those is her 1995 dissertation, "What Happened to the Iroquois Clans?"[8] It looks at nineteenth-century clan histories of the Tonawanda Seneca, Tyendinaga, and Six Nations of the Grand River communities. While her analysis was deeply rooted in Haudenosaunee thought, she did often default to problematic secondary literature. Her dissertation is one of the most utilized pieces of graduate student work I know, referenced often by scholars working in history, philosophy, education, literature, Indigenous studies, anthropology, American studies, and other fields as well. Unfortunately, she passed away just a few years after completing the dissertation and before she could publish it. She didn't get a chance to proceed with her research – but with more time, I believe she would have replaced the areas where she relied on poor secondary sources. Her work is extremely influential on my work. She also did a lot of great writing in the arts. She curated museum exhibits. A lot of her philosophical material is found in her curatorial essays.[9] You don't read a lot of historians who are referring to curators' notes and essays to inform how they do history. But often Indigenous historians, particularly Indigenous women's historians, end up going to those unexpected places for inspiration as well as for those theoretical structures that the field has missed.

Mary Jane: This is such a great reminder of the vast and diverse points of entry
into our field: family and community history, photos, art and curating, and
ethnography just to name a few. I think I was initially interested in the Canadian
state and Indian policy – in social history rather than anthropology, and in
legal and moral regulation alongside cultural history. When I was a teenager, I
"became" a status Indian and a band member through a revision to the Indian Act
that allowed us to apply to the government to have our heritage and community
membership formally acknowledged. My parents did the work of "applying" for
our recognition in the highly precarious Indian Affairs registry. This involved
trying to sort through complicated Indian Affairs forms and rules and making
records of all of our family members' vital statistics. This process probably
started me thinking about what I'd later call "race" and "gender": about how and
why women in my family lost rights to live on the reserve, to be band members,
and to inherit property. For my grandmother, this was because of who she
married and the legal status of their relationship. To come to this knowledge and
think through it as an adolescent seems significant now. To connect this lived
experience to a law helped to see that it wasn't inevitable or "natural" that she
was disenfranchised and us as well. Yet these definitions remained real. While
one-sided infatuations and crushes were safe, dating and especially requited love
were associated with potential risk of unspeakable loss. Much of the Canadian
women's history I read in my MA studies – work by Veronica Strong-Boag,
Franca Iacovetta, Karen Dubinsky, Joan Sangster, and others[10] – described the
kinds of Victorian notions of race, gender relations, and roles of women and men
that informed the Indian Act. I started to see some of these things differently,
I think – as learned behaviours and social constructions that had histories with
vitally important implications for women.

   I then began to read some of the books that used women's history to make
interventions into Indigenous histories that previously had little to say about
women – work by Sarah Carter, Sylvia Van Kirk, Jo-Anne Fiske, and Jennifer
Brown.[11] That work of using different primary sources and new approaches
to conventional primary sources to see women in history where they had been
cast as unimportant was very compelling to me. Feminist historians, or those
who examine gender relations and inequality, made a significant challenge to
Indigenous history – they discussed family, marriage, children, governance, and
labour. They also identified patterns and trends in representations of Indigenous
women and connected these to other inequities. In my Native studies course
we read work by Indigenous women like Winona Wheeler (Stevenson), Kim
Anderson, Maria Campbell, Rayna Green, Paula Gunn Allan, and Janice Acoose,
who used techniques like life writing, cultural history, and speaking from
experience to identify multiple forms of oppression and to uncover Indigenous

women's diverse lives and distinct experiences of oppression.[12] I was compelled by this work on representations, patriarchy, Indian policy, and state relations because it seemed to offer a way to articulate some of the paradoxes and limitations our family had experienced firsthand.

At one point, John Milloy referred me to Adele Perry's article "Fair Ones of a Purer Caste: White Women and Colonialism in Nineteenth-Century British Columbia."[13] At the time I was thinking through the Girl Guide program and especially its citizenship training goals for girls who were at these assimilatory residential schools. The article helped me to think about how gender, race, and age functioned together in the history I was looking at and seemed to put the history I was doing on a much larger scale, connecting it to our broader national history and huge global movements. I loved thinking of that photo of the Girl Guides in Aklavik in that way, and it compelled me to pursue studying Indigenous women's history at the University of Manitoba just as Adele Perry was about to start a Canada Research Chair in Western Canadian Social History there.

Part Two: Our Current History Work as Historians of Indigenous Women

What interests you in Indigenous women's history these days? What research are you doing?

Susan: For me, it often isn't the material you're reading – rather it's the stuff that people ask you about. "Hey, did you ever come across this document?" "Did you ever see this list of names?" And that's what I always find very fulfilling. We are quite fortunate – even though it's a double-edged sword in many ways, we (Haudenosaunee) are so heavily researched, but that means that there's so much information in archives that is quite rich in our cultural information, that for many reasons families have been separated from. So I like to help facilitate connections of families to these resources. Again, because we are a matrilineal society, it almost always starts with women. It includes men and women, because, you know, we're generally 50-50. In the end, women's history is history. First of all, there's no new people without women. We're partners in that process, but there's no big important man without a whole bunch of women. That's a piece that typical historical training does not teach enough. For example, those archival encounters where we come across things that we know will be useful to families, to communities, and helping to convey that information for those people and with those people. This reclaiming has to be collaborative or all you are doing is making copies. It's not truly reclaimed until it rests with those people who it belongs to. That's the kind of stuff I love doing. Rarely does it make a piece of writing. But that's ok. We're really fortunate to be in positions to assist with that kind of historical work. Akin to this are also language materials that again are often housed in archives and other repositories of various types hundreds and thousands of miles from the communities of origin or communities of connection. Things that could have been written about Manhattan in the seventeenth century, for example, are highly relevant to your (Delaware) communities in southern Ontario – even if you do not have an immediate connection, you may have a lineal and a cultural inheritance connection. If you do not know that history, you might not see why someone in Oklahoma might see this as part of their (Delaware) cultural history because they won't know that connection. Or why someone at Six Nations who is a Mohawk is connected to that seventeenth-century Delaware history, too. That's not something that you can learn overnight; it's not something that you can learn in a book. You learn it by being around people, by listening to people over years and years and years. You often don't understand it until you see it.

I'm also really interested in what Jennifer Denetdale is doing. She is mentoring young scholars working on border-town violence against Indigenous people. She's also doing research on traditional Diné (Navajo) stories around gender that are informing Diné society about the present. That's tough work. Finding a way and a means for that to be useful for her professional career must also be challenging given that her key audience is a Diné audience. She finds a way to balance her academic obligations with her community scholarly work. There's also some amazing work coming out of Hawaii – Noelani Arista and Marie Alohalani Brown, for example, using Hawaiian language archives to frame their interpretations within a Hawaiian view of the world that centres women and centres gender.[14]

Mary Jane: I love their work as well. Two major trends stand out to me. The first is work that critically examines gender, settler colonialism, and the state. This analysis insists that we study the ideas behind and the diverse and diffuse nature of colonialism and how it is put to work in the world, including at home in Canada. To think about history in this way has, in some (not all) quarters, had an enormous impact on the writing of history in Canada and challenged a significant trend to write Canadian history as a "good" story of national progress and independent development that resulted in equality for all who live here. Much of this work demonstrates how women and men – and ideas about "womanliness" and "manliness" – are informed by notions of white cultural and racial superiority and acts of violence on land and people in settler colonies like Canada.

There's also a lot of great new work on Indigenous women and activism. So much of our history has been concerned with identifying forms of oppression, regulation, punishment, surveillance, and their effects. It's necessary that we critically study Indigenous people's resistance and agency in the past as well. We do always seem to get caught in this "either/or" kind of depiction of our history – that's one of the things I struggled with in my book[15] – how to acknowledge women's labour histories within a canon that depicted Indigenous women either as uniformly subjugated or as "strong women." Yet how do we reconcile this with the many violent elements of our past when essentialist tropes of the "strong Indigenous woman" are so appealing? Erica Violet Lee has recently raised the question of how to discuss our vulnerabilities as Indigenous women in critical ways, so that these stories do not get individualized and compartmentalized. In many ways we still need to make visible to the broader public in Canada how the historical and contemporary material realities of many Indigenous women were and are vulnerable.[16]

And yet there is so much value to histories of Indigenous women's activism, in understanding the fundamentally important but often forgotten roles of women in activism in the areas of Indigenous-state relations, health, education, policing, child welfare, Indian policy, and the justice system, to name a few.[17] The current interest in histories of activism reflects the climate and in particular the Idle No More movements and the work being done in the name of Missing and Murdered Indigenous Women (MMIW). But much of this scholarship also connects to feminist work at a more local level and comes to grips with Indigenous change and persistence in the modern era. I'm thinking here of work like Christine Taitano DeLisle's. She studies Chamorro midwife nurses who acted as intermediaries between Indigenous communities and modern hospitals in early twentieth-century Guam. She argues that they "negotiated" pregnancy and child-birthing work and asserted cultural determination in their work, which continued Chamorro practices including those concerning the care of placentas, thus resisting colonialism in gendered ways. They took on, she argues, "new ways of being and enacting what it means to be native without necessarily abandoning earlier concepts of progress, propriety, and in relation to self and community and stewardship of the land."[18]

For many historians of Indigenous women, our work is embedded in our politics and our lives and vice versa. Our work is often "activist" of sorts in that we seek to identify change and stasis over time in ways that can inform our present for the better. Methodologies that guide us on this are sometimes explicitly feminist and sometimes not, but they are often driven by an interconnected critique of colonialism, patriarchy, and capitalism and a desire to identify Indigenous actors, methodologies, and participants of history in order to learn from them.

What kinds of primary sources do you work with in women's history?

Susan: It varies, depending on what I have access to. The work I do is mostly
related to primary historical documents, produced by Haudenosaunee people
as well as by colonial governments. I'm really fortunate doing research on my
own community that there's often a government source and a community source
so there are opportunities for comparison – for example, what's included in this
source that's not included in the other and why might that be. For most of us as
historians we run into things that are so fascinating but the trail just stops – and
we wonder, "What happened?" The Indian Affairs files are full of those things.
There are more than many lifetimes to keep us busy with those things. No one
really sets out to be an archival historian. When is the last time you spoke to a
five-year-old or a twelve-year-old or even a thirty-year-old who said they wanted
to be an archival historian? It's something that happens. If you end up being in a
place where you can gain skills in that process and you see value in it, that's how
you end up there. I wouldn't do it if I didn't enjoy it. I've gained a lot of skills
doing this kind of work – in accessing information; being able to navigate an
archive is not something that just happens.

When you're doing your initial research it becomes organic after a while, and
it's only when you're put into a situation of unfamiliarity that you are able to
identify the skills you have, and need. Indian Affairs files for British Columbia,
for example, are really different – in part because of the minimal existence of
Treaty and the later entry of Indian Affairs on a full scale. This means that a
lot of the issues we can easily identify in Ontario do not exist in that fashion in
BC. What I've been reminded of is you need to be aware of the different names
a place may have, all of the different spellings it may have, names of Indian
Agencies which often change, and when communities are shifted in and out of
different agencies. That happens in the east, but it is much easier to track in the
records. It's funny how few people know the answers to those questions. I think
that the reduction of archivists at Library and Archives Canada (LAC) and this
push to digitization has actually really made it more difficult in some ways,
particularly in those areas that are not traditionally documented.

I also wonder about the digitization process – who's determining what is
and what isn't digitized? I'm pretty confident it is not Indigenous scholars
setting that agenda.[19] I'm confident that these decisions are made by those who
wouldn't have the knowledge of what it is that communities are looking for.
Instead, they're going to be trained in government, bureaucratic ways. And this
has implications for women's history, as the actual information that directly
pertains to women's history is almost never there. That's when you have to have
the community information and cultural knowledge to interpret the records of

women (specifically) and the communities (generally). To train students in how to do that – no one person could teach this. You have to experience it, you have to live it, you have to work with different people to hone those skills.

Mary Jane: My experience is that there's quite a lot of information about women in the Indian Affairs records. They seem to worry about Indian women an awful lot.

Susan: That's because they're trying to regulate us.

Mary Jane: But the problem is in how to interpret and ethically use all of this information. As you mentioned, we need an understanding of local knowledge to put it into context. But I think there are also ethical issues about using these records, even those that aren't restricted by law. I have used microfilms that contain names of individuals and their personal information. I think for most historians, we tend to aggregate information about individuals to tell a general story or make a broader argument about something, Indian policy for example. But this individual information is sometimes the most valuable to Indigenous communities you are writing about. We struggle then with reading, analysing, and sharing too much or not enough of the archive.[20] I often use government documents that are legally regulated and so it is difficult not to be able to directly share knowledge I have gained as a result of that research. It seems almost antithetical to our larger goals of knowledge sharing and oddly seems to protect the state. I am interested when the public engages with the topic I'm studying, even in instances where I'm not able to directly address questions. Usually once or twice a month I get an email asking if I have come across a particular name, or if I know how to find out more information about particular circumstances. Often these are very difficult research questions concerning where family members are buried and what happened to them. These questions come when, as you said, the "trail just stopped," sometimes well before satisfying information was found. Records concerning health, death, and burial are often very difficult to find in part because of the way it was recorded and the way records survived. Moreover, this kind of information is more often than not protected by access-to-information laws. This forces researchers to re-enact those structures that take the information away from communities or failed to share it in the first place. This is one of the issues that we twentieth-century historians uniquely face because our records often fall under these laws and our historical research topics occurred within living memory.[21] Of course, government documents aren't the only sources we look at – what other kinds of primary sources are you interested in?

Susan: While I'm primarily a documentary historian, I also have an avid interest in maps. They illuminate aspects of women's history that are often left out. Maps from this (Six Nations) territory that talk about different cornfields and gardens, for example. Rarely, but sometimes, you encounter survey maps of harvesting areas for berries. More often you see trails – but that's where being able to combine textual information with information that is held by people in communities comes in. If you talk to someone who has plant knowledge, you learn things such as, "My grandmother taught me about this plant and it used to grow in that place." And sometimes too, in contemporary times, what you find in that kind of information is the documentation of decimation. There's going to be that lineage of medicine people who know that grandma and great-grandma used to harvest there. And they dammed that stream and it flooded that area. Again, in cases such as these there's no sign that says, "This is a source of women's history"; rarely is it even noted that stories like these relate to environmental history and Indigenous land rights.

I have a lot of interest in historical photos and that's an area that I'm moving towards in my work. Many of the early ethnologists who did work in my community also commissioned photographs – of their "informants," of buildings (especially longhouses), and of parades and other community events. These all intrigue me. And of course, photographs of "everyday people" doing "everyday things" become amazing sources of information – and sources that provide excellent opportunities for collaborative research. The Woodland Cultural Centre (WCC), for example, has a program they hold semi-annually called "Ancestors in the Archives." At those events, cultural centre staff share parts of the WCC photo collection and invite community members from Six Nations (and related communities) to look through the photos in attempts to identify people, often relatives and ancestors. Often people also bring in photos from their own family collections. There are opportunities to copy pictures and to document living knowledge of historic photos. I also have an interest in our original documents, too, that aren't written, in a traditional sense, such as our wampum belts and our artwork, such as pottery. What can we learn from these pieces that reflects cultural and contemporary history? A lot of this material culture, as it's often referred to, is women's work. Having a more in-depth cultural knowledge to understand our symbols – and what has a connection to female aspects of things – again adds illumination to the historical record. We need to have a strong cultural background, particularly of visual literacy, to interpret these pieces of evidence on that level.

Mary Jane: These are great resources as well, and help to balance out some of the state-centred evidence we use. I find that using artefacts and photographs also helps to mitigate the effects of working with what are often quite violent and disturbing records directed at our ancestors, ourselves. On the one hand, we have a kind of insider's view on the workings of the federal government with respect to Indigenous people, and on the other we can directly see the structures and legacies that have been left from that. How do we continually read records and yet be as healthy as we can in our own relationships, our personal lives, and in our professional work and work relations? I've been thinking a lot about how I can hone my methodology to work with state records concerning Indigenous people as, after years, this work does affect the way that you see the world. I do a lot of writing while researching, usually in the evenings after a day of work. I kind of "write back" to those who created the records. It doesn't ever go anywhere, but it's a way of gaining a bit more perspective I guess and of questioning the decisions and work of government employees while their words are still fresh in my mind. Also, I try to limit the intensity of my exposure to the records – if possible. Sue, I remember a great lecture you did that identified how strange it can be to do this kind of work – in particular, you talked about what it's like to be doing Indian Affairs records research on your own community at the LAC in Ottawa.

Susan: Oh yes, the experience is a mixed bag. On an emotional level, here you are: you make this trip to Ottawa – fortunately in southern/eastern Ontario, we can drive – but for others it takes considerable time and expense to access information that your community should have but rarely does. So you're already perhaps a bit bitter? There's no obligation of sharing with the communities of course. Once you get through that, generally archivists are very helpful, lovely people – but they hold the key and you have to follow rules and procedures. I understand that there are reasons for that. But you need to get permission to access quite basic information from your community, from people who know nothing about it.

You also may not be prepared for the information you encounter. For example, one night, I was sitting in the reading room at the LAC, looking at Six Nations Council records, and came across records about a family mediation over a marriage separation. I realized fairly quickly it was my grandparents. And I didn't know about that part of my family's history. My father's mother died when he was very young, and I don't think he even knew that his parents were divorced. He went to residential school at the age of six, and I don't know what he knew about the specific family dynamics that were going on at the time. I had no idea that my grandparents were divorced – and there it was on the microfilm reel at the LAC one evening – for anyone to see.

In my dissertation and the subsequent book,[22] I use my family story and how my grandparents dealt with a custody issue and a land matter. These are the kinds of things that one encounters looking at families' histories. And almost always those looking at those stories do not know the specific histories or the people involved (or descended). In the end when we're writing about this stuff, and publishing books about it, we're airing families' dirty laundry. So I decided if I'm going to be airing dirty laundry of families who I may not know, but who are my neighbours, I had better air my own family's dirty laundry. In my grandparents' dispute, the chiefs conducted the separation in a manner that was consistent with their other dealings and it becomes a good example of how they dealt with land and custody of children. Therein was a cultural interpretation of morality that was central to the government decision made in that case. It was consistent with other cases. I could have used another case – but I didn't because in the end it always feels a bit like exploitation. That said, however, I've never run into a family that said, "I can't believe that you wrote that about my family"; rather, I hear, "I'm really glad that you found that and that you wrote that."

Mary Jane: That's good to hear. In the tuberculosis research, I'm facing very different types of information derived from oral history versus what I'm learning in the records. Because the sanatoriums I'm looking at closed in the 1960s, most of the people I have spoken with were children at the time that they were treated. Their knowledge about the institutions is thus very different than what I'm getting in the archives. Moreover, many frame the story of their treatment in a larger life history about recovery from TB that often celebrates the hospitals as having "saved their lives." I have a hard time reconciling this with the records – this is one instance where primary sources seem not to speak to each other and in fact constitute two very different kinds of history. For example, thanks to a government records archivist at the LAC, Leah Sander, I was made aware of a highly unique set of correspondence written by Inuit people in the late 1950s and 1960s, and within this file were several letters by patients in sanatoriums undergoing treatment for tuberculosis. This is one of the only sources of information by Indigenous people that describes what it is like to be a patient at the time. In addition to describing abuse, homesickness, boredom, and dislike of staff and other patients, the letter writers constantly discuss their concern about families back home and ask for definite information about when they will be able to return. Many were worried about who would undertake their roles at home and what would happen to their families when they were not there. Inuit women were particularly concerned about their family's clothing and who would sew, mend, and alter boots, coats, and mittens for the winter. They were worried that if they were not there to do the work, their families would not have proper clothing; they could get sick or would have to call on someone else to do this work. The letters are invariably polite – and state something like, "I understand that you are doing the best you can, but my worries are this and these are my responsibilities and they are not being done."

Susan: Can you imagine what someone who could read Inuktitut would be able to find out in these letters?

Mary Jane: I know – and this is one of the practical limitations on my work on Indian hospitals in Manitoba. Currently, reading the letters together with oral histories, it just doesn't seem to work – it seems like two different kinds of projects – one on the management of TB by the government and one on the way this past is remembered and how memories of hospitals were processed by Indigenous people. The scant photos of this history are also telling about the system. In one in particular, there were about ten officials – all men, doctors, surgeons, Indian Health Services administrators – standing around a girl patient who was in bed, presumably recovering from TB. Every one of the officials was named and given a title. The patient, however, was not even mentioned.

What methods do you use to interpret the primary sources that you work with?

Susan: I've tried to immerse myself in cultural structures and cultural history in order to situate things in larger ways. Without this you're limited. A key piece in this is in terms of Indigenous language knowledge. I've studied Mohawk and Cayuga. And that is also helpful in understanding the way that our people use English, because the way we use English is not the same way that those who have taught us English use it. It often ties to how our people translated our original knowledge into English. We use it in a slightly different way. If you have that lens to use, that offers you another layer of interpretation compared to if you don't have that background. And the more language that you know, the more you're going to understand. It's an area that I continually try to work towards. I'm fortunate in that I'm able to go to longhouse and see it used in ways that recall our history. Our ceremonial expressions are all tied to historical consciousness. We don't talk about it that way but that's what it is. We celebrate and recreate creation in our ceremonies – we recall what happened at the beginning of time, which instils in us a sense of appreciation for history.

Yesterday I was having a conversation about the Great Law. There's a lot of work happening in our communities right now about knowledge sharing around the Great Law and our governance system and how we obtained it. People are investigating the written documents that pertain to the story of the founding of the law as well as the written versions of the law itself. Our people love to read when they can access material that interests them, and the archival documents around the documentation of the Great Law are very popular. In these conversations around the Great Law, the current focus is internal. While there has long been extensive interest from outside of our communities, the leadership has chosen to limit access to outsiders presently. We have to build up our own knowledge in our communities before we're in a place to share it, to take the time to share it with other people. We need to focus on building our own base, which gives us the capacity to share it beyond ourselves. There is a growing number of Haudenosaunee scholars and amongst us there is a debate about access to materials produced around the Great Law recitals and other internal examinations of our cultural histories and heritage. Requests by our own academics for access to this material have sometimes been denied – my response is that that person can attend and participate. I encourage people to experience something in person before you try to write about it. For example, I read a lot about the ritual of condolence (a key aspect of the Great Law) – but what I learned from reading paled in comparison with participating in an actual condolence ceremony. There's a part that recalls our ancient villages – at that time we walk and remind ourselves of what our ancestors did. In that way, we're walking with them (our ancestors). Reading and talking about condolence is powerful historical research, but participating can lead you to an understanding beyond the spoken or written word. You are connecting to your ancestors in a way that no document is ever going to allow you to do. And it connects you to place. We are often told that those stories are held by places which in turn get labelled as "sacred places"; from our cultural perspective all places are sacred because they all help to support life. There is no hierarchy, but there are places of historical relevance that help us to connect with that history. For me it's about being in a place of our ancestors to help to understand their decisions and why they made them.

Part Three: Thinking Critically about Indigenous Women's History

Who are your favourite historians and books about women's history at the moment? Where are some of the gaps in our field?

Mary Jane: For me, and I imagine for you as well, NAISA [the Native American and Indigenous Studies Association] has been a really important site for conversations about Indigenous history. I'm so fortunate to have had exposure there to the work of people like Brenda Child, Tsianina Lomawaima, Jennifer Denetdale, Jeani O'Brien, Audra Simpson, Aroha Harris, Crystal Fraser, Jessica Kolopenuk, Rob Innes, Brendan Hokowithu, Vince Diaz, and many others. Many of my favourite panels from conferences this year dealt with biography actually – which continues to be so important in our field. And one panel in particular with Caitlin Keliiaa, Victoria Haskins, Colleen O'Neill, and Catherine Nolan-Ferrell looked at Indigenous women, labour, and state policy in the United States, Australia, and Guatemala and was really exciting to see. Keliiaa, for example, talked about two Native women who worked in a US Japanese internment camp in the Second World War. This work melded histories that are often thought to be separate and discontiguous. Another great panel I saw this year was at the Canadian Historical Association and featured Allyson Stevenson, Cheryl Troupe, and Tara Turner that centred Métis family, land, and bodies in western Canadian history and Métis historical consciousness. These discussions of family were so vibrant and illustrative of how we come to know, understand, and use history. I also really enjoyed a recent panel at the University of Saskatchewan that asked Kim Tallbear, Kim Anderson, and Audra Simpson to discuss how they came to feminism in their work; it was really useful in thinking about the use of feminist approaches in Indigenous history.[23] You know, a lot of the great material I'm getting these days is online. In addition to lectures, many scholars and activists have their own websites and do short pieces on other sites about a particular issue or event from the past in light of specific concerns about inequality, marginalization, and justice.[24] And then of course, there's also "Indigenous Twitterati," those who are using social media to develop and apply Indigenous methods.

Susan: Connections and parallels to things that are happening right now – that's for me the ultimate test of good history. If it is able to tell us about the life that we're living today, then it has relevance. In the end, most of the students we teach are not going to be professional historians. We didn't even have those plans when we were in undergraduate history classes. They're going to be lawyers, teachers, bank managers – but all of them have something useful to gain from knowing something about Indigenous history.

Borrowing Maori historian Aroha Harris's phrase, "You can't have good New Zealand history without good Maori history" – you also can't have good Native history without good Native women's history. If you only talk about men, if you only analyse things from a men's context – you cannot actually understand men. You cannot have one without the other. No matter what issues may arise around gender tensions, all of our traditional teachings are based in concepts of equity and gender balance. I have yet to encounter in a North American context where our traditional teachings don't come from that concept of balance. You can't write the story of Indigenous men if you don't include the story of women in that process.

Mary Jane: I remember in the early presentations of work on Indigenous masculinity that there was some concern that the focus would turn again to men, and that it would be just another way of centring men in our histories, and perhaps also uncritically celebrate heteromasculinity. To date, rather, there seems to have been a real focus on researching the history and consequences of the colonization of Indigenous genders.

Susan: That tends to be the scholarly focus, yes. Most of our communities aren't real keen on the "colonized" and "decolonized" terminology, however. It's one of those gears you have to shift between conversations in the academy vs. conversations in the community. It's about respect and understanding what are the problems – particularly around agency. We reacted as well – and what is the responsibility side of that? It often comes from our older people too. To me, that's the message they're trying to share – be careful in allowing yourself to be a victim – it's more complicated than that.

Those in the field of Indigenous masculinities are doing good work – I think that many of the leaders of the field are really talking about gender balance and helping communities and families restore gender balance. In anything, the risk is that people use it for self-glorification – that's a pitfall for all academic work because the academy is built on the premise of self-glorification – there are examples of where that has happened. But at its core, there's this premise of understanding the concept of gender, and the intention to encourage men to take responsibility for what they inherit as men, and how that plays out in our communities. At its core it is entrenching responsibility around healthy gender relationships in living in Indigenous communities. It's going to take lots of different approaches to be truly effective.

Many who started that field would probably consider themselves to be Indigenous feminists – or Indigenous thinkers who don't need feminism as a title per se. I haven't seen too much of that element – I would expect a correlation between the pushback with the feminism label, too. But I don't know how much of this is being talked about at the grassroots level. The I Am a Kind Man project – they don't talk about masculinities per se but rather about how to be a healthy man who has good relationships.[25] There are scores of community-based projects working directly with Indigenous men on being healthy people, primarily through Friendship Centres. They focus on men, but it is about wellness for individuals, families, and communities. This is similar to how Indigenous women's research began as well. But I think this is a bit different – there is still a lot of research funding going to grassroots women's groups – but not so much in terms of Indigenous masculinities at the grassroots level. There's also exponentially less exposure of sexual and gendered violence against males.

In terms of other kinds of work, there are a lot more collaborations in women's history. I think that's good – work like that of Paige Raibmon and Leslie Robertson.[26] But what I want to know is what are collaborating scholars doing to make space for Indigenous-community-based scholars to have a voice in the institution beyond a particular publication. Are they getting scholarships? Are they getting them into graduate programs? Are they helping them get publications of their own where an allied scholar is not the lead?

Moreover, the "as told bys" are not that revolutionary. It depends on how they're doing it. There are some really truly collaborative examples, but you won't always know it by reading it. It's only when you work with them that you find this out.

Mary Jane: I notice that a lot of this kind of work seems to happen in BC and the Yukon.

Susan: It may be a product of the social structures of those communities.

Mary Jane: Alyssa Mt. Pleasant raises the excellent point that Indigenous history is often focused on the nineteenth and twentieth centuries – this is true of Indigenous women's history as well. There is so little on the seventeenth and eighteenth centuries.

Susan: A lot of it focuses on Native women guides and wives, still only important because of their connections to white men. In terms of the more contemporary histories, much of it is inspired by the Native women's movement – these primarily informed those strong women stories. Those were the ones that were getting media attention. That's the narrative that gets put forward, that has the political weight – it's tied to current political events that are popular in the media but it often misses so much of what is happening in communities and Native organizations in terms of women's issues and female leadership.

Mary Jane: I love studying the modern era. In my work on Indigenous women's labour history in the twentieth century, I was so frustrated with the assumption that Indigenous women had no significant role in the history of waged labour, or even in modern Indigenous and Canadian history more generally. We have to think about what goes into those assumptions – and the commonplace ideas about what "counts" as labour and what "counts" as history.

Susan: Are there any other gaps or problems that you find with the field?

Mary Jane: Certainly – and these are reflected too in our selected readings section. I would like to see more work on the north, on Atlantic Canada and on Quebec. As a peer reviewer in the field, we also see important oversights. In particular, far too often, I see manuscripts that fail to take Indigenous scholarship into consideration. This is especially problematic in work that deals with Indigenous historical topics. The false impression given is that either there isn't any scholarship to refer to, or that it's not relevant or worthwhile to the topic at hand. But this means that the scholarship here does not genuinely speak to, engage with, or benefit us. For this reason, we focus on Indigenous scholarship in our suggested readings section at the end of this chapter.

Part Four: Teaching Indigenous Women's History

How do you teach Indigenous women's history? What are the major topics, issues?

Susan: I would say that I teach in a very integrated way – so that women are rarely a single page in a PowerPoint but rather incorporated. I generally start my survey courses with Indigenous stories of creation, which almost always have women early on in the story. Women are a central aspect to some things – but are not always represented or documented in others – such as treaties. So you need to do a lot more interpretation and analysis. You have to do more work on kinship – such as who decided who would sign, and what was the state saying about women, and how is the state regulating things like marriage and childbirth. These are all topics that connect to women. The students wouldn't necessarily know that there's a plan. But there is.

It certainly helps when it's the type of course where you can start with Indigenous constructions of history first. In teaching on the twentieth century – I teach the Native women's movement as an aspect of Indigenous history in Canada, a piece of the Indigenous rights movement. And I make connections to what was happening in the United States and Australia at the same time for comparative purposes. The understanding of the regulating and defining of women as an effort to control land is almost always missed. The canon often forgets this extension; historians also usually fail to fully connect Indigenous men or the state agenda to land (even though that is the state agenda).

Mary Jane: I developed a third-year course on Indigenous women's history that I intentionally teach as a "long twentieth-century" history course. Often Indigenous history courses aren't given the "gift" of chronology so important to the structures of Canadian, US, and other history courses. After a few introductory classes on historiography, Indigenous feminism, and sources, we discuss Education, Work, Law, and Life 1870s–1940s; Sexuality, Gender, and Canadian Law; Visibility and Invisibility, 1940s–1970s; Aboriginal Women and Organized Political Action, 1970s–2000; and Reflections on Indigenous Women's History and Historians. There's no prerequisite and it's also cross-listed with women's and gender studies.

Susan: What texts do you use?

Mary Jane: Most texts about Indigenous women's history are not by Indigenous people, although that is now just starting to change. At the same time texts by Indigenous authors that do deal with women, gender, and Indigenous studies include very little historical analysis. So in a way I had to choose one or the other, and in the end my preference was to support Indigenous scholars where possible. I supplement the text *Restoring the Balance: First Nations Women, Community, and Culture* (edited by Valaskakis, Dion Stout, and Guimond) with biography and a number of great articles on Indigenous women's history from Canada and beyond – I've used Beatrice Mosinier's *Come Walk with Me: A Memoir* and Blair Stonechild's *Buffy Sainte Marie: It's My Way* so far, and I think my secondary reading list is second to none. I was actually a bit surprised that very few history majors have signed up for the course – students mostly came from women's and gender studies, Indigenous studies, criminology, education, urban and inner city studies, and politics. I know that you get a lot more senior history students in your courses. What kind of advice do you give students who want to go on to study Indigenous history at graduate levels?

Susan: Committing to learn an Indigenous language is vital. This will improve the quality of students who are in this field. Mindset and learning the language are central to a deeper analysis of sources. By studying a Native language, you also start to have a better understanding of how a Native community uses English. This leads to a deeper understanding of the historical records you encounter.

Gaining a sense of cultural metaphors is also really critical and often tied to language as well. Particularly, the earlier historical records are full of these metaphors that the transcriber may not have understood. Even understanding how some non-Native people were able to build alliances, to understand how they were able to get the concepts of cultural metaphors. This becomes really important to having a more nuanced analysis of the historic record.

Make sure you talk to living people about how they understand the past to be. Don't steal their ideas, but have communications and dialogues, because that's another form of fact-checking. You need to be careful, err on the side of caution, and have an understanding of how to apply Indigenous research ethics – but this may seem different in different contexts.

For anyone doing advanced historical studies, you have a responsibility to give something back. When you find information, make a copy, make sure it gets into the hands of people who can and will use it.

When you encounter archivists and librarians, share what you have learned with them as well. It's important for them to understand the value of the material they have. And make sure they know you will be sharing the information with communities, who may in turn come knocking on their door. Assure them you know they will be welcoming to those communities, as welcoming to those after you as they were for you.

Finally, it doesn't hurt to know a good lawyer. You are responsible, and you have to think about that before you say or publish anything, because it does impact people's lives now and into the future.

Mary Jane: I recall a discussion you and I had about mentoring students in Indigenous history. One of the points you made was that much of our mentorship work deals with undergraduate, rather than graduate, students; at the same time, mentorship with Indigenous students is often not seen as "teaching" in the same way as our work with non-Indigenous students. Ironically, many of the mentors that we had going through school – those who taught us skills to undertake historical research – are non-Indigenous scholars, and more particular, white men. Currently, in spite of what you might think of when you hear the term "mentor," many of our mentors are not older than us or at more advanced stages in their careers. Rather, they are Indigenous scholars who we work with and who talk with us about their experience of survival in a department of history (or related fields), provide professional advice, share course outlines, and think about how to reframe university work in thoughtful and helpful ways. They read our stuff over and provide helpful questions, and are models of how to exist as an Indigenous scholar. This kind of mentoring is not hierarchical or generational, but across generations, and often is transnational as well.

I do have some concerns about the mentorship of Indigenous scholars in history at present. There's a tendency to rely heavily on these scholars, who often, at least in history departments, are utterly under-represented. They are given a lot of work and may not have the ability to refuse, especially in a climate where there is so little hiring going on. While some universities have started to increase Indigenous representation among faculty through, for example, efforts to recruit and retain Indigenous faculty, little hiring has been done in history departments and many of the historically focused Indigenous scholars, and the intellectual communities and spaces they build on campus, are found in departments outside of history. History departments can do a lot to mentor Indigenous scholars. Providing a supportive, scholarly, collegial, and informed environment is critical. Ensuring that Indigenous scholars are not too weighed down by service commitments is also important. Obviously, one Indigenous faculty member is never enough. I hope that as we look forward to a period in which our universities fully acknowledge the contributions of Indigenous scholars and provide the necessary space and support to allow them to flourish to their full potential. Academic leadership needs to consistently take up the cause of diversity at an intellectual and human resources level.

Susan: Also, Indigenous students continue to be extremely under-represented in graduate history programs. Most of the Indigenous graduate students I work with are in other departments, including sociology, anthropology, kinesiology, and education. Most of them have a deep interest in history but found other fields more welcoming of their work. So our graduate student mentoring is often much more active outside of history departments than within.

Mary Jane: Speaking of mentorship, students also inform our work – often by asking really thought-provoking questions that stay with us. I guest-lectured in a Sources and Methods in History class last year and after telling a few stories about my research, a student asked me something like, "What makes you want to study history, especially in a context in which most people dismiss it, and when these histories are so heartbreaking to write and to read?" At the time I didn't see it this way, but now I think this question was about where motivation to research comes from. For me, I have a genuine fascination in the lives of my family and my ancestors that drives me to learn more about them. While they connect me to certain places and ways of thinking, they lived such different, often difficult lives. Sometimes I am astounded at what the documentary record can tell me about their lives. I love to share these leads and learn about other information by talking to relatives. Our family history quite literally fascinates me and propels me.

As historians we constantly revisit a historiography that fails to acknowledge Indigenous people's agency and activity in shaping our history. In fact, this historiography informs our practice – our methods. Why do we still care about academic history then? Aroha Harris has a fabulous essay entitled "Why I'm Still Keen Even Though You're So Mean," and in it, she is writing to the discipline of history itself and explains her participation as a "sense of duty and a challenge that it is our turn to write our history for ourselves and for our children in the first instance and then for the world." History teaches us, she argues, "how to see ourselves, not only in the past but also in the present. History has been used as a powerful colonizing tool; and it can also be a powerful liberating tool. It's in our interests to learn how to make History work for us." Harris reasons that,

If you shape History, you can shape the nation's stories about itself. And as Maori, as colonized Indigenous people, we must be interested in that. To not be interested is to accept the histories our colonisers will tell about us, which in fact risks not being spoken about at all. Now, I'm not saying here that colonisers can only write bad history or no history. I'm just saying that we put ourselves in a far more powerful position if we write our histories ourselves, on our own terms, according to our own values and priorities … So I like to think I will be keen on History for as long as I can imagine; imagine our key messages about the past occurring in everyday lives and events; imagine our history becoming not only the nation's reading but also the nation's memory; imagine ourselves writing our histories, and writing ourselves powerful.[27]

Part Five: "Our Moment" of Indigenous Women's History in Broader Historical Context – Concluding Thoughts

Mary Jane: Indigenous history is now seen as more important than it ever has been before. If anything, I think it's the most vibrant field of history in Canada right now.

Susan: Again, borrowing from Aroha – you can't have good Canadian history if you don't have a good understanding of Indigenous history. You need both a historical and a contemporary understanding of the realities of Indigenous people in Canada if you are to truly understand the Canadian nation state.

Mary Jane: The issue of MMIW has entered the consciousness of many Canadians. We write now in the midst of one of the most important and energetic social movements in Canadian history – the Idle No More movement, which was initiated by Indigenous women and has popularized an understanding about the importance of Indigenous history to our contemporary society. With the work of the Truth and Reconciliation Commission (TRC), Indigenous history – indeed also the otherwise almost invisible work of Indigenous archival research – gained unprecedented media attention. The TRC's recommendations included broad public education about Indigenous history, racism, and Indigenous treaty and other rights in Canada. Our university and others have taken this up in part through the development of its mandatory Indigenous Course Requirement.[28] In Winnipeg, issues like anti-Indigenous racism are being publicly discussed in important, if not completely unprecedented, ways. For example, many in our city have seriously begun to consider where our drinking water comes from and at what costs. In most of these discussions, there is at least a nod to history – even if it's a sort of passing interest and sometimes not very rigorous. I think as well, efforts in the project of "reconciliation" have drawn many non-Indigenous scholars to see their work as part of a broader purpose – to identify and "acknowledge" the problem of colonization in Canada. In a very immediate way, we write women's history amidst unprecedented media attention on Indigenous women's lives and bodies in Canada. What does it mean to think historically in this context?

Susan: This brings to mind Theresa Spence's hunger strike. Harper's Conservative government was quick to release to media information on the millions of government dollars allocated to the community, but those reports were short on the details of northern living expenses. They also failed to highlight that a significant portion of those funds were spent on a new school to replace the one the government had built on a toxic waste site in the community. The media reports about Chief Spence and her First Nation were characteristic of Canadian cultural representations of modern Native people, and of modern Native women. These reports were fraught with social expectations of how a modern Native woman should be. Not a chief and certainly not a disgruntled chief. And all the reports (and related commentary) lacked historical context. Chief Spence and many of the Idle No More activists were trying to raise awareness of contemporary issues within a context of historical understanding. In this, they followed the footsteps of many ancestors who fought to bring awareness of the Indigenous past to the broader public.

Within the TRC I see very little about gender. In the media around the TRC there has been little about gender. Yet, from survivors' stories (including those of our own family members), we know the experiences of residential schools were extremely gendered. As you've pointed out in your work on Indigenous labour history, the history of residential school "training" impacts on our present Indigenous labour force in very gendered ways. That analysis is missing from the report. From a historian's perspective, you can read the report and know who from the Commission made specific recommendations. While still useful, many of them are not national in scope. There's a lot about the creation of Canada that is not spelled out there, and that is an area where work needs to be taken up and moved forward.

Similarly, the publicly released investigative reports on MMIW have focused on Indigenous men as perpetrators with little critique of systemic racism, poverty, and the role of police and government agencies. And yet that whole inquiry has lots of meaning for both men and women, particularly when you look at families. At the same time, murdered and missing Indigenous men tend to be quite invisible. Both of those stories are vital and important because these are our relatives. In the end, regardless of someone's gender identification, having your relative murdered is an awful thing, a life ended before it should have been. Regardless of your gender, you will not be able to change that, and it will have an impact on your life. We should remember the community and family understandings of those losses, including but not limited to gender.

Mary Jane: For me, writing Indigenous women's history today presents many challenges and rewards. Unlike those writing Indigenous women's history before, say, 2000, we do so in some ways in a far more supportive context. Often our work is also given attention and voice as it is seen to have immediate and broad relevance to the lived lives of Indigenous women and other Canadians, and this is not commonly the case for academic historical work. At the same time, there is a way in which media attention on Indigenous women's issues tends to narrow the otherwise diverse experiences of Indigenous women, and in some ways the lives and bodies of Indigenous women have become symbols of a singular yet powerful narrative of a gendered experience of colonialism and modernity in Canada, including poverty, sexism, ill health, substandard housing, sexual danger, over- and under-policing. This narrative is powerful in that it motivates change and helps to explain broader social and economic circumstances which put Indigenous women in particular kinds of racialized and sexualized danger. Indeed, this narrative shapes our realities everyday – what we tell our kids, how we interact with our neighbours, what informs our interactions with our universities and our profession more broadly. In a very real way we too confront people's "common-sense" ideas about our bodies and our lives and those of our children – ideas that we had no role in shaping and have no real way of escaping.

How do we account for the multiple experiences of Indigenous women's lives in this context? How do we interpret their lives in ways that have meaning for Indigenous people today and which reflect our particular concern about and care for Indigenous lives lived in the past and the integrity of Indigenous history?

The goal of resolution and reconciliation in some ways interrupts my work, I find. At certain moments, I feel the need to press my scholarship into the service of reconciliation when really what I want to do is to name and identify things I'm not willing to reconcile with now or ever.

As historians, our responsibilities are to the past – whatever era you are looking at. We can never write or research history outside of the present, but we do care about the past in ways that other disciplines don't.[29] We care about our sources as well in unique ways and come to have very odd relationships with them that are also unique to those in our discipline. When our histories are "watered down" or condensed in particular ways, even when it serves a distinct purpose, I always feel a sense of loss somehow.

Susan: As Indigenous historians, we are often looked at to answer all questions around social grievances, political disputes, and identity. This is not new for us, but many of the question askers are new. The media coverage of Idle No More, MMIW, and the TRC has raised the profile of Indigenous history and Indigenous studies, especially within Canadian universities. And as always, the reactions to our answers – answers which are pretty consistent with what they were a decade ago, by the way – will be met with a combination of belief and disbelief. While more people are asking questions and are actually open to our answers, a significant portion of society will only believe what they already believe to be true regardless of evidence presented.

Mary Jane: In Indigenous history, we are also constantly writing back to a narrative of history that marginalized and erased us from the past. Some of us write back in ways that "include" us in the narrative of the nation; others of us write back in ways that seek alternative ways of analysing the past that are rooted in Indigenous epistemologies and methods of history keeping and telling. And lots of us do both. Sue, I'd say we inherited a fairly colonized, white-supremacist, and patriarchal canon of Indigenous and women's history when we entered school. Do you see this as changing? What things need to be in place in order for us to "decolonize" or "liberate" our history?

Susan: Change has happened and is happening at great rates, yet much of what we experienced as undergraduate history students in Canada and the United States still persists. We still have very few textbooks written by Indigenous scholars. Very few history departments employ tenured/tenure-track Indigenous historians. Most students can get a Canadian undergraduate history degree without any substantial knowledge of Indigenous history within Canada or elsewhere in the world. The issues continue to be around content, context, and human resources. I'm hesitant around decolonization terminology because it is often co-opted with other non-Indigenous agendas. Whether one calls it "decolonization" or "liberation" or "reconciliation" is of far less concern than what actually is done; Canada (and the United States) needs to take a broader, more critical, and more inclusive look at its past if it is to face the future in a well-informed manner.

Mary Jane: Thank you so much for this great conversation. Anushiik.

Susan: Nyaweh.

NOTES

Mary Jane Logan McCallum and Susan M. Hill have worked together for over a decade on several collaborative projects seeking to advance Indigenous historical scholarship.
1 John S. Milloy, "The Early Indian Acts: Developmental Strategy and Constitutional Change," in *As Long as the Sun Shines and the Water Flows: A Reader in*

Canadian Native Studies, ed. Ian Getty and Antoine Lussier (Vancouver: UBC Press, 1993), 56–64.

2 J.N.B. Hewitt (Tuscarora Nation) was a linguist and ethnographer who worked for the Bureau of American Ethnology.

3 Reuben Gold Thwaites, ed., *Jesuit Relations and Allied Documents: Travels and Explorations of the Jesuit Missionaries in New France, 1610–1791* (Cleveland: Burrows Brothers Company, 1986). See also Olive P. Dickason, *The Myth of the Savage and the Beginnings of French Colonialism in the Americas* (Edmonton: University of Alberta Press, 1984); Karen L. Anderson, *Chain Her by One Foot: The Subjugation of Native Women in Seventeenth-Century New France* (New York: Routledge, 1993); Susan Sleeper-Smith, *Indian Women and French Men: Rethinking Cultural Encounter in the Western Great Lakes* (Amherst: University of Massachusetts Press, 2001); Mary Dunn, "Neither One Thing nor the Other: Discursive Polyvalence and Representations of Amerindian Women in the Jesuit Relations," *Journal of Jesuit Studies* 3 (2016): 179–96.

4 John Arthur Gibson and Hanni Woodbury, trans., *Concerning the League: The Iroquois League Tradition as Dictated in Onondaga* (Syracuse: Syracuse University Press, 1992).

5 Sally M. Weaver, "Seth Newhouse and the Grand River Confederacy at Mid-Nineteenth Century," in *Extending the Rafters: Interdisciplinary Approaches to Iroquoian Studies*, ed. Michael K. Foster, Jack Campisi, and Marianne Mithun (Albany: SUNY Press, 1984), 165–82.

6 An example of this can be found in John Mohawk's 2005 *Iroquois Creation Story*, where he misidentifies John Arthur Gibson (Seneca Nation) as an Onondaga because he worked in the Onondaga language. John C. Mohawk, *Iroquois Creation Story: John Arthur Gibson and J.N.B. Hewitt's Myth of the Earth Grasper* (Buffalo: Mohawk Publications, 2005).

7 Deborah Doxtator, "What Happened to the Iroquois Clans? A Study of Clans in Three Nineteenth-Century Rotiononhsyonni Communities" (PhD diss., University of Western Ontario, 1996). See also Deborah Doxtator, "Inclusive and Exclusive Perceptions of Difference: Native and Euro-Based Concepts of Time, History, and Change," in *Decentring the Renaissance: Canada and Europe in Multidisciplinary Perspective, 1500–1700*, ed. Germaine Warkentin and Carolyn Podruchny (Toronto: University of Toronto Press, 2001), 33–47.

8 For example, see Deborah Doxtator, *Godi'nigoha': The Women's Mind* (Brantford, ON: Woodland Cultural Center, 1997).

9 Veronica Strong-Boag, *The New Day Recalled: Lives of Girls and Women in English Canada, 1919–1939* (Toronto: Copp, Clark, Pitman and Penguin Books,

1988); Franca Iacovetta and Mariana Valverde, eds, *Gender Conflicts: New Essays in Women's History* (Toronto: University of Toronto Press, 1992); Karen Dubinsky, *Improper Advances: Rape and Heterosexual Conflict in Ontario, 1880–1929* (Chicago: University of Chicago Press, 1993); Joan Sangster, *Earning Respect: The Lives of Working Women in Small-Town Ontario, 1920–1960* (Toronto: University of Toronto Press, 1995), and *Regulating Girls and Women: Sexuality, Family, and the Law in Ontario, 1920–1960* (Toronto: Oxford University Press, 2001); Carolyn Strange, *Toronto's Girl Problem: The Perils and Pleasures of the City, 1880–1939* (Toronto: University of Toronto Press, 1995); and Mariana Valverde, *The Age of Light, Soap, and Water: Moral Reform in English Canada, 1885–1925* (Toronto: McClelland and Stewart, 1991).

10 Sarah Carter, *Capturing Women: The Manipulation of Cultural Imagery in Canada's Prairie West* (Montreal: McGill-Queen's University Press, 1997); Sylvia Van Kirk, *Many Tender Ties: Women in Fur-Trade Society, 1670–1870* (Winnipeg: Watson and Dwyer, 1996); Jo-Anne Fiske, "'The Womb Is to the Nation as the Heart Is to the Body': Ethnopolitical Discourses of the Canadian Indigenous Women's Movement," *Studies in Political Economy* 51 (1996): 65–96, and "Child of the State, Mother of the Nation: Aboriginal Women and the Ideology of Motherhood," *Culture* 13, 1 (1993): 17–35; and Jennifer Brown, *Strangers in Blood: Fur Trade Company Families in Indian Country* (Norman: University of Oklahoma Press, 1996).

11 Kim Anderson, *A Recognition of Being: Reconstructing Native Womanhood* (Toronto: Canadian Scholars Press, 2001); Maria Campbell, *Halfbreed* (Toronto: McClelland and Stewart, 1973); Janice Acoose, *Iskwewak – kah'ki yaw ni wahko-makanak: Neither Indian Princesses nor Easy Squaws* (Toronto: Women's Press, 1992); Winona Stevenson, "Colonialism and First Nations Women," in *Scratching the Surface: Canadian Anti-Racist Feminist Thought*, ed. Enakshi Dua and Angela Roberts (Toronto: Canadian Scholars Press, 1999), 49–80; Rayna Green, "The Pocahontas Perplex: The Image of American Indian Women in American Culture," *Massachusetts Review* 16 (1975): 698–714; Paula Gunn Allan, *The Sacred Hoop: Recovering the Feminine in American Indian Traditions* (Boston: Beacon Press, 1992); Christine Miller and Patricia Churchyk, eds, *Women of the First Nations: Power, Wisdom, and Strength* (Winnipeg: University of Manitoba Press, 1996).

12 Adele Perry, "Fair Ones of a Purer Caste: White Women and Colonialism in Nineteenth-Century British Columbia," *Feminist Studies* 23, 3 (Fall 1997): 501–24.

13 See, for example, Jennifer Denetdale, "'No Explanation, No Resolution, and No Answers': Border Town Violence and Navajo Resistance to Settler Colonialism," *Wicazo Sa Review* 31, 1 (Spring 2016): 111–31; Noelani Arista, "Ka Waihona Palapala Manaleo: Research in a Time of Plenty: Colonialism and Ignoring the

Hawaiian Language Archive," in *Indigenous Textual Cultures*, ed. Lachlan Paterson and Tony Ballantyne (Durham, NC: Duke University Press, forthcoming), and *Histories of Unequal Measure: Euro-American Encounters with Hawaiian Governance and Law, 1796–1827* (Philadelphia: University of Pennsylvania Press, forthcoming); Marie Alohalani Brown, "Mauna Kea: Ho'omana Hawai'i and Protecting the Sacred," *Journal for the Study of Religion, Nature, and Culture* 10, 2 (2016): 150–69.

14   Mary Jane Logan McCallum, *Indigenous Women, Work, and History: 1940–1980* (Winnipeg: University of Manitoba Press, 2014).

15   Erica Violet Lee, "My Optimism Wears Moccasins and Is Loud: On Paris, Heavy Metal, and Chasing Freedom," 30 April 2016, Moontime Warrior, https://moontimewarrior.com/2016/04/30/my-optimism-wears-moccasins-and-is-loud/. See also Andrea Smith, *Conquest: Sexual Violence and American Indian Genocide* (Durham, NC: Duke University Press, 2015).

16   For example, a recent book re-examines the history of Wahbung, the Manitoba Indian Brotherhood's 1971 response to the proposal of the White Paper, by centring the story on women who worked to develop the document. Dave Courchene Jr, Janet Fontaine, and Kathi Avery Kinew, *Our Tomorrows, Today: Wahbung 1971* (Winnipeg: Manitoba First Nations Education Resource Centre, 2017).

17   Christine Taitano DeLisle, "A History of Chamorro Nurse-Midwives in Guam and a 'Placental Politics' for Indigenous Feminism," *Intersections: Gender and Sexuality in Asia and the Pacific* 37 (March 2015), http://intersections.anu.edu.au/issue37/delisle.htm.

18   For more on digitization, see Siobhan Senier, "Digitizing Indigenous History: Trends and Challenges," *Journal of Victorian Culture* 19, 3 (2014): 396–402.

19   See for example Laura L. Terrance, "Resisting Colonial Education: Zitkala-Sa and Native Feminist Archival Refusal," *International Journal of Qualitative Studies in Education*, 24, 5 (September–October 2011): 621–6.

20   For more on Access to Information and Privacy (ATIP), see Dominique Clement, "'Freedom of Information': Implications for Historical Research," *Labour / Le Travail* 75 (Spring 2015): 101–31.

21   Susan M. Hill, *The Clay We Are Made Of: Haudenosaunee Land Tenure on the Grand River* (Winnipeg: University of Manitoba Press, 2017).

22   Kim Anderson, Kim Tallbear, and Audra Simpson, "Indigenous Feminism Power Panel," moderated by Alex Wilson, 15 March 2016, Saskatoon, Saskatchewan, https://www.youtube.com/watch?v=-HnEvaVXoto.

23   These include work by Leanne Simpson (www.leannesimpson.ca), Christine Sy (https://giizismoon.wordpress.com), Chelsea Vowel (apihtawikosisan.com), Joanne Barker (www.tequilasovereign.com), Erika Violet Lee (moontimewarrior.com), Zoe S.C. Todd (zoesctodd.wordpress.com), and others.

24 The I Am a Kind Man project is a special project of the Ontario Federation of Indian Friendship Centres. More information can be found at www.iamakindman.ca.
25 Elsie Paul with Paige Raibmon and Harmony Johnson, *Written as I Remember
It: Teachings (ʔəms taʔaw) from the Life of a Sliammon Elder* (Vancouver: UBC
Press, 2014); Leslie A. Robertson and the Kwagu'ł Gixsam Clan, *Standing Up
with Ga'axsta'las: Jane Constance Cook and the Politics of Memory, Church, and
Custom* (Vancouver: UBC Press, 2012).
26 Aroha Harris, "Why I'm Still Keen Even Though You're So Mean," paper presented
to the Berkshire Conference on the History of Women, May 2014, Toronto, Ontario,
Canada.
27 For a more detailed discussion among Indigenous scholars in Canada on
their research and teaching, see Crystal Fraser, ed., "Indigenous Histories"
blog series, *Active History*, January 2016, http://activehistory.ca/papers/
indigenous-histories/.
28 Thank you to Adele Perry for the conversations about how the present begins our
work and historians' distinctive attention to and care for the past as the past.

SELECTED READINGS

Acoose, Janice. *Iskwewak Kah'Ki Yaw Ni Wahkomakanak: Neither Indian Princesses
nor Easy Squaws*. 2nd ed. Toronto: Women's Press, 2016.
Anderson, Kim. *Life Stages and Native Women: Memory, Teachings, and Story
Medicine*. Winnipeg: University of Manitoba Press, 2011.
– *Recognition of Being: Reconstructing Native Womanhood*. 2nd ed. Toronto:
Women's Press, 2016.
Anderson, Kim, Robert Alexander Innes, and John Swift. "Indigenous Masculinities:
Carrying the Bones of the Ancestors." In *Canadian Men and Masculinities:
Historical and Contemporary Perspectives*, edited by Christopher Greig and Wayne
Martino, 266–84. Toronto: Canadian Scholars Press, 2012.
Anderson, Kim, and Bonita Lawrence, eds. *Strong Women Stories: Native Vision and
Community Survival*. Toronto: Sumach Press, 2003.
Backhouse, Constance. *Carnal Crimes: Sexual Assault Law in Canada, 1900–1975*.
Toronto: Irwin Law, 2008.
Barker, Joanne. "Gender, Sovereignty, and the Discourse of Rights in Native Women's
Activism." *Meridians: Feminism, Race, Transnationalism* 7, 1 (2007): 127–61.
https://doi.org/10.2979/MER.2006.7.1.127
– "Gender, Sovereignty, Rights: Native Women's Activism against Social Inequality
and Violence in Canada." *American Indian Quarterly* 60, 2 (June 2008): 259–66.
https://doi.org/10.1353/aq.0.0002

Barker, Joanne, ed. *Critically Sovereign: Indigenous Gender, Sexuality, and Feminist Studies*. Durham, NC: Duke University Press, 2017.

Barman, Jean. *French Canadians, Furs, and Indigenous Women in the Making of the Pacific Northwest*. Vancouver: UBC Press, 2014.

Brownlie, Robin Jarvis. *A Fatherly Eye: Indian Agents, Government Power, and Aboriginal Resistance in Ontario, 1918–1939*. Don Mills, ON: Oxford University Press, 2003.

– "Intimate Surveillance: Indian Affairs, Colonization, and the Regulation of Aboriginal Women's Sexuality." In *Contact Zones: Aboriginal and Settler Women in Canada's Colonial Past*, edited by Katie Pickles and Myra Rutherdale, 160–78. Vancouver: UBC Press, 2005.

– "'Living the Same as the White People': Mohawk and Anishinabe Women's Labour in Southern Ontario, 1920–1940." *Labour / Le Travail* 61 (Spring 2008): 41–68.

Burnett, Kristin. *Taking Medicine: Women's Healing Work and Colonial Contact in Southern Alberta, 1880–1930*. Vancouver: UBC Press, 2010.

Cahill, Cathleen. *Federal Fathers and Mothers: A Social History of the United States Indian Service, 1869–1933*. Chapel Hill: University of North Carolina Press, 2011.

Carlson, Nellie, and Kathleen Steinhauer as told to Linda Goyette. *Disinherited Generations: Our Struggle to Reclaim Treaty Rights for First Nations Women and Their Descendants*. Edmonton: University of Alberta Press, 2012.

Carter, Sarah. *The Importance of Being Monogamous: Marriage and Nation Building in Western Canada to 1915*. Edmonton: Athabasca University Press and University of Alberta Press, 2008.

Carter, Sarah, Lesley Erickson, Patricia Roome, and Char Smith. *Unsettled Pasts: Reconceiving the West through Women's History*. Calgary: University of Calgary Press, 2005.

Carter, Sarah, and Patricia A. McCormack, eds. *Recollecting: Lives of Aboriginal Women of the Canadian Northwest and Borderlands*. Edmonton: Athabasca University Press, 2011.

Chacaby, Ma-Nee, and Mary Louisa Plummer. *A Two-Spirit Journey: The Autobiography of a Lesbian Ojibwa-Cree Elder*. Winnipeg: University of Manitoba Press, 2016.

Child, Brenda. *Holding Our World Together: Ojibwe Women and the Survival of Community*. New York: Penguin, 2013.

Courchene, Dave Jr., Janet Fontaine, and Kathi Avery Kinew. *Our Tomorrows, Today: Wahbung, 1971*. Winnipeg: Manitoba First Nations Education Resource Centre, 2017.

Daum Shanks, Signa. "A Story of Marguerite: A Tale about Panis, Case Comment, and Social History." *Native Studies Review* 22, 1–2 (2013): 113–37.

Deer, Sarah. *The Beginning and End of Rape: Confronting Sexual Violence in Native America*. Minneapolis: University of Minnesota Press, 2015.

DeLisle, Christine Taitano. "A History of Chamorro Nurse-Midwives in Guam and a 'Placental Politics' for Indigenous Feminism." *Intersections: Gender and Sexuality in Asia and the Pacific* 37 (March 2015). http://intersections.anu.edu.au/issue37/delisle.htm

– "'Tumuge'Påpa' (Writing It Down): Chamorro Midwives and the Delivery of Native History." *Pacific Studies* 30, 1 (2007): 20–32.

Denetdale, Jennifer. "Chairmen, Presidents, and Princesses: The Navajo Nation, Gender, and Politics of Tradition." *Wicazo Sa Review* 21, 1 (Spring 2006): 9–28. https://doi.org/10.1353/wic.2006.0004

Ekberg, Carl. *Stealing Indian Women: Native Slavery in the Illinois Country*. Champaign: University of Illinois Press, 2010.

Farrell Racette, Sherry. "Looking for Stories and Unbroken Threads: Museum Artifacts as Women's History and Cultural Legacy." In *Restoring the Balance: First Nations Women, Community, and Culture*, edited by Gail Guthrie Valaskakis, Madeline Dion Stout, and Eric Guimond, 283–312. Winnipeg: University of Manitoba Press, 2009.

– "Sewing Ourselves Together: Clothing, Decorative Art, and the Expression of Métis and Half Breed Identity." PhD diss., University of Manitoba, 2004.

Fur, Gunlog. "Some Women Are Wiser Than Some Men: Gender and Native American History." In *Clearing a Path: Theorizing the Past in Native American Studies*, edited by Nancy Shoemaker, 75–103. New York: Routledge, 2002.

George, Corinne. "'If I Didn't Do Something, My Spirit Would Die': Grassroots Activism of Aboriginal Women in Calgary and Edmonton, 1951–1985." MA thesis, University of Calgary, 2007.

Goeman, Mishuana. "Indigenous Interventions and Feminist Methods." In *Sources and Methods in Indigenous Studies*, edited by Chris Andersen and Jean M. O'Brien, 185–94. London: Routledge, 2016.

Green, Joyce. "Canaries in the Mines of Citizenship: Indian Women in Canada." *Canadian Journal of Political Science* 34, 4 (December 2001): 715–39. https://doi.org/10.1017/S0008423901778067

– *Making Space for Indigenous Feminism*. Black Point, NS: Fernwood, 2007.

Green, Rayna. "The Pocahontas Perplex: The Image of the Indian Woman in American Culture." In *Native Women's History in Eastern North America before 1900: A Guide to Research and Writing*, edited by Rebecca Kugel and Lucy Eldersveld Murphy, 7–26. Lincoln: University of Nebraska Press, 2007.

Greer, Allan. *Mohawk Saint: Catherine Tekakwitha and the Jesuits*. New York: Oxford University Press, 2005.

Harris, Aroha. "History with Nana: Family, Life, and the Spoken Source." In *Sources and Methods in Indigenous Studies*, edited by Chris Andersen and Jean M. O'Brien, 128–34. London: Routledge, 2016.

Harris, Aroha, and Mary Jane Logan McCallum. "'Assaulting the Ears of Government': The Work of the Maori Women's Welfare League and the Indian Homemakers' Clubs in the 1950s and 60s." In *Indigenous Women and Work: From Labour to Activism*, edited by Carol Williams, 225–39. Champaign: University of Illinois Press, 2012.

Haskins, Victoria, and Claire Lowrie. *Colonization and Domestic Service: Historical and Contemporary Perspectives*. New York: Routledge, 2015.

– *Matrons and Maids: Regulating Indian Domestic Service in Tucson, 1914–1934*. Tucson: University of Arizona Press, 2012.

Hill, Susan M. *The Clay We Are Made Of: Haudenosaunee Land Tenure on the Grand River*. Winnipeg: University of Manitoba Press, 2017.

Hokowhitu, Brendan. "History and Masculinity." In *Sources and Methods in Indigenous Studies*, edited by Chris Andersen and Jean M. O'Brien, 195–204. London: Routledge, 2016.

Howard, Heather. "Women's Class Strategies as Activism in Native Community Building in Toronto, 1950–1975." In *Keeping the Campfires Going: Native Women's Activism in Urban Communities*, edited by Susan Applegate Krouse and Heather Howard, 105–24. Lincoln: University of Nebraska Press, 2009.

Innes, Robert Alexander, and Kim Anderson, eds. *Indigenous Men and Masculinities: Legacies, Identities, Regeneration*. Winnipeg: University of Manitoba Press, 2015.

Jacobs, Margaret. *White Mother to a Dark Race: Settler Colonialism, Maternalism, and the Removal of Indigenous Children in the American West and Australia, 1880–1940*. Lincoln: University of Nebraska Press, 2009.

Janovicek, Nancy. "'Assisting Our Own': Urban Migration, Self-Governance, and Native Women's Organizing in Thunder Bay, 1972–1989." In *Keeping the Campfires Going: Native Women's Activism in Urban Communities*, edited by Susan Applegate Krouse and Heather Howard, 56–75. Lincoln: University of Nebraska Press, 2009.

Jasen, Patricia. "Race, Culture, and the Colonization of Childbirth in Northern Canada." In *Rethinking Canada: The Promise of Women's History*, 4th ed., edited by Veronica Strong-Boag, Mona Gleason, and Adele Perry, 353–66. Don Mills, ON: Oxford University Press, 2002.

Kelm, Mary-Ellen, and Lorna Townsend, eds. *In the Days of Our Grandmothers: A Reader in Aboriginal Women's History in Canada*. Toronto: University of Toronto Press, 2006.

Kolopenuk, Jessica. "My Girl." *Aboriginal Policy Studies* 3, 3 (2014): 109–14.

Labelle, Kathryn Magee. *Dispersed but Not Destroyed: A History of the Seventeenth-Century Wendat People*. Vancouver: UBC Press, 2013.

Lavell-Harvard, D. Memee, and Kim Anderson, eds. *Mothers of the Nations: Indigenous Mothering as Global Resistance, Reclaiming and Recovery*. Toronto: Demeter Press, 2014.

Lawrence, Bonita. "Gender, Race, and the Regulation of Native Identity in Canada and the United States: An Overview." *Hypatia: A Journal of Feminist Philosophy* 18, 2 (Spring 2003): 3–31. https://doi.org/10.1111/j.1527-2001.2003.tb00799.x

– *"Real" Indians and Others: Mixed-Blood Urban Native Peoples and Indigenous Nationhood*. Lincoln: University of Nebraska Press, 2004.

– "Rewriting Histories of the Land: Colonialization and Indigenous Resistance in Eastern Canada." In *Race, Space, and the Law: Unwrapping a White Settler Society*, edited by Sherene Razack, 21–46. Toronto: Between the Lines, 2002.

Leddy, Lianne. "Interviewing Nookomis and Other Reflections of an Indigenous Historian." Special Issue, *Oral History Forum d'histoire orale* 30 (2010): 1–18.

– "'Mostly Just as a Social Gathering': Anishinaabe Kwewak and the Indian Homemakers' Club, 1945–1960." In *Aboriginal History: A Reader*, 2nd ed., edited by Kristin Burnett and Geoff Read, 353–63. Don Mills, ON: Oxford University Press, 2016.

Luby, Brittany. "From Milk-Medicine to Public (Re)Education Programs: An Examination of Anishinabek Mothers' Responses to Hydroelectric Flooding in the Treaty #3 District, 1900–1975." *Canadian Bulletin of Medical History* 32, 5 (2015): 363–89. https://doi.org/10.3138/cbmh.32.2.363

Macdougall, Brenda. *One of the Family: Métis Culture in Nineteenth-Century Northwestern Saskatchewan*. Vancouver: UBC Press, 2010.

Magee, Kathryn. "'For Home and Country': Education, Activism, and Agency in Native Homemakers' Clubs, 1942–1970." *Native Studies Review* 18, 2 (2009): 27–49.

– "Oky Ontatechiata: Wendat Witchcraft and the Panic of 1635–1645." *Journal of Early American History* 4, 3 (2014): 187–211.

– "'They Are the Life of the Nation': Women and War in Nadouek Society." *Canadian Journal of Native Studies* 28, 1 (2008): 119–38.

McCallum, Mary Jane Logan. *Indigenous Women, Work, and History: 1940–1980*. Winnipeg: University of Manitoba Press, 2014.

– "'I Would Like the Girls at Home': Domestic Labour and the Age of Discharge at Canadian Indian Residential Schools." In *Colonization and Domestic Service: Historical and Contemporary Perspectives*, edited by Victoria Haskins and Claire Lowry, 191–209. New York: Routledge, 2014.

McCallum, Mary Jane Logan, and Shelisa Klassen. "Because It's 1951: The Non-History of First Nations Female Band Suffrage and Leadership." In *Surviving Canada: Indigenous Peoples Celebrate 150 Years of Betrayal*, edited by Kiera Ladner and Myra Tait. Winnipeg: ARP Books, 2017.

McKegney, Sam. *Masculindians: Conversations about Indigenous Manhood.* Winnipeg: University of Manitoba Press, 2014.

– "Warriors, Healers, Lovers, and Leaders: Colonial Impositions on Indigenous Male Roles and Responsibilities." In *Men and Masculinities: An Interdisciplinary Reader*, edited by Jason A. Laker, 241–68. Don Mills, ON: Oxford University Press, 2012.

McNab, Miriam. "George Gordon First Nations Women: Partners in Survival." PhD diss., University of Saskatchewan, 2016.

Meijer Drees, Laurie. "Indian Hospitals and Aboriginal Nurses." *Canadian Bulletin of Medical History* 27, 1 (2010): 139–61. https://doi.org/10.3138/cbmh.27.1.139

Million, Dian. "Felt Theory: An Indigenous Feminist Approach to Affect and History." *Wicazo Sa Review* 24, 9 (Fall 2009): 53–76. https://doi.org10.1353/wic.0.0043

– *Therapeutic Nations: Healing in an Age of Indigenous Human Rights.* Tucson: University of Arizona Press, 2013.

Nason, Dory. "We Hold Our Hands Up: On Indigenous Women's Love and Resistance." *Decolonization: Indigeneity, Education, and Society*, blog, 12 February 2013. decolonization.wordpress.com/2013/02/12/we-hold-our-hands-up-on-indigenous-womens-love-and-resistance/

Nickel, Sarah A. "'I Am Not a Women's Libber, Although Sometimes I Sound Like One': Indigenous Feminism and Politicized Motherhood in British Columbia, 1950s to 1980s." *American Indian Quarterly* 41, 4 (2017): 299–335. https://muse.jhu.edu/article/679037

– "'United We Stand, Divided We Perish': Negotiating Pan-Tribal Unity in the Union of BC Indian Chiefs." PhD diss., Simon Fraser University, 2015.

– "'You'll Probably Tell Me That Your Grandmother Was an Indian Princess': Identity, Community, and Politics in the Oral History of the Union of BC Indian Chiefs, 1969–1983." *Oral History Forum d'histoire orale* 34 (2014): 1–19.

Nickel, Sarah, and Erica Violet Lee. *Intergenerational Indigenous Feminisms.* Winnipeg: University of Manitoba Press, forthcoming.

Ouellette, Grace. *The Fourth World: An Indigenous Perspective on Feminism and Indigenous Women's Activism.* Halifax: Fernwood Publishing, 2002.

Paul, Elsie, with Paige Raibmon and Harmony Johnson. *Written as I Remember It: Teachings (ʔems taʔaw) from the Life of a Sliammon Elder.* Vancouver: UBC Press, 2014.

Perry, Adele. *Colonial Relations: The Douglas-Connolly Family and the Nineteenth-Century Imperial World.* Cambridge: Cambridge University Press, 2015.

– "Historiography That Breaks Your Heart: Van Kirk and the Writing of Feminist History." In *Finding a Way to the Heart: Feminist Writings on Aboriginal and Women's History in Canada*, edited by Robin Jarvis Brownlie and Valerie J. Korinek, 81–97. Winnipeg: University of Manitoba Press, 2012.

Raibmon, Paige. "Living on Display: Colonial Visions of Aboriginal Domestic Spaces." *BC Studies* 140 (Winter 2003–4): 69–89.

– "The Practice of Everyday Colonialism: Indigenous Women at Work in the Hop Fields and Tourist Industry of Puget Sound." *Labour: Studies in Working-Class History of the Americas* 3 (2006): 23–56. https://doi.org/10.1215/15476715-2006-004

Razack, Sherene. "Gendered Racial Violence and Spatialized Justice: The Murder of Pamela George." *Canadian Journal of Law and Society* 15, 2 (2000): 91–130. https://doi.org/10.1017/S0829320100006384

Razack, Sherene, ed. *Race, Space, and the Law: Unmapping a White Settler Society*. Toronto: Sumach Press, 2002.

Rifkin, Mark. *When Did Indians Become Straight? Kinship, the History of Sexuality, and Native Sovereignty*. New York: Oxford University Press, 2011.

Robertson, Leslie A., and the Kwagu'ł Gixsam Clan. *Standing Up with Ga'axsta'las: Jane Constance Cook and the Politics of Memory, Church, and Custom*. Vancouver: UBC Press, 2012.

Rutherdale, Myra. *Women and the White Man's God: Gender and Race in the Canadian Mission Field*. Vancouver: UBC Press, 2002.

Rutherdale, Myra, and Katie Pickles, eds. *Contact Zones: Aboriginal and Settler Women in Canada's Colonial Past*. Vancouver: UBC Press, 2007.

Sangster, Joan. *The Iconic North: Cultural Constructions of Aboriginal Life in Postwar Canada*. Vancouver: UBC Press, 2016.

Silman, Janet. *Enough Is Enough: Aboriginal Women Speak out*. Toronto: Women's Press, 1992.

Simonsen, Jane E. *Making Home Work: Domesticity and Native American Assimilation in the American West, 1860–1919*. Chapel Hill: University of North Carolina Press, 2006.

Simpson, Audra. "Captivating Eunice: Membership, Colonialism, and Gendered Citizenships of Grief." *Wicazo Sa Review* 24 (2009): 105–29. https://doi.org/10.1353/wic.0.0031

– *Mohawk Interruptus: Political Life across the Borders of Settler States*. Durham, NC: Duke University Press, 2014.

Slater, Sandra, and Fay A. Yarbrough, eds. *Gender and Sexuality in Indigenous North America, 1400–1850*. Columbia: University of South Carolina Press, 2011.

Smith, Andrea. *Conquest: Sexual Violence and American Indian Genocide*. Cambridge, MA: South End Press, 2005.

Speed, Shannon. "Representations of Violence: (Re)Telling Indigenous Women's Stories and the Politics of Knowledge Production." In *Sources and Methods in Indigenous Studies*, edited by Chris Andersen and Jean M. O'Brien, 178–84. London: Routledge, 2016.

Stevenson, Allyson. "The Adoption of Frances T: Blood, Belonging, and Aboriginal Transracial Adoption in Twentieth-Century Canada." *Canadian Journal of History* 50, 3 (2015): 469–91. https://doi.org/10.3138/cjh.ach.50.3.004

– "Vibrations across a Continent: The 1978 Indian Child Welfare Act and the Politicization of First Nations Leaders in Saskatchewan." *American Indian Quarterly* 37, 1–2: Special Issue: *Native Adoption in Canada, the United States, New Zealand, and Australia* (Winter–Spring 2013): 218–36. https://doi.org/10.1353/aiq.2013.0007

St. Onge, Nicole, Carolyn Podruchny, and Brenda Macdougall. *Contours of a People: Métis Family, Mobility, and History*. Norman: University of Oklahoma Press, 2012.

Stote, Karen. "The Coercive Sterilization of Aboriginal Women in Canada." *American Indian Culture and Research Journal* 36, 3 (2012): 117–50. https://doi.org//10.17953/aicr.36.3.7280728r6479j650

Strong-Boag, Veronica, and Carole Gerson. *Paddling Her Own Canoe: The Times and Texts of E. Pauline Johnson (Tekahionwake)*. Toronto: University of Toronto Press, 2000.

Sunseri, Lina. *Being Again of One Mind: Oneida Women and the Struggle for Decolonization*. Vancouver: UBC Press, 2010.

Suzack, Cheryl, Shari M. Huhndorf, Jeanne Perreault, and Jean Barman, eds. *Indigenous Women and Feminism: Politics, Activism, Culture*. Vancouver: UBC Press, 2010.

Tallbear, Kim. "Standing with and Speaking as Faith: A Feminist-Indigenous Approach to Inquiry." In *Sources and Methods in Indigenous Studies*, edited by Chris Andersen and Jean M. O'Brien, 78–85. London: Routledge, 2016.

Thompson Rand, Jacki. "Status, Sustainability, and American Indian Women in the Twentieth Century." In *Sources and Methods in Indigenous Studies*, edited by Chris Andersen and Jean M. O'Brien, 171–7. London: Routledge, 2016.

Valaskakis, Gail Guthrie, Madeleine Dion Stout, and Eric Guimond, eds. *Restoring the Balance: First Nations Women, Community, and Culture*. Winnipeg: University of Manitoba Press, 2009.

Van Kirk, Sylvia. "From 'Marrying-In' to 'Marrying-Out': Changing Patterns of Aboriginal/Non-Aboriginal Marriage in Colonial Canada." *Frontiers: A Journal of Women Studies* 23, 3 (2002): 1–11. https://doi.org/10.1353/fro.2003.0010

Voyageur, Cora. *Firekeepers of the Twenty-First Century: First Nations Women Chiefs*. Montreal: McGill-Queen's University Press, 2008.

Wanhalla, Angela. *In/Visible Sight: The Mixed-Descent Families of Southern New Zealand*. Wellington, New Zealand: Bridget Williams Books, 2009.

– *Matters of the Heart: A History of Interracial Marriage in New Zealand*. Auckland, New Zealand: Auckland University Press, 2013.

– "Women 'Living across the Line': Intermarriage on the Canadian Prairies and in Southern New Zealand, 1870–1900." *Ethnohistory* 55, 1: 29–49. https://doi.org/10.1215/00141801-2007-045

Wheeler, Winona. "Cree Intellectual Traditions in History." In *The West and Beyond: New Perspectives on an Imagined Region*, edited by Alvin Finkel, Sarah Carter, and Peter Fortna, 47–61. Edmonton: Athabasca University Press, 2010.

Williams, Carol, ed. *Indigenous Women and Work: From Labour to Activism*. Champaign: University of Illinois Press, 2012.

3 Writing Black Canadian Women's History: Where We Have Been and Where We Are Going

KAREN FLYNN AND FUNKÉ ALADEJEBI

Introduction

"On September 2, 1964 at 10:50 a.m., I applied for a position on the staff at the Queen Elizabeth Hotel. This job was advertised in the paper. They advertised for a full-time and part-time Registered Nurse. I filled out an application form. I then saw the Personnel Manager. He informed me that the job was filled. I told him that I was applying for the part-time job. He informed me a second time that the job was filled."[1]

On 23 March 1965, Gloria Clarke Baylis, with the assistance of Negro Citizenship Association (NCA), sued Hilton of Canada Ltd. for discrimination. On 26 March, Baylis appeared in the New Courthouse in Montreal to testify about her experience at the Queen Elizabeth Hotel (QEH). Trained as an RN with midwifery in London, England, Baylis, a bilingual nurse with extensive administrative and bedside experience, was refused employment by personnel staff at the QEH. The court ruled in favour of Baylis and imposed the minimum penalty fine of $25 against Hilton of Canada Ltd. This particular case remains important for a number of reasons, one of which is how it sheds light on the assumption that Canada is a raceless society. For this chapter, this case is significant for what it yields about the value of intersectionality – where race, gender, class, and language serve as important vectors of analysis. Given that this case is the first in Canada following legislation (An Act Respecting Discrimination in Employment) that specifically defined discrimination, how is it that so very little is known about the case?[2] How is it that, besides a brief mention in a women's history text,[3] Baylis remains virtually absent from the historical record? What should Baylis's almost erasure and under-recognition mean for the cultivation of Canadian women's history?

The writing of Black Canadian women's history is still in its recovery stages, punctuated by small spurts and then disappearances. The absented presence that characterizes how and when Black women enter the historical record gives the impression that they have made little or no contribution to the development of the Canadian nation. That Baylis was adamant about exposing discrimination at the Queen Elizabeth Hotel should be interpreted as one of the multiple ways in which Black women participated in Canada's nation-building project. Unless one has access to the archival materials associated with the Hilton of Canada Ltd. lawsuit or conducted an interview with Baylis, her story, along with those of other Black women, remains hidden due to a range of factors.

The reality is that those who are committed to excavating and producing knowledge about Black women are confronted by a number of mitigating and interrelated factors. The paucity of and challenge of locating available sources, coupled with their relevance and legitimacy within various academic disciplines, particularly history, is a key issue. Indeed, what counts as an acceptable source has implications for the overall methodological, epistemological, and political project of documenting Black Canadian women's history. In tandem with the aforementioned, there is also the task of how to situate Black women in the larger Canadian narrative, given its exclusionary framing and ongoing denial of gendered racism, particularly through an acknowledgment of how racism and sexism shapes Black women's material and lived realities. Thus, it makes sense that in the process of recovery, the focus has been to foreground "rootedness" as a trope – a strategy of sorts – to disrupt Canada's amnesia as it relates to Black women's presence on its soil.[4]

As practitioners undertake and explore new avenues of study that highlight the multifaceted subjectivities of Black womanhood, the limitations mentioned here must be acknowledged. Equally significant, care must be taken to avoid the propensity to compare the pace of Black women's history to that of Canadian women's history generally. Simply put, practitioners' themes, trajectories, and focus might appear passé in light of new and recent interventions in Canadian women's and gender history. The objectives of this chapter are twofold. The first builds and expands on the work of scholars who are not necessarily historians or feminist(s) with the intent to complicate notions of rootedness and disrupt the proclivity of writing Black women's experiences as linear, unchanging, and homogeneous. In elucidating the evolving nature of Black Canadian women's history and the kinds of feminist history tools and approaches required, our second objective insists that this epistemological project utilize an anti-racist, Black Canadian feminist lens as a framework that recognizes Black women's social location. That is, attention must be paid to the intersections of race, culture, religion, identity, nation, sexuality, and gender, which will ultimately transform how Black women's history is conceptualized and articulated. Taking seriously the directive from Peggy Bristow and her co-authors, who insist that "a Black feminist historiography would begin with the writings ... of Mary Ann Shadd Cary," we begin with her and foreground her for what she reveals regarding the difficulties and possibilities of recovering Black Canadian women's submerged histories.[5]

Mary Ann Shadd Cary: A Window into Black Women's Submerged Histories

Reflected in the genesis of Canadian women's history, it has been "great women" – those who have left imprints or facets of their lives behind – who ostensibly become worthy subjects. Therefore, it is not surprising that Shadd Cary, who has the distinction of being the first woman to edit and publish a newspaper in North America, is remembered as an important symbol of Black Canadian womanhood and presence in Black Canadian studies. As editor of the *Provincial Freeman*, Shadd Cary used the paper as a vehicle to articulate her views on abolition, women's rights, integration, education, and migration. But the majority of ordinary women (and men) who belonged to the community she lived in left little or no written sources behind. Thus, the *Provincial Freeman* and Shadd Cary's other writings are invaluable resources that are easily accessible to researchers. Ironically, even though these sources are available, this has not resulted in the kind of sustained analysis of Shadd Cary's life in Canada that has appeared about her in the United States. According to Rinaldo Walcott, Shadd Cary "enjoys a place of importance within African-American studies, in particular African-American feminist historiography," but remains a marginal figure in Canadian history and feminist scholarship.[6] If, despite her accomplishments, Shadd Cary occupies such a minimal presence in Canadian history, what are the implications for writing about Black women who do not share her status?

However, an ongoing commitment to recover the narratives of faceless and nameless Black women should not preclude further exploration of Shadd Cary's life and writings. As a free Black woman and educated female activist, Shadd Cary, who migrated to Canada West in 1851, serves as a potent reminder of how race, gender, class, education, religion, and nation intersect to simultaneously circumscribe and shape women's choices and resistive strategies at specific historical junctures. Writing about Shadd Cary, Carla Peterson explains, "given the attitude of both the dominant culture and the Black male elite toward Black women, Shadd Cary found herself time and time again forced to confront the boundaries of race, gender and even nationality."[7] Regardless of how she was positioned in relation to her public disagreement with Henry Bibb, editor of *Voice of the Fugitive*, and other notable abolitionists like Frederick Douglass, it is hard to dismiss or ignore the role gender played (with)in these interactions. Indeed, the gender conventions of the time period valorized and supported Black male leadership, which Shadd Cary was hardly oblivious to. Surely, some of Shadd Cary's behaviour and motivations were a response to and recognition of the marginal position women occupied.

While Shadd Cary's gender has been well discussed in historical scholarship, her class background and religious leanings are often alluded to, but the latter in particular is often left unexamined as a critical aspect of her identity formation. As Calloway-Thomas explains, Shadd Cary, "unlike many free Blacks ... was a member of the Black elite, moistened by an intellectual environment that created a quintessentially middle-class Black family."[8] Whether historian Shirley Yee attributed Shadd Cary's attitude to her family's background is unclear, but she nonetheless also pointed out that Shadd Cary "reinscribed ... classist views" reflected in criticisms levelled at Black settlers who imitated the "materialism of middle-class whites."[9] Yee further added, "Shadd herself carried with her particular ideas and assumptions that reflected a middle-class reformist and Christian sensibility."[10] Similarly, Yee's identification of Shadd Cary as a "middle-class Protestant" woman demands further commentary, particularly in light of the role of religion in discussions of slavery and abolition. The notion that class can be manifested as a form of identity for Shadd Cary or structurally, as it related to ex-slaves and free Black newcomers, is worth pursuing.

In addition to acknowledging how Shadd Cary's lived experiences were shaped by race, gender, class, and religion, an acknowledgment of their fluidity and how these concepts are constituted and remade discursively and historically is critical. Often race, gender, class, sexuality, and nation are presented as a litany, transparent and easily identifiable. However, this was not always the case for Black women who (re)crossed and moulded these markers of difference based on personal experiences and philosophies. Therefore, when focusing on an individual such as Shadd Cary, it would be worthwhile to consider how and under what circumstances her perspectives changed over time. Surely, the views and perspectives of the woman who arrived in Canada in 1850 and returned to the United States in 1863 did not remain static.

To account for change over time and geographic spaces, we turn to Shadd Cary's *Notes on Canada West* to help in the intellectual and epistemological enterprise of relying on an intersectional framework to advance the writing of

Black women's history. As she was someone who had access to the public and influenced particular viewpoints, are there lessons to be gleaned from Shadd Cary's life? As already discussed, how did discourses of class, religion, and gender help to frame Shadd Cary's articulation of the possibilities "for a Black homeland"?[11] To be sure, Shadd Cary viewed Canada West as a place where all Black people from the United States could succeed. Despite her specific references to men, she ardently set out to convince the enslaved and free Black populations of its vast potential. However, considering Shadd Cary's middle-class elitist views, was the practical advice and information she provided to prospective settlers a reflection of her beliefs and thoughts? Or can these ideals be also read as mere responses to the exigencies of time?

Regardless of whether they were "men of small means or with no capital," there were no limits to what Canada offered, and Shadd Cary provided the evidence.[12] She explained, "If a farmer determines to keep out of debt, and be satisfied with what his farm yields, independence in a few years will be the result."[13] Conscious that the majority of fugitive slaves lacked resources, she further assured them that "from the many instances of success under my observation, (particularly of formally totally destitute colored persons), I firmly believe that with an axe and a little energy, an independent position would result in a short period."[14] Clearly, notions of class are implicitly and explicitly imbued in Shadd Cary's statements and opinions and are reflected in her expectations of the new settlers. She was especially critical of settlers who idled and refused to work.

Notes on Canada West demonstrated that Shadd Cary's expectations were firmly rooted in class assumptions, which had both symbolic and structural meanings for her; the former appears to be connected to notions of citizenship and the latter about behaviour and attitudes. Shadd Cary's extensive focus on land and farming endorsed the "agrarian doctrine," whereby farming was viewed as the basic economic endeavour upon which the nation's prosperity and morality depended.[15] The structural and symbolic meanings of class would reverberate throughout Shadd Cary's reflections on the newcomers.

To be sure, Shadd Cary had an image of the ideal Black citizen subject and chastised those who were unable to live up to her expectations. Still, her repeated expression of disdain towards those who "idled" and were "lazy" has to be acknowledged in conjunction with how much Shadd Cary desired a home for enslaved populations. She emphasized that hard work, thrift, self-determination, and independence – intricately connected to "Protestant and republican values" – are valuable to the development of the Canadian nation.[16] As long as they embodied and reproduced the norms and values of acceptable citizenship, the settlers were proving themselves valuable and

worthy of belonging to the Canadian nation. Shadd Cary's response to philanthropic efforts by ministers or other anti-slavery advocates on behalf of fugitive
slaves suggests that her views were far from fixed. She vehemently opposed
what she characterized as begging, and for those who received any assistance,
equalling about $3,000, Shadd Cary claimed, "not more than half of them re-
quired it had they been willing to work."[17] She quickly pointed out that the
other 27,000 settlers were self-supporting and did not require "handouts." Even
as Shadd Cary held "classist views," she was hardly oblivious to the fact that
there were settlers who required assistance "due to sickness or old age."[18] Pay-
ing attention *only* to how class as a concept was manifested in Shadd Cary's
migration and settlement philosophies prevents a particular kind of flexibility
that allows for examining nuances that otherwise might not be obvious.

Shadd Cary's expectations of the newcomers cannot be explored in isolation
or predicated entirely on her middle-class values. The demeaning manner in
which ex-slaves were viewed clearly influenced Shadd Cary's writing, as did the
belief propagated by slaveholders that Canada was unsuitable for ex-slaves. She
viewed insinuations regarding the inability of ex-slaves to be self-determined
and independent as orchestrated by "our enemies," who circulated this "foul
slander" in both Canada and the United States "to our prejudice."[19] Exploring Shadd Cary's responses to such opinions serves as a reminder that context,
space, and place matters. In other words, the history of enslavement in British
North America, which on the surface epitomized "freedom" – coupled with
the gender, race, and class ideologies of the period – shaped her reaction to
Black settlers. One lesson that can be gleaned from *Notes in Canada West* is
that Shadd Cary was still very much a product of her time. By situating Shadd
Cary's comments alongside dominant ideologies about race and freedom in
nineteenth-century Canada, historians might be less likely to judge female subjects when they fail to live up to whatever ideals have been imposed upon them.

To understand Black women's philosophies and complicated influences,
the importance of language not as a fixed window into a reality but rather
as a series of processes, fluid and open to multiple interpretations, cannot be
ignored in excavating Black women's narratives. When, for example, Shadd
Cary insisted that the "colored man ... should 'plant his tree' deep in the soil,"
what did she mean?[20] Should the language Shadd Cary used be taken literally
or symbolically, or does it reflect both? It bears repeating that Shadd Cary's
comments have to be considered against the backdrop of her motivation for
compiling *Notes on Canada West*. Shadd Cary fundamentally believed that
Canada West was the "Promised Land." Planting the tree deep into the soil
signified a level of permanency, and what better way of solidifying one's stake
in a nation than through the acquisition of land, which Shadd Cary mentioned

was inexpensive and available? Thus, planting the tree is definitely linked to the idea of rootedness which is visible in Black Canadian discussions about their place in the nation, as reflected in Bristow's *"We're Rooted Here and They Can't Pull Us Up"* or Katherine McKittrick's "Their Blood Is There, and They Can't Throw It Out."[21] Shadd Cary's language about who was able to plant was decidedly gendered in that it encoded particular assumptions about the role of (Black) settler men in the formation of a homeland within the nation. In this case, an intersectional framework that incorporates discourse analysis, and attention to language, can further enrich the writing of Black women's history.

Excavating Black Women's Stories through Transnational Citizenship

If the African diaspora is viewed as not only a condition or position but also a process and set of practices, as articulated by historian Jared G. Toney, it is hardly surprising that language and discourses of community and nation travel across borders and geographical spaces. There are varied manifestations of these border crossings and transnational exchanges evidenced in Toney's urging to examine the permeability of national borders in relation to migration and the relationships between Black people from Canada, the Caribbean, and the United States. Even if the gendering of the African diaspora in Canada foregrounds the experiences of heterosexual men, Toney provides examples of how transnationalism was enacted in practical ways for African Canadian communities that included women. Claire Clarke, for example, was introduced to African American authors, such as Langston Hughes, by Black railroad porters. Toney effectively shows how migration and movement marked Black women's lives in unconventional ways.[22] Toney and other scholars, who insist that attention be paid to transnational exchanges, circuits, and flows that Black women participated in, point to the permeability of the nation state. This raises the question of whether rootedness can still be claimed as a desired condition.[23]

Engagement in transnational circuits and exchanges should not be interpreted as a dismissal or a negation of a desire to belong to the nation state, as reflected in Sarah-Jane Mathieu's *North of the Color Line*. According to Mathieu, regardless of attempts to construct Black men as outside of the nation, their labour allowed them to feel some semblance of belonging. Even as they occupied less than desirable positions, Mathieu notes, "Canada's railways, so often recognized as a unifying Canadian icon, solidified a national sense of belonging and 'Canadianness' for blacks in the dominion as well."[24] As a result of the labour performed by Black men on the transcontinental railway, Black communities helped to "thrust Canada into the industrial age."[25]

While Mathieu demonstrates how Black Canadian encounters across geographic boundaries disrupted notions of rootedness to create a transnational race consciousness among African-descended peoples, her discussion of the ways in which racism and sexism intersected not only in labour and employment patterns but also with family and community development is particularly important for uncovering Black women's stories.[26] Mathieu explains that although the separate spheres ideology was pervasive in African Canadian communities, Black women exercised their citizenships by being "dedicated wives, educators, consumer advocates, shrewd voters, caregivers to the sick, and guardians of their communities' histories."[27] Black women spearheaded organizations such as the Montreal Coloured Women's Club, which not only gave them access to transnational networks akin to those found through men's employment on the railways, but also gave them a platform to carry out political and social activism nationally and internationally.[28]

A more sustained analysis of Black Canadian-born women's relationship to citizenship practices and the meanings they attributed to this enterprise is sorely needed. How might Black Canadian-born women's investment in *being* Canadian citizens lend to understandings of their identity formation? Moreover, how do the specific ways Black Canadian-born women exercised their citizenship, as identified by Mathieu, force a rethinking of citizenship when considering the labour of Caribbean domestic workers? Surely, rootedness had different meanings for Black women recruited under the government-sponsored domestic schemes of the 1920s and 1955 than it did for Canadian-born Black women whose relationship to the nation-state may have fostered different constructions of belonging.

Some of the tasks that Mathieu identifies as embodying practices of citizenship were also performed by Caribbean women who worked in white middle-class homes. As Joane Nagel and others have argued, the nation-building enterprise is highly gendered and racialized. Stemming from nineteenth-century notions of femininity, mothers were expected to reproduce the nation by inculcating the values and norms of national culture into its new members.[29] When Caribbean-born women assumed the responsibilities of child-rearing and domestic labour, they also freed white women of these roles and granted them access to the public sphere of paid work. However, this meant that Caribbean-born women inadvertently also participated in the nation-building project.

There is no shortage of scholarship on the dimensions of the various government-sponsored programs involving Caribbean domestic workers. The work of sociologists Daiva Stasiulis and Abigail B. Bakan is especially insightful in challenging assumed notions of citizenship in the age of neoliberalism and globalization.[30] They elucidate how Caribbean and Filipina domestic workers were caught in a global nexus of players, or gatekeepers, who were instrumental in circumscribing their citizenship rights. Female migrants of colour were then placed in an unenviable liminal position of negotiating citizenship, a much-desired acquisition. Historians can enrich this available scholarship by making visible the links between the reproductive activities that Caribbean domestics performed, the separate spheres ideology, and nation-building. The first domestic scheme in 1910, which is all but forgotten, can serve as the genesis.[31] In addition to the aforementioned, a historicized comparative account of Finnish, British, Greek, Caribbean, and Filipina domestic workers and how they were situated temporally in Canada's political economy would offer a more nuanced analysis of the matrix in which these women found themselves as potential immigrants, temporary workers, and legitimate migrants. Drawing on critical race studies would further shed light on how whiteness was harnessed in constructing domestic workers from Britain, Greece, and other locations as legitimate citizens.[32] Attempts to write integrated histories that include Black women are necessary if historians of women and gender are interested in transforming the dominant narrative that continues to centre white subjects as the norm. Similar to the ways in which Marlene Epp and Franca Iacovetta encourage us in this volume to think beyond the dichotomies of sisters or strangers, including transnational diasporic women's stories can help link women's multiple identities in a way that includes various intersectionalities, such as regionalism, gender, race, ethnicity, sexuality, and much more.[33]

As part of integrating Black women's presence within broader discussions of Canadian history, the work of Nina Reid-Maroney, Agnes Calliste, Annette Henry, Makeda Silvera, and the scholars mentioned thus far have been instrumental in disrupting the idea of Black women's marginality in relation to the nation state. Together these authors bear witness to how Black women in their various overlapping capacities also built community institutions that promoted racial and social uplift, expanding their contributions beyond the confines and limits of paid work.[34] These stories not only showcase Black women's contributions to the nation but also challenge the myth of Canada as the Great White North.

As these authors highlight the nation-building activities of both Canadian-born and Caribbean-born Black women, the emphasis that Black women as a group are differentiated by sexuality, class, and citizenship status is critical. It is worth underscoring that to capture the polyvocality of Black women's voices, essentialist compositions of women – fuelled by a racist and sexist society – should not be used to eschew the differences that exist between and among them. In other words, to get at the full range of Black womanhood in Canada requires avoiding the proclivity to privilege Caribbean women at the expense of Black Canadian-born women, Ontario as the main geographical location, English as the main language, professional women versus working-class and poorer women. Citizenship and all that it encompasses was not and could not be easily pursued, evoked, or even imagined equally by all Black women.

Thus, an attachment to and insistence of rootedness may be more pronounced for Black Canadian-born women, who might foreground their presence on Canadian soil differently than, for example, Caribbean domestic workers on temporary visas or permanent residents. Recent immigrants from the continent might be further disadvantaged depending on how they enter Canada. What is patently clear is that Black women are situated unequally in the Canadian nation, which affects the kinds of formal citizenship claims each group can make. Unpacking these relationships allows for more sustained material and discursive renderings of nation-building that acknowledges that Black women are not necessarily positioned in identical ways under the categorical umbrella of Blackness. Minimizing or ignoring the "difference" within "difference" reinforces the idea that Black women are a monolithic group and misses the specificities, nuances, and complexities of particular groups, such as those that identify as mixed race or biracial. Clara Ford is one such example. Ford, a mixed-raced seamstress who occasionally dressed as a man, was accused of killing Frank Westwood, a wealthy white youth, in November 1894 after he had taken "improper liberties" with her.[35] While popular media outlets attributed Ford's "bizarre" behaviour of cross-dressing to her "Africanness," historian Carolyn Strange explains that Ford's disruption of mainstream gendered norms intersected with popular notions of Black inferiority. Ford was exonerated, despite her dramatic testimony admitting to the crime, owing to her feminine and racial frailties.[36] It is in unlikely places, such as courtroom proceedings and testimonials, that Black women's complicated and messy histories of "difference" can be unearthed. The use of trial records then can serve as an indispensable resource in light of continued concern regarding the kinds of methods and available sources with which to recuperate Black women's history.

In terms of finding and accessing sources and the appropriate methods for writing about Black women's lives, Afua Cooper asks relevant questions: How do we do it? How do we get to it?[37] While there is resounding agreement on the need to write Black women's history, the process itself can be daunting if there are no actual finding aids that explicitly address the researcher's topic. Sarah-Jane Mathieu poignantly captures this dilemma when she writes, "Facing hundreds of archival files and seemingly endless microfilm reels – none of them reassuringly labeled 'black/Negroes/colored' – made these eyes fear indeed."[38] Archivists' knowledge, response, and willingness to comb through repositories to support the work of scholars interested in Black women is also a concern. Katherine McKittrick recounted how she was rebuffed by an archivist when undertaking research for *Demonic Grounds: Black Women and the Cartographies of Struggle.*[39] Regardless of the many challenges, Black women's history is being written, albeit gradually, by scholars who use both traditional and non-traditional sources to access these stories. Other scholars outside of the discipline of history are also suggesting creative and innovative ways to document Black women's history. There are sources, such as autobiographies written by and about Black women, that have yet to be utilized and others that have yet to be considered. Together, these sources and methods, what they currently yield, their utility, and directions for future research, will be the focus of the next section.

Rethinking Sources: Autobiography, Biography, and Diaries

Memoirs, autobiographies, biographies, and oral histories surprisingly remain an underutilized source in Black Canadian history. These sources are significant for what they can reveal about the multiple and varied ways Black women exercised their citizenship and provide a window into Black women's lives. Books such as Rosemary Sadlier, *Leading the Way: Black Women in Canada*, Lawrence Hill, *Women of Vision: The Story of the Canadian Negro Women's Association, 1951–1976*, and Rella Braithwaite and Tessa Benn-Ireland, *Some Black Women: Profiles of Black Women in Canada*, include partial biographical information about Black women across historical time periods. Carrie Best's *The Lonesome Road* and Rosemary Brown's *Being Brown: A Very Public Life* are examples of autobiographies replete with information about how Black citizenship was manifested in Canada, including details about their childhood and specific geographies, which in turn shaped their identity and subjectivity formation. For Best, it was Glasgow, Nova Scotia, and for Brown, Jamaica and later Canada.

The texts by Sadlier, Hill, and Braithwaite and Benn-Ireland share certain similarities in that the biographical information, albeit partial, short, and incomplete, almost entirely focuses on activism in its broadest conception. The authors also share a similar objective, which is to make visible Black women's presence in and contributions to Canada. The Black women featured are famous figures, such as Best and Brown, and others who are less well known. Despite the brevity of some of the biographical profiles, they offer glimpses into the lived experiences of Black Canadian women and the ways in which these encounters informed their social, economic, and political philosophies. What else can be gleaned from these partial biographies in relation to the construction of identities and Black women's representation of the self? How might some of the more extensive profiles be used in conjunction with other sources to advance the scholarship of Black women?

Too often, as reflected by some of the books mentioned, Black women's public life – their activism and paid work – is the focus. Less is known about their private lives as it was lived relationally and in the inner sanctuary of their homes. Here is perhaps where Best's and Brown's autobiographies might help to fill in the void. Despite incredible accolades, Best, like Shadd Cary, is hardly canonized in Canadian women's history. Best was a publisher who used her newspaper, the *Clarion*, to bring attention to the inequality Blacks faced across the nation. One noteworthy example is how Best galvanized support for Viola Desmond, who, in 1946, was ejected from the Roseland Theatre for sitting in a seat reserved for whites. Similar to Baylis, Best's place in Canadian legal history is negligible, prompting legal scholar Constance Backhouse to write that she "deserves equal attention for her effort to promote racial equality in Canadian legal history."[40] *The Lonesome Road* cannot be read entirely as a reflection of Best's life but rather as a way to cement the Black presence on Canadian soil. That Best begins her autobiography with the arrival of Black people on Canadian soil speaks to a desire, similar to those of the authors mentioned earlier, to remind, lest one forget, that the Black presence in Canada is neither arbitrary nor recent. Since Best's widespread activism is already well known, at least in her community, the information about her formative years and the influence of her mother helps to fill in the lacuna regarding Black womanhood at the beginning of the twentieth century. Best's provocative retelling of a story involving her mother, Georgina Prevoe, is worth mentioning for what it reveals about how her actions departed from accepted racial and gendered norms.

Best writes, "Black womanhood was held in low esteem during the early part of the twentieth century and only the home afforded the protection needed to ensure security from outside influences."[41] She then proceeds to tell the story of how her mother, a domestic worker and a quiet woman who rarely uttered unkind words, found her son and brought him home during a race riot. Insults and threats by the rioters did not deter Prevoe as she walked through the crowd. At one point, a young man recognized Prevoe and inquired about her destination, to which she replied, "I'm going to the Norfolk House for my son."[42] The individual "ordered the crowd back," and Best's mother brought her frightened son safely home. In this narrative, home emerged as a sanctuary, a space where protection against a racist and hostile world was almost guaranteed, as reiterated in the works of scholars such as Hazel Carby and bell hooks.[43]

Nevertheless, the importance of home and family as a place of safety and refuge from societal prejudice, and its role in the construction of activist identities as exemplified by Prevoe's influence on Best, cannot be understood one-dimensionally, for it minimizes or obscures how as an institution, the Black Canadian family and home did not *always* provide safe spaces for Black women. This area of scholarship has recently been given attention by historian Barrington Walker, who documents the problematic ways in which violence was (re)enacted on the Black female body. Similar to Strange, Walker uses the tools of legal history and coroners' reports to examine the complicated and vexed nature of family and home life in nineteenth-century Canada. In his analysis of the deaths of Martha Veney and Hannah Richardson at the hands of their husbands, Walker explains, "Although black men and women both had to endure racism, black men enjoyed relative privilege compared with black women and they could exercise patriarchal violence against 'their' women."[44] These two separate criminal cases offer a brief glimpse into how the family was far from a respite for Black women, albeit through "white patriarchal legal" apparatuses. The white judge and all-white jury, coupled with the coroners' reports – they all reinforced stereotypes of Black inferiority. More studies are needed to explore how the home and family reinforced patriarchal values and attitudes that limited Black women's potential and growth. How Black women internalized conservative views of family and relationships offers another area of critical inquiry. Indeed, there are missing pieces to a much larger narrative on the private, intimate, and personal aspects of Black families.

Given the scholarly focus on domestic workers, it is surprising how little information is available on their relationships with children and other family members left behind in the Caribbean or at home while they sought opportunities in Canada. As a result of their positions as workers, Black women rarely enter into the Canadian literature as mothering their own children. What, if any, has been the impact of mothers' relationships with their children? How do Black extended families continue to challenge the logic of nuclear families as the locus of stability? How has globalization and transnationalism as processes and systems affected Caribbean families who continue to see migration as the only route to upward mobility? Exploring the family broadens historical and contemporary discussions that emphasize Black women's productive as opposed to their reproductive labour.

Rosemary Brown's *Being Brown: A Very Public Life* captures both. In a fascinating story that begins in Jamaica and continues in Canada, *Being Brown* is the compelling journey of the first Black woman elected to a provincial legislature (Legislative Assembly of British Columbia) and the first to run for the leadership at the federal level in the New Democratic Party (NDP). In keeping with the trajectory of this chapter, Brown's inclusion of private and painful family life stories can serve as the starting point for further investigating Black familial structures. A difficult period for Brown was giving birth to a still-born daughter. She also expressed fears of raising her children, especially her daughter, in a society where white standards of beauty were valorized. There was also the issue of the division of labour in the household. Her husband Bill was pursuing his psychiatric residency at the time of Brown's second pregnancy, which forced a rethinking of her own career goals. As with women generally, Brown was primarily responsible for the household, which led her to question her ability to "juggle parenting, homemaking, and studying."[45] While Brown managed to navigate the dilemma of her multiple roles and became a successful politician, the patriarchal ideology that insisted that women are biologically suited for child-rearing was and is still a reality for Black women. Lisa Pasolli and Julia Smith's exploration of working-class women's private and public work in chapter 12 of this volume speaks to the importance of this issue.[46]

The history of Black women's sexuality is another under-researched area. Prior to having children, Brown mentioned her fears about sex, marriage, and intimacy. She writes, "Over the years, throughout my relationships with boys and men there had always existed two Rosemary's. There was the cool, sure, sophisticated woman on the outside and insecure, old fashioned little girl on the inside. There was clearly a great deal of confusion around my sexual identity."[47] Specific examples of how she navigated the confusion around her sexual subjectivity are excluded, but that Brown bothered to include such information given Black women's contested sexual histories cannot be overlooked. The writing of Black women's sexual histories has to be an interdisciplinary effort that not only recognizes the specificity of space and place, but also captures all the dimensions of it, as exemplified by Strange's discussion of Clara Ford. Even with an acknowledgment that Black women share similarities regarding their sexual histories, theories developed in the context of a particular geographical arena cannot be uncritically applied to the Canadian context. Practitioners interested in writing Black Canadian women's sexual histories can broadly draw on the works of feminist and literary scholars such as Rosamund Elwin, Makeda Silvera, Wesley Crichlow, Shana Calixte, Erica Lawson, Dionne Brand, Becki Ross, and Kim Greenwell.[48]

Both Best and Brown had the privilege of writing autobiographies, using sources they had at their disposal, including their own writing, newspaper clippings, and photographs. Shadd Cary, of course, left behind her newspaper editorials and other documents. Still, the gnawing question remains: What about Black women who left few or no sources behind? Two additional monographs – Nina Reid-Maroney's *The Reverend Jennie Johnson and African-Canadian History, 1868–1967* and Afua Cooper's *The Hanging of Angélique: The Untold*

Story of Canadian Slavery and the Burning of Montreal – provide additional examples of how sources can be creatively harnessed. Jennie Johnson, who was the first ordained woman in Canada to be a full-time minister with her own church, "left behind two brief biographical works and some letters," but no cadre of sermons from which to reconstruct her theological journey.[49] For Reid-Maroney, the lack of materials was further intensified by a "deep and protective silence that emanates from much of Johnson's community."[50] Reid-Maroney admits that her book "cannot be called a biography" because the sources that are available "do not tell us the things we would like to know about her."[51] From the fragments left by Johnson coupled with archival and published and unpublished sources, Reid-Maroney paints a provocative portrait, however incomplete, of a remarkable, intelligent, and astute woman, who in her lifetime preached in her own church, traversed national borders, founded a mission, and sustained lifelong relationships across racial lines. *The Reverend Jennie Johnson* is a stark reminder not only of the significance of religion in the lives of Black women, but also of its transnational iteration, embodied in the scholarship of Carol Duncan and Njoki Wane.[52]

These scholars encourage us to refocus our attention on reading the silences within the limited sources available. While hers is not necessarily a biography in the traditional sense, Afua Cooper uses a variety of sources such as legal documents, baptismal records, and newspaper accounts to tell the story of female enslavement in early Canada. Like Strange and Walker, Cooper also relies on court records and incorporated Marie-Joseph Angélique's transcript as a window into her thoughts. Obviously, the words spoken by Angélique at her trial are limited in what they revealed about her, but this did not preclude Cooper from attempting to reconstruct her subject's life. Similar to Reid-Maroney, Cooper places Angélique's life within a larger historical context of the Atlantic slave trade. To unearth the subaltern female voice, particularly of the enslaved, Cooper builds on Maureen Elgerson Lee's analysis of Black female enslavement which encourages the use of "newspaper advertisements, bills of sale, bills of hire, and contracts between slaveholders" as authentic evidence of the Black presence in Canada."[53] Of course, the use of piecemeal sources might be viewed as problematic if one is attempting to write all-encompassing histories of Black women, which is highly impossible. The value lies in the actual attempt to resurrect Black women from historical obscurity, and this might mean an unfinished narrative or devising creative ways to write these histories. This begs the question: To what length should a historian go to accomplish the task of writing Black women histories?

There is a popular Jamaican proverb saying, "every mickle meck a muckle" – essentially meaning using whatever is at one's disposal to make, for example, dinner.[54] The same perspective can be applied to sources. Can a historian use her imagination in conjunction with other sources to gain insights into the lives of ordinary Black women who left little or no trace of themselves behind? How does one grapple with the impossibility of knowing? In response to this question, literary scholar Omise'eke Natasha Tinsley, influenced by the scholarship of M. Jacqui Alexander and Saidiya Hartman, insists that to "tell meaningful stories of Black womanhood – and particularly Black women's sexuality – traditional scholarship, especially academic work that relies on the archive, can never suffice."[55] She maintains that "scholars must turn to creative methodologies to intuit and imagine narratives of Black women's freedom: a freedom that has remained an impossibility in official discourses but that must be invented even where it did not exist in the past, in order that it might exist in the future."[56] In discussing her historical novel *Water, Shoulders, Into the Black Pacific*, Tinsley also notes how after scouring the archives, she was forced to rely on her imagination in tandem with oral interviews to discuss the intersections of migration, work, and desire experienced by African and Caribbean American women who came from the Mississippi Delta to the San Francisco Bay to work in Kaiser shipyards.[57] What kinds of liberties can one assume with the creative imagination? Are there particular themes or historical periods that require the use of the imagination more than others? Can the imagination be used for other topics besides Black women's sexuality and slavery? What about a combination of fiction and history?

Another way to address the "impossibility of knowing" might be to use a combination of fiction and historical documents similar to Lawrence Hill's *The Book of Negroes*, based on a document of the same name kept by British naval officers. According to Gillian Roberts in her analysis of the manuscript, Hill has "commented that the Book of Negroes is an important document about which Canadians are largely ignorant."[58] A novelist, Hill is gesturing to the larger absence of Blacks generally from the Canadian landscape. The document includes the names of 3,000 Blacks who fought on the side of the British in the American Revolutionary War and wanted to flee from Manhattan for Canada in 1783. According to Hill, "unless you were in The Book of Negroes, you couldn't escape to Canada."[59] Instead of creating a male subject, which would be in line with the majority of slave narratives, Hill's main character is an enslaved young woman named Aminata, whose experience begins on a Southern plantation, where she was displaced throughout various American states, Nova Scotia, and then Sierra Leone. According to Gillian Roberts, Hill "has taken liberties with the history of visual culture, by imagining an African woman, escaping from her owner, as the document's scribe."[60] In much the same way, Winfried Siemerling also encourages us to reconsider the use of imagination when transforming available information to recode the historical narratives of

Black Canadian experiences. Like Roberts, Siemerling argues that contemporary Black Canadian writers transform discursive scripts and the possibilities of the historical past to create "a *practice* of relation that connects times, spaces and texts in a 'shared knowledge.'"[61] Perhaps the subgenres of nonfictional history, fictionalized history, or historicized fiction as part of the larger historical enterprise is another way that Black women's histories can be documented. Is there a way to confront the apparent absence of finding aids in archives that do not explicitly deal with Black women?

While it is probable that records on Caribbean domestic workers are non-existent, it could also mean that they are buried within broader subject categories, such as immigration or domestic workers more generally.[62] The same can be said about Caribbean nurses, who were also recruited to help alleviate the labour shortage after the Second World War. Notwithstanding this possibility, there are no subject headings for Caribbean nurses in the provincial and national archives; they exist but are submerged in health care and nursing records. What these examples illustrate is that the lives of some Black women, such as nurses, will have to be meticulously excavated by painstakingly examining whatever sources are available. In addition to the information that can be gleaned from institutional records, it also means relying on sources such as student records, yearbooks, newspapers, obituaries, tombstones, wills, or the census more generally. Another avenue is to utilize archival information available about white women to determine what these sources might reveal about Black women, with the larger intention to at least write more integrated histories.

Oral histories, while we acknowledge that like biographies they pose a number of interpretive challenges, remain a critical source. As much as archival sources are useful, they too are limited in what they can reveal about subjects' lives, as Karen Flynn argues in her book *Moving beyond Borders*: *A History of Black Canadian and Caribbean Women in the Diaspora*. In addition to providing information about family, migration, and work experiences that can only be culled from oral interviews, these sources also serve another purpose. Flynn maintains that "oral history locates women as subjects, not objects, and as producers of knowledge and agents of social change embodied within the complexities and contradictions of different histories and cultures."[63] Yet two interrelated issues are at play here: convincing Black women that their stories are worthy of being told and preserved and determining which subjects archives and museums deem valuable. Collections classifications are limited in their scope and prioritize technology, great events, and people, marginalizing those who intersect under categories such disability, sexuality, race, and ethnicity.

The very act of documenting Black women's history is political and requires commitment on the part of Black women, scholars, churches, community centres, and archives. How do we create and maintain a sustained interest in recuperating Black women's history? What roles do archives, schools, and universities have in ensuring that Black Canadian history/studies include women and girls? How do we reach Black women who have documents and encourage them to deposit them to the appropriate archives? Hill, in reference to the Canadian Negro Women's Association (CANEWA), notes how "many of the documents were incidentally thrown out" but that three members – Phyllis Brooks, Penny Hodge, and Aileen Williams – "refused to let their story lie down and die."[64] Indeed, Brooks, Hodge, and Williams are the custodians of CANEWA's legacy. The vexing issue of safeguarding and storing materials for archival purposes will continue to plague those interested in writing Black Canadian women's history. Who will solicit Black women for their materials? Who will encourage and convince them that their stories are worth preserving and retelling? Where are the women like Brooks, Hodge, and Williams, who understood the work of CANEWA and commissioned Hill to write the organization's remarkable story? What the aforementioned example reveals is that Black women's presence has long been in Canada; sometimes it is thrown out, and on other occasions, if, like an archaeologist, one digs long enough, sometimes sources can be found in unexpected places.

Such is the case of Claudine Bonner, who came across Nina Mae Alexander's diary, a rare find, at the Buxton Museum in southwestern Ontario. Notwithstanding the fact that the diary spans only four months, Bonner provides a partial glimpse into the life of twenty-seven-year-old Alexander, a teacher who taught in white schools in early nineteenth- and twentieth-century Ontario.[65] This fascinating young woman lived life on her own terms despite the social and racial conventions of the period. The diary provided information about teaching and family as well as her social and dating life. Alexander dated men across racial lines, and some questions were even raised about their suitability. Alexander had a very active dating life, but one wonders whether she was sexually active. What role did religion play in dictating Alexander's life, especially as she had grown up in a religious family? As with Hill's *Book of Negroes*, perhaps the diary and a historian's imagination can build on what Bonner has done thus far.

Conclusion

Despite attempts to erase, dismiss, and ignore Black Canadian women's presence in Canada, the scholarship presented here, however fragmented and partial, is an attempt both to make claims to rootedness as a response to the historical erasure of Black womanhood on Canadian soil and also to demonstrate that Black womanhood beckons to Blackness beyond the confines of the Canadian nation state. As scholars are working vigilantly to document the stories of Black women in Canada, this chapter has worked to demonstrate that there continue to be several avenues for further research and expansion on work already done. While more famous women like Mary Ann Shadd Cary provide us with a lens for understanding Black settlement and migration in the colonial period, Shadd Cary represents much more than this. Utilizing an anti-racist/Black Canadian feminist framework, we can begin to understand how class, religion, space and place, gendered notions of belonging, and various modes of intersectionality influenced Shadd Cary's conceptions of rootedness in Canada. Conversely, lesser-known historical actors, such as Clara Ford, urge us to look beyond categorical binaries of race and gender to interrogate the in-between spaces of difference and defiance that Black Canadian women occupied. Although access to sources continues to remain a tremendous challenge for scholars of Black Canadian women's history, re-conceptualizing the ways in which we use these limited sources gives credence to the importance of biographical sketches, court transcriptions, and – dare we say it – imagination in broadening the scope of what and how we can learn about Black women's lives. There is much value in the uncovering and (re)telling of Black Canadian women. We hope that this chapter reminds us of their presence both within the margins and on the frontiers of Canadian history.

NOTES

1 Gloria Clarke Baylis, Application for Employment, Queen Elizabeth Hotel, 2 September 1964; Karen Flynn, "'I'm Glad That Someone Is Telling the Nursing Story': Writing Black Canadian Women's History" (paper presented at the annual Berkshire Conference on the History of Women, Toronto, Ontario, 22–5 May 2014).

2 Her Majesty, the Queen Complainant vs. Hilton of Canada Ltd., Court of Sessions, Montreal, 4 October 1965.

3 Alison Prentice, Paula Bourne, Gail Cuthbert Brandt, Beth Light, Wendy Mitchinson, and Naomi Black, *Canadian Women: A History*, 2nd ed. (Toronto: Harcourt, Brace, Jovanovich, 1996), 32–3.

4 Since the publication of the seminal text titled *"We're Rooted Here and They Can't Pull Us Up": Essays in African Canadian Women's History* in 1994, Peggy Bristow, Dionne Brand, and others sought to lend a feminist framework to the writing of Black Canadian history. These authors worked to "challenge prevailing notions of Canadian history" by rooting the experiences of Black women within

a larger and longer trajectory of Black enslavement beginning in the seventeenth century. Peggy Bristow, ed., *"We're Rooted Here and They Can't Pull Us Up":* *Essays in African Canadian Women's History* (Toronto: University of Toronto Press, 1994), 9.

5 Approximately a decade after Bristow's book, historian Afua Cooper pointed out the challenges associated with writing Black Canadian women's history. See Afua Cooper, "Constructing Black Women's Historical Knowledge," *Atlantis* 25, 1 (2000): 39.

6 Rinaldo Walcott, "'Who Is She and What Is She to You?': Mary Ann Shadd Cary and the (Im)possibility of Black/Canadian Studies," in *Rude: Contemporary Black Canadian Cultural Criticism* (Toronto: Insomniac Press, 2000), 138.

7 Walcott, "Who Is She," 139.

8 Carolyn Calloway-Thomas, "Crafting Black Culture through Empirical and Moral Arguments," *Howard Journal of Communications* 24 (2013): 244.

9 Shirley J. Yee, "Finding a Place: Mary Ann Shadd Cary and the Dilemmas of Black Migration to Canada, 1850–1870," *Frontiers: A Journal of Women Studies* 18, 3 (1997): 2, 4.

10 Yee, "Finding a Place," 4.

11 Walcott, "Who Is She," 140.

12 Mary A. Shadd, *A plea for emigration, or, Notes of Canada West: In its moral, social, and political aspect; with suggestions respecting Mexico, West Indies, and Vancouver's Island, for the information of colored emigrants* (Detroit: George W. Pattison, 1852), 10.

13 Shadd, *Plea for emigration*, 10.

14 Shadd, *Plea for emigration*, 10.

15 Rebecca J. Mancuso, "Three Thousand Families: English Canada's Colonizing Vision and British Family Settlement, 1919–39," *Journal of Canadian Studies* 45, 3 (2011): 9.

16 Calloway-Thomas, "Crafting Black Culture," 251.

17 Shadd, *Plea for emigration*, 32.

18 Shadd, *Plea for emigration*, 32.

19 Shadd, *Plea for emigration*, 32.

20 Moira Ferguson, ed., *Nine Black Women: An Anthology of Nineteenth-Century Writers from the United States, Canada, Bermuda, and the Caribbean* (New York: Routledge, 1998), quoted in Walcott, *Rude*, 140.

21 Bristow, *"We're Rooted Here"*; Katherine McKittrick, "'Their Blood Is There, and They Can't Throw It Out': Honouring Black Canadian Geographies," *Topia: Canadian Journal of Cultural Studies* 7 (2002): 27–37.

22 Jared G. Toney, "Locating Diaspora: Afro-Caribbean Narratives of Migration and Settlement in Toronto, 1914–1929," *Urban History Review* 28, 2 (2010): 81.

23 Alissa Trotz, "Rethinking Caribbean Transnational Connections: Conceptual Itineraries," *Global Networks* 6, 1 (2006): 41–60.

24 Sarah-Jane Mathieu, *North of the Color Line: Migration and Black Resistance in Canada, 1870–1995* (Chapel Hill: University of North Carolina Press, 2010), 18.

25 Mathieu, *North of the Color Line*, 8.

26 Mathieu, *North of the Color Line*, 145.

27 Mathieu, *North of the Color Line*, 152–3.

28 Mathieu, *North of the Color Line*, 161.

29 Joane Nagel, *Race, Ethnicity, and Sexuality: Intimate Intersections, Forbidden Frontiers* (New York: Oxford University Press, 2003).

30 Daiva Stasiulis and Abigail B. Bakan, "Negotiating Citizenship: The Case of Foreign Domestic Workers in Canada," *Feminist Review* 57 (Autumn 1997): 112–39.

31 Agnes Calliste argues that the first Caribbean Domestic Scheme was initiated between 1910 and 1911 to bring in 100 women from Guadeloupe to work in Canada as domestic workers. Agnes Calliste, "Canada's Immigration Policy and Domestics from the Caribbean: The Second Domestic Scheme," in *Race, Class, Gender: Bonds and Barriers*, ed. Jesse Vorst (Toronto: Between the Lines, 1989), 133–65.

32 For more on the politics of whiteness and domestic workers, see Noula Mina, "Taming and Training Greek 'Peasant Girls' and the Gendered Politics of Whiteness in Postwar Canada: Canadian Bureaucrats and Immigrant Domestics, 1950s–1960s," *Canadian Historical Review* 94, 4 (2013): 514–39; Franca Iacovetta, "'Primitive Villagers and Uneducated Girls': Canada Recruits Domestics from Italy, 1951–52," *Canadian Woman Studies* 7, 4 (1986): 14–18; Abigail B. Bakan and Daiva Stasiulis, eds, *Not One of the Family: Foreign Domestic Workers in Canada* (Toronto: University of Toronto Press, 1997); K. England and B. Stiell, "'They Think You're as Stupid as Your English Is': Constructing Foreign Domestic Workers in Toronto," *Environment and Planning A* 2, 9 (1997): 195–215, https://doi.org/10.1068/a290195.

33 See Marlene Epp and Franca Iacovetta's chapter in this volume.

34 Makeda Silvera, *Silenced: Caribbean Domestic Workers Talk with Makeda Silvera* (Toronto: Sister Vision Press, 1989); Agnes Calliste, "Women of 'Exceptional Merit': Immigration of Caribbean Nurses to Canada," *Canadian Journal of Women and Labour* 6 (1993): 85–102; Linda Carty and Dionne Brand, "Visible Minority Women – A Creation of the Canadian State," *Resources for Feminist Research* 12, 3 (1988): 39–42; Annette Henry, *Taking Back Control: African Canadian Women Teachers' Lives and Practice* (New York: University of New York Press, 1998); Nina Reid-Maroney, "African Canadian Women and New World Diaspora, circa 1865," *Canadian Woman Studies* 23, 2 (Winter 2004): 92–6; Shirley Yee, "Gender Ideology and Black Women: Community Builders in Ontario, 1850–1870," *Canadian Historical Review* 75 (March 1994): 53–73.

35 Carolyn Strange, "Wounded Womanhood and Dead Men: Chivalry and the Trials of Clara Ford and Carrie Davies," in *Gender Conflicts: New Essays in Women's History*, ed. Franca Iacovetta and Mariana Valverde (Toronto: University of Toronto Press, 1993), 155.

36 Strange, "Wounded Womanhood," 178.

37 Cooper, "Constructing Black Women's Historical Knowledge," 39.

38 Mathieu, *North of the Color Line*, xiii.

39 Katherine McKittrick, *Demonic Grounds: Black Women and the Cartographies of Struggle* (Minneapolis: University of Minnesota Press, 2006).

40 Constance Backhouse, "'I Was Unable to Identify with Topsy': Carrie M. Best's Struggle Against Racial Segregation in Nova Scotia, 1942," *Atlantis* 22, 2 (Spring 1998): 16.

41 Carrie M. Best, *That Lonesome Road: The Autobiography of Carrie M. Best* (New Glasgow, NS: Clarion Publishing Company, 1977), 43.

42 Best, *That Lonesome Road*, 44.

43 Hazel V. Carby, "White Woman Listen! Black Feminism and the Boundaries of Sisterhood," in *The Empire Strikes Back: Race and Racism in 70s Britain*, ed. Centre for Contemporary Cultural Studies (London: Hutchinson, 1982), 212–35; bell hooks, *Rock My Soul: Black People and Self-Esteem* (New York: Atria Books, 2003).

44 Barrington Walker, "Killing the Black Female Body: Black Womanhood, Black Patriarchy, and Spousal Murder in Two Ontario Criminal Trials, 1892–1894," in *Sisters or Strangers? Immigrant, Ethnic, and Racialized Women in Canadian History*, ed. Marlene Epp, Franca Iacovetta, and Frances Swyripa (Toronto: University of Toronto Press, 2004), 94.

45 Rosemary Brown, *Being Brown: A Very Public Life* (Toronto: Random House, 1989), 57.

46 See Lisa Pasolli and Julia Smith's discussion in this volume.

47 Brown, *Being Brown*, 44.

48 Rosamund Elwin, *Tongues on Fire: Caribbean Lesbian Lives and Stories* (Toronto: Women's Press, 1997); Silvera, *Silenced*; Wesley Crichlow, *Buller Men and Batty Bwoys: Hidden Men in Toronto and Halifax Black Communities* (Toronto: University of Toronto Press, 2003); May Friedman and Shana L. Calixte, eds, *Mothering and Blogging: The Radical Act of the MommyBlog* (Toronto: Demeter Press, 2009); Erica Lawson, "Images in Black: Black Women, Media and the Mythology of an Orderly Society," in *Back to the Drawing Board: African-Canadian Feminisms*, ed. Njoki Nathani Wane, Katerina Deliovsky, and Erica Lawson (Toronto: Sumach Press, 2002), 199–223; Dionne Brand, *Bread out of Stone: Recollections on Sex, Recognitions, Race, Dreaming, and Politics* (Toronto: Coach House Press, 1994); Becki Ross and Kim Greenwell,

"Spectacular Striptease: Performing the Sexual and Racial Other in Vancouver, B.C., 1950–1975," *Journal of Women's History* 17, 1 (2005): 137–64.

49 Nina Reid-Maroney, *The Reverend Jennie Johnson and African-Canadian History, 1868–1967* (Rochester, NY: University of Rochester Press, 2013), 8.

50 Reid-Maroney, *The Reverend Jennie Johnson*, 3.

51 Reid-Maroney, *The Reverend Jennie Johnson*, 1.

52 Carol Duncan, "'This Spot of Ground': Migration, Community, and Identity among Spiritual Baptists in Toronto," *Canadian Woman Studies* 17, 1 (1997): 32–5; Njoki Nathani Wane, "African Women and Spirituality: Harmonizing the Balance of Life," in Wane, Deliovsky, and Lawson, *Back to the Drawing Board*, 275–8.

53 Afua Cooper, *The Hanging of Angélique: The Untold Story of Canadian Slavery and the Burning of Montreal* (Athens: University of Georgia Press, 2007), 302–3.

54 A special thank you from Karen Flynn to the following: Nicklaus Schoultz, Marsha Clarke, Jennifer Harris, Terry Ann-Jones, Omege Rose, Neil Armstrong, Karen C. Tomlinson, Sharon Beckford-Foster, Debbie Miles-Senior, Audrey Taylor, Marvette Camille, and Arlene Edwards for a fruitful discussion on the various Jamaican proverbs and sayings that can be found in the writing of Black Canadian women's history.

55 Jafari S. Allen and Omise'eke Natasha Tinsley, "A Conversation Overflowing with Memory: On Omise'eke Natasha Tinsley's *Water, Shoulders, into the Black Pacific*," *GLQ: A Journal of Lesbian and Gay Studies* 18, 2 (2012): 251; M. Jacqui Alexander, *Pedagogies of Crossing: Meditations on Feminism, Sexual Politics, Memory, and the Sacred* (Durham, NC: Duke University Press, 2005); Saidiya V. Hartman, *Lose Your Mother: A Journey along the Atlantic Slave Route* (New York: Farrar, Straus and Giroux, 2007).

56 Allen and Tinsley, "A Conversation," 251.

57 Allen and Tinsley, "A Conversation," 252–3.

58 Gillian Roberts, "'The Book of Negroes' Illustrated Edition: Circulating African-Canadian History through the Middlebrow," *International Journal of Canadian Studies* 48 (2014): 53–66, https://doi.org/10.3138/ijcs.48.53.

59 Lawrence Hill, "Why I'm Not Allowed My Book Title," *Guardian,* 20 May 2008, http://www.theguardian.com/books/booksblog/2008/may/20/whyimnotallowedmybooktit.

60 Roberts, "'The Book of Negroes' Illustrated Edition," 57.

61 Winfried Siemerling, *The Black Atlantic Reconsidered: Black Canadian Writing, Cultural History, and the Presence of the Past* (Montreal: McGill-Queen's University Press, 2015), 27 (emphasis in the original).

62 Karen Flynn, "'I'm Glad That Someone Is Telling the Nursing Story': Writing Black Canadian Women's History," *Journal of Black Studies* 38, 2 (January 2008): 444.

63   Karen Flynn, *Moving beyond Borders: A History of Black Canadian and Caribbean Women in the Diaspora* (Toronto: University of Toronto Press, 2011), 14.
64   Lawrence Hill, *Women of Vision: The Story of the Canadian Negro Women's Association, 1951–1976* (Toronto: Umbrella Press, 1996), 10.
65   Claudine Bonner, "Nina Mae Alexander: Daughter of Promise," in *The Promised Land: History and Historiography of the Black Experience in Chatham-Kent's Settlements and Beyond*, ed. Boulou Ebanda de B'beri, Nina Reid-Maroney, and Handel Kashope Wright (Toronto: University of Toronto Press, 2014), 91–105.

SELECTED READINGS

Alexander, M. Jacqui. *Pedagogies of Crossing: Meditations on Feminism, Sexual Politics, Memory, and the Sacred*. Durham, NC: Duke University Press, 2005.
Allen, Jafari S., and Omise'eke Natasha Tinsley. "A Conversation Overflowing with Memory: On Omise'eke Natasha Tinsley's *Water, Shoulders, into the Black Pacific*." *GLQ: A Journal of Lesbian and Gay Studies* 18, 2 (2012): 252–3. https://doi.org/10.1215/10642684-1472881
Backhouse, Constance. "'I Was Unable to Identify with Topsy': Carrie M. Best's Struggle Against Racial Segregation in Nova Scotia, 1942." *Atlantis* 22, 2 (Spring 1998): 16–26. https://ssrn.com/abstract=2263419
Bakan, Abigail B., and Daiva Stasiulis, eds. *Not One of the Family: Foreign Domestic Workers in Canada*. Toronto: University of Toronto Press, 1997.
Best, Carrie M. *That Lonesome Road: The Autobiography of Carrie M. Best*. New Glasgow, NS: Clarion Publishing Company, 1977.
Bonner, Claudine. "Nina Mae Alexander: Daughter of Promise." In *The Promised Land: History and Historiography of the Black Experience in Chatham-Kent's Settlements and Beyond*, edited by Boulou Ebanda de B'beri, Nina Reid-Maroney, and Handel Kashope Wright, 91–105. Toronto: University of Toronto Press, 2014.
Brand, Dionne. *Bread out of Stone: Recollections on Sex, Recognitions, Race, Dreaming, and Politics*. Toronto: Coach House Press, 1994.
Bristow, Peggy, ed. *"We're Rooted Here and They Can't Pull Us Up": Essays in African Canadian Women's History*. Toronto: University of Toronto Press, 1994.
Calliste, Agnes. "Canada's Immigration Policy and Domestics from the Caribbean: The Second Domestic Scheme." In *Race, Class, Gender: Bonds and Barriers*, edited by Jesse Vorst, 133–65. Toronto: Between the Lines, 1989.
–   "Women of 'Exceptional Merit': Immigration of Caribbean Nurses to Canada." *Canadian Journal of Women and Labour* 6 (1993): 85–102.

Calloway-Thomas, Carolyn. "Crafting Black Culture through Empirical and Moral Arguments." *Howard Journal of Communications* 24 (2013): 239–56. https://doi.or g/10.1080/10646175.2013.805978

Carby, Hazel V. "White Woman Listen! Black Feminism and the Boundaries of Sisterhood." In *The Empire Strikes Back: Race and Racism in 70s Britain*, edited by Centre for Contemporary Cultural Studies, 212–35. London: Hutchinson, 1982.

Carty, Linda, and Dionne Brand. "Visible Minority Women – A Creation of the Canadian State." *Resources for Feminist Research* 12, 3 (1988): 39–42.

Cary Shadd, Mary A. *A plea for emigration, or, Notes of Canada West: In its moral, social, and political aspect; with suggestions respecting Mexico, West Indies, and Vancouver's Island, for the information of colored emigrants.* Detroit: George W. Pattison, 1852.

Cooper, Afua. "Constructing Black Women's Historical Knowledge." *Atlantis* 25, 1 (2000): 39–50.

– *The Hanging of Angélique: The Untold Story of Canadian Slavery and the Burning of Montreal.* Athens: University of Georgia Press, 2007.

Crichlow, Warren. *Buller Men and Batty Bwoys: Hidden Men in Toronto and Halifax Black Communities.* Toronto: University of Toronto Press, 2003.

Duncan, Carol. "'This Spot of Ground': Migration, Community, and Identity among Spiritual Baptists in Toronto." *Canadian Woman Studies* 17, 1 (1997): 32–5.

Elwin, Rosamund. *Tongues on Fire: Caribbean Lesbian Lives and Stories.* Toronto: Women's Press, 1997.

Epp, Marlene, Franca Iacovetta, and Frances Swyripa, eds. *Sisters or Strangers? Immigrant, Ethnic, and Racialized Women in Canadian History.* Toronto: University of Toronto Press, 2004.

Ferguson, Moira, ed. *Nine Black Women: An Anthology of Nineteenth-Century Writers from the United States, Canada, Bermuda, and the Caribbean.* New York: Routledge, 1998.

Flynn, Karen. "Black Canadian Feminist Theorizing: Possibilities and Prospects." *The CLR James Journal* 20, 1/2 (Fall 2014): 179–93. https://doi.org/10.5840/ clrjames20149158

– "'I'm Glad That Someone Is Telling the Nursing Story': Writing Black Canadian Women's History." *Journal of Black Studies* 38, 2 (January 2008): 443–60. https:// doi.org/10.1177/0021934707306586

– *Moving beyond Borders: A History of Black Canadian and Caribbean Women in the Diaspora.* Toronto: University of Toronto Press, 2011.

Friedman, May, and Shana L. Calixte, eds. *Mothering and Blogging: The Radical Act of the MommyBlog.* Toronto: Demeter Press, 2009.

Hartman, Saidiya V. *Lose Your Mother: A Journey along the Atlantic Slave Route.* New York: Farrar, Straus and Giroux, 2007.

Henry, Annette. *Taking Back Control: African Canadian Women Teachers' Lives and Practice*. New York: University of New York Press, 1998.

Hill, Lawrence. "Why I'm Not Allowed My Book Title." *Guardian*, 20 May 2008. http://www.theguardian.com/books/booksblog/2008/may/20/whyimnotallowedmybooktit

– *Women of Vision: The Story of the Canadian Negro Women's Association, 1951–1976*. Toronto: Umbrella Press, 1996.

hooks, bell. *Rock My Soul: Black People and Self-Esteem*. New York: Atria Books, 2003.

Iacovetta, Franca. "'Primitive Villagers and Uneducated Girls': Canada Recruits Domestics from Italy, 1951–52." *Canadian Woman Studies* 7, 4 (1986): 14–18. https://doi.org/10.3138/jcs.45.3.5

Iacovetta, Franca, and Mariana Valverde, eds. *Gender Conflicts: New Essays in Women's History*. Toronto: University of Toronto Press, 1993.

Mancuso, Rebecca J. "Three Thousand Families: English Canada's Colonizing Vision and British Family Settlement, 1919–39." *Journal of Canadian Studies* 45, 3 (2011): 5–33. https://doi.org/10.3138/jcs.45.3.5

Mathieu, Sarah-Jane. *North of the Color Line: Migration and Black Resistance in Canada, 1870–1995*. Chapel Hill: University of North Carolina Press, 2010.

McKittrick, Katherine. *Demonic Grounds: Black Women and the Cartographies of Struggle*. Minneapolis: University of Minnesota Press, 2006.

– "'Their Blood Is There, and They Can't Throw It Out': Honouring Black Canadian Geographies." *Topia: Canadian Journal of Cultural Studies* 7 (2002): 27–37. https://doi.org/10.3138/topia.7.27

Nagel, Joane. *Race, Ethnicity, and Sexuality: Intimate Intersections, Forbidden Frontiers*. New York: Oxford University Press, 2003.

Reid-Maroney, Nina. "African Canadian Women and New World Diaspora, circa 1865." *Canadian Woman Studies* 23, 2 (Winter 2004): 92–6.

– *The Reverend Jennie Johnson and African-Canadian History, 1868–1967*. Rochester, NY: University of Rochester Press, 2013.

Roberts, Gillian. "'The Book of Negroes' Illustrated Edition: Circulating African-Canadian History through the Middlebrow." *International Journal of Canadian Studies* 48 (2014): 53–66. https://doi.org/10.3138/ijcs.48.53

Ross, Becki, and Kim Greenwell. "Spectacular Striptease: Performing the Sexual and Racial Other in Vancouver, B.C., 1950–1975." *Journal of Women's History* 17, 1 (2005): 137–64. https://doi.org/10.1353/jowh.2005.0012

Siemerling, Winfried. *The Black Atlantic Reconsidered: Black Canadian Writing, Cultural History, and the Presence of the Past*. Montreal: McGill-Queen's University Press, 2015.

Silvera, Makeda. *Silenced: Caribbean Domestic Workers Talk with Makeda Silvera*. Toronto: Sister Vision Press, 1983.

Stasiulis, Daiva, and Abigail B. Bakan. "Negotiating Citizenship: The Case of Foreign Domestic Workers in Canada." *Feminist Review* 57 (Autumn 1997): 112–39. https://doi.org/10.1080/014177897339687

Toney, Jared G. "Locating Diaspora: Afro-Caribbean Narratives of Migration and Settlement in Toronto, 1914–1929." *Urban History Review* 28, 2 (2010): 75–87. https://doi.org/10.7202/039676ar

Trotz, Alissa. "Rethinking Caribbean Transnational Connections: Conceptual Itineraries." *Global Networks* 6, 1 (2006): 41–60. https://doi.org/10.1111/j.1471-0374.2006.00132.x

Vorst, Jesse, ed. *Race, Class, Gender: Bonds and Barriers*. Toronto: Between the Lines, 1989.

Walcott, Rinaldo. *Rude: Contemporary Black Canadian Cultural Criticism*. Toronto: Insomniac Press, 2000.

Wane, Njoki Nathani, Katerina Deliovsky, and Erica Lawson, eds. *Back to the Drawing Board: African-Canadian Feminisms*. Toronto: Sumach Press, 2002.

Yee, Shirley J. "Finding a Place: Mary Ann Shadd Cary and the Dilemmas of Black Migration to Canada, 1850–1870." *Frontiers: A Journal of Women Studies* 18, 3 (1997): 1–16. https://doi.org/10.2307/3347171

– "Gender Ideology and Black Women: Community Builders in Ontario, 1850–1870." *Canadian Historical Review* 75 (March 1994): 53–73. https://doi.org/10.3138/CHR-075-01-03

4 Quebec Nationalism and the History of Women and Gender

DENYSE BAILLARGEON

TRANSLATED BY ZOË BLOWEN-LEDOUX

Micheline Dumont, a pioneer in Quebec women's history and sometime polemicist, bitterly lamented in an article published about fifteen years ago that this area of historical research had not been able to carve out the place it deserved despite much valuable research and, especially, that it had not fundamentally transformed the interpretation of Quebec history.[1] Returning vigorously to this issue in her most recent book, published in 2013, she took the example of Éric Bédard's *Quebec History for Dummies*[2] as proof of certain (male) colleagues' resistance to including women in historical narratives to better maintain "the old conception of history summed up by traditionally defined politics."[3]

Of course, *Quebec History for Dummies* is popular history and should not serve as the basis on which to judge the whole of Quebec historiography, particularly in French. Nevertheless, it is true that in Quebec's French-speaking university settings, women's and gender history has taken longer to emerge and has had a harder time taking hold than elsewhere in Canada.[4] How can this widespread avoidance or incapacity to truly consider feminist thought in history and include women and gender in the historical framework be explained? I argue that interpretations of Quebec history that have dominated the historiographic landscape since the 1970s and have sought to offer new versions of this history (especially of the Franco-Quebecois national destiny) are plausible explanations. Rather than present an exhaustive overview of the research produced on Quebec history over the last forty years, this chapter will examine these different interpretations, which the history of women sometimes helped inform, in light of the debates they generated. In so doing, it will also show how and why these interpretations cannot easily "accommodate" women's and gender history.

This chapter is available in French on UTP's website, utorontopress.com: click on the "Downloads and Links" tab featured on the detail page for this book.

A Modern Quebec

There is no doubt that the interpretations of Quebec history have undergone profound change since the 1970s. Those who have analysed the historical production of the 1970s through the 1990s have unanimously highlighted Quebec historians' almost radical shift in perspective at the same time they turned their focus to the study of the post-industrial period. Identified as "revisionist" by historian Ronald Rudin[5] and as "modernist" by those he included in this movement,[6] this new interpretive framework suggested that historians of Quebec no longer insist on its specificities, but rather draw out Quebec's similarities with other Western societies, such as English-speaking Canada, particularly Ontario.

Overall, this new interpretation mainly showed that instead of being politically, economically, socially, ideologically, or culturally "behind," as the Montreal and Laval schools of historical thought argued,[7] Quebec developed at the same pace and along the same lines as its neighbours. Rejecting the unequivocal portrait of a society dominated by the Catholic Church, bound by its rural roots, economically underdeveloped, and culturally behind the times, a new generation of researchers painted a portrait of Quebec as a society marked since the 1850s by industrialization, urbanization, and laicization, and by the rise of liberalism and the predominance of class rather than ethnic conflicts. From this perspective, the 1960s – the Quiet Revolution – were no longer considered a sudden left turn into modernity but the end of a long road to maturation that dated back to the Second World War or even the nineteenth century.[8] As many modernist historians pointed out, their analyses and conclusions have often been more refined, complex, and nuanced than existing assessments would lead us to believe.[9] But if we can agree that they did not completely ignore the deep-seated conservatism of Quebec society and the iron grip that the Catholic Church had over Quebec society and institutions, this portrait of modernist historiography is on the whole correct.[10]

It should be noted that women's history, a field of study that arose at the same time the modernist interpretation of history began taking hold, contributed a great deal to this new vision of a "modern" Quebec. As I pointed out in 1995, this field of research did not evolve in a vacuum; it proved to be quite amendable to the modernist historiographic framework, which provided an opportunity to re-evaluate the historical experience of Quebec women, particularly its French-speaking women, and to go beyond the stereotyped image of them portrayed in history.[11] Like their modernist colleagues, feminist historians have particularly insisted on what was similar between French-speaking Quebec women and women of other Western societies, particularly English-speaking Canadian women and, more specifically, women in Ontario.

For instance, childcare centres founded by the Grey Nuns in the nineteenth century led Suzanne D. Cross to argue that many married French Canadian women were obliged to join the labour market from the very start of industrialization, despite opposition from clergy.[12] Marta Danylewycz, who studied two female religious communities between 1840 and 1920, put forth that economic and social factors (and not just spiritual ones) had contributed to the explosion in these communities' numbers, with nuns and feminists joining forces on certain issues.[13] In the same vein, Micheline Dumont came to the conclusion that, far from being just proof of the Catholic Church's domination over women, joining a religious order was, in fact, an outlet for French speakers, who thus escaped marriage and could more easily undertake a teaching or nursing career. Under the guise of these vocations, one could detect a "diverted" feminism that placed early twentieth-century Quebec women, otherwise deemed little inclined to advocacy, on the same footing as other Western women.[14] Marie Lavigne showed how it was not true that all Quebec women gave birth to dozens of children. This demographic pattern, she argued, was found mostly in rural areas, where many hands were still necessary to ensure family subsistence. Urban Quebec women adjusted the size of their families to the new reality of the city, and thus necessarily used some sort of contraception, despite Church prohibitions.[15] Andrée Lévesque took an interest in women who strayed from prescribed norms, particularly with regard to sexuality and maternity, thus even more radically deconstructing the image of the "chaste and virtuous" French Canadian woman.[16] Among the first to shed light on phenomena like maternity outside of marriage, prostitution, infanticide, and abortion, through her work she has inspired other female historians, notably Marie-Aimée Cliche and Danielle Lacasse, who have aimed their inquiry at decidedly unconventional women.[17]

These few examples show how this generation's most prominent female historians reassessed the historical experience of Quebec's French-speaking women to revise the stereotyped vision of either the matriarch of a large family confined to her home or the nun trapped in an alienating vocation; instead, they gave voice to women who refused to conform or who had no other choice but to live on the margins – a completely alien phenomenon up until then. As these studies sought to highlight, French-speaking women in Quebec have acted like all North American women at least since the second half of the nineteenth century and, when this was not so, it was for strategic reasons. Female historians did not necessarily concur with these interpretations, some of which have since been questioned or nuanced by subsequent research.[18] But beyond the debate it stirred, this body of work offered a much more complex view of French-speaking women's past and, especially, was very much in line with the modernist interpretation that was changing the field.

However, the contribution of modernist female historians was largely ignored when this historiography began to be the focus of reflection and critique in the early 1990s. Even in their re-evaluations of the historiographical venture to which they had contributed, male historians continued to skip over the work their female colleagues had contributed to this new vision of Quebec history.[19] Moreover, the female historians themselves did not take part in these debates, perhaps because the grounds on which the discussions were conducted necessarily excluded them.

Beyond how much the history of women and gender has been incorporated into each so-called modernist study – an assessment beyond the scope of this chapter[20] – the production that gave rise to these discussions clearly shows the "virilizing" intentions of the modernist historiographic venture, with which female historians struggle to identify. In fact, we can surmise that if the modernist interpretation inspired them, it was because this perspective allowed them to better assert the historical experience of Quebec's women (one of the major objectives of women's history at the time), to affirm its complexity and therefore its importance, and to insist on past feminine and feminist struggles. Their goal was to draw out the feminine part of this history, not exacerbate its masculine part, which is rather exactly what modernist historiography set out to do. Echoing Micheline Dumont's findings that Quebecois (male) historians who were "compulsively focused on the new Quebec identity had the most trouble incorporating theoretical perspectives that questioned masculine presumptions of this identity,"[21] I would argue that a very masculine vision of modernist historiography has clearly commandeered these discussions, regardless of how these historians may have taken women and gender into account in their respective works.

As Ronald Rudin has demonstrated, the modernist version of Quebec's past drew its source from the transformations of the 1960s – a fact many of these historians have acknowledged. Speaking of his generation, Paul-André Linteau said, for instance, that it was "marked by the ideology of the modernization of the Quiet Revolution and by the new Québécois nationalism,"[22] and that this led his generation to reorient its inquiry. Contemporary history, the territory of Quebec (rather than of French Canada), and its population as a whole (rather than just the French speakers) have since become central to this generation's research, which draws inspiration from classic social history and its quantitative methods to explore aspects of Quebec's past that, until then, had been completely neglected, particularly the development of industrial capitalism.[23] As Jacques Rouillard mentions, this generation of historians not only explored new avenues of study but, in doing so, also questioned the notion of Quebec society's "backwardness" that had been developed in the 1950s by sociologists who, he specifies, did not spend much time in the archives.[24] For Gérard Bouchard, the new light shed on Quebec's past was clearly in line with the new identity that the Quebecois were forging: "In the minds of many 'Franco-Québécois,' a regained collective confidence, enthusiasm, and hope ushered in by the Quiet Revolution made the panoply of depressing myths associated in many minds with the defeatist paradigm of survival meaningless and intolerable [...] This pantheon of vanquished or downtrodden figures became incompatible with the emerging Québécois, standing tall at long last, and with his new world view and vision of the New World."[25]

In sum, to modernists, Quebec history as it was portrayed by their predecessors was unsatisfactory on at least two accounts. First, it was not founded on the ideals of scientific research, and second, it drew a reductionist and defeatist portrait of Quebec society that fit poorly with the rising hopes of the 1960s. Modernist works therefore had a twofold aim: establish the discipline on new bases and find in Quebec's past the origins of this modernity unfolding before their eyes. The result was a true historiographic revolution, the magnitude and scope of which could not be underestimated; beyond the criticism it attracted, modernist historiography substantially altered the vision of Quebec's past. To this day, what is retained most especially is that it sought to portray Quebec history in a modern light; in my opinion, this new interpretation of Quebec history was also an operation to "masculinize" historical practice and narrative, a process that was just as significant but that went almost unnoticed and that may well explain why there was practically no mention of women and gender in the debate it spurred.

This double phenomenon can be seen first of all in the way male modernists sought to present their approach. Acknowledging that their historiographical project was greatly influenced by the context in which it was emerging and that it aimed for a new version of history that would reflect a less depressing picture of the past, and thus admitting that this renewed narrative also held its share of subjectivity, these historians have nonetheless reiterated that their work drew on an arsenal of historical science to better establish its credibility. On this subject, Bouchard said, "We are talking about a full-fledged scientific movement that projected a new vision of Quebec's past. It managed to do so by drawing on reformed scientific method, that produced very high-quality work."[26] As this quote illustrates, the "scientific methods" of the inquiry into the past would produce – in the eyes of many modernists – a history that was fairer, truer, and therefore more "objective."

In my opinion, the importance the modernists lent their scientific methods of inquiry can be interpreted as a desire to present the discipline in a more masculine light. As Bonnie Smith demonstrated, scientific history that rose in the nineteenth century simultaneously with its professionalization was clearly associated with masculinity, while amateurism – henceforth disqualified in the eyes of these new professionals – became a synonym for femininity.[27]

Rigorous archival research, scrupulous criticism of sources, exercise of impartial judgment, and factual writing stripped of all emotion were considered necessary to the pursuit of scientific knowledge. More to the point, these ingredients call on the intellectual dispositions and rationality deemed masculine and which "historians" without university training could no longer pretend to possess.[28] Examining the Canadian experience, Donald Wright, building on work by Alison Prentice and Beverly Boutilier, also pointed out that the professionalization of history in Canada drew on a valorization of so-called masculine attributes (reason, objectivity, and knowledge), which were presented as the exact opposites of feminine qualities (emotion, subjectivity, and experience), considered to be inferior.[29]

From this perspective, it could be said that by insisting on the scientific dimension of their work, the modern school led us to believe that they had taken on their discipline with more virility than their forerunners, whom they generally criticized for having been, as Jacques Rouillard put it, "little enamoured of historical research."[30] Their scientific rigour and ability to present their results in a detached manner[31] (the foundation of their professionalism) appeared to guarantee the virility – and, therefore, the superiority – of the history they practised.

While claiming this "objectivity" and "rationality" that referred to the discipline's masculinity, the modernists also put forth a masculine interpretation of Quebec history that served as a counterweight to the feminine image their predecessors had built. This is at least what this historiography's many analysts suggest. Although associated with the movement, Gérard Bouchard, one of its primary critics, summarized the modern school's contributions as "the new historical consciousness that downplayed the legendary figures of the survival and the heroes of the French and Catholic movement to populate the land [...] It sought to turn its back on the old and depressing myths and replace the image of the downtrodden and humiliated French Canadian with that of the resilient Québécois, master of his own destiny."[32] Thus, Bouchard lays out a very contrasting vision of Quebec's past. In his view, the new historiography replaced an outdated and (especially) humiliating representation of the colonized "French Canadian" unable to face the socio-economic changes under way with the image of the "Quebecois" perfectly mastering his own destiny and able to take a stand. Juxtaposing the subjection and disempowerment of a "traditional" Quebec to the free will and the assurance of a "modern" Quebec, these two portraits could not refer more clearly to symbolic femininity and masculinity. While the gender of modernity was debated among researchers for a decade and many affirmed it could very well indeed be feminine,[33] it remains that in this case, the image of Quebec's past that the modern school sought to project was decidedly virile: not only did it seem to be incarnated by its only male component (the French Canadian, the Quebecois), it also referred to resolutely masculine attributes (self-mastery, mastery of one's destiny, self-affirmation, etc.).

Of course, all historians of the modern school did not explain their new vision of Quebec history in such explicitly gendered terms. However, the various assessments that have been carried out tend to confirm that the modernist agenda was indeed the masculinization of Quebec's past. Ronald Rudin, for example, stated that the revisionist movement aimed to prove that Quebecois French speakers "were able to make it in the world"[34] or, in other words, that they were able to fight for their rightful place. For Jocelyn Létourneau, the new version of Quebec history "sanctioned the passage from a vanquished, humiliated, and greatly demoralized collective Subject (the French Canadian of the past) into an accomplished, enterprising, and ambitious Subject."[35] Clearly, for these critics of the modernist movement, confidence, self-assurance, and a conquering mindset – all incontestable indications of virility – were also the primary characteristics this new historiography attributed to the French Canadian nation. We might argue that the pre-modernist historiography was just as infatuated with masculinity and that the likes of Lionel Groulx (to mention this period's most famous historian) heavily insisted on the valour of his "petit peuple" who courageously fought for their Catholic and French society against the British invader – indeed the most masculine behaviour.[36] But for the modern school, the idea of survival at the centre of the Groulxian interpretation seemed to be a form of closing in on oneself and on one's traditions caused by "feminine" disempowerment, a strategy that reflected Quebec's inferiority and translated into the docility generally associated with women. This demeaning view of a feminine Quebec can be found in the work of historians and sociologists in the 1950s who trained or influenced the modernists. By questioning, as Linteau said, "their predecessors' assumptions and interpretations"[37] and by taking the opposite line of their positions, the modern school constructed a representation of Quebec's past that highlighted masculine characteristics that for them could not be dissociated from modernity. Under these conditions, it is probably not surprising that those who spoke out about this new interpretation of Quebec history – both those who helped make it and wished to elucidate their venture, and those who offered critical analysis – had not considered what women's and gender history had brought to it. Even if some feminist historians borrowed the interpretative grid of Quebec modernity, as we saw, they did not conclude any less that women – here as elsewhere in the Western world – had been victims of domination, oppression, and discrimination by a profoundly patriarchal society. Much more interested in proving Quebecois progressivism (a way among others of demonstrating that they had, in fact, been modern), historians in the modern school could less easily take into account these kind of findings. Yvan Lamonde draws a similar conclusion in explaining the absence of cultural history in these historiographical debates: "For the proponents of the 'normal' society or a precocious 'modernity,' it was more difficult to base their analysis or view on close consideration of the destiny of nineteenth-century Ultramontanism and liberalism; on conservatism or its ideological variations over the first third of the [twentieth] century."[38] In other words, whatever got in the way of the modernist vision was removed, if not from the research used to build it, then at least from the subsequent representation of that research. This is how, like cultural or intellectual history, women's and gender history struggled to find its place in the portrait of the "modern" Quebec this interpretation created.

Quebecois Language, Faith, and American Orientation

The modern school's thesis has certainly exercised the greatest influence on Quebec historiography in recent decades; it is also the perspective that has prompted the greatest amount of debate among historians.[39] However, at the dawn of the twenty-first century, at least two other interpretations of the history of French-speaking Quebec – one focused on its Americanness, the other on its Catholic and French heritage – were also put forth, though neither were more inclined to take women or gender into consideration. With only a few exceptions, critics of these new interpretations did not highlight this exclusion. Yet, at the start of this century while these new perspectives were developed, the two fields of historical research had matured and their perspectives considerably widened to include reflections on connections between women, religious institutions, state formation, and the national issue.

For example, in a synthesis published in the early 1980s, Susan Mann-Trofimenkoff had already shown how the national issue brought together French-speaking nationalists and feminists while also deeply dividing them, as the nationalists were unable to accommodate women's quest for autonomy, which was counter to the reproduction of the community on which preservation of the French language and Catholic culture depended.[40] Stéphanie Lanthier had also highlighted the profoundly misogynous narrative of the 1970s radical nationalism in which Quebec, associated with a feminine figure, who became territory to conquer, even by rape.[41] Like that of Allan Greer, who had emphasized the republican – and therefore most masculine – conception of the

Patriotes' citizenship,[42] Lanthier's work inspired Micheline Dumont to write an article exploring the difficulty of meshing women's history and national history.[43] Bettina Bradbury's early work on the debates around the abolition of dowries in the nineteenth century had already demonstrated how women's rights had been a key issue in developing capitalism, just as the civil institution of marriage and the protection of widows had been central to the political battle between nationalists and their opponents.[44] My own research on the fight against infant mortality had also illustrated the nationalism of the priests and doctors who led the *Gouttes de lait montréalaises* and how these political and religious convictions overrode children's protection, leading them to defend the inadequate socio-sanitary infrastructure from which they had eradicated the feminists.[45] Lastly, let us mention Nicole Laurin, Danielle Juteau, and Lorraine Duchesne's very detailed study, which had clearly established the invaluable contribution of female religious communities to the edification of the Quebec Catholic Church's works and emphasized the appropriation of their (unpaid) work by male clerical authorities, who used it to consolidate their own power within Quebec society.[46] Placing gender at the centre of their analysis, these studies (all published prior to 2000), among others, were an invitation to reconsider the narrative framework of Quebec nationalism and to take into account not only the ethnic conflicts and French speakers' desire for self-affirmation, but also the tension within this community regarding women's role in the endeavour. In other words, they suggested the question be reformulated to include all the power relationships that shaped French Canadian nationalism and to explore these right into the private areas of family relationships. But, as we will see in the coming pages, these considerations hardly influenced the new historiographical proposals of the twenty-first century, perhaps due to the much less unified image of the national struggles that emerged from these works.

Although associated with the modernist movement, Gérard Bouchard formulated certain critiques of this historiography starting in the early 1990s because he felt it had reached its heuristic limits.[47] In his opinion, it was becoming ever more urgent to overcome this paradigm to examine, instead, the "Americanness" of Quebec – how indeed it fit into this continent – and assess how the collective imagination has symbolically appropriated this space to build a national identity. He took on just such an exercise in *Genèse des nations et cultures du Nouveau Monde*. Therein, he postulates that, beginning in the 1840s, there was a break between the culture of the elites – who turned to Europe in general and to France in particular – and that of the people, who were solidly anchored on the American continent. The first "projected into false identities,"[48] insisting on French traditions and the French Canadians' distinctive traits that constituted their heritage, in such a way as to better focus on the imperative of survival. The second did not hesitate to fully embrace their American destiny and integrate a set of myths based on conquering their immediate surroundings. Echoing the radical nationalist discourse of the 1960s that accused "traditional" French Canadian nationalism of having been the source of the people's (especially men's) oppression,[49] Bouchard postulated that the dominant "*élitaire*" memory "long portrayed an emasculated image of the settler (accompanied by his double: the procreative, devoted, and pious mother) [...] that made him a supine being of nationality coiled up in the clergy's bosom."[50] In a completely contrasting way, popular culture proceeded to mix French and American traditions, giving rise to a "gallery of masculine archetypes, like the *coureur de bois*, the *voyageur*, the working woodsman, the porter, the jobber, the fixer-upper, the water carrier, the settler, the *canayen*, the transitory factory worker, or the rich uncle from the States [...] And for women, emerged the characters of the saintly wife, the mother hen, the perfect spouse, the glamour girl and the jolly wife – a much more limited repertory, indeed. Clearly, the new collective imagination was masculine."[51]

In this portrayal the *élitaire* and European-flavoured culture that especially valued tradition adopted a feminine configuration, while the Americanized and all-conquering popular culture adopted an exclusively masculine dimension. Bouchard recognizes this but without, however, examining the meaning and consequences of such an association. According to his analysis, elite culture managed to take hold in the century between the 1840s and the 1940s, as the images of the settler emasculated by the Church and by his pious wife dominated Quebec collective imagination at the expense of the more virile figures of the new world adventurers. This interpretation seems to reinforce the idea that the Quebec of this era was more traditional than modern, as Jacques Rouillard argued,[52] but examined under the light of gender, Bouchard's argumentation simply falls into line with the modern school historiography.

By decreeing that the culture of the elites forged "false identities" and broke with American and modern popular culture, Bouchard did not really seek to return to earlier interpretations so much as he sought to disqualify the learned identity-based discourse, which built a feminine image of French Canadians, in order to better reaffirm the masculinity of Quebecois people and history. The more "authentic" popular culture was in the end the only one that really counted and that was truly virile, even if it was stifled right up to the Quiet Revolution. As sociologist Joseph Yvon Thériault says, "National representation is just an optical illusion resulting from an erroneous collective representation: the French Canadian fiction. By bringing these representations back to the facts, Americanism re-established the truth and wiped away the backwardness."[53] In other words, if Bouchard lingered so long on the *élitaire* discourse, it was to better show the narrow, feminine nature of the elites' conservative ideology and its discrepancy with the reality of the people who did not hesitate to embrace a most masculine Americanness. In so doing, Bouchard invited Quebec history to be reinterpreted through a modernist filter. Moreover – and Thériault failed to raise this point – this desire to revisit Quebec history to better match it with its American destiny was an eminently gendered undertaking. After all, it was not the women confined to the domestic sphere who spurred on the national imagination of territorial conquest – a fundamental element in the Americanist thesis.

The "Americanist" interpretation of Quebec history was not taken up by academic historians. The argument of the parallel existence of the two cultures – *élitaire* to the one side and popular to the other – left many sceptical, but not because this interpretation marginalized half of the population's historical experience. Joseph Yvon Thériault's critique of Bouchard for creating a radical break with what he called "French Canadian filiation" and for undermining the foundations of a national undertaking that was made obsolete without reference to a distinctive past, as well as Jacques Beauchemin's discomfort with the French Canadians' relationship with their so-called shameful past,[54] was nonetheless picked up by a new generation of researchers, including a few historians, who purported a "new sensitivity." This group's flagship, almost manifesto-like, work entitled *Les idées mènent le Québec* rejected wholesale the heritage of the Quiet Revolution and the modern school's overly positive assessment of it, which, in these authors' opinions, finished cutting the French Canadians off from their cultural roots. In fact, taking the opposite of the dichotomous view of the French Canadian national imagination Bouchard had suggested, some of the young historians in this collective sought instead to offer up a consensual vision, while also emphasizing the necessity of reconciling with the past. This was the only way, in their view, to revive declining nationalist fervour.[55] Éric Bédard and Xavier Gélinas criticized the neo-nationalist historians (i.e., the modernists) for having reconstructed the story of the nation "by negation." They felt that by obliterating, if not denigrating, the French Canadian society's traditional and religious aspects to better affirm Quebec's modernity, they showed "ingratitude towards French Canadians of yesteryear."[56] They considered it imperative to return to a less materialistic vision of history, one that was less obsessed with the evolution of social structures, less likely to denigrate tradition and demote the Church to the simple rank of "institution," and more likely to be attentive to "the meaningful world" of past generations.[57] In other words, these two historians suggested a return to the study of the ideas, collective representations, and, especially, religious beliefs that, along with French cultural references, were the foundations of "our traditions." To counter the materialism of the social history defended by the modernists, the co-authors went so far as to state that "the action, thought, and faith of the people of the past" should be considered as "causal explanations as worthy of our sustained and empathetic attention as the underlying currents in which they form."[58]

This new historiographic project was criticized for many reasons, especially by Thierry Nootens, Jean-Marie Fecteau, and Martin Petitclerc.[59] Most particularly targeted by critics were the "*passéism*" of this "new sensitivity," which was demonstrated by the virulent denunciation of the Quiet Revolution's gains, as well as the fragile scientific basis of a movement that advocated gratitude to the ancestors and made the autonomy of ideas and the quest for meaning (in particular via religion) the main driver for studying history and understanding the past. As Petitclerc pointed out, this historiographic agenda, which would have us return to a history of ideas by analysing them with respectful consideration of the ancestors' intentionality, "ran the risk of having little to say about the experience of these women who had not be been given the 'privilege' of having autonomous ideas. At least, maybe we will succeed," he goes on to say, "if the deference for the ancestors does not prohibit asking a few delicate questions, to reconstitute the wealth of this world of meaning that made it possible to justify this exploitation."[60]

By adopting the mandate to reinstate the value of traditional French Canadian heritage to better revive nationalist fervour, the historiographic agenda of the authors of the "new sensitivity" could, in a way, be read as a return to a feminine vision of Quebec history in the purest of Groulxian tradition. But although it is true that this interpretation sought to reinstate the main characteristics of the nation that gave rise to the survival thesis, it did so out of a desire to highlight a unit of thought and action, an obstinacy, and an assurance in the struggle that can also be seen as a sign of virility. Regardless, it is obvious, as Petitclerc aptly pointed out, that this historiographic endeavour did not foresee any space for the historic experience of women and especially for their oppression.[61] In one of his more recent writings, Éric Bédard lamented that social history had emphasized the study of various "sociological or minority 'us'" – notably the workers, marginalized populations, women, ethnic groups, etc. – that would have had "the effect of distancing us from the study of a national 'us'" and led to believe "that a nation is nothing but an aggregate of individuals fiercely fighting to get their piece of the pie."[62] Over a conflictual interpretation of social relations, Bédard preferred the vision of a French Canada and a Quebec designed as "moral communities [...] that inspired excellence and solidarity." Like Jacques Beauchemin, he felt the nation, "by the devotion it traditionally stirred, [kept in check] the egoism freed by an emancipating momentum of modernity."[63] That some groups more than others – like women – had to restrain their emancipating "egoism" in the name of national solidarity does not appear to bother him. Like the early twentieth-century traditionalist nationalists Bédard seems to admire so ardently, he undoubtedly believes that this cost would not be too high to maintain this community.

Thus, since the 1970s, the modernist, Americanist, and "new sensitivity" theses have in their own ways proposed a vision of Quebec history modelled on a renewed way of perceiving the nation and its identity. Confronted with a "feminine" representation of history that was fed by a strong sense of inferiority to anglophones, the modernist and Americanist interpretations sought to distance themselves from this view, leading them to build an opposing and "masculine" image of Quebec's past by insisting on its modernity or Americanness. If proponents of the "new sensitivity" sometimes seem to return to the very Groulxian ideas that modernists had earlier judged too "feminizing," the value they ascribe to French Canadian heritage fits into the same desire to "virilize" the past. From their perspective, indeed, defending tradition was an act of courage when modernity sought to do away with it, and the demonstration of resistance by French Canadians of yesterday should serve as inspiration for today's nationalists.

As presented in the debates they stirred, these ideas and their interpretations did not encompass women, and certainly not gender, despite the multiplication of research in these two areas over the years. This comes as no surprise: affirming Quebec's modernity or its Americanness, insisting on its ability to fit into the North American or Western evolution, required emphasizing whole processes and realizations in which women were most often excluded, while ignoring the reasons for this exclusion. Bringing them to the core of the analysis would undoubtedly not have eradicated all ideas of modernity or Americanness, but it would have shifted the focus to men and women's contribution to building this so-called modern or American society, which would have led to a much more nuanced appreciation of these realities. Among other results, such a shift would have led these historians to recognize that, for most French-speaking male elites, support for modernity or the appropriation of Americanness most often stopped where the defence of a distinctive and "traditional"-based collective identity began. Inversely, such a light would have shown how many women sought to shed the very traditions of which they had been declared the "guardians" by fighting to gain recognition of their rights as free individuals – a resolutely modern conception of themselves.

The attachment that proponents of the "new sensitivity" held to tradition seems to have made them incapable of examining it with a critical eye and of taking stock of its inherent gender inequities. In their opinion, these inequities simply did not exist or, if they did, they were a necessary evil, a trifle in the face of the imperative need to preserve French Canadian heritage. Their even minimal consideration of gender would have made completely unbearable the vision of Quebec history they sought to defend. Taking gender into account would indeed have required acknowledgment that affinity to the nation is in and of itself eminently gendered, wherein men and women play different roles, which are determined by the social construction of masculinity and femininity in a given era and by the resulting power relationships.[64] This would have required both admitting that women had long been included in the nation in the name of their maternity and highlighting that it was not an option for many nationalists to grant women the rights that would have allowed them to emancipate themselves from this role of group survival. In other words, it would have required acknowledgment that, hardly unifying, nationalism has always stirred tension, particularly around women's bodies.

We can therefore say that neither the modernists nor the proponents of a "new sensitivity" have shown any particular concern with the role of women in their conceptualizations of Quebec history. This is because, more often than not, women's historical experience confronted their interpretations, so much so that to take this experience into consideration would have required a thorough reworking, if not a completely overhaul, of their interpretations. Nonetheless, it would seem to me that, while resolutely disregarding the issue of gender, these interpretations could not escape it: in fact, implicitly, the issue of gender is the very core of their historiographic (re)constructions.

ACKNOWLEDGMENTS

Many thanks to Andrée Lévesque, Suzanne Morton, Thomas Wien, and Brian Young, who generously agreed to comment on previous versions of this text. I remain the only one responsible for the ideas expressed here.

NOTES

1 Micheline Dumont, "Un champ bien clos: L'histoire des femmes au Québec," *Atlantis* 25, 1 (2000): 102–18.
2 Éric Bédard, *L'histoire du Québec pour les nuls* (Paris: First Éditions, 2012).
3 Micheline Dumont, *Pas d'histoire les femmes! Réflexions d'une historienne indignée* (Montreal: Remue-ménage, 2013), 10; our translation. See also the debate between Dumont and Bédard in *Le Devoir*, 21 December 2012. For other critiques of Bédard's book, see Andrée Lévesque, "Où sont-elles?," *HistoireEngagée. ca*, 8 January 2013, http://histoireengagee.ca/lactualite-en-debat-ou-sont-elles/;

and Jocelyn Létourneau, "La fin de l'histoire québécoise?," *Recherches socio-graphiques (RS)* LIV: 1 (2013): 165–82.

4   Andrée Lévesque, "Réflexions sur l'histoire des femmes dans l'histoire du Québec," *Revue d'histoire de l'Amérique française (RHAF)* 51, 2 (1997): 271–84.

5   Ronald Rudin, "Revisionism and the Search for a Normal Society: A Critique of Recent Quebec Historical Writing," *Canadian Historical Review (CHR)* 73, 1 (1992): 30–61, and *Making History in Twentieth-Century Quebec* (Toronto: University of Toronto Press, 1997).

6   Gérard Bouchard, "Sur les mutations de l'historiographie québécoise: Les chemins de la maturité," in *La société québécoise après 30 ans de changements*, ed. Fernand Dumont (Quebec: Institut québécois de recherche sur la culture [IQRC], 1990), 253–67.

7   Jean Lamarre, *Le devenir de la nation québécoise selon Maurice Séguin, Guy Frégault, et Michel Brunet (1944–1969)* (Sillery, Quebec: Septentrion, 1993); Serge Gagnon, *Le Québec et ses historiens de 1840 à 1920; la Nouvelle-France de Garneau à Groulx* (Quebec: Presses de l'Université Laval, 1978), and *Le passé composé: De Ouellet à Rudin* (Montreal: VLB Éditeur, 1999).

8   Rudin, "Revisionism and the Search for a Normal Society"; Bouchard, "Sur les mutations"; and Jacques Rouillard, "La révolution tranquille: Rupture ou tournant?," *Journal of Canadian Studies / Revue d'études canadiennes (JCS/RÉC)* 32, 4 (1997–8): 23–51.

9   See for example the responses by Brian Young, Paul-André Linteau, and John Dickinson to Rudin's article in *Bulletin d'histoire politique (BHP)* 4, 2 (1995): 7–24.

10   As Bouchard recognizes in "Sur les mutations."

11   Denyse Baillargeon, "Des voies/x parallèles: L'histoire des femmes au Québec et au Canada anglais, 1970–1995," *Sextant* 4 (1995): 133–68.

12   Suzanne D. Cross, "La majorité oubliée: Le rôle des femmes à Montréal au 19e siècle," in *Travailleuses et féministes: Les femmes dans la société québécoise*, ed. Marie Lavigne and Yolande Pinard (Montreal: Boréal, 1983), 61–84.

13   Marta Danylewycz, *Profession: religieuse. Un choix pour les Québécoises, 1840–1920* (Montreal: Boréal, 1985); "Une nouvelle complicité: Féministes et religieuses à Montréal, 1890–1925," in Lavigne and Pinard, *Travailleuses et féministes*, 245–70.

14   Micheline Dumont, "Vocation religieuse et condition féminine," in Lavigne and Pinard, *Travailleuses et féministes*, 271–92; and *Les religieuses sont-elles féministes?* (Montreal: Bellarmin, 1995).

15   Marie Lavigne, "Réflexions féministes autour de la fertilité des Québécoises," in *Maîtresses de maison, maîtresses d'école: Femmes, familles, et éducation dans l'histoire du Québec*, ed. Nadia Fahmy-Eid and Micheline Dumont (Montreal: Boréal, 1983), 319–38.

16 Andrée Lévesque, *La norme et les déviantes: Des femmes au Québec pendant l'entre-deux-guerres* (Montreal: Remue-ménage, 1989).

17 Marie-Aimée Cliche, "L'infanticide dans la région de Québec (1660–1969)," *RHAF* 44, 1 (1990): 31–59; "Filles-mères, familles, et société sous le Régime français," *Histoire sociale / Social History (HS/SH)* 21, 41 (1988): 39–70; and "Un secret bien gardé: L'inceste dans la société traditionnelle québécoise, 1858–1938," *RHAF* 50, 2 (1996): 201–26; Danielle Lacasse, *La prostitution féminine à Montréal, 1945–1970* (Montreal: Boréal, 1994).

18 On this question, see Baillargeon, "Des voies/x parallèles."

19 Except for Rudin, who dedicates some pages to the contribution of Quebec women historians to modernist historiography in his book. But this was because I had pointed out to him that he had not taken their work into account in his 1992 article, which he graciously recognized (see Rudin, *Making History*, 265n92).

20 Micheline Dumont has done this analysis, developing a four-level typology: 1) exclusionary; 2) compensatory presence; 3) partial integration; and 4) conceptual integration. For more details, see her article "Un champ bien clos."

21 Dumont, "Un champ bien clos," 113; our translation.

22 Paul-André Linteau, "La nouvelle histoire du Québec vue de l'intérieur," *Liberté* 147 (1983), reproduced in *Paroles d'historiens: Anthologie des réflexions sur l'histoire au Québec*, ed. Éric Bédard and Julien Goyette (Montreal: Presses de l'Université de Montréal, 2006), 264.

23 Linteau, "La nouvelle histoire du Québec," 264.

24 Rouillard, "La révolution tranquille," 24.

25 Gérard Bouchard, "Une crise de la conscience historique: Anciens et nouveaux mythes fondateurs dans l'imaginaire québécois," in *Les idées mènent le Québec: Essais sur une sensibilité historique*, ed. Stéphane Kelly (Quebec: Presses de l'Université Laval, 2003), 36; our translation.

26 Gérard Bouchard, *Genèse des nations et cultures du Nouveau Monde* (Montreal: Boréal, 2000), 72; our translation.

27 Bonnie G. Smith, *The Gender of History* (Cambridge, MA: Harvard University Press, 1998).

28 Smith, *Gender of History*, 131.

29 Donald Wright, "Gender and the Professionalization of History in English Canada Before 1960," *Canadian Historical Review (CHA)* 81, 1 (2000): 66; Alison Prentice and Beverly Boutilier, eds, *Creating Historical Memory: English-Canadian Women and the Work of History* (Vancouver: UBC Press, 1997). For a discussion about amateur historians in English Canada, see Cecilia Morgan, "History, Nation, and Empire: Gender and Southern Ontario Historical Societies, 1890–1920s," *CHR* 82, 3 (2001): 491–528.

30 Jacques Rouillard, "À propos de Genèse des nations et cultures du Nouveau Monde de Gérard Bouchard," *BHP* 11, 1 (2002): 144–9; our translation.

31 As Ronald Rudin pointed out, reviews of both volumes of *Histoire du Québec contemporain* praised their authors for precisely this reason (Rudin, *Making History*, 200).

32 Bouchard, *Genèse des nations*, 166; our translation.

33 For a discussion on the gender of modernity, see in particular Rita Felski, *The Gender of Modernity* (Cambridge, MA: Harvard University Press, 1995).

34 Quoted in Jacques Rouillard, "À propos de Genèse des nations et cultures du Nouveau Monde de Gérard Bouchard," *BHP* 11, 1 (Autumn 2002): 144.

35 Jocelyn Létourneau, "La production historienne courante portant sur le Québec et ses rapports avec la construction des figures identitaires d'une communauté communicationnelle," *RS*, 36, 1 (1995): 12; our translation. From the same author about the same topic, see also "Le Québec moderne: Un chapitre du grand récit collectif des Québécois," *Revue française de science politique* 42, 5 (1992): 765–85.

36 For a gendered analysis of the discourse of French Canadian male elites at the beginning of the twentieth century and their desire to represent modern Quebec as masculine, see Jeffery Vacante, *National Manhood and the Creation of Modern Quebec* (Vancouver: UBC Press, 2017).

37 Paul-André Linteau, "De l'équilibre et de la nuance dans l'interprétation de l'histoire du Québec," *BHP* 4, 2 (1995): 14; our translation.

38 Yvan Lamonde, "L'histoire culturelle comme domaine historiographique au Québec," *RHAF* 51, 2 (1997): 294; our translation.

39 For another perspective on this historiography, which retraces its genesis and ramifications, see Martin Petitclerc, "Notre maître le passé? Le projet critique de l'histoire sociale et l'émergence d'une nouvelle sensibilité historiographique," *RHAF* 63, 1 (2009): 83–113.

40 Susan Mann-Trofimenkoff, *Visions Nationales* (Montreal: Éditions du Trécarré, 1986).

41 Stéphanie Lanthier, "*L'impossible réciprocité des rapports politiques et symboliques entre le féminisme radical et le nationalisme radical au Québec, 1960–1971*," master's thesis, University of Sherbrooke, 1998.

42 Allan Greer, "La république des hommes: Les Patriotes de 1837 face aux femmes," *RHAF* 44, 4 (1991): 507–28.

43 Micheline Dumont, "L'histoire nationale peut-elle intégrer la réflexion féministe sur l'histoire," in *À propos de l'histoire nationale*, ed. Robert Comeau and Bernard Dionne (Montreal: Septentrion, 1998), 6–26.

44 Bettina Bradbury, "Debating Dower: Patriarchy, Capitalism, and Widows' Rights in Lower Canada," in *Power, Place, and Identity: Historical Studies of Social and Legal Regulation in Quebec*, ed. Tamara Myers, Kate Boyer, Mary Anne

Poutanen, and Steven Watt (Montreal: Montreal History Group, 1998), 55–78. See also "Wife to Widow: Class, Culture, Family, and the Law in Nineteenth-Century Quebec," in *Programme d'études sur le Québec de l'Université McGill* (Les Grandes Conférences Desjardins, Montreal, 1997).

45   Denyse Baillargeon, "Gouttes de lait et soif de pouvoir: Les dessous de la lutte contre la mortalité infantile à Montréal, 1910–1953," *Canadian Bulletin of Medical History / Bulletin canadien d'histoire de la médecine* 15 (1998): 27–56.

46   Nicole Laurin, Danielle Juteau, and Lorraine Duchesne, *À la recherche d'un monde oublié: Les communautés religieuses de femmes au Québec de 1900 à 1970* (Montreal: Le Jour Éditeur, 1991).

47   Bouchard, "Sur les mutations."

48   Bouchard, *Genèse des nations*, 82; our translation.

49   Lanthier, *L'impossible réciprocité*; Jean-Philippe Warren, "Un parti pris sexuel: Sexualité et masculinité dans la revue *Parti Pris*," *Globe* 12, 2 (2009): 129–57.

50   Bouchard, *Genèse des nations*, 153.

51   Bouchard, *Genèse des nations*, 151; our translation. Emphasis in the original.

52   See Jacques Rouillard's review, "À propos de *Genèse des nations*"; compare to Éric Bédard, who saw this work as the magnum opus of modernist historiography (Éric Bédard, "Genèse des nations et cultures du Nouveau Monde: le magnum opus de l'historiographie moderniste,"*BHP* 9, 2 (2001): 161.

53   Joseph Yvon Thériault, *Critique de l'américanité* (Montreal: Québec/Amérique, 2002), 93; our translation.

54   Jacques Beauchemin, *L'histoire en trop: La mauvaise conscience des souverainistes québécois* (Montreal: VLB Éditeur, 2002).

55   The decline in support for sovereignty in Quebec after the 1995 referendum is not unrelated, indeed, to this historiographical program.

56   Éric Bédard and Xavier Gélinas, "Critique d'un néo-nationalisme en histoire du Québec," in Kelly, *Les idées mènent le Québec*, 75; our translation.

57   Bédard and Gélinas, "Critique d'un néo-nationalisme," 80.

58   Bédard and Gélinas, "Critique d'un néo-nationalisme," 91; our translation.

59   Thierry Nootens (in collaboration with Jean-Marie Fecteau), "'Les idées mènent le Québec'? Sur une 'nouvelle sensibilité' historique et ses apories," *BHP* 12, 1 (2003): 161–9; and Petitclerc, "Notre maître le passé?"

60   Petitclerc, "Notre maître le passé?," 113; our translation.

61   See in particular the answer of Charles-Phillipe Courtois to Martin Petitclerc's article in which he argued that it was never demonstrated that sexism or motherhood were "harder to bear by French-Canadian women [...] for cultural reasons which would fall to French-Canadian nationalism" (in "Le débat sur les sensibilités historiques au Québec: Connaissance historique ou projet politique?," *RHAF* 64, 1 (2010): 81).

62 Éric Bédard, "Passé dénationalisé, avenir incertain," in Bédard, *Recours aux sources: Essais sur notre rapport au passé* (Montreal: Boréal, 2011), 44; our translation.
63 Bédard, "Passé dénationalisé," 45.
64 A large body of literature exists on this topic. See in particular the special issue of the *JCS/RÉC*, Women and Nationalisms: Canadian Experiences / Les femmes et les nationalismes: les expériences canadiennes 35, 2 (2000).

SELECTED READINGS

Baillargeon, Denyse. *Babies for the Nation: The Medicalization of Maternity in Quebec, 1910–1970* (trans. D.W. Wilson). Waterloo: Wilfrid Laurier University Press, 2009.
– *A Brief History of Women in Quebec* (trans. D.W. Wilson). Waterloo: Wilfrid Laurier University Press, 2014.
– *Making Do: Women, Family, and Home in Montreal during the Great Depression* (trans. Yvonne Klein). Waterloo: Wilfrid Laurier University Press, 1999.
Bradbury, Bettina. *Wife to Widow: Lives, Laws, and Politics in Nineteenth-Century Montreal*. Vancouver: UBC Press, 2011.
– *Working Families: Age, Gender, and Daily Survival in Industrializing Montreal*. Toronto: University of Toronto Press, 1991.
Chamberland, Line. *Mémoires lesbiennes*. Montreal: Remue-ménage, 1996.
Charles, Aline. *Quand devient-on vieille? Femmes, âge, et travail au Québec, 1940–1980*. Quebec: Presses de l'Université Laval / Institut québécois de recherche sur la culture, 2007.
Danylewycz, Marta. *Taking the Veil: An Alternative to Marriage, Motherhood, and Spinsterhood in Quebec, 1840–1920*. Toronto: McClelland and Stewart, 1987.
Detellier, Élise. *Mises au jeu: Les sports féminins à Montréal, 1919–1961*. Montreal: Remue-ménage, 2015.
Dumont, Micheline. *Le Féminisme québécois raconté à Camille*. Montreal: Remue-ménage, 2008.
Dumont, Micheline, and Louise Toupin. *La Pensée féministe au Québec: Anthologie [1900–1985]*. Montreal: Remue-ménage, 2003.
Fahrni, Magda. *Household Politics: Montreal Families and Postwar Reconstruction*. Toronto: University of Toronto Press, 2005.
Gray, Colleen. *The Congrégation de Notre-Dame, Superiors, and the Paradox of Power, 1693–1796*. Montreal: McGill-Queen's University Press, 2007.
Greer, Allan. *Mohawk Saint: Catherine Tekakwitha and the Jesuits*. New York: Oxford University Press, 2005.

Lamoureux, Diane. *L'Amère Patrie: Féminisme et nationalisme dans le Québec contemporain*. Montreal: Remue-ménage, 2001.

Lévesque, Andrée. *Making and Breaking the Rules: Women in Quebec, 1919–1939* (trans. Yvonne Klein). Toronto: University of Toronto Press, 2001.

– *Freethinker: The Life and Works of Éva Circé-Côté* (trans. Lazer Lederhendler). Toronto: Between the Lines, 2017.

Myers, Tamara. *Caught: Montreal's Modern Girls and the Law, 1869–1945*. Toronto: University of Toronto Press, 2006.

Noel, Jan. *Along a River: The First French-Canadian Women*. Toronto: University of Toronto Press, 2013.

Piché, Lucie. *Femmes et changement social au Québec: L'apport de la Jeunesse ouvrière catholique féminine, 1931–1966*. Quebec: Presses de l'Université Laval, 2003.

Poutanen, Mary Anne. *Beyond Brutal Passions: Prostitution in Early Nineteenth-Century Montreal*. Montreal: McGill-Queen's University Press, 2015.

Rousseau, Nicole, and Johanne Daigle. *Infirmières de colonie: Soins et médicalisation dans les régions du Québec, 1932–1972*. Quebec: Presses de l'Université Laval, 2013.

Rivard, Andrée. *Histoire de l'accouchement dans un Québec modern*. Montreal: Remue-ménage, 2014.

Young, Brian. *Patrician Families and the Making of Quebec*. Montreal: McGill-Queen's University Press, 2014.

5 Class, Race, and Gender Roles in Early British North America

KATHERINE M.J. MCKENNA

Arriving in the backwoods of Upper Canada in the early 1830s, the genteel Susanna Moodie was advised by a garrulous sleigh driver who conveyed the family to their new home, "To tell you the truth, Mrs. Moodie, ladies and gentlemen have no business in the woods. Eddication spoils man or woman for that location."[1] In contrast, it seems that typical working-class immigrants found themselves well suited to this new environment. "They no sooner set foot upon the Canadian shores," Susanna complained of former servants, "than they become possessed with this ultra-republican spirit. All respect for their employers, all subordination is at an end; the very air of Canada severs the tie of mutual obligation which bound you together."[2] Class relationships were challenged and often contested in colonial Canada, and a gentlewoman like Susanna Moodie was thrown into a life where the rank and gender norms of old England were not always respected. As settlement progressed, towns and cities grew, and Canadians gained control of their own political destiny, social relationships became more aligned with the new middle-class values first promoted by the evangelical reformers of England.[3] Accompanying this were new standards of masculinity and femininity that we would recognize today as typically "Victorian" and the ideal (if not always the reality) of separate spheres for men and women – the notion that public space was gendered male and the private home female. This chapter focuses on the early period of the English-speaking British North American colonies from about 1780 to 1850, in order to examine these changes.[4] The irony is that as English Canada became a place where white middle-class men could exercise their independence and master their destiny, for women, the roles they could play and the spaces they could occupy became increasingly restricted. Compounding this inequality was the fact that Indigenous peoples and other racialized persons were excluded from a role in the developing new liberal state.

What Jane Errington and Cecilia Morgan noted almost twenty years ago of women's history in Ontario still generally holds true today. "The period that remains mostly untouched," Morgan observed, "is that of the 'pre-Confed' era."[5] Errington agreed that women's history in the colonial era was "still in its infancy."[6] As Allan Greer has noted, the overwhelmingly greater focus of Canadian historians has been on the post-1850 period.[7] Even in comprehensive surveys of Canadian women's and gender history, this time is usually glossed over as a preface to the post-Confederation era, which has themes that are often seen as more relevant to our lives and research interests in the twenty-first century.[8]

The work on English-speaking Canada that has focused on class, race, and gender before 1850 is limited and concentrates predominantly on Upper Canada. In terms of book-length studies on women's and gender history, Jane Errington's exemplary and comprehensive treatment of women in early Upper Canada gives a progressive narrative that emphasizes the evolution from hardy pioneer woman to middle-class domestic lady.[9] Janice Potter-MacKinnon examines the suffering of uprooted Loyalist women.[10] Katherine McKenna's work on the Powell family and the Upper Canadian elite deals with the shift from the vital public social roles of the women of the Family Compact to the newly developing sense of female domesticity.[11] Cecilia Morgan's important scholarship on the growth of the middle-class gendered language of public religious and political values focuses on the development of ideals of masculinity as well as femininity.[12] François Noël investigates family life and sociability in Upper and Lower Canada.[13]

It is decidedly easier to document the lives of those who were closer to the status of Susanna Moodie than to her supposedly disloyal servants. Letters and diaries are rarely left by those who may not even have known how to write and for whom paper was an expensive luxury. It is generally the case that we are forced to rely on observations made by class-biased commentators, like Moodie, or the surviving official records from the period. Lynne Marks has made fruitful use of church records to document how intrusive evangelical church authorities censored the sinful activities of their congregations.[14] J.K. Johnson has gleaned glimpses of ordinary women from petitions to government in Upper Canada.[15] Cecilia Morgan and Julia Roberts have both made extensive use of early newspapers. Roberts, in her innovative work on Upper Canadian taverns, has drawn on a wide variety of sources, from account books to court records.[16] The latter have been mined quite successfully in a number of works, including McKenna's work on early Prescott, Ontario, based on local Board of Police records.[17] Julian Gwyn studied poor widows who were litigants in late eighteenth-century Nova Scotia,[18] while Rusty Bittermann employed a variety of colonial government records in discussing rural women's participation in the escheat movement on Prince Edward Island.[19] In addition to letters and household journals, Elizabeth Manke examined court records to reveal the broad range of women's economic activity in eighteenth-century Horton, Nova Scotia, while Gail Campbell consulted women's petitions to the Legislature in mid-nineteenth-century New Brunswick to reveal their assertion of their political rights.[20] Willeen Keough drew on British authorities' and Catholic Church records, as well as oral tradition, to examine the active working lives of Irish women immigrants in eighteenth- and nineteenth-century Newfoundland.[21] All these records can be problematic in that they often represent the viewpoint of those in power, and the way that women express themselves can be highly formulaic (as in petitions). However, when used with sensitivity to these concerns, such sources can provide valuable insights.

Although most of this scholarship addresses issues of male and female gender roles, and much has been written on the history of men in the colonial period, there is much less specifically focused on masculinity. Exceptions are the work of Catharine Wilson on work bees and plowing matches,[22] that of Kevin Walmsley and of Greg Gillespie on sport,[23] and that of Kevin Walmsley and Robert Kossuth on tavern fighting.[24]

In terms of race and ethnicity, the historical work is still in a developing stage. Much of the scholarship on women and gender in Indigenous communities focuses not on the period of British North American settlement, but rather on the fur trade and the impact of western expansion on the prairies. Gender roles and sexuality were more fluid in Indigenous societies; women performed valued labour and could be leaders in many communities, even participating in warfare.[25] They played an important part as cultural brokers for many European fur traders, who established family relationships with Indigenous women.[26] As McCallum and Hill note in this volume, Indigenous women were viewed as important primarily because of their connections to these white European men. These relationships, as Sylvia Van Kirk and Sarah Carter have observed, were discredited in the Canadian West in the late nineteenth century by the introduction of European settlement, which imposed Victorian middle-class codes of womanhood and the regulation of sexuality upon Indigenous peoples.[27] In British North America, Indigenous settlements had been seriously disrupted by European incursion before the late eighteenth century. Their land rights were systematically eroded through multiple treaties that pushed them west and north in the face of increasing settlement, as well as onto reservation lands that defined and limited their territory. Women settlers in nineteenth-century Upper Canada shared with their Indigenous neighbours what Carole Gerson has called "marginal space on the outskirts of frontier culture."[28] Settlers in the bush, such as Susanna Moodie, frequently interacted with their Denesuline (Chippewan) neighbours in a friendly way, but, influenced by European notions of "noble savages," she viewed them as social outsiders. The Moodies admitted them to their table – unlike their servants, who dined separately – and although Susanna wrote many positive things about their courteous manners and generosity, she did not think much of their women. One wife, who was generally considered "very handsome" and clever, did not meet with her approval. She declared, "In what her superiority consisted, I never could discover, often as I visited the wigwam. She was very dirty, and appeared quite indifferent to the claims of common decency (in the disposal of the few filthy rags that covered her). She was, however, very expert in all Indian craft."[29] Clearly the standards by which she was judged in her own culture were very different from those of English settlers. As Cecilia Morgan has observed, despite the efforts of Christian missionaries in Upper Canada to inculcate European notions of appropriate female and male behaviour into First Nations communities, Indigenous women "could never aspire to the status of 'ladies'" by definition.[30] Some responded by rejecting the pressure to conform. The Kanyen'kehaka (Mohawk) leader Mary Brant was a powerful cultural broker who served the British in the American Revolution by keeping her people loyal to them. She was granted a government pension and settled in Kingston, Upper Canada, where she lived out her days among white settlers. Even though her daughters assimilated and married British men[31] and she was held in high regard in Kingston society, Brant refused to conform to European standards. She retained her native dress and declined to speak English (in which she was fluent) in her later years.[32]

As with all ordinary women, sources are a serious issue in the scholarship of Indigenous peoples, meaning that either oral tradition or the writings of European settlers and official government records must be relied upon for information. Similar issues are found when we look at African Canadian women's history. Only recently have scholars of the early period documented the frequent presence of slaves across British North America, mostly pulled from diverse sources such as personal correspondence of their owners, court cases, and newspapers. Maureen Lee has provided an overview of female slaves in this early period, while Afua Cooper has begun the work of documenting the agency and resistance of enslaved Black women in Upper Canada.[33] Sylvia Hamilton has focused on the important roles Black women played in their communities in Nova Scotia, which had successive waves of migration of freed slaves from the United States and Jamaica from 1783 to 1816.[34] The largest migration occurred during the years of the Underground Railroad starting in 1815, and especially after 1850, when African Canadian settlements were established in southwestern Ontario. Adrienne Shad highlights the roles of Black women in the Underground Railroad, while Shirley Yee and Peggy Bristow examine the important work they undertook in building these settlements. This was despite, as Yee observes, the prevailing gender ideology that prescribed the unattainable middle-class ideals of female domesticity.[35] As Karen Flynn and Funké Aladejebi point out in their chapter in this volume, journalist, activist, and writer Mary Ann Shadd Cary was an outstanding female leader in this period, even though her sojourn in Canada, from 1851 to 1862, was short.[36] Shadd Cary argued ardently for equality and integration of the races in Canadian society, but, as Yee has observed, this meant adopting the same patriarchal gender role standards that she struggled against as a politically involved woman.[37] African Canadian women, however, shared with Indigenous women the impossibility of their conforming to middle-class gender models, which were encoded with the race and class biases of their day, yet they were expected to nonetheless aspire to this ideal.

If there is anything on which this work on women, men, race, and gender concurs, it is that the middle-class doctrine of separate spheres is not the best explanatory framework for understanding this early period. Prior to the mid-nineteenth century, classes tended to be polarized at opposite ends of the social scale, with dominant oligarchies at the top and a rural population beneath them who lived radically different lives and were usually more common folk. This does not mean that there were not many others, such as Susanna Moodie, who came from higher classes in their native country and found their view of themselves challenged by their lives in rural Canada. In the small towns and cities, a class of male professionals and merchants developed as settlement progressed. Many rural farmers, especially those who came with capital, grew prosperous and aspired to minor government offices and appointments as officers in the local militia. They were to establish their claim to social pre-eminence as the nineteenth century progressed. However, in the earliest decades of settlement, they were not a dominant group, although many aspired to join the ranks of the colonial leaders.

What forms of masculinity and femininity do we find in English Canada before 1850? Kevin Walmsley describes two main types of masculinity in early Canada: "bush masculinity" and "gentry masculinity," which held quite different values. Bush masculinity had roots in the old *coureurs de bois* and focused on physical strength relating to hard work in a challenging wilderness environment. Although settlers in the bush in Canada did not live quite the same rough lifestyle, it was still a model they admired. "Men engaged in more settled and less rugged occupations such as farming, greatly revered the romantic sense of manhood embodied in notions of bush masculinity."[38] Wilson shows how this is reflected in the competitive nature of neighbourhood work bees and plowing matches. These neighbourhood events were occasions where men tested their mettle against each other and work tasks were assigned according to the recognized skill and strength of the participants. Even as they competed with each other, they bonded together as a community and enforced standards of male behaviour. Often these manly contests were accompanied by heavy drinking, which could erupt into conflict. Sometimes these could be channelled into physical competition such as arm wrestling, tree chopping, or weightlifting, but all too often violence occurred. Forced by circumstance and need to participate in this communal activity, Susanna Moodie was disdainful about the social values and behaviour displayed at them. She saw them as a "necessary evil" and complained that "these gatherings are considered indispensable, and much has been written in their praise; but, to me, they present the most disgusting picture of a bush life. They are noisy, riotous, drunken meetings, often terminating in violent quarrels, sometimes even in bloodshed."[39] Julia Roberts has made a convincing case that taverns in Upper Canada were community places of socializing where classes and genders mixed, but that "there is no question that colonial social relations included a high level of tolerance for violence." Furthermore, "some men sometimes found fighting a seductive way to showcase their masculinity in a public setting."[40]

Violence, however, was not the main characteristic of bush masculinity. It was certainly about physical power but also pride in self-sufficiency and hardiness. Corresponding to these hardy men were the women who worked alongside them. Men rarely ventured into the kitchen, but women performed all sorts of physical labour when needed on pioneer farms. As one Loyalist daughter, Catherine White, recalled, her mother "used to help chop trees, attended the household duties and as the children grew up, they were trained to industrious habits, we were very useful to her, attended the cattle, churned the butter, making cheese, dressing the flax, spinning, in those days the spinning Wheel looked cheerful, made our own cloth, and stockings."[41] Women's responsibilities were so great that pioneer gentlewoman Anne Langton complained that a woman was "a bit of a slave in this country."[42] Women could take equal pride with men in the fruits of their labour, however. Catharine Wilson has noted how women were evaluated on the quality of the spread they laid for the hungry men at bees and competed to provide the most impressive feast. Their skill made a significant difference to the success of such an event. For their logging bee, Susanna Moodie provided thirty-two men with a meal consisting of the "best fare that could be procured in the bush. Pea-soup, legs of pork, venison, eel, and raspberry pies, garnished with plenty of potatoes, and whiskey to wash them down, besides a large iron kettle of tea."[43] This substantial meal took her and a servant two days to prepare. The values of the day were patriarchal, and legally women were considered subservient to men in every way. But in practical terms, on pioneer farms they needed to work together as a unit if they were to survive and thrive in rural life.

Although prowess in physical pursuits was not a sign of status for farm women, they were not averse to aggressive action when required. Rusty Bittermann has shown how rural women on Prince Edward Island actively participated in the rural protest against absentee landlords known as the escheat movement. Like their husbands, they turned out armed with whatever weapons came to hand. Women were part of a group that confronted a local constable charged with seizing their goods in lieu of unpaid rent. They drove him out of their neighbourhood, and it was Isabella MacDonald who whacked him with a board to hasten him on his way.[44] Although stories of such women are hard to come by, they show up at times in early court records in a small-town context. Prescott's Board of Police, an early local court, gives us many examples of women taking direct action in defence of their interests with little concern for ladylike demeanour. In the early years of the court's existence, they were very active in pressing charges against anyone who offended them, and the records of testimony give a glimpse into the lives of women considered to belong to the "lower orders" of society. We see them hurling insults at each other in the streets, running disorderly houses, smashing windows to extract their goods seized in lieu of rent, and in one case, a woman abusing a neighbour who had pleaded for quiet – by shouting that she "had a right to make as much noise as she pleased and told complainant to kiss his arse and go to hell."[45]

Women's public activities were not always so transgressive, however. Although they may have been confined to the house at times by the sheer demands of labour, women in the colonial era fully participated in public activities. Julia Roberts has shown that they were routinely present in the inns and taverns of Upper Canada, as workers, owners, and patrons. Gwyn's study of female litigants, mostly widows, in Halifax in the late eighteenth century concluded, "It is clear that women's work, as found in these civil cases, was almost never domestic, even though the place of work or the store or shop was part of the house itself."[46] As women moved into the growing towns, they took on all kinds of roles to survive economically and were not restricted to the private sphere.

To turn to the other major class group in early Canada, we need to look at the exclusive groups composing the ruling oligarchies. Like bush masculinity, the gentry masculinity characteristic of the ruling colonial elites also focused on outward displays of power and status, but not in contests of brute physical prowess. Instead, it was highly focused on notions of honour and a gentlemanly code of behaviour. Paired with this was the display of conspicuous markers of wealth and class status: grand homes, lavish entertaining, and fine clothes. In

Nova Scotia, the elite, first led by the Duke of Kent, the king's fourth son, brought with him his French mistress and built a large estate with magnificent gardens. He was supported by Lieutenant Governor Sir John Wentworth, the former governor of New Hampshire, who threw lavish parties for his visits and built an official residence for himself that ultimately cost the immense sum of £300,000.[47] Managing this luxurious lifestyle, particularly in the earliest years of frontier settlement with an imperfectly subservient class of servants, was a challenge but was considered absolutely essential. Elizabeth Simcoe, wife of the lieutenant governor of Upper Canada, observed in 1793, "The worse inconvenience in this country are want of servants which are not to be got. The worst of people do you a favour if they merely wash dishes for twenty shillings a month." "Servants need not have been afraid of coming to this country," she remarked caustically. "They have here immense Wages are well treated & work very little."[48] Indeed, as Anne, wife of Chief Justice William Dummer Powell, complained in 1818, the "want of a servant" was "an evil so generally" encountered that it seemed "to be irremediable."[49] As settlement progressed, the situation did not improve. Susanna Moodie noted that the power in the relationship was not on the master's side in the new world. She complained that the slightest reproof could cause a servant to quit, knowing they were a valued commodity and could always get other work "and such always can command the highest wages ... They turn upon you with a torrent of abuse ... And away they bounce, leaving you to finish a large wash, or a heavy job of ironing, in the best way you can."[50]

Because of the small size and insularity of these oligarchies and the fact that success was dependent upon being the favoured recipient of royal patronage, sometimes the minutest signs of slighting someone's position in the colonial hierarchy became explosive incidents that fractured elite society. The male gentry of British North America shared with their so-called inferiors a propensity to violence. Mob action was certainly not unknown, as in 1825 when a large group of elite youth disguised themselves and attacked the reform journalist William Lyon Mackenzie's print shop, smashing his press and dumping his type in Lake Ontario. However, more often disputes between gentlemen were printed up and posted as public declarations – and in extreme cases could result in a challenge to a duel. One such missive printed for R. Hervy in 1858 informed the public that he had been "grossly and wantonly insulted yesterday, in the streets of Bytown," which had prompted him to challenge the offender to a duel that the man had declined. Because the offender had not responded to this challenge to his honour, Hervy felt justified in calling him a "cowardly miscreant" as well as "a mean and contemptible liar, slanderer, and ruffian; a miserable, drivelling, cowardly scoundrel, a pitiful poltroon, and utterly unworthy of the notice of any one having pretensions to the character of a gentleman."[51] When gentlemen met with pistols at dawn, injury or death could occur, not to mention prosecution, since duelling was illegal. Yet such challenges persisted throughout the colonial period. As Cecilia Morgan has observed, "the central, unifying tenet of this code was the right and responsibility of certain men to defend their reputations with a public display of physical courage."[52] This was not dissimilar to the objectives of the tree-chopping contests or fistfights at the drunken parties following bees in the backwoods.

Women of the oligarchy may not have resorted to duels, but they had their own means of establishing and defending status. Although living surrounded by a wilderness, the members of the elite concocted elaborate social rituals to celebrate and assert their rank. For example, on the occasion of the queen's birthday in 1809, the *York Gazette* reported that the elite enjoyed an elegant reception. Following dinner, dancing started at 10:00 p.m. in a ballroom that had been "tastefully and elegantly fitted up and decorated for the occasion." At 1:30 a.m. "the Supper Room was thrown open, when the Company, amounting to about an hundred persons, partook of a very sumptuous banquet, consisting of every delicacy and a variety of the choicest Wines." This was not the end of the evening, however. "Dancing was resumed after Supper, and kept up with great spirit, till near eight o'clock in the morning." Finally, "the Company retired highly gratified with the Splendour of the Entertainment and the condescending attention of the Lieutenant Governor and Mrs. Gore."[53] As Bruce Curtis demonstrates, perhaps the apotheosis of this style of entertainment was achieved by the elaborate and very expensive gatherings hosted by Lord and Lady Durham during his brief tenure as governor general of British North America from 1838 to 1839. At a ball held in honour of the coronation, his guests drank upwards of 500 bottles of champagne.[54] Alcohol consumption, often to excess, was just as common at these grand events as it was at the backwoods bees, except with more refined beverages.

As hosts and attendees of these elaborate occasions, women of the elite had important roles to play. Proper dress and correct manners were required. Visiting rituals, which consisted of the higher-ranking ladies receiving visits from those just under them in the hierarchy, established a social pecking order that was violated at one's peril. Elizabeth Small was to learn this the hard way. In the earliest days of Upper Canadian society, she and her husband (the clerk of the Executive Council) moved in the highest circles of the elite. However, at one of the elegant balls so popular at the time, Elizabeth Small and Mrs Elmsley (wife of the chief justice) "publicly slighted Mrs. White," wife of the attorney general, "in a most pointed manner" by "passing her by without noticing her or making any return to her advances of Civility."[55] Such a seemingly trivial incident was to have far-reaching, even tragic, consequences. Vicious gossip, further social slights, a celebrated duel, a fatal wounding, a sensational sex scandal court case, and the social ostracism of Mrs Small were among the events that followed in the wake of Mrs White's humiliation.[56] Mrs Small was publicly discredited because slurs to her moral reputation were repeated in a court of law in defence of her husband, in order to show the provocation for the fatal duel he participated in. He was let off on a technicality, but she was condemned, not because she had committed these acts of immorality but because they had been stated publicly. Status was about display and appearances, not inner morality. Similarly, it was generally known that Lieutenant Governor Wentworth's wife had been for a time the mistress of a royal prince, but this was ignored because she was never accused publicly.[57] Most of the elite of Upper Canada attended the Anglican Church and were more concerned about the rank of their assigned pew than about the lessons they were taught in sermons. Their minister, Reverend George Stuart, was "tempted to despond" because "a more lukewarm set of Christians (if they can at all be so called) can scarcely be found."[58]

Women of the elite in colonial Canada were just as subject to patriarchy as were their sisters in the bush and the small towns. Mrs Small's social exclusion because of slurs on her sexual honour is proof of the double standards that existed for men and women. Law and access to the world of political power were just as closed to them. However, what they also shared with the common woman was a sphere of activity that was not confined to the private realm. Errington has observed, "The wives and daughters of the colonial gentry were frequently seen (and active) in the public sphere."[59] In fact, it was an important part of their role to be on display at all important civic functions and even at public entertainments such as plays.[60] In a society characterized by a hierarchy of power and ruled by patronage, their role was a crucial one, and their husband's success or failure was heavily reliant on their social skills and ability to manoeuvre through the maze of social rules and requirements.

Both the modes of masculinity and femininity, the bush masculinity that characterized men on the farm and in the towns and the gentry masculinity of the ruling elite, each with their corresponding modes of femininity, were supplanted as the century progressed. The professional and merchant middle class that dominated after the rebellions and political unrest of 1837–8 wrested power from the old oligarchy and instituted new social standards. With the establishment of responsible government, they set out to create a society that would reflect their own brand of patriarchy. We see this in their enforcing of new professional standards that, for example, locked women out of any practice of medicine.[61] They instituted a wave of legal reforms that established police forces, introduced tougher by-laws to keep the peace, and implemented measures that reduced the role of juries in favour of a professional judiciary who would apply the law in keeping with liberal principles.[62] They implemented what John Weaver has called "a moral order crusade,"[63] attacking lawlessness and disorderly behaviour, as well as conduct they considered morally suspect. Vagrancy charges became a convenient means to clear destitute persons and dubious women from the streets. Indeed, any woman unescorted in public was regarded with a suspicious eye. We also see this shift in the Prescott Board of Police record. In the late 1840s, charges brought before it at the instigation of ordinary women precipitously dropped, and for the first time by-laws were passed that specifically targeted prostitutes and houses of ill fame occupied by "loose" women.[64] Charges against women accused of this behaviour were now brought by the leading middle-class men of the town, and the fines set were so steep that they virtually ensured that those convicted would be unable to pay them and would be forced to serve jail terms. Drunkenness in women, or even their consumption of alcohol in inns and taverns, was increasingly frowned upon. "By the 1880s any public (or private) drinking had become unacceptable for respectable women."[65] The heavy imbibing of alcohol so characteristic of social life for all classes in Canada was attacked as unseemly, and the temperance movement became a force to be reckoned with.[66] Evangelical Protestants led the way in enforcing this new social order and regulating the behaviour of both men and women to ensure compliance with these moral standards.[67]

Although, of course, many women continued to be actively engaged in public occupations, it was less and less socially acceptable to do so if one had aspirations to a higher class of society.[68] A middle-class woman now had to adhere to a new standard, which banned her from most public places unless supervised by a man, and as if in compensation, idealized her role as a domestic angel who was the guardian of purity and morality in the sanctity of the middle-class man's private home.[69]

The Canada that emerged in the late nineteenth century has been characterized as what Ian McKay called a "liberal order framework" distinguished by a focus on the individual's actualization through their own self-determination "and whose freedom should be limited only by voluntary obligations to others or to God, and by the rules necessary to obtain the equal freedom of other individuals."[70] McKay acknowledges that this liberalism, as it was articulated in the early days of the Canadian state, was a selective political ideal, only applying to white men who had at least attained the rank of middle-class: "Women, workers, ethnic minorities, and Amerindians ... can all be related to each other by noting the consistency of a liberal model which tended to mark them all out as 'Other,' and which, in the nineteenth century, excluded them from the burdens and responsibility of full individuality."[71] I would add to this that it also excluded them from the privileges that this full expression of white male individuality brought with it: access to education, the ability to participate in democratic political life, property ownership, and unfettered participation in capitalist free enterprise. For white middle-class men, this was a positive new world, but it "forged a political culture that was emphatically hostile to the political participation of women." In fact, they made an "effort to deprive women of even the limited openings then available to them in the public sphere."[72] For Indigenous, Black, and lower-class women, the disadvantages were even more pronounced.

The liberal view of Canadian history that sees the ascendancy of white middle-class men as a positive step on the road to democracy and equality tends to colour our view of the early settlement period of British North America as an undeveloped prelude. Oligarchy is not a political system that is at all admirable, nor was it fair and equitable for the peoples of English Canada's colonial past, but it did not reach into and regulate the lives of ordinary people in the way that the new middle-class regime did. Today, as many struggle to extend the promise of liberalism – asserting the rights of people of all genders, races, and classes – we can find inspiration by looking into a past where women, even with the patriarchal restrictions of European political dominance, were able to act with greater agency in their own lives. Despite the difficulties with sources, we need to learn more about the insubordinate servants who troubled Susanna Moodie, the Indigenous women who held respected roles in their cultures, and the African Canadian women who were community builders across Canada.

NOTES

1 Susanna Moodie, *Life in the Backwoods: A Sequel to Roughing It in the Bush* (New York: J.W. Lovell Co., 1887), 11.

2 Susanna Moodie, *Roughing It in the Bush, or Forest Life in Canada* (Toronto: Maclear & Co., 1871), 241.

3 The still-classic work on this theme is Leonore Davidoff and Catherine Hall, *Family Fortunes: Men and Women of the English Middle Class, 1780–1850* (London: Hutchinson, 1987).

4 This paper does not discuss French Canada because of its very different culture, legal situation, and status of women in the pre-confederation period.

5 Cecilia Morgan, "'Old Ontario' through the Lens of Feminist Scholarship, 1970s–1990s," *Atlantis* 25, 1 (2000): 89.

6 E. Jane Errington, "'And What about the Women?': Changing Ontario's History," *Ontario History* 90, 2 (1998): 142.

7   Allan Greer, "Canadian History: Ancient and Modern," *Canadian Historical Review* 77, 4 (2001): 575–90.

8   See, for example, the excellent multi-edition *Rethinking Canada: The Promise of Women's History* series. Other recent examples are Gail Cuthbert Brant, Naomi Black, Paula Bourne, and Magda Fahrni, *Canadian Women: A History*, 3rd ed. (Toronto: Nelson, 2011); Catherine Carstairs and Nancy Janovicek, eds, *Feminist History in Canada: New Essays on Women, Gender, Work, and Nation* (Vancouver: UBC Press, 2014); Willeen Keough and Lara Campbell, eds, *Gender History: Canadian Perspectives* (Don Mills, ON: Oxford University Press, 2014). Kathryn McPherson, Cecilia Morgan, and Nancy M. Forestell, eds, *Gendered Pasts: Historical Essays in Femininity and Masculinity in Canada* (Toronto: University of Toronto Press, 1993), is exceptional in having three chapters out of eleven focusing on the pre-1850 period.

9   Elizabeth Jane Errington, *Wives and Mothers, School Mistresses, and Scullery Maids: Working Women in Upper Canada, 1790–1840* (Montreal: McGill-Queen's University Press, 1995).

10 Janice Potter-MacKinnon, *While the Women Only Wept: Loyalist Refugee Women* (Montreal: McGill-Queen's University Press, 1993).

11 Katherine M.J. McKenna, *A Life of Propriety: Anne Murray Powell and Her Family, 1755–1849* (Montreal: McGill-Queen's University Press, 1994); "Options for Elite Women in Early Upper Canadian Society: The Case of the Powell Family," in *Historical Essays on Upper Canada: New Perspectives*, ed. J.K. Johnson and Bruce G. Wilson (Ottawa: Carleton University Press, 1989), 401–23; "The Role of Women in the Establishment of Social Status in Early Upper Canada," *Ontario History* 83, 3 (1990): 179–205; and "'The Union between Faith and Good Works': The Life of Harriet Dobbs Cartwright 1808–1887," in *Changing Roles of Women within the Christian Church in Canada*, ed. Marilyn Färdig Whiteley and Elizabeth Gillian Muir (Toronto: University of Toronto Press, 1995), 284–98.

12 Cecilia Morgan, *Public Men and Virtuous Women: The Gendered Languages of Religion and Politics in Upper Canada, 1791–1850* (Toronto: University of Toronto Press, 1996).

13 François Noël, *Family Life and Sociability in Upper and Lower Canada, 1780–1870* (Montreal: McGill-Queen's University Press, 2003).

14 Lynne Marks, "No Double Standard? Leisure, Sex, and Sin in Upper Canadian Church Records, 1800–1860," in *Gendered Pasts: Historical Essays in Femininity and Masculinity in Canada*, ed. Kathryn McPherson, Cecilia Morgan, and Nancy M. Forestell (Toronto: Oxford University Press, 1999), 48–64; "Railing, Tattling, and General Rumour: Gossip, Gender, and Church Regulation in Upper Canada," *Canadian Historical Review* 81, 3 (2000): 380–402.

15 J.K. Johnson, *In Duty Bound: Men, Women, and the State in Upper Canada, 1783–1841* (Montreal: McGill-Queen's University Press, 2014).

16 Julia Roberts, *In Mixed Company: Taverns and Public Life in Upper Canada* (Vancouver: UBC Press, 2008).

17 Katherine M.J. McKenna, "Women's Agency in Upper Canada: Prescott's Board of Police Record, 1830–1850," *Histoire sociale / Social History* 36, 72 (2003): 347–70.

18 Julian Gwyn, "Female Litigants before the Civil Courts of Nova Scotia, 1749–1801," *Histoire sociale / Social History* 36, 72 (2003): 311–46.

19 Rusty Bittermann, "Women and the Escheat Movement: The Politics of Everyday Life on Prince Edward Island," in *Separate Spheres: Women's Worlds in the 19th-Century Maritimes*, ed. Janet Guildford and Suzanne Morton (Fredericton, NB: Acadiensis Press, 1994), 35–8. Even military records can prove to be fruitful sources for women's history. See Katherine M.J. McKenna, "Women's History, Gender Politics, and the Interpretation of Canadian Historic Sites," *Atlantis* 30, 1 (2005): 21–30.

20 Elizabeth Mancke, "At the Counter of the General Store: Women and the Economy in Eighteenth-Century Horton, Nova Scotia," in *Intimate Relations: Family and Community in Planter Nova Scotia, 1750–1800*, ed. Margaret Conrad (Fredericton, NB: Acadiensis Press, 1995), 167–81; Gail G. Campbell, "Disenfranchised but Not Quiescent: Women Petitioners in New Brunswick in the Mid-19th Century," in Guildford and Morton, 39–66.

21 Willeen G. Keough, "Unpacking the Discursive Irish Woman Immigrant in Eighteenth-and Nineteenth-Century Newfoundland," *Irish Studies Review* 21, 1 (2013): 55–70.

22 Catharine Anne Wilson, "A Manly Art: Plowing, Plowing Matches, and Rural Masculinity in Ontario, 1800–1930," *Canadian Historical Review* 95, 2 (2014): 157–86; and "Reciprocal Work Bees and the Meaning of Neighbourhood," *Canadian Historical Review* 82, 3 (2001): 431–64.

23 Kevin B. Walmsley, "The Public Importance of Men and the Importance of Public Men: Sport and Masculinities in Nineteenth-Century Canada," in *Sport and Gender in Canada*, 2nd ed., ed. Kevin Young and Philip White (Don Mills, ON: Oxford University Press, 2007), 75–91; Greg Gillespie, "Sport and 'Masculinities' in Early-Nineteenth-Century Ontario: The British Traveller's Image," *Ontario History* 92, 2 (2000): 113–26.

24 Kevin B. Walmsley and Robert S. Kossuth, "Fighting It Out in Nineteenth-Century Upper Canada / Canada West: Masculinities and Physical Challenges in the Tavern," *Journal of Sport History* 27, 3 (2000): 405–30.

25 Kathryn Magee, "They Are the Life of the Nation: Women and War in Traditional Nadouek Society," in *Rethinking Canada: The Promise of Women's History*,

6th ed., ed. Mona Gleason, Tamara Myers, and Adele Perry (Don Mills, ON: Oxford University Press, 2011), 13–24.

26 Bruce M. White, "The Woman Who Married a Beaver: Trade Patterns and Gender Roles in the Ojibwa Fur Trade," in *In the Days of Our Grandmothers: A Reader in Aboriginal Women's History*, ed. Mary-Ellen Kelm and Lorna Townsend (Toronto: University of Toronto Press, 2006), 56–92.

27 Sarah Carter, *The Importance of Being Monogamous: Marriage and Nation Building in Western Canada to 1915* (Edmonton: Athabasca University Press, 2008); Sylvia Van Kirk, *Many Tender Ties: Women in Fur-Trade Society in Western Canada, 1670–1870* (Winnipeg: Watson and Dwyer, 1980).

28 Carole Gerson, "Nobler Savages: Representations of Native Women in the Writings of Susanna Moodie and Catharine Parr Traill," in *Rethinking Canada: The Promise of Women's History*, 4th ed., ed. Veronica Strong-Boag, Mona Gleason, and Adele Perry (Don Mills, ON: Oxford University Press, 2002), 78.

29 Moodie, *Life in the Backwoods*, 31.

30 Cecilia Morgan, "Turning Strangers into Sisters? Missionaries and Colonization in Upper Canada," in *Sisters or Strangers? Immigrant, Ethnic, and Racialized Women in Canadian History*, ed. Marlene Epp, Franca Iacovetta, and Frances Swyripa (Toronto: University of Toronto Press, 2004), 35.

31 Gretchen Green, "Molly Brant, Catharine Brant, and Their Daughters: A Study in Colonial Acculturation," *Ontario History* 81, 3 (1989): 235–50.

32 Katherine M.J. McKenna, "Mary Brant Konwatsi'tsiaienni Degonwadonti: 'Miss Molly,' Feminist Role Model or Mohawk Princess?," in *The Human Tradition in the American Revolution*, ed. Nancy L. Rhoden and Ian Steele (Wilmington, DE: Scholarly Resources, 2000), 183–202.

33 Maureen Elgerson Lee, "Slavery in Early Canada: Making Black Women Subject," in *Rethinking Canada: The Promise of Women's History*, 5th ed., ed. Mona Gleason and Adele Perry (Don Mills, ON: Oxford University Press, 2006), 45–60; Afua Cooper, "Acts of Resistance: Black Men and Women Engage Slavery in Upper Canada, 1793–1803," in Gleason and Perry, *Rethinking Canada*, 5th ed., 71–9.

34 Sylvia Hamilton, "Naming Names, Naming Ourselves: A Survey of Early Black Women in Nova Scotia," in *"We're Rooted Here and They Can't Pull Us Up": Essays in African Canadian Women's History*, ed. Peggy Bristow (Toronto: University of Toronto Press, 1994), 13–40.

35 Adrienne Shad, "'The Lord Seemed to Say "Go"': Women and the Underground Railroad Movement," in Bristow, *"We're Rooted Here,"* 41–68; Peggy Bristow, "'Whatever You Raise in the Ground You Can Sell It in Chatham': Black Women in Buxton and Chatham, 1850–65," in Bristow, *"We're Rooted Here,"* 69–142; Shirley J. Yee, "Gender Ideology and Black Women as Community-Builders in

Ontario, 1850–70," in *Rethinking Canada: The Promise of Women's History*, 3rd ed., ed. Veronica Strong-Boag and Anita Clair Fellman (Don Mills, ON: Oxford University Press, 1997), 135–53.

36 Jason H. Silverman, "Mary Ann Shadd and the Search for Equality," in *A Nation of Immigrants: Women, Workers, and Communities in Canadian History, 1840s–1960s*, ed. Franca Iacovetta, Paula Draper, and Robert Ventresca (Toronto: University of Toronto Press, 1998), 101–14.

37 Shirley J. Yee, "Finding a Place: Mary Ann Shadd Cary and the Dilemmas of Black Migration to Canada, 1850–70," *Frontiers* 18, 3 (1997): 1–16.

38 Walmsley and Kossuth, "Fighting It Out," 408.

39 Moodie, *Life in the Backwoods*, 58–9.

40 Roberts, *In Mixed Company*, 95.

41 "Reminiscence of Mrs. White," in *Loyalist Narratives from Upper Canada*, ed. J.J. Talman (Toronto: Champlain Society, 1946), 354.

42 Helen E.H. Smith and Lisa M. Sullivan, "'Now That I Know How to Manage': Work and Identity in the Journals of Anne Langton," *Ontario History* 87, 9 (1995): 263.

43 Moodie, *Life in the Backwoods*, 64.

44 Bittermann, "Women and the Escheat Movement," 24.

45 McKenna, "Women's Agency," 358.

46 Gwyn, "Female Litigants," 343.

47 Judith Fingard, "WENTWORTH, Sir JOHN," in *Dictionary of Canadian Biography*, vol. 5 (University of Toronto / Université Laval, 2003), http://www.biographi. ca/en/bio/wentworth_john_1737_1820_5E.html.

48 McKenna, "The Role of Women," 188.

49 McKenna, *A Life of Propriety*, 81.

50 Moodie, *Roughing It in the Bush*, 242–3.

51 Hugh A. Halliday, *Murder among Gentlemen: A History of Duelling in Canada* (Toronto: Robin Brass Studio, 1999), ii.

52 Cecilia Morgan, "'In Search of the Phantom Misnamed Honor': Duelling in Upper Canada," *Canadian Historical Review* 76, 4 (1995): 531.

53 Edith Firth, *The Town of York, 1793–1815* (Toronto: Champlain Society, 1962), 273.

54 Bruce Curtis, "The 'Most Splendid Pageant Ever Seen': Grandeur, the Domestic, and Condescension in Lord Durham's Political Theatre," *Canadian Historical Review* 89, 1 (2008): 68.

55 Peter Russell to E.B. Littlehales, York, 15 February 1800, Russell Papers, Public Archives of Ontario.

56 McKenna, *A Life of Propriety*, 70–2.

57 Fingard, "WENTWORTH, Sir JOHN."

58 Rev. John Stuart to James Stuart, Kingston, 28 June 1804, Stuart Papers, Public Archives of Ontario.

59 Elizabeth Jane Errington, "Suitable Diversions: Women, Gentility, and Entertainment in an Imperial Outpost," *Ontario History* 102, 2 (2010): 188.

60 Michel S. Beaulieu, "'Not That I Lov'd Fleas Less, but That I Lov'd England More': Entertainment in Kingston, 1816–1837," *Ontario History* 102, 2 (2010): 204–5.

61 Lykke de la Cour, Cecilia Morgan, and Mariana Valverde, "Gender Regulation and State Formation in Nineteenth-Century Canada," in *Colonial Leviathan: State Formation in Mid-Nineteenth-Century Canada*, ed. Allan Greer and Ian Radforth (Toronto: University of Toronto Press, 1992), 163–91.

62 R. Blake Brown, *A Trying Question: The Jury in Nineteenth-Century Canada* (Toronto: University of Toronto Press, 2009).

63 John C. Weaver, *Crimes, Constables, and Courts: Order and Transgression in a Canadian City, 1816–1970* (Montreal: McGill-Queen's University Press, 1995), 48.

64 McKenna, *Women's Agency*, 367.

65 Cheryl Krasnick Warsh, "'Oh Lord, Pour a Cordial in Her Wounded Heart': The Drinking Woman in Victorian and Edwardian Canada," in *Drink in Canada*, ed. Cheryl Krasnick Warsh (Montreal: McGill-Queen's University Press, 1993), 75.

66 Jan Noel, *Canada Dry: Temperance Crusades before Confederation* (Toronto: University of Toronto Press, 1995).

67 Lynne Marks, *Revivals and Roller Rinks: Religion, Leisure, and Identity in Late-Nineteenth-Century Small-Town Ontario* (Toronto: University of Toronto Press, 1996).

68 Lori Chambers, "Married Women and Businesses," *Ontario History* 104, 2 (2012): 45–62; Janet Guildford, "'Whate'er the Duty of the Hour Demands': The Work of Middle-Class Women in Halifax, 1840–1880," *Histoire sociale / Social History* 30, 59 (1997): 1–20.

69 On the development of middle-class values in the late eighteenth century, see Andrew C. Holman, *A Sense of Their Duty: Middle-Class Formation in Victorian Ontario Town* (Montreal: McGill-Queen's University Press, 2000). On the idealization of middle-class women's roles, see Cecilia Morgan, "'Better Than Diamonds': Sentimental Strategies and Middle-Class Culture in Canada West," *Journal of Canadian Studies* 32, 4 (1998): 125–48.

70 Ian McKay, "The Liberal Order Framework: A Prospectus for a Reconnaissance of Canadian History," *Canadian Historical Review* 81, 4 (2000): 623.

71 McKay, "Liberal Order Framework," 626.

72 Alan Gregg, "Historical Roots of Canadian Democracy," *Journal of Canadian Studies* 34, 1 (1999): 15.

SELECTED READINGS

Bittermann, Rusty. "Women and the Escheat Movement: The Politics of Everyday Life on Prince Edward Island." In *Separate Spheres: Women's Worlds in the
19th-Century Maritimes*, edited by Janet Guildford and Suzanne Morton, 23–8.
Fredericton, NB: Acadiensis Press, 1994.

Campbell, Gail G. "Disenfranchised but Not Quiescent: Women Petitioners in New
Brunswick in the Mid-19th Century." In *Separate Spheres: Women's Worlds in the
19th-Century Maritimes*, edited by Janet Guildford and Suzanne Morton, 39–66.
Fredericton, NB: Acadiensis Press, 1994.

Chambers, Lori. "Married Women and Businesses." *Ontario History* 104, 2 (2012):
45–62.

Cooper, Afua. "Acts of Resistance: Black Men and Women Engage Slavery in Upper
Canada, 1793–1803." In *Rethinking Canada: The Promise of Women's History*,
6th ed., edited by Mona Gleason, Tamara Myers, and Adele Perry, 71–9. Don Mills,
ON: Oxford University Press, 2011.

Errington, Elizabeth Jane. *Wives and Mothers, Schoolmistresses, and Scullery Maids:
Working Women in Upper Canada, 1790–1840*. Montreal: McGill-Queen's
University Press, 1995.

Gerson, Carole. "Nobler Savages: Representations of Native Women in the Writings
of Susanna Moodie and Catharine Parr Traill." In *Rethinking Canada: The Promise
of Women's History*, 4th ed., edited by Veronica Strong-Boag, Mona Gleason, and
Adele Perry, 75–86. Don Mills, ON: Oxford University Press, 2002.

Guildford, Janet. "'Whate'er the Duty of the Hour Demands': The Work of Middle-Class
Women in Halifax, 1840–1880." *Histoire sociale / Social History* 30, 59 (1997): 1–20.

Gwyn, Julian. "Female Litigants before the Civil Courts of Nova Scotia, 1749–1801."
Histoire sociale / Social History 36, 72 (2003): 311–46.

Hamilton, Sylvia. "Naming Names, Naming Ourselves: A Survey of Early Black
Women in Nova Scotia." In *"We're Rooted Here and They Can't Pull Us Up":
Essays in African Canadian Women's History*, edited by Peggy Bristow, 13–40.
Toronto: University of Toronto Press, 1994.

Keough, Willeen G. "Unpacking the Discursive Irish Woman Immigrant in
Eighteenth- and Nineteenth-Century Newfoundland." *Irish Studies Review* 21, 1
(2013): 55–70. https://doi.org/10.1080/09670882.2012.759709

Lee, Maureen Elgerson. "Slavery in Early Canada: Making Black Women Subject."
In *Rethinking Canada: The Promise of Women's History*, 5th ed., edited by Mona
Gleason and Adele Perry, 45–60. Don Mills, ON: Oxford University Press, 2006.

Magee, Kathryn. "They Are the Life of the Nation: Women and War in Traditional
Nadouek Society." In *Rethinking Canada: The Promise of Women's History*, 6th ed.,

edited by Mona Gleason, Tamara Myers, and Adele Perry, 13–24. Don Mills, ON: Oxford University Press, 2011.

Manke, Elizabeth. "At the Counter of the General Store: Women and the Economy in Eighteenth-Century Horton, Nova Scotia." In *Intimate Relations: Family and Community in Planter Nova Scotia, 1750–1800*, edited by Margaret Conrad, 167–81. Fredericton, NB: Acadiensis Press, 1995.

Marks, Lynne. "No Double Standard? Leisure, Sex, and Sin in Upper Canadian Church Records, 1800–1860." In *Gendered Pasts: Historical Essays in Femininity and Masculinity in Canada*, edited by Kathryn McPherson, Cecilia Morgan, and Nancy M. Forestell, 48–64. Toronto: Oxford University Press, 1999.

– "Railing, Tattling, and General Rumour: Gossip, Gender, and Church Regulation in Upper Canada." *Canadian Historical Review* 81, 3 (2000): 380–402. https://doi.org/10.3138/chr.81.3.380

– *Revivals and Roller Rinks: Religion, Leisure, and Identity in Late-Nineteenth-Century Small-Town Ontario*. Toronto: University of Toronto Press, 1996.

McKenna, Katherine M.J. *A Life of Propriety: Anne Murray Powell and Her Family, 1755–1849*. Montreal: McGill-Queen's University Press, 1994.

– "'The Union between Faith and Good Works': The Life of Harriet Dobbs Cartwright, 1808–1887." In *Changing Roles of Women within the Christian Church in Canada*, edited by Marilyn Färdig Whiteley and Elizabeth Gillian Muir, 284–98. Toronto: University of Toronto Press, 1995.

– "Women's Agency in Upper Canada: Prescott's Board of Police Record, 1830–1850." *Histoire sociale / Social History* 36, 72 (2003): 347–70.

Morgan, Cecilia. "'In Search of the Phantom Misnamed Honor': Duelling in Upper Canada." *Canadian Historical Review* 76, 4 (1995): 529–62. https://doi.org/10.3138/chr-076-04-01

– *Public Men and Virtuous Women: The Gendered Languages of Religion and Politics in Upper Canada, 1791–1850*. Toronto: University of Toronto Press, 1996.

– "Turning Strangers into Sisters? Missionaries and Colonization in Upper Canada." In *Sisters or Strangers? Immigrant, Ethnic, and Racialized Women in Canadian History*, edited by Marlene Epp, Franca Iacovetta, and Frances Swyripa, 23–48. Toronto: University of Toronto Press, 2004.

Noël, François. *Family Life and Sociability in Upper and Lower Canada, 1780–1870*. Montreal: McGill-Queen's University Press, 2003.

Roberts, Julia. *In Mixed Company: Taverns and Public Life in Upper Canada*. Vancouver: UBC Press, 2008.

Shadd, Adrienne. "'The Lord Seemed to Say "Go"': Women and the Underground Railroad Movement." In *"We're Rooted Here and They Can't Pull Us Up": Essays in African Canadian Women's History*, edited by Peggy Bristow, 41–68. Toronto: University of Toronto Press, 1994.

Silverman, Jason H. "Mary Ann Shadd and the Search for Equality." In *A Nation of Immigrants: Women, Workers, and Communities in Canadian History, 1840s–1960s*, edited by Franca Iacovetta, Paula Draper, and Robert Ventresca, 101–14. Toronto: University of Toronto Press, 1998.

Walmsley, Kevin B., and Robert S. Kossuth. "Fighting It out in Nineteenth-Century Upper Canada / Canada West: Masculinities and Physical Challenges in the Tavern." *Journal of Sport History* 27, 3 (2000): 405–30. www.jstor.org/stable/43609777

White, Bruce M. "The Woman Who Married a Beaver: Trade Patterns and Gender Roles in the Ojibwa Fur Trade." In *In the Days of Our Grandmothers: A Reader in Aboriginal Women's History*, edited by Mary-Ellen Kelm and Lorna Townsend, 56–92. Toronto: University of Toronto Press, 2006.

Wilson, Catharine Anne. "A Manly Art: Plowing, Plowing Matches, and Rural Masculinity in Ontario, 1800–1930." *Canadian Historical Review* 95, 2 (2014): 157–86. https://doi.org/10.3138/chr.1918

– "Reciprocal Work Bees and the Meaning of Neighbourhood." *Canadian Historical Review* 82, 3 (2001): 431–64. https://doi.org/10.3138/chr.82.3.431

6 Performative (Ir)rationality: Rethinking Agency in Canadian Histories of Gender, Religion, Reason, and Beyond

BETH A. ROBERTSON

Introduction

The niqab in Canada became a major election issue in October 2015. It emerged from a 2011 federal ban on the wearing of face-coverings for people taking their oath of citizenship. Zunera Ishaq, a woman of Pakistani descent who wished to become a Canadian citizen, objected to the requirement. She brought her case to court, and she won – twice. Yet the Conservatives' election promise to appeal their second legal defeat over the ban gave the party a considerable boost in the polls. To justify their actions, Conservative leader Stephen Harper argued that the niqab is "anti-woman" and runs contrary to Canadian "values."[1] Much as Marlene Epp and Franca Iacovetta write in their chapter for this volume, this moment powerfully illustrates how immigrant women of racial and religious minorities have historically been targeted by political leaders and lawmakers. Troubling and more than just subtly racist, these debates also shed a great deal of light on pervading views of women and religion within Canada and far beyond.

As these controversies illustrated, women have been conceived of as able to assert their will and desires only once freed from spiritual or religious doctrine. This attitude has in part been supported by Western feminism and secularist ideals that position religion as fundamentally unredeemable from patriarchal frameworks. Women of faith, in turn, have been characterized as passive recipients of misogynist dogma, at best suffering from a false consciousness that leads them to participate in spiritual practices ultimately intended to oppress them.[2] To counter or complicate this narrative, numerous scholars of religion have addressed women's ability to assert themselves and direct their own paths.[3] Yet arguably this endeavour has been fraught, as even the idea of "agency" itself has too often been based upon the assumption that the desire for autonomy and a liberalist notion of "freedom" is a universal and ahistorical aspiration.[4]

This chapter explores the Canadian historiography that has crossed into such debates, asking not solely how agency has been identified when investigating women of faith, but also how the term itself has been defined in relation to larger histories of religion and rationality, and what consequences such signification means when examining the histories of women associated with certain forms of spiritual practice. To help illustrate my argument, in the last section of this chapter, I focus on Canadian women of the early twentieth century who engaged in what is often classified as the more marginal spiritualist practice of mediumship or trance. Their participation in seances and enactment of possession has often been viewed as the epitome of irrationality, making it that much more difficult to situate these women in a discourse of agency that is largely framed in relation to reasonable and self-conscious decision-making. Taking into consideration the ideas of Saba Mahmood and Judith Butler's theorization of embodiment and performance, I argue for alternative means to understand women's sense of agency. I propose that Canadian historians join other international scholars of religion and beyond to reassess the origins of the term "agency" and how it has been associated or disassociated with women and belief. It is at this juncture where we can begin to contemplate how the past actions of the women we study complicate pervading definitions of agency. In other words, rather than fit these women within a conceptual box that conforms to highly gendered historical constructions of rationality and autonomy, Canadian historians have the option of letting these women, and their embodied performances, restructure the terms of agency itself.

Agency, Religion, and Rationality

The concept of agency has had a long lineage in feminist theory. Sumi Madhok, Anne Phillips, and Kalpana Wilson argue that from the moment that British philosopher Mary Wollstonecraft penned *Vindication of the Rights of Woman* in 1792, feminists have argued for women's capacity for "rationality, reflection and responsible action."[5] Other scholars give the term a much more recent history, contending that it emerged alongside feminist thought since the 1970s, primarily to "refine the rather one-sided language of patriarchal oppression that characterized first wave feminism."[6] The rise of post-structuralist theory in the 1980s again drew the conception of agency to the forefront, as feminist scholars struggled with what was often feared to be a form of discourse determinism: making women unable to act on their own accord apart from the cultural constructions of their experiences.[7]

As even these origin stories of agency attest to, the meaning of agency has historically been framed in reference to a particular conception of a rational subject, able and willing to adhere to a neoliberal valorization of individual choice and autonomy. Scholars such as Clare Hemmings and Amal Treacher Kabesh have identified that this association seems hard to break, even for those who openly critique these very same definitions of agency. Difficulties arise due not only to the problematic tendency to ascribe everyone with the same degree of options from which to choose, but also to the fact that even when a choice is being recognizably made, it is not one which several Western feminists would approve of. As Hemmings and Kabesh describe in relation to the wearing of the hijab, for instance, "it is common for women to be thought of as agentic if they veil as a part of resistance to Western imperialism, but as anything from less agentic to pure victims of patriarchal culture if they veil for religious reasons."[8]

The example from Hemmings and Kabesh vividly articulates the women who often rest at the centre of these debates – women who are designated as "other" by virtue of their race, class position, and geographical and cultural location, as well as their religious or spiritual affiliations. An application of Kimberlé W. Crenshaw's formative theories of intersectionality would quickly lead to the conclusion that these various signs of difference are in many ways bound up with one another as they simultaneously serve to define the debates surrounding the idea of agency and its invocations.[9] Inseparable as they are, I will, for a moment, focus on why religion in particular has come to play a role in discussions around agency and its contested definitions.

The fact that religion or spirituality remains so central to these debates is far from coincidental. Religion, often cast in binary opposition to liberal secularism, serves as yet one more means to highlight the racial, gendered, and class privilege that largely underscores and even animates these debates.[10] An even deeper, historical examination into the place of religion in these conflicts helps unravel the vexed relationship between agency and rationality that stretches as far back as the European Enlightenment.

Feminist scholars have pointed out that agency, frequently defined as the ability to act autonomously in a rational, responsible way, was itself a gendered ideal. Men were coded active and rational, as well as somehow separate from the subjective influences around them, whereas women remained passive, irrational, and dependent upon others.[11] This same mode of understanding rationality would eventually marginalize certain forms of faith and spiritual devotion. This in part had to do with the invention of the category of religion that emerged as a direct result of early modern controversies attempting to define, articulate, and ultimately rationalize what legitimate devotion entailed. As Peter Harrison explains, "In keeping with the developing spirit of the Enlightenment, reason came to be the ultimate arbiter of true religion, thus confirming the objective, rationalist orientation of the new entity."[12]

This manner of defining religion continued for the following centuries, with faith expressions that could not (or would not) be rationalized according to these modern conceptions faring the worst. Anne Taves, Heather Curtis, and others have discussed how religion – particularly its more marginal, enthusiastic, or embodied expressions – became increasingly pathologized in the late nineteenth and early twentieth century. Beginning largely with the work of Jean-Martin Charcot, learned men applied theories of psychology and psychoanalysis to certain forms of ecstatic faith expressions in an effort to render decipherable what was once thought indecipherable – the repressed, the uncanny, and other supposedly primal and thereby "irrational" aspects of the human psyche. Still replete with racial, class, and gendered associations, the spiritual became an effeminate object of study to be investigated by chiefly white, European men of a particular social standing.[13] The binaries of passive and active were evoked, much as they had been in earlier centuries, to describe the chiefly male investigator who sought after objective knowledge of the world by scrutinizing female bodies, the natural world, or both as each were described as ultimately submissive, mysterious, even esoteric, destined to be probed by the rational male gaze.[14]

Agency in Feminist Historiographies of Religion

It is largely due to this lineage that agency has come to occupy such a significant position in feminist scholarship and historiographies of religion in particular. Agency as a concept came to the fore in feminist thought to challenge the idea that white, European men were the only ones able to act rationally, whereas women remained passive vehicles, unable to exert their own wills or direct their lives in a responsible and reasonable fashion. Although this reassessment of women's capacity for action successfully undermined sexist assumptions of what women were capable of, the underlying logic of agency still remained entangled with certain gendered conceptions of rationality and autonomy. Women of faith have been consequently marginalized since their adherence to male religious authority is characterized as an unthinking act of compliance with a patriarchal world view. Such difficulties are compounded by a veneration of submission within the accounts of many religious women themselves. International scholars of women and religion have thus dedicated much of their time to unravelling these apparent contradictions by examining how believing women straddle divides between passive and active, oppressed and free.[15]

Canadian gender historians of religion have joined this much broader debate by seeking to address how women can exert agency, even within certain cultural and institutional constraints that demand their submission. One fairly prominent example is how Canadian women and gender historians have entered into discussions surrounding the agency of nuns, female mystics, and other devout women. Marta Danylewycz's work on French Catholic nuns in Quebec and especially her posthumously published *Taking the Veil: An Alternative to Marriage, Motherhood, and Spinsterhood in Quebec, 1840–1920* was groundbreaking in this respect. At the time of her writing, studies focusing on nuns in New France and Quebec were scarce, albeit growing due to the inroads of women's history.[16] One of Danylewycz's main reasons for writing was to challenge the stereotype of nuns as "tight-lipped troubled souls," "cruel disciplinarians," or, the most relevant to a discussion of agency, "the unquestioning and obedient servants of bishops and priests."[17]

Other Canadian historians would follow in Danylewycz's footsteps by challenging the uncomplicated assumption that nuns passively accepted the dictates of male religious authority. Scholars such as Micheline Dumont, one of Danylewycz's contemporaries, as well as an ongoing and significant voice in the discussion of women in the history of Quebec, continued to write on the role of nuns in New France. Similar to Danylewycz, she has written on the more visible, public acts of nuns, including their engagement with the rise of feminism in Quebec.[18] Dominique Deslandres's seminal work on Catholic missionary work in New France, meanwhile, focused on highly influential women saints, including Marie Guyart de l'Incarnation.[19] In one chapter published in the edited collection *Colonial Saints: Discovering the Holy in the Americas, 1500–1800*, Deslandres specifically explores "the role of women ... especially that of saintly women," which had ultimately compelled her "to reconsider the relationship between female holiness and the society that feeds it and is fed by it – a relationship that, as we will see, is one part power and one part seduction."[20]

Deslandres examines how these holy women were fundamental to the construction of not only early colonial French society but the narratives of sanctity that legitimized and animated settler culture as well. They set clear goals for the completion of grand projects, whether convents, hospitals, or schools, and in this way made themselves exceptional and thereby "holy." As Deslandres describes, "They were select women, women who chose. They cleared their very own paths to power and succeeded in winning over their fellow settlers."[21]

Deslandres identifies how the seventeenth century provided an especially rich historical moment when French women remade the models of holiness that were bequeathed them through theologians and hagiographers – models that were "both mystical and active."[22] These women constructed an identity of sainthood that was their own, sometimes in ways that more modern audiences would find troubling and in direct opposition to contemporary feminist ideals, including mortifications, self-imposed poverty, and chastity.[23]

Deslandres's work identifies some of the more challenging aspects of examining the agency of French Catholic nuns in New France and Quebec. Acts of self-mortification proved particularly contentious, as did the complicated relationships between nuns and male priestly authorities.[24] Allan Greer approached both of these questions, especially in the context of colonialism, in his 2005 study *Mohawk Saint: Catherine Tekakwitha and the Jesuits*. Here he focused not only on Tekakwitha, but on her influence on the life and world view of her biographer, Catholic priest Claude Chauchetière. Although Chauchetière did not know Tekakwitha in life, he witnessed her premature death and served as the main investigator for her canonization.[25]

For Chauchetière to tell this women's story through the scripts of hagiography, Greer relates how the priest became both a "gender cross-dresser" and a "cultural cross-dresser," an act that was, in both cases, perceived as a move to a humbler status. This imaginative "downward" progression that Greer describes may have offered the Jesuit "an unavowed thrill in temporarily shedding the burdens and responsibilities of power without really relinquishing its privileges."[26] Yet Greer argues that Chauchetière's position of power did not necessarily negate the possibility that he could have been transformed by his experience, primarily by his encounter with Tekakwitha. As Greer relates, Chauchetière "seems to have found ways to reconcile his initial stance of mystical exoticism, the projection outward of inverted forms of European norms, with his personal experience of a real human community struggling to find its way in a shifting world of war, epidemics and colonialism."[27]

This transformation of Chauchetière occurred and found expression in his perceived sense of intimacy with Tekakwitha on her deathbed and beyond. Although recognizing that his time with her was probably more important to him than to her, Chauchetière nevertheless related deeply to Tekakwitha, finding through her new meaning.[28] Tekakwitha was in this sense instrumental to fundamentally altering Chauchetière's world view.

Greer identifies how Tekakwitha was an active agent in other ways as well as she assumed and re-adjusted Catholic practice while carving out an identity for herself that would be ultimately deemed holy. Similar to Deslandres's observations, present-day readers may very well judge her acts of self-inflicted flagellations as counter to feminist aims. Yet as Greer points out, Tekakwitha's behaviour cannot simply be read as a passive adoption of Catholic forms of penance; instead it serves as an example of a hybrid spiritual practice that was as much a part of Iroquois custom as it was Christian.[29] Greer insists that the life of Tekakwitha points to how "there was far more to [Tekakwitha's] encounter with Christianity than anything that can be measured on a scale of acquiescence and resistance."[30]

Colleen Gray approached some very similar questions two years later in *The Congrégation de Notre-Dame, Superiors, and the Politics of Power, 1693–1796.* Much as the title of her work suggests, Gray sought "to examine the more concrete dimensions of power, for one cannot study women in history without exploring power and its pervasive influence upon them."[31] Gray thus engages with the concept of agency in her work alongside the complexities of the lives and motivations of women devotees. Examining Marie Barbier, for instance, Gray investigates not only the real sense of authority that this nun exercised as a superior of the Congrégation de Notre-Dame, but also how that power operated in parallel to her "passionate desire to suffer" through self-mortification, as well as her relationship to male religious authorities, most especially with her confessor Charles de Glandelet.[32] Gray explains Barbier's self-afflicted wounds as a means to join her body with Christ's suffering, "expiating both individual and collective sins," and thus as one central aspect of a host of other administrative, social, and spiritual expressions of personal power.[33] Barbier's relationship with Glandelet was nevertheless "more complex," and Gray admits that he "possessed absolute power over her." The intimacy that characterized their relationship, as well as his insistence of her power over him, even urging her to take "charge" over his soul, suggests a relationship that was more reciprocal, despite church hierarchies that placed him in a position of authority over her.[34]

The analysis that these historians have put forward undoubtedly presents a more complex understanding of religious women's expression of agency. Especially by the early twenty-first century, several Canadian scholars of religion paralleled Deslandres, Greer, and Gray in addressing expressions of agency by women of faith, albeit in contexts other than French Catholic convents. In studies ranging from Methodists, Mennonites, and Anglicans to missionaries, evangelicals, and faith healers, historians have probed women's ability to exercise different levels of personal, and sometimes collective, forms of agency.

In 2002, Ruth Brouwer considered the response of Indigenous women to the efforts of white women missionaries, arguing that an espoused Christian devotion did not render Indigenous actors passive to colonial power. Rather, they exercised "considerable agency in adopting only what they wanted from the menu of missionary offerings, and a few were agitating vigorously for deletions and additions."[35] Myra Rutherdale similarly argued in the context of Canadian Anglican missionary work of the consistent presence of "hybridity" on the mission field, as Indigenous women navigated difficult terrains between Western Christianity and their own cultural practices and belief systems.[36] Marguerite Van Die, when writing of Victorian women and religion in her study *Religion, Family, and Community in Victorian Canada*, acknowledged that women seemed to adhere to the dictates articulated by male theologians and preachers. Yet they also adjusted and revised these doctrines to foster their own spiritual identities, formed in conjunction with specific gendered, middle-class ideals. Religious belief, Van Die posits, intertwined with women's "valorization of self," which encouraged "the development and strengthening of their inner identity and sense of agency" deemed necessary for their "participation in the host of gendered religiopolitical organizations that emerged after the 1860s."[37] The effect of such histories has been much more nuanced accounts of women and their ability to act and even change their life circumstances, confirming James Opp's argument that women of faith can be characterized as neither "liberal crusaders" nor passively accepting the religious and cultural norms that were offered them.[38]

This scholarship is indeed promising in the way it wrestles with the complex behaviour of women of faith. Yet arguably, what still seems to be missing is a deeper analysis of the terms we are using. By identifying instances of agency in the lives of believing women without first contemplating the teleology of the discourses we use, are we nevertheless continuing to place these women within a very particular understanding of rational action? Or do we need to join our colleagues in broader international discussions about agency, and in turn let the lives of these women be as transformative as they promise to be? Do we, as Saba Mahmood has suggested, need to disinvest ourselves from a certain brand of liberalist, Western, even feminist politics so that the idea of agency is more fluid and indeterminate, one that is left to "emerge through an analysis of the particular concepts that enable specific modes of being, responsibility and effectivity"?[39] Instead of rendering believing women comprehensible to a particularly Western conception of rationality, neoliberal choice, and progressive politics, we are therefore in a position to allow the historical experiences of these women to remake our theories.

Women at the Margins of Spirit and Reason

As this chapter has thus far illustrated, the focus in discussions of religion, gender, and agency in Canada has remained largely on Christian expressions of faith. Historical studies of women within Jewish, Muslim, and other ethnic and religious communities in Canada, meanwhile, focus mostly on important issues related to labour, migration, settlement, class, and culture, leaving to others the question of how the faith of these women has been framed in relation to agency.[40] And although a large international literature exists that speaks to agency and women mediums, often in association with the occult and spiritualist movements, Canadian histories of such women is limited – but this seems to be changing.[41] The lack of attention on faith expressions beyond a strictly Christian viewpoint may be one reason why the Canadian literature has yet to fully engage in international debates about the contested meaning of agency in the lives of believing women.

One very influential voice in this international debate, particularly from a non-Christian perspective, is Saba Mahmood. Mahmood questions the emphasis on autonomy, especially when it is applied to the lives of women who exist in some sense beyond "nonliberal traditions," as she describes.[42] Mahmood similarly critiques feminist scholars' undue emphasis on resistance, identifying how even the idea of resistance is based upon a liberatory politics, one that prizes "freedom" and thus resurrects the reliance upon an autonomous, singular actor. Insistent upon the need to contextualize how agency is understood within a particular cultural and historical moment, Mahmood argues that one must not allow the meanings of agency to be "fixed in advance."[43] Thus, rather than only recognize certain forms of action, such as resistance or subversion, Mahmood argues that scholars must investigate how women have negotiated norms at very diverse moments in time and space.[44]

It is important to recognize the context in which Mahmood has focused her attention – namely on Egyptian Muslim women involved with the mosque movement, an extension of the larger Islamic revival in Cairo. Yet her ideas are not exclusive to this specific cultural and political landscape and can, in fact, be applied fruitfully to faith practices that have emerged from the Western world, and Canadian women who engaged in mediumship and trance in particular. In fact, this application of Mahmood's theories to the Canadian context may very well continue to unsettle the notion that autonomous and rational self-direction must be the uniform desire and sole option of every women throughout history, regardless of their location in the Western hemisphere or not.

Canadian women's practice of mediumship and trance, particularly in the nineteenth and early twentieth centuries, has historically been associated with the larger, much more global movement of spiritualism, and there is some good reason for making this link. Women acting as mediums and entering trance rested at the heart of spiritualist practice, playing a central role in seances and, at least in the nineteenth century, other more public displays of supernatural power.[45] Yet it is important to note that women mediums did not always espouse spiritualist beliefs; neither did they always practise their gifts in the company of other spiritualists. Much like Janet Oppenheim and others since have identified in contexts outside Canada, typically men but some women donned the label of psychical researchers from the late nineteenth century onward, intent on investigating what they understood to be the scientific value of trance and possession.[46] Psychical researchers such as Thomas Glendenning Hamilton, for instance, a man from Winnipeg, Manitoba, who became celebrated internationally for his work in the 1920s and 1930s, did not view his experiments with female mediums as religious but rather as empirical investigations. The mediums he studied acknowledged his perspective and in many ways enthusiastically facilitated and supported Hamilton's experiments.[47]

Canadian women's engagement with mediumship thus did not always fall so neatly into the category of religion but were at moments thrust into what was at least perceived as objective experiments, meant to test the limits of the natural world and perhaps even the bounds of science itself. By resting so uncomfortably between science and religion, both powerful discourses that are historically invested in certain understandings of rationality, these women's experiences provide a vivid window into how understandings of reason and reliable knowledge continue to flex and shift depending on very particular historical circumstances. The position of these women to discourses of rationality, in turn, can open new avenues by which to re-examine the very terms upon which agency is performed and enacted.

A prominent theme that feminist scholars have recognized when examining mediumship in the international literature is that the practice epitomized stereotypes of female passivity, irrationality, and the loss of the self. In Alex Owen's seminal work on women mediums of Victorian Britain, she claims that this alignment was by no means coincidental. Rather, she argues, mediumship represented a host of Victorian conceptions of ideal femininity, including that of passivity and lack of will, which were considered fundamental qualities for someone to act as a conduit between this world and the next. Only in laying their conscious selves aside for a spirit to possess them could women achieve the promised power of mediumship.[48] Represented as a climax of female passivity, mediumship blatantly challenged autonomy and rational action as ideals to be courted. And it did so in ways that extended even further than the negation of self it proposed, which scholars have identified as a feature of not only spiritualism but a variety of more "enthusiastic" forms of devotion as well.[49]

In addition to the negation of self, mediumship also involved being joined with and expressing oneself through or in combination with a radical other. And it is here where most become uncomfortable. Feminist theory at times seems to lack the tools with which to analyse such experiences without first denying the existence of one crucial element of that communal performance of agency – the spirits themselves. As a result, it becomes that much more tempting for historians, Canadian or otherwise, to characterize mediums as simply using the guise of spirit possession to assert their own goals and opinions.

This explanation of women mediums is problematic, however. Not only does it too easily toss aside the acclaimed beliefs of women in order to disprove, at some level, that these women actually, even emphatically, rejected many of the qualities Western feminists have come to recognize as necessary for agency. This perspective of women mediums also seems to uncritically replicate the criticism female mediums received from their contemporaries, mostly men intent on asserting their own gendered abilities for rationality and objectivity in contrast to the women they studied. Women in this equation were cast as liars, and pathologically so – their unstable minds providing the justification for "scientific" and "professional" men to assert authority over them. Much of the international literature on spiritualism and the occult critiques and analyses this gendered power struggle.[50] Yet by ignoring persistent links between progressive, even feminist, politics and a certain brand of rational knowledge and self-conscious capacity for choice and action, scholars perhaps inadvertently validate the troubling perspectives of the men they ultimately endeavour to challenge.

The alternative is to not shy away from this much more complicated, unsettling material imagery through which women asserted themselves as actors. Embracing Mahmood's suggestion to not let agency be "fixed in advance," this approach can help disentangle agency with longer and problematic historical definitions of rationality – definitions that are in many ways structured according to gendered perceptions of reliable knowledge. This involves not only stepping outside previous definitions of women's agency, but also considering alternative theoretical approaches that problematize what agency looks like.

One such approach is queer theory and the ideas of Judith Butler in particular. Butler's analysis of agency as it relates to gender, the body, and sexuality has in many ways become a model that others have either expanded upon or sometimes critiqued. This critique has largely focused on Butler's tendency to link agency with resistance or subversion, to the point that the transgression of norms seems to be the only legitimate and recognizable form of agency. In response, some have proposed a "generative theoretical framework" to use the words of Lois McNay, one that seeks to identify more creative and indeterminate moments of self-interpretation.[51] But arguably, even these approaches still seem routed within a certain valorization of autonomy and individualism, and thus reminiscent of contemporary Western values, as well as of historical idealizations of rational and responsible action that prize the ability of a singular, individual person (usually male) to act independently, free from political, cultural, and social influences.[52]

Mahmood critiques Butler along similar lines, in that she problematizes how Butler, like other feminist scholars, has so closely linked agency with resistance. Yet Mahmood notably does not reject Butler altogether and in fact uses Butler's theorization of performance as central to her own. Mahmood emphasizes alternative modes of agency that are often expressed and made possible through embodied performances. In the context of Mahmood's analysis, these enactments are neither wholly transgressive nor affirmative, but provide a critical means through which women navigate particular gendered norms – norms that are not only "consolidated and/or subverted" but also perpetually "performed, inhabited and experienced in a variety of ways."[53]

Mahmood's employment of Butler reveals the merits of applying queer theory to the question of believing women's capacity for agency in the Canadian historiography. In the context of women's involvement as mediums, a consideration of Butler could very well become critical. In *Gender Trouble* Butler asserts how "the gendered body is performative," with "no ontological status apart from the various acts that constitute its reality." An interior essence, identity, or, by extension, religious or spiritual sensibility are "*fabrications* manufactured and sustained through corporeal signs and other discursive means."[54] Although this claim could be read as dismissive of spiritual belief and thus counterproductive to any discussion of women and religion, Butler's insights are nevertheless open to alternative interpretations.

Butler's insistence on performance and discourse as constitutive to identity challenges the persistent divide between inward and outward, in that she argues that an interior sense of the self does not exist in isolation from exterior social acts and influences; rather each are co-constitutive and mutually reinforcing. Taken a step further, Butler's theorization subverts the prioritization of what is understood as inward, particularly as it relates to agency – the mind, consciousness, and the ability for autonomous choice. In this re-evaluation of the inward, the conception of rationality as inherently and invisibly routed within particular gendered bodies arguably becomes just as performatively "manufactured" as any supernatural belief.[55] Such constructions, as Butler recognizes, and clarifies in her following work *Bodies That Matter*, are not somehow "artificial and dispensable." They are, in fact, formative, even essential, in that "we could not operate without them."[56] By arguing that projections of the inward, whether supernatural manifestation or so-called "mindful" rationality, are repeatedly constituted through a series of bodily acts, it draws into question why one is prioritized, whereas the other is deemed illusory; why one is perceived as formative to exercising agency, whereas the other is deemed an impediment.

Embodied performance is agentic but not, in and of itself, always transgressive, Butler contends, even though she herself seems to focus on the resistive. Rather performance, the enacted repetition of norms, is how gendered stereotypes are first materialized upon the body. Yet this "materialization is never quite complete" and thus allows for "instabilities, the possibilities for rematerializations."[57] In the 1920s and 1930s seance room, Canadian women often complied with the terms of mediumship in that they evacuated their own selves to make room for the spirits. Yet this act of trance fundamentally reconstituted what their bodies represented and, in turn, broadened the possibilities for performance within the space of the seance. Susan Marshall, a working-class medium living in Winnipeg during the 1920s, in many ways encapsulated this potential. She was prized for her gifts of trance, which was viewed as so utterly complete that it at times resembled "rigor mortis."[58] Through this state, striking, even unsettling spirit manifestations emerged, including the ghost of the renowned chemist William Crookes. Crookes was credited with building an array of metaphysical contraptions and helped facilitate spirit communication and paranormal experiments. Men such as Thomas Glendenning Hamilton, in keeping with his own commitments, viewed such performance not as irrational or superstitious acts but as demonstrable, empirical proofs of as yet unexplored complexities in the natural world.[59]

International scholars of nineteenth- and twentieth-century spirituality may view the performance of Susan Marshall as a continuation of the "paradox of power" in the seance room. Women obtained great influence as mediums but could not wield an "authoritative voice" understood as their own.[60] Yet this diminishing of Marshall's performance of possession seems to rest upon the premise that acts of agency must be recognizable as coming from a single, isolated person, self-consciously and, by extension rationally, directing their own life. These acts must come from a visible expression of individuality that rests somehow beyond, even in opposition to, external, outward acts or influences. Marshall's act of joining herself with a radical, indecipherable other to re-enforce the goals of male authority therefore makes her performance less agentic, if not anti-agentic altogether.

Yet arguably, such an interpretation not only "remains encumbered by the binary terms of resistance and subordination," to use the words of Mahmood, but also insists upon the inward coherency of a singular subject.[61] It is based on the conviction of an indivisible self with the potential to be unencumbered by social realities. Marshall's mediumship challenges this perspective as it represents a moment in which the self becomes joined with another through embodied performances. Her experiences become a powerful testament to the mutability of the body and the identities that are associated with it. The performance of Marshall and many other women mediums can be read as either affirmative or transgressive in some respects, much like other Canadian historians have recognized of women's actions in other religious contexts. Rather than simply identify this tension, however, perhaps we must allow such instances to help reconfigure the very terms by which we understand agency. Is there another way to envision women's ability to either singularly or collectively alter their material circumstances? Without, that is, making agency merely a synonym for particular ideals of rational individualism, autonomy, progressive politics, and liberal choice, concepts that are steeped in historical gendered ideals that ultimately reinforce inequality by prioritizing which experience of agency is authentic or "truly" feminist?

Conclusion

Canadian historians have indeed begun to recognize the complexity of examining the agency of women within religious frameworks. As this chapter has demonstrated, Canadian scholars have increasingly identified through the historical record how women of faith cannot simply be read as transparently resisting patriarchal norms. The insistence to highlight this resistance, however, may indicate that Canadian historians must now direct their analysis to even deeper, more probing questions about the very conceptual frameworks we employ.

By thinking through the origins of the term "agency," in conjunction with the dynamic international scholarship, pervading commitments that seem to most literally haunt the term "agency" can be unravelled. In the process, agency itself becomes much more open-ended and indeterminate, not solely resting upon binaries of passive and active, submission and dominance. Instead of simply imposing certain ideals and concepts upon historical actors, possibilities are created to allow the experiences and embodied performances of historical actors to change our theoretical models altogether. Canadian historians have indeed become more sensitive to considering how religious women have exercised their will and pursued different, even controversial forms of self-realization that stray from straightforward resistance or contemporary Western feminist ideals. The next step is to ask how these categories have shaped the very means by which we are analysing our subjects.

Women's engagement with mediumship and trance in nineteenth- and twentieth-century Canada can provide a useful example with which to begin this journey. Not only do such experiences speak very forcefully to questions of agency, but they also allow for some creative approaches that deconstruct the alleged disconnect between some women's actions and neoliberal idealizations of rational action and autonomous choice. Some of these approaches, articulated by Saba Mahmood, Judith Butler, and others, have not inconsequently been formative to the re-articulation of agency within a much broader international literature pertaining to gender, embodiment, and the construction of knowledge. By considering these approaches in more depth, how might Canadian historians' ideas about agency and women's ability to wield it be transformed as a result?

NOTES

1 John Barber, "Veil Debate Becomes Big Issue in Canada Election, Putting Conservatives into Lead," *Guardian,* 1 October 2015, accessed 23 February 2017, https://www.theguardian.com/world/2015/oct/01/zunera-ishaq-veil-canada-election-conservatives; "Niqab Ban Prevented 2 Women from Proceeding to Citizenship Oath: Controversy over Niqab Swells into an Election Issue," *CBC News*, 29 September 2015, accessed 23 February 2017, http://www.cbc.ca/news/politics/niqab-ban-zunera-ishaq-1.3249495.
2 Joan Wallach Scott, *The Politics of the Veil* (Princeton, NJ: Princeton University Press, 2007), 1–20.
3 As addressed by Pamela Klassen, "Agency, Embodiment, and Scrupulous Women," *Journal of Religion* 84, 4 (October 2004): 592–603.
4 Saba Mahmood, *Politics of Piety: The Islamic Revival and the Feminist Subject* (Princeton, NJ: Princeton University Press, 2011), 14.
5 Sumi Madhok, Anne Phillips, and Kalpana Wilson, "Introduction," in *Gender, Agency, and Coercion*, ed. Sumi Madhok, Anne Phillips, and Kalpana Wilson (Houndmills, UK: Palgrave Macmillan, 2013), 1.
6 Lois McNay, "Agency, Anticipation, and Indeterminacy in Feminist Theory," *Feminist Theory* 4, 2 (2003): 139.
7 John Schlueter, "Beyond Reform: Agency 'after Theory,'" *Feminist Theory* 8, 3 (2007): 316.
8 Clare Hemmings and Amal Treacher Kabesh, "The Feminist Subject of Agency: Recognition and Affect in Encounters with 'the Other,'" in Madhok, Phillips, and Wilson, *Gender, Agency, and Coercion*, 31.
9 Kimberlé W. Crenshaw, "Demarginalizing the Intersection of Race and Sex: A Black Feminist Critique of Antidiscrimination Doctrine, Feminist Theory, and Antiracist Politics," *University of Chicago Legal Forum* 140 (1989): 139–67.
10 Scott, *Politics of the Veil*, 13–16.
11 Donna Haraway, *Modest_Witness@Second_Millennium. FemaleMan_Meets_OncoMouse: Feminism in Technoscience* (New York: Routledge, 1997), 32; Mary

Evans, "The Meaning of Agency," in Madhok, Phillips, and Wilson, *Gender, Agency, and Coercion*, 49–51; Madhok, Phillips, and Wilson, "Introduction," 2–3.

12 Peter Harrison, "'Science' and 'Religion': Constructing the Boundaries," *Journal of Religion* 86, 1 (January 2006): 92. This desire to make religion (and its study) rational has still not passed away, as witnessed in the heated 2012 debate after the publication of Luther H. Martin and Donald Wiebe, "Religious Studies as a Scientific Discipline: The Persistence of a Delusion," *Journal of the American Academy of Religion* 80, 3 (2012): 587–97.

13 Ann Taves, *Fits, Trances, and Visions: Experiencing Religion and Explaining Experience from Wesley to James* (Princeton, NJ: Princeton University Press, 1999), 242–8; Heather Curtis, "A Sane Gospel: Radical Evangelicals, Psychology, and Pentecostal Revival in the Early Twentieth Century," *Religion and American Culture: A Journal of Interpretation* 21, 2 (2011): 195–226; Ann Braude, *Radical Spirits: Spiritualism and Women's Rights in Nineteenth-Century America*, 2nd ed. (Bloomington: Indiana University Press, 2001), 157–61; Elaine Showalter, *The Female Malady: Women, Madness, and English Culture, 1830–1980* (New York: Pantheon Books, 1985), 18–19.

14 Evelyn Fox Keller, *Secrets of Life, Secrets of Death: Essays on Language, Gender, and Science* (New York: Routledge, 1992), 40–1.

15 Examples of this literature include Heather Curtis, *Faith in the Great Physician: Suffering and Divine Healing in American Culture* (Baltimore: Johns Hopkins University Press, 2007); Marie Griffith, *God's Daughters: Evangelical Women and the Power of Submission* (Berkeley: University of California Press, 1997); Phyllis Mack, *Visionary Women: Ecstatic Prophecy in Seventeenth-Century England* (Berkeley: University of California Press, 1992).

16 An example of the contemporary work being done alongside Danylewycz's includes the work of Micheline Dumont-Johnson, such as "Les communautés religieuses et la condition féminine," *Researches sociographiques* 19, 1 (January–April 1978): 79–102; as well as Micheline Dumont and Nadia Fahmy-Eid, *Les couventines: L'éducation des filles au Québec dans les congrégations religieuses enseignantes, 1840–1960* (Montreal: Boréal, 1986).

17 Marta Danylewycz, *Taking the Veil: An Alternative to Marriage, Motherhood, and Spinsterhood in Quebec, 1840–1920* (Toronto: McClelland and Stewart, 1987), 14–16.

18 Micheline Dumont, *Les religieuses sont-elles féministes?* (Montreal: Bellarmin, 1995).

19 Dominique Deslandres, *Croire et faire croire: Les missions françaises au XVIIe siècle (1600–1650)* (Paris: Fayard, 2003); Dominique Deslandres, John A. Dickinson, and Ollivier Hubert, dir., *Les sulpiciens de Montréal, 1657–2007: Une histoire de pouvoir et de discretion* (Montreal: Fides, 2007), in addition to various articles and book chapters.

20 Dominique Deslandres, "In the Shadow of the Cloister: Representations of Female Holiness in New France," in *Colonial Saints: Discovering the Holy in the Americas, 1500–1800*, ed. Allan Greer and Jodi Bilinkoff (New York: Routledge, 2003), 130.

21 Deslandres, "In the Shadow of the Cloister," 131–2.

22 Deslandres, "In the Shadow of the Cloister," 135.

23 Deslandres, "In the Shadow of the Cloister," 138.

24 This attention came at least partly in response to Carolyn Bynum's seminal study of medieval female mysticism in Western Europe, *Holy Feast and Holy Fast: The Religious Significance of Food to Medieval Women* (Berkeley: University of California Press, 1987). While Bynum's emphasis on the role of the body in the expression of women's agency was monumental in how historians approached gender and religion in Canada and beyond, others would claim this was a disturbing misunderstanding of patriarchal power in convents and even a step backwards in feminist analysis. Marie-Florine Brunea, *Women Mystics Confront the Modern World* (New York: State of New York University Press, 1998); Julia B. Miller, "Eroticized Violence in Medieval Women's Mystical Literature," *Journal of Feminist Studies in Religion* 15 (1999): 25–49.

25 Allan Greer, *Mohawk Saint: Catherine Tekakwitha and the Jesuits* (Oxford: Oxford University Press, 2005), ix.

26 Greer, *Mohawk Saint*, 83–4.

27 Greer, *Mohawk Saint*, 87.

28 Greer, *Mohawk Saint*, 87–8.

29 Greer, *Mohawk Saint*, 116–24, 134–9.

30 Greer, *Mohawk Saint*, 124.

31 Colleen Gray, *Congrégation de Notre-Dame, Superiors, and the Politics of Power, 1693–1796* (Montreal: McGill-Queen's University Press, 2007), 6.

32 Gray, *Congrégation de Notre-Dame*, 129–30.

33 Gray, *Congrégation de Notre-Dame*, 133–4.

34 Gray, *Congrégation de Notre-Dame*, 137–8.

35 Ruth Brouwer, *Modern Women Modernizing Men: The Changing Missions of Three Professional Women in Asia and Africa, 1902–1969* (Vancouver: UBC Press, 2002), 7.

36 Myra Rutherdale, *Women and the White Man's God: Gender and Race in the Canadian Mission Field* (Vancouver: UBC Press, 2002); Myra Rutherdale, "'She Was a Ragged Little Thing': Missionaries, Embodiment, and Refashioning Aboriginal Womanhood in Northern Canada," in *Contact Zones: Aboriginal and Settler Women in Canada's Colonial Past*, ed. Katie Pickles and Myra Rutherdale (Vancouver: UBC Press, 2005), 242.

37 Marguerite Van Die, *Religion, Family, and Community in Victorian Canada: The Colbys of Carrollcroft* (Montreal: McGill-Queen's University Press, 2005), 53.

38 James Opp, *The Lord for the Body: Religion, Medicine, and Protestant Faith Healing in Canada, 1880–1930* (Montreal: McGill-Queen's University Press, 2005), 206. Other histories that contributed to this discussion include Nancy Christie, ed., *Households of Faith: Family, Gender, and Community in Canada, 1760–1969* (Montreal: McGill-Queen's University Press, 2002); Joanna Dean, *Religious Experience and the New Woman: The Life of Lily Dougall* (Bloomington: Indiana University Press, 2007); Marlene Epp, *Mennonite Women in Canada: A History* (Winnipeg: University of Manitoba, 2008).

39 Mahmood, *Politics of Piety*, 14.

40 Andrea Eidinger, "Looking Jewish: The Embodiment of Gender, Class, and Ethnicity Among Ashkenazi Jewish Women in Montreal," *Histoire sociale / Social History* 47, 95 (2014): 729–46; Ruth Frager, *Sweatshop Strife: Class, Ethnicity, and Gender in the Jewish Labour Movement, 1900–1939* (Toronto: University of Toronto Press, 1992); Ruth Frager and Carmela Patrias, *Discounted Labour: Women Workers in Canada, 1870–1939* (Toronto: University of Toronto Press, 2005); Nadia Lewis, "Iraqi Women, Identity, and Islam in Toronto: Reflections on a New Diaspora," *Canadian Ethnic Studies* 40, 3 (2008): 131–47.

41 For instance, Gillian McCann, *Vanguard of the New Age: The Toronto Theosophical Society, 1891–1945* (Montreal: McGill-Queen's University Press, 2012) discusses Canadian women involved with theosophy, as does Claudie Massicotte's *Trance Speakers: Femininity and Authorship in Spiritual Séances, 1850–1930* (Montreal: McGill-Queen's University Press, 2016), and my own recently published book, Beth A. Robertson, *Science of the Séance: Transnational Networks and Gendered Bodies in the Study of Psychic Phenomena, 1918–1940* (Vancouver: UBC Press, 2016).

42 Saba Mahmood, "Feminist Theory, Agency, and the Liberatory Subject: Some Reflections on the Islamic Revival in Egypt," *Temenos* 42, 1 (2006): 33.

43 Mahmood, *Politics of Piety*, 14.

44 Mahmood, *Politics of Piety*, 22.

45 Braude, *Radical Spirits,* 23–5; Molly McGarry, *Ghosts of Futures Past: Spiritualism and the Cultural Politics of Nineteenth-Century America* (Berkeley: University of California Press, 2008), 32–6; Alex Owen, *The Darkened Room: Women, Power, and Spiritualism in Late Victorian England* (Chicago: University of Chicago Press, 1989), 5–6.

46 Janet Oppenheim, *The Other World: Spiritualism and Psychical Research in England, 1850–1914* (Cambridge: Cambridge University Press, 1985), 111–58, 326–90; Deborah Blum, *Ghost Hunters: William James and the Search for Scientific Proof of Life After Death* (New York: Penguin, 2006), 106–30; Pamela Thurschwell, *Literature, Technology, and Magical Thinking, 1880–1920* (Cambridge: Cambridge University Press, 2001), 12–36.

47 Robertson, *Science of the Séance*, 11, 13.
48 Owen, *Darkened Room*, 10–11.
49 Mack, *Visionary Women*, 33.
50 For example, Barbara Goldsmith, *Other Powers: The Age of Suffrage, Spiritualism, and the Scandalous Victoria Woodhill* (New York: Alfred A. Knopf, 1998); Diane Basham, *The Trial of Woman: Feminism and the Occult Sciences in Victorian Literature and Society* (Houndmills: Macmillan, 1992); Marlene Tromp, *Altered States: Sex, Nation, Drugs, and Self-Transformation in Victorian Spiritualism* (New York: State University of New York Press, 2006).
51 Lois McNay, *Gender and Agency: Reconfiguring the Subject in Feminist and Social Theory* (Cambridge: Polity Press, 2000), 2–3; McNay, "Agency, Anticipation, and Indeterminacy," 141; Miri Rozmarin, *Creating Oneself: Agency, Desire, and Feminist Transformations* (Oxford: Peter Lang, 2011), 9–38.
52 Haraway, *Modest_Witness*, 23–4, 32.
53 Mahmood, *Politics of Piety*, 22.
54 Judith Butler, *Gender Trouble: Feminism and the Subversion of Identity* (New York: Routledge, 1990), 136; emphasis in original.
55 Butler, *Gender Trouble*.
56 Judith Butler, *Bodies That Matter: On the Discursive Limits of "Sex"* (New York: Routledge, 1993), xi.
57 Butler, *Bodies That Matter*, 2.
58 T.G. Hamilton, "A Study of the Winnipeg Group Mediumship in Its Relation to the Dawn Teleplasms," *Psychic Research* 29, 2 (February 1934): 118.
59 T.G. Hamilton, "The Shell of Katie Appears, Sitting #329," 23 April 1933, Hamilton Family Fonds MSS14 (A.79-41), box 16, folder 11, University of Manitoba Archives and Special Collections, Winnipeg.
60 Owen, *Darkened Room*, 233.
61 Mahmood, *Politics of Piety*, 15.

SELECTED READINGS

Androsoff, Ashleigh. "A Larger Frame: 'Redressing' the Image of Doukhobor-Canadian Women in the Twentieth Century." *Journal of the Canadian Historical Association* 18, 1 (2007): 81–105. https://doi.org/10.7202/018255ar
Avishai, Orit, Afshan Jafar, and Rachel Rinaldo. "A Gender Lens on Religion." *Gender and Society* 29, 1 (2015): 5–25. https://doi.org/10.1177/0891243214548920
Brouwer, Ruth Compton. *New Women for God: Canadian Presbyterian Women and India Missions, 1876–1914*. Toronto: University of Toronto Press, 1990.

Burnett, Kristin. *Taking Medicine: Women's Healing Work and Colonial Contact in Southern Alberta, 1880–1930*. Vancouver: UBC Press, 2010.

Bynum, Carolyn Walker. *Fragmentation and Redemption: Essays on Gender and the Human Body in Medieval Religion*. New York: Zone Books, 1991.

Devens, Carol. *Countering Colonialization: Native American Women and Great Lakes Missions, 1630–1900*. Berkeley: University of California Press, 1992.

Evans, Jennifer Hough, and Katrina Srigley. "'Women of the North, Ministering in the North': Understanding the Sisters of St Joseph through Memory and Space, 1940–1980." *Histoire sociale / Social history* 47, 93 (May 2014): 37–61. https://muse.jhu.edu/article/546759

Greer, Allan. "Iroquois Virgin: The Story of Catherine Tekakwitha in New France and New Spain." In *Colonial Saints: Discovering the Holy in the Americas, 1500–1800*, edited by Allan Greer and Jodi Bilinkoff, 235–50. New York: Routledge, 2003.

Griffith, Marie. *Born Again Bodies: Flesh and Spirit in American Christianity*. Berkeley: University of California Press, 2004.

Hollett, Calvin. *Shouting, Embracing, and Dancing with Ecstasy: The Growth of Methodism in Newfoundland*. Montreal: McGill-Queen's University Press, 2010.

Klassen, Pamela. "Review Article: Agency, Embodiment, and Scrupulous Women." *Journal of Religion* 84, 4 (October 2004): 592–603.

– *Spirits of Protestantism: Medicine, Healing, and Liberal Christianity*. Berkeley: University of California Press, 2011.

Klassen, Pamela, Shari Golberg, and Danielle Lafebvre, eds. *Women and Religion: Critical Concepts in Religious Studies*. London: Routledge, 2009.

Marks, Lynne. *Revivals and Roller Rinks: Religion, Leisure, and Identity in Late-Nineteenth-Century Small-Town Ontario*. Toronto: University of Toronto Press, 1996.

Morgan, Cecilia. *Public Men and Virtuous Women: The Gendered Language of Religion and Politics in Upper Canada, 1791–1850*. Toronto: University of Toronto Press, 1996.

Muir, Elizabeth Gillan. *Petticoats in the Pulpit: The Story of Early Nineteenth-Century Methodist Women Preachers in Upper Canada*. Toronto: United Church Public House, 1991.

Selles, Johanna M. *Methodists and Women's Education in Ontario, 1836–1925*. Montreal: McGill-Queen's University Press, 1996.

Sleeper-Smith, Susan. "Women, Kin, and Catholicism: New Perspectives on the Fur Trade." *Ethnohistory* 47, 2 (2000): 423–52. https://doi.org/10.1215/00141801-47-2-423

Valverde, Mariana. *The Age of Light, Soap, and Water: Moral Reform in English Canada, 1885–1925*. Toronto: McClelland and Stewart, 1991.

Whitehouse-Strong, Derek. "Purveyors of 'Religion, Morality, and Industry': Race, Status, and the Role of Missionary Wives in the Church Missionary Society's North-West American Mission." *Histoire sociale / Social History* 40, 79 (May 2007): 143–68.

Whitely, Marilyn Färdig. *Canadian Methodist Women, 1766–1925: Marys, Marthas, Mothers in Israel*. Waterloo: Wilfrid Laurier University Press, 2005.

Whitely, Marilyn Färdig, and Elizabeth Muir, eds. *Changing Roles of Women within the Christian Church in Canada*. Toronto: University of Toronto Press, 1995.

7 Home Fronts and Front Lines: A Gendered History of War and Peace

TARAH BROOKFIELD AND SARAH GLASSFORD

"There from the troubled sea had Evangeline landed, an exile," wrote Henry Wadsworth Longfellow in a tragic poem depicting his heroine's wedding day deportation from her Acadian homeland.[1] Known as the *grand derangement*, the 1755 Acadian expulsion affected 20,000 men, women, and children, who faced massacres, fires, scalping, and rape. Wives and daughters were murdered or "abused" in front of their husbands and fathers. Survivors, like the fictional Evangeline, violently separated from their kin, found their identities and life cycles permanently disrupted.[2] Despite a prevailing image of Canada as a peaceable kingdom, episodes of violence like the Acadian expulsion and long periods of war at home and abroad have arguably been the norm.[3] Even a cursory glimpse through the early history of North America reveals pre-contact Indigenous conflicts, imperial and colonial wars, armed uprisings, coastal and border raids, genocidal intentions, sectarian violence, and population displacements. The image of Canada as warrior nation emerges even more clearly when we consider the Canadian military and government's involvement in international wars and conflicts since 1867.[4] Woven throughout the warrior narrative are moments where Canadians strove for peace and compromise through treaty-making, individual pacifism, collective peace activism, support for international humanitarian law and mediation, and military peacekeeping missions – but the fact remains that Canada and its inhabitants have been and continue to be fundamentally shaped by war.

The gendered scholarship on Canadian warfare and peace activism, crafted primarily by women's history scholars but also more broadly by historians interested in military history and the social history of war, strives to study the ways in which war informs, changes, and pushes the boundaries of gender. These histories demonstrate that before enfranchisement, women rarely held formal positions of authority to influence, stop, or start a war – queens and clan mothers were the exceptions. Despite these constraints, women, especially mothers, were singled out as having exceptional responsibilities in maintaining recruitment and wartime morale, as well as in advocating less destructive alternatives to war. At the same time, women's material contributions in households, volunteer organizations, or industry have been critical factors in every war, as has their caregiving work. Historically, women living near battlefields or sites of contested territory embodied a vulnerability that arose in part from their proximity to violence, but also from the gendered ideology that shaped laws and social norms restricting women's movements, earning power, and control of their property, while simultaneously fostering a view of their bodies as potential sites of conquest. Women who took up arms or risked their lives to assist the military have been celebrated in research and public memory for their bravery, loyalty, and challenge to the notion of female fragility; concurrently, the formal entry of women into the armed forces in non-combatant and later combatant roles provoked widespread debate over gender and sexuality in the military. Much of the focus has been on women and war; however, the recent development of masculinity studies has enriched our understandings of historical expectations for military service among men and boys.

Despite making great strides in understanding the gendered nature of war and the individual experiences of women and men, the historiography disproportionately emphasizes certain topics, people, and wars, which inhibits a broader understanding of the relationship between gender and war across time and space in Canadian history. Most significantly, gendered analyses of the two world wars have dominated the literature, while men's and women's experiences of warfare and peacemaking before the twentieth century and after 1945 have made only limited inroads. The prevailing tendency to study specific groups of women in different theatres of war or wartime roles has fragmented our understanding of what may be constant, transformative, or unusual in these experiences. At the same time, men's and women's experiences in war are rarely studied in conjunction with one another and are often framed in ways that may overemphasize the idea of separate spheres. For these reasons, this chapter reflects on what has been learned thus far, but it also works to broaden the terms of reference and begin the task of making comparisons across time periods and between different conflicts and theatres of war.

Questions of Liberation: Women and the World Wars

During the summer of 2014 we surveyed the existing studies on women, war, and peace in Canada, with the addition of research specifically relating to masculinity and war, ultimately compiling a bibliography of more than

450 individual articles or chapters, edited or oral history collections, and monographs.[5] While we cannot claim it is comprehensive, this bibliography enables us to draw broad conclusions about the state of the field as a whole. In terms of sheer volume of work, the First (1914–1918) and Second (1939–1945) World Wars dominate the literature: roughly half of the works dealt explicitly with these two wars (split almost exactly in half between them); that number increases slightly if works dealing with pacifism in these periods are included. This predominance partly reflects the availability of sources: "total war" deliberately engaged all citizens, and this wide involvement combined with increased state intervention produced a wealth of materials with which to study these periods. The vast scope of these conflicts, their dramatic and enduring influence on global geopolitics, their prominent place in Canadian narratives of nationhood, and interest among the general public, also contribute to this wealth of scholarship.

Both halves of our bibliography (the world wars and everything else) explore a wide range of experiences and employ a variety of methodologies. In other words, the field is richer than the initial numbers might suggest. Women emerge from these studies not only as victims of war or passive observers but also as active agents supporting or resisting war, *acting* as much as – or more than – they are *acted upon*. The larger trajectory of growth within women's and gender history overall is clearly reflected in the evolution of studies of gender, war, and peace. Before the 1970s, the existing literature on Canadian women and war arose principally from the tradition of popular biographies and dictionary entries about pre-Confederation heroines: young Madeleine de Verchères's defence of her seigneury (1692), War of 1812 heroine Laura Secord, and Loyalist women of the American Revolutionary War (1775–83), including Molly Brant (Koñwatsiãtsiaiéñni), were enduringly popular members of this pantheon. As Canadian women's history developed during the 1970s into a coherent field of study interested in questions of liberty, labour, and power, historians moved beyond individual portraits of women affected by war to consider war as a collective experience that reinforced and challenged gender norms. At the forefront was historian and feminist activist Ruth Roach Pierson.

During the spring 1975 semester, Pierson taught the first course on women's history to be offered at Memorial University of Newfoundland, one of a handful of similar courses being pioneered at Canadian universities in the early 1970s. Inspired by a mature student in her class who had served as a member of the Royal Canadian Air Force (Women's Division), Pierson began researching the history of women's labour during the Second World War.[6] Pierson's examination of women's paid and unpaid labour in war industries, as members of the armed forces, and in voluntary associations would later appear in her path-breaking 1986 monograph *"They're Still Women after All": The Second World War and Canadian Womanhood*, which asked whether the Second World War liberated women.[7] Pierson's question was necessary because the decades after 1945 saw American propaganda icon "Rosie the Riveter" and her "We Can Do It!" image gradually assume a prominent place in Canadian public memory of women's involvement in the two world wars, along with a corresponding assumption that women's wartime actions proved their worth and changed their status.[8] Pierson's work was groundbreaking because it not only brought women into the academic discussion of Canadian wartime history, but it also challenged popular assumptions about women's war work, offering fresh insights and taking the conversation in new directions.

Pierson argued that the government and military used women's paid and voluntary labour to win the war, then forced them back into conventional gender roles when the crisis ended; any wartime "liberation" experienced by Canadian women was deliberately partial and temporary. Scholars like Tina Davidson, Helen Smith, and Pamela Wakewich picked up Pierson's debunking torch at the end of the twentieth century, noting that for every advance into a non-traditional field or behaviour, women faced an equal or greater onslaught of conventional expectations for respectable femininity.[9] More recently, Cynthia Toman and Jeff Keshen have suggested a middle ground between the war-as-liberation and war-as-oppression-dressed-as-liberation camps, in their respective studies of military nurses and civilian women during the Second World War. Toman suggests that nurses did experience real wartime gains overseas, although they did not translate well to domestic postwar nursing. Keshen argues that Pierson "sets the bar too high" in her assessment of what constituted real progress for women, and he makes the case for a "two steps forward, one step back" interpretation of the war's legacy for Canadian women.[10]

The question of whether war is a liberating and/or transformative experience for women remains an area of lively historiographical debate in the second decade of the twenty-first century – not only in Canada, but in the United States and Britain too – and now also extends its reach to the historiography of the First World War. Linda J. Quiney's research on Volunteer Aid Detachment (VAD) nurses in the First World War critically assesses the degree to which the war opened doors for women's employment and leadership.[11] Tarah Brookfield shows how women's collective contribution to the war was the turning point in overcoming long-held government opposition to women's voting rights. Yet the war caused deep ruptures within the suffrage community, whose members held different views on the legitimacy of militarism, conscription, the Wartime Elections Act, and the decision to continue campaigning for suffrage during the war.[12] Barbara Roberts's pioneering work on Canadian women's feminist-pacifism during the First World War similarly complicates any simplistic or universalized view of women's wartime responses and experiences.[13] The twelve essays in *A Sisterhood of Suffering and Service: Women and Girls of Canada and Newfoundland during the First World War* deliberately engage with Pierson's question of war's role in transforming women's lives, and often contradict one another in answering this unifying question of the volume. Editors Sarah Glassford and Amy Shaw conclude that "each woman's experience of the war was unique" and "gender alone did not produce a single, universal wartime experience," liberating or otherwise.[14]

The first studies of women and the world wars took gender as their principal category of analysis, primarily examining the experiences of white, English-speaking, urban Canadian women. Little space was allotted to considering how similar or different the experiences of non-white, rural, or francophone Canadian women may have been. During the 1990s, the growth of studies on racialized and immigrant women's history, and new understandings of how race and gender intersect to shape women's lives, offered insights into non-white Canadian women's wartime experiences. Dionne Brand's path-breaking article "We Weren't Allowed to Go into Factory Work until Hitler Started the War," about African Canadian women's employment in war industries, enriched the discourse of women and war by making visible the intersections between race, gender, and privilege that determined wartime opportunities and hardships.[15] A decade later, Pamela Sugiman's oral history research with Japanese Canadian women forcibly relocated from coastal British Columbia and often separated from interned male kin during the Second World War provides a strikingly different narrative of Canadian women's wartime lives.[16] These women's experiences of wartime oppression, violence, and displacement make it clear that while the war years may have been transformative, they were far from liberating.

The absence of certain groups of women in this historiography may not be solely attributable to scholarly myopia. Rather, the silences suggest that the world wars were not a major turning point in all women's histories. For example, there is very little scholarship on the support or resistance of Indigenous women or francophone women in Quebec during either world war. Alison Norman's recent study of the voluntary war work of Six Nations women at Grand River highlights the promise of these neglected areas of wartime social history,[17] but feminist scholars already working in these fields have clearly found other subjects or time periods more significant within the broader trajectories of Quebecoise and Indigenous women's histories. Clearly, there is no "universal" wartime experience for Canadian women, and the world wars have not played as critical a role in determining some women's status as they may have done for others.

Still, the dynamic conversation around war's transformative or liberating impact, started by Pierson in the 1970s, has yielded rich results. Collectively, the more than 200 world war–related works in our bibliography explain how labour shortages and a sense of wartime emergency offered opportunities for some women to break out of long-standing gender norms, while those same gender norms were manipulated to mobilize men as soldiers and workers and women in supportive and caring roles. The overturning of conventional gender roles upset many Canadians and prompted increased social surveillance, while government, private industry, and social pressure eroded many of women's wartime gains in peacetime. Women believed themselves to have important roles in wartime; government, industry, and war charities reinforced this sense and turned it to their own ends. Rituals of collective mourning and commemoration took gendered forms, privileging the fallen (male) soldier above all other forms of wartime participation, but some women fought to assert a similar place of privilege for the figure of the grieving mother. Child-rearing, housekeeping, food preparation, nursing, and acts of care were asserted as forms of fighting, as much as were taking on new jobs in industry, the military, or the white-collar sector. Contemporaries recognized that wartime changed women's place in society, at least temporarily, but historians assess the long-term implications of this "liberation" in different ways.

As Sugiman's research on Japanese Canadian women demonstrates, the idea of wartime as potentially liberating is not a useful framework for studying all women in the world wars, let alone other conflicts. War-as-liberation assumes a particular type of state-sanctioned, industrialized "total war" that is non-nuclear, non-civil, lengthy, and fought at a great distance from the "home front." In other words, more or less exclusively the two world wars – conflicts that stand out as anomalies in the broader sweep of Canadian history. The distance of most Canadian women from the violence and territorial upheaval of the world wars created a very particular home front culture and corresponding array of opportunities very different from those of refugees and all who lived in occupied countries or near the frontlines. Were women in *Patriote* families concerned with overturning gender roles in the midst of supporting the cause of liberation from Anglo-dominated political overlords? What of the female members of the Canadian Forces in Afghanistan, or Voice of Women's anti-nuclear activists during the Cold War? As an overarching framework for understanding women and war through all of Canadian history, the liberation/transformation question proves insufficient to grapple with the diverse array of women and wars involved. The fact that this question is rarely (if ever) asked of men and war further illustrates its limits as an entry point for understanding gender and war as broadly as possible.

Scholars *are* pursuing other themes within their studies of the world wars, but these other questions are often overshadowed by the question of war's transformative impact. Happily, the vast documentary record left by the two world wars means there are ample sources to support new directions for scholarship on women and gender in the two conflicts. A host of tasks present themselves as obvious paths to pursue. The first major task is to broaden, integrate, and compare, viewing the two wars not as discrete units of four or six years but in terms of a *longue durée* within the broader twentieth-century context. Tracing individual case studies of women's lives during and after a war, for example, could help determine whether wartime accelerated, delayed, or foretold later changes. There are intimate histories of women's sexuality, sexual danger, family dynamics, and grief waiting to be written; attention to the impact of age and of religious affiliation (beyond the historic peace churches) on wartime experience will yield further important insights. Areas of existing study can also benefit from being integrated with one another: women's traditional and non-traditional work, as well as pacifism and support for the war, existed and were defined in relationship to one another. Many Canadian men were ineligible to enlist, so women's and men's home front work (both paid and voluntary) deserves to be considered in tandem, staying alert to the ways that gender dictated its respective forms – Ian Mosby's *Food Will Win the War* is an excellent example of this approach.[18] Fruitful comparative work – some of it transnational – also waits to be tackled: for instance, the experiences of military nurses and members of the Second World War women's armed services; interned enemy alien women of both wars; women's voluntary work for different organizations or campaigns; women's experiences in different regions of the country; or rural versus urban settings. A survey and comparison of women's experiences in both wars would also reveal trends in voluntary and paid labour, military participation, social attitudes, grief, and commemoration. A further task is to continue expanding the study of women and the world wars beyond the urban, anglophone, and white women who still populate the majority of existing studies. In short, despite already dominating the literature on women, war, and peace, there are giant gaps in the literature on the world wars, which means exciting work still to come.

Women's Vulnerability and Resilience in Wars of the Colonial and Post-1945 Periods

Wars fought at a safe distance from home may offer a chance for liberation from gender norms, but armed conflicts fought *at* home occurred far more often throughout Canadian history. When there is little distinction between the home front and the battlefield, civilians become collateral damage, or even targets; consequently, vulnerability and resilience shape women's wartime lives. Even if a war ultimately results in a more democratic state focused on improving the lives of women, in the interim women's lived experiences are marked by what Helene Moussa calls "sharp, if not violent discontinuities of identities, social and economic status, culture, family and community relationships."[19] This was certainly true for the native and settler women living in colonial-era Canada, when "home" was frequently the site of warfare or smaller-scale raids between rival Indigenous groups and colonial interlopers. Wars and armed uprisings remained real (and sometimes endemic) possibilities in many eighteenth- and nineteenth-century women's lives until the conclusion of the 1885 uprising of Métis and Plains nations, after which military attacks on Canadian soil principally existed in the form of imagined threats. Throughout the twentieth century, Canadian-born civilians largely remained safe, a rarity in a period which witnessed the invention of total war, genocide, and nuclear weapons; meanwhile, survivors of overseas wars migrated to Canada – many of them women arriving alone or with families – bringing with them physical and emotional traces of their trauma and loss.

Despite wars of close proximity being the most prevalent and recurring sort in Canadian history, only a quarter of the texts in our bibliography focus on them. The most significant representation in this group comes from studies of Loyalist women, a standing which is likely the result of the importance of the American Revolutionary War and Loyalist diaspora in American, British, and Canadian history alike. The most significant study of Canadian Loyalist women is Janice Potter-MacKinnon's 1993 monograph *While the Women Only Wept: Loyalist Refugee Women in Eastern Ontario*. She argues that the war exacerbated whatever constraints women faced in their peacetime lives, making it even more challenging to seek safety and subsistence, but shows that Loyalist women seized upon the very same understandings of their gender that put them at risk in war and turned them instead into survival tools. In their petitions to the Crown for compensation, for instance, they used contemporary notions of femininity as a measure of their success or an excuse for their failures during their flight to Canada.[20] Since the 1970s scholars have noted the lack of homogeneity in the Loyalist experience and demonstrated how much class and race mattered: enslaved, free Black, and white Loyalist women would have had vastly different relationships to the British Crown, affecting their resettlement process in Canada.[21] There were other types of outliers as well, such as Molly Brant. Elizabeth Elbourne has shown how, during the American Revolution, Brant's matrilineal Kanyen'kehaka (Mohawk) ancestry and the status she held as the sister and wife of prominent men worked together to enable her to play a crucial role as intermediary between the British and their Indigenous allies.[22] Brant's powerful role existed within the wider context of Aboriginal "feminism" discussed by Nancy Forestell in this volume.

Outside of the Loyalist experience, gendered analyses of other seventeenth-to nineteenth-century colonial conflicts are much more fragmented: women's wartime experiences as observers, targets of violence, refugees, prisoners of war, camp followers, prostitutes, collaborators, or war resisters are peripherally glimpsed in military histories, annotated primary sources, or general histories of the period. In the twentieth-century context, the Cold War has recently received new attention, particularly in regard to the settlement of Cold War refugees, women's engagement in the disarmament and anti–Vietnam War movements, the impact of Cold War ideology on families, and the surveillance of gay and lesbian Canadians during the Red Scare.[23] Later-twentieth- and early twenty-first-century conflicts still await significant historical attention, although feminist scholars in other disciplines are working to contextualize the gendered landscape of modern war, particularly the experiences of refugee women coming to Canada. What the existing historiography lacks in quantity, it makes up for in possibility, represented by innovative ways of researching and thinking about women and war, including the freedom to compare and contrast common experiences across time.

Even though each historic conflict is grounded in era-specific and culturally specific understandings of gender, patriarchy, codes of war, and human rights, reading through the historiography reveals seemingly enduring similarities in the way war collides with women's lives. The oral history work of Steven High and his team of university and community researchers in Montreal brings to light particularly striking parallels in terms of gendered vulnerability and a capacity for resilience.[24] Read alongside each other, the more than 500 life stories gathered from male and female survivors of the Holocaust, the Cambodian Killing Fields, the Rwandan genocide, and state violence in Haiti reveal that women and girls were more likely than their male counterparts to experience violence and poverty in their war-torn homelands, while travelling to sites of refuge, and again while establishing lives in Canada. The reasons for this include women's economic disadvantages, a higher likelihood of being burdened with the care of children or aged parents, and the ever-present threat of sexual violence. We also see multiple examples of how killing, hurting, or raping a woman in these wars was a symbolically powerful way to mock the masculinity of male refugees, emphasizing their inability to protect female kin.

Recognizing recurring patterns in modern warfare and refugee experiences and applying them to the past can also be useful for historians studying colonial women and war, where primary sources by or about women are scarce and frequently silent on taboo subjects like rape. This is demonstrated most effectively by Elsbeth Heaman's 2013 article on the probability of sexual violence in the War of 1812.[25] After a student commented that Laura Secord was lucky not to have been sexually assaulted during her famous trek, Heaman considered the reasons behind the rape discourse – or lack thereof – in the Canadian press and other forms of war propaganda. While the invisibility of rape in the historic record left some earlier historians confident that American soldiers acted like gentlemen around Canadian women, Heaman found evidence in court records and personal papers that proved rape and sexual violence occurred in occupied towns and other war zones during the War of 1812, although newspapers rarely connected it to the context of the war. The sexual violence took many forms, including grey areas of consent when women traded sex with enemy soldiers for survival. This choice is well documented in other historic cases involving female prisoners of war or women living in occupied zones, such as Barbara Austen's studies on New England female captives assimilated into Indigenous or French society through marriage, or Marlene Epp's work on Mennonite refugee women's relationships with Soviet soldiers in the Second World War.[26] Heaman concludes by reflecting on the need for historians to revisit earlier portrayals of war and offer a "counter narrative" that allows speculation that women such as "Laura Secord may have braved and overcome more obstacles than perhaps has been generally understood – more, indeed, than can be understood unless feminist historical analysis and public commemoration continue to interrogate one another."[27]

While we may be able to paint a portrait in broad strokes about the similarities of women's exposure to risk in war zones, we are still missing the finer detail of how war disrupted women's lives or challenged gender norms in the sixteenth to nineteenth centuries. Much more work is needed in this field. In part, this can be accomplished through informed speculation (as in Heaman's article), applying what is known about women and war in better-studied eras, and re-reading primary sources in new ways – or uncovering entirely new ones. Another fruitful undertaking would be for social historians to delve more confidently into the territory of military history (and vice versa), looking for traces of women's existence or gendered clues amid military records and casualty reports.[28] More generally, if more scholars of women's history were to work on early Canada, we would gain a richer understanding of how colonial warfare intruded (or did not) on the domestic and work lives of Indigenous and settler women. Feminist historians working in all eras might be able to reframe narratives of war by considering the impact of war alongside episodes of armed conflict that are not traditionally defined or studied as wars, yet shared much of the same destructive impact on women's lives and livelihoods, including localized cases of violent disputes between neighbours and landlords, tavern brawls, duels, and domestic violence.[29] By the same token, how differently might we understand the Métis migration from Saskatchewan to Alberta in the aftermath of the Red River Resistance (1869–70) if we framed it as a refugee experience? What can we learn about the intersections of gender, resistance, and militarism by studying historic episodes in which a portion of the population is at war with the armed forces, such as during the Winnipeg General Strike (1919), the October Crisis (1970), or the Oka Crisis (1990)? It would also be revealing if historians were to consider the broader range of ways in which men experience war. Not all men were soldiers, and not all men soldiered in the same manner.

Masculinity, War, and Peace

"Daddy, what did YOU do in the Great War?" ask a young son and daughter in Savile Lumley's infamous recruitment poster for the British Expeditionary Force in 1915. Presumably, the father's only acceptable answer – one that will confirm his patriotism, validate his masculinity, and avoid shaming his children – is to acknowledge that he took up arms to defend his homeland and empire. Canadian men's participation in warfare has never been habitual or guaranteed, but before 1945 most generations of men in Canada would have had opportunities to participate in war parties, militias, and armies. The threat of an enemy attack combined with promises of profit and adventure made volunteer or professional soldiering a critical role for men to play. Unsurprisingly, much of the scholarship dealing with men and war in Canada focuses on men's military commitments.

The writing of military and wartime history has a long, robust tradition in Canada, encompassing under its broad umbrella such contributions as the propaganda-infused First World War publications of Max Aitken's Canadian War Records Office, official histories commissioned by the Department of National Defence, academic scholarship by leading Canadian historians of their generation like J.L. Granatstein, and rigorous but popularly accessible recent works by Tim Cook.[30] The impact of gender, however, has rarely been a focus in this scholarship, nor has commentary on the patriarchal framework of war. Yet even when the gender analysis is not implicit, such as in Terry Copp's and Bill McAndrew's work on the armed forces' complex history with shell shock, or Jonathan Vance's study of prisoners of war, the subject itself provides insights into how war works to assemble and shatter concepts of masculinity.[31]

If the legacy of Ruth Pierson has a counterpart in military history, it would be the work of Desmond Morton. While Pierson's work marked a deliberate attempt to recuperate women's history and analyse gendered wartime discourses, Morton dedicated his illustrious career to military history – but an increasingly social-history-infused version of military history. This eventually led him to consider women and family in *Fight or Pay: Soldiers' Families in the Great War*,[32] his study of the Canadian Patriotic Fund, but his earlier work (on the cadet movement, postwar provisions for veterans, and trench life) had already examined many aspects of military masculinity – even if he did not explicitly label it as such.[33]

Historians, joined by scholars of masculinity studies, are increasingly shaping our understandings of how men and boys are groomed to be soldiers and of the gendered, heterosexual expectations that inform recruitment campaigns, military training and culture, and wartime propaganda. Yet such studies remain relatively few in number. If any period can be considered a particular focus for this burgeoning field, it is the century leading up to the First World War, including the War of 1812, the Rebellions (1837–8), and the South African War (1899–1902). Gendered analyses by Cecilia Morgan, Allan Greer, Jarett Henderson, Mary G. Chaktsiris, and Mark Moss demonstrate how amid each of these highly charged imperial interludes the Canadian men who took up arms and the boys who trained as cadets re-negotiated their position as British subjects through expressions of masculine sacrifice.[34] Until falling enlistment rates in the First World War dictated otherwise, Canada's military masculinity was also cloaked in whiteness: racist ideology dictated that non-white men were presumed to lack sufficient "valour, discipline, and intelligence" to serve effectively.[35] More recently, historians have probed the gendered nuances of the veteran experience, particularly those struggling with disability and mental health issues, as they navigated re-entry into civilian life. As monuments were built to honour the sacrifice of the war dead, surviving veterans came under attack from a society and government unprepared to handle their financial, emotional, or health care needs.[36]

Few historians have grounded their studies of masculinity and militarism beyond the First World War, perhaps because the recent centenary of the Great War drew the attention of historians to this conflict, while more contemporary histories of war, gender, and military culture remain the domain of political scientists and interdisciplinary scholars. The historians who have waded into these subjects have uncovered previous silences that complicate assumptions about masculinity and soldiering. For example, Paul Jackson's *One of the Boys: Homosexuality in the Military during World War II* plumbs court martial and medical records to reveal the often punishing and occasionally welcoming way queer serviceman were treated in their units and by the military brass.[37] Similarly, Claire Cookson-Hills uses court martial records to uncover the plethora of Canadian soldiers charged with, if rarely found guilty of, sexual violence against German women in the Second World War. Her work asserts a narrative of Canadian soldiers as emboldened, violent men in addition to the more traditional image of Canadian soldiers as heroic liberators.[38] When considering the criminal acts of soldiers in subsequent peacekeeping scandals, as well as military culture more broadly, political scientist Sandra Whitworth insists that "soldiers are not born, they are made; and part of what goes into the making of a soldier is a celebration and reinforcement of some of the most aggressive, and most insecure, elements of masculinity: those that promote violence, misogyny, homophobia, and racism."[39] Future studies will need to consider the impact of the slow but persistent gender integration of the Canadian Forces on prevailing notions of who and what a soldier is expected to be in both wartime and peacetime.[40] Moving forward, it would be both useful and interesting to broaden the study of men's experiences of war. Until recently, men were almost exclusively studied in terms of their military service; men's wartime experiences out of uniform have rarely been considered in gendered terms. This contrasts with the study of women and war, in which everything women have done in wartime – work, fight, resist, volunteer, survive, or die – is considered first and foremost "women's history," making gender the dominant frame of analysis. What would change if men's wartime history was painted in similarly gendered brushstrokes? What if we thought about all the men who did not fight *as men*, rather than as individual cases of cowardice, apathy, neutrality, pacifism, or essential worker classification? Has there ever been a men's peace movement, or only different pockets of men's war resistance based on their identities as scientists, clergymen, draft dodgers, or conscientious objectors? What about studying war's impact on the civilian men who were ineligible or unable to serve in popularly supported wars and conflicts? Looking at men's wartime experiences and ideologies beyond soldiering would open windows onto a wider range of masculine behaviours and social expectations. It might also highlight situations in which gender was not the defining experience of war for men. This in turn could either reinforce or challenge our prevailing assumption that men and women experience war in entirely different terms.

Conclusion

Since the history of gender, war, and peace became a distinct area of study in the 1970s, social historians, military historians, and other scholars have produced a rich body of work dealing with many types of violence, upheaval, and armed conflict in which Canadians have participated at home or overseas. The heavy concentration on the First and Second World Wars (particularly on the home front) has enriched our understanding of these two total wars but has simultaneously obscured other important experiences and made it difficult to get a more holistic sense of the field. The question of whether war liberated women, which has informed a significant proportion of these world-war-focused studies, has led to many valuable insights into the changes and continuities in women's lives during the first half of the twentieth century, but it is not a universally appropriate question to ask of women's – or men's – wartime experiences. Persistent popular interest and public commemorations are probably responsible for the preponderance of attention paid to the two world wars. A later-twentieth- and early twenty-first-century desire to find and celebrate the trailblazers and milestones that led to the very different roles, rights, and expectations women enjoy today is likely behind the liberation question's persistence. But other questions beckon: the collection *Worth Fighting For: Canada's Tradition of War Resistance from 1812 to the War on Terror*, for instance, highlights the fact that Canadians' responses to conflict have historically been complicated and diverse.[41] The book's broad time frame and expansion beyond the world wars and any concern with liberation points to a path future research could profitably follow.

We close here with some preliminary conclusions arising from Canadian history and the historiography of gender, war, and peace overall. To start with, if we define sacrifice as the key characteristic of war, then it is fair to say that men and women experience warfare on similar terms: war brings loss, regardless of gender. Similarly, in the chaos of war both men and women may emerge and be remembered as heroes and martyrs, victims and victors, aggressors and profiteers, cowards and warriors. Yet the significance of these identities, and the opportunities and consequences associated with them, are inherently gendered. War is ultimately an expression of power, one that more often emphasizes than erases or eases peacetime inequities, and thus it presents gender-specific risks and privileges that serve to determine wartime opportunities and oppressions. These risks and privileges are modified by social constructions of race, ethnicity, class, and other variables, which shift depending on the location and scale of warfare. The history of Canada's engagement in warfare and peacemaking therefore provides an important setting in which to better understand the way gender operates and can be disrupted in critical moments of nation-building and times of great distress. In turn, a gendered analysis of warfare and peacemaking illuminates the ways in which ingrained societal processes and ideologies can shape the way wars are fought, resolved, or avoided.

NOTES

1 Henry Wadsworth Longfellow, *Evangeline: A Tale of Acadie* (New York: Macmillan, 1902).
2 John Mack Faragher, "A Great and Noble Scheme: Thoughts on the Expulsion of the Acadians," *Acadiensis* 36, 1 (Autumn 2006): 82.

3   On the peaceable kingdom image, see Paul Rutherford, "Made in America: The
    Problem of Mass Culture in Canada," in *The Beaver Bites Back? American Pop-
    ular Culture in Canada*, ed. David H. Flaherty and Frank E. Manning (Montreal:
    McGill-Queen's University Press, 1993), 278. Louise Dechêne explores the
    impact of frequent warfare in New France in *Le Peuple, l'État, et la Guerre au
    Canada sous le Régime français* (Montreal: Boréal, 2008).

4   Ian McKay and Jamie Swift, *Warrior Nation: Rebranding Canada in the Age of
    Anxiety* (Toronto: Between the Lines, 2012), xi.

5   Journals dedicated to the study of gender history and women's history pub-
    lished the most articles on our list (21 per cent). Not far behind were locally
    or regionally focused journals (19 per cent); those with a national focus
    (Canadian, American, or British) published 18 per cent. Another 8 per cent
    came from military history journals, and the remainder (34 per cent) from
    journals dedicated to a wide array of social, political, and cultural themes and
    subthemes.

6   Deborah Gorham, "Women's History: Founding a New Field," in *Creating His-
    torical Memory: English-Canadian Women and the Work of History*, ed. Beverly
    Boutilier and Alison Prentice (Vancouver: UBC Press, 1997), 282–5.

7   Ruth Roach Pierson, *"They're Still Women after All": The Second World War and
    Canadian Womanhood* (Toronto: McClelland and Stewart, 1986).

8   On 9 October 2018, the user-created Wikipedia page for "Canadian Women in the
    World Wars" included the iconic (American) Rosie the Riveter poster and focused
    primarily on women entering new fields of work during the wars. "Canadian
    Women in the World Wars," https://en.wikipedia.org/wiki/Canadian_women_in_
    the_World_Wars (accessed 9 October 2018).

9   Tina Davidson, "'A Woman's Right to Charm and Beauty': Maintaining the Fem-
    inine Ideal in the Canadian Women's Army Corps," *Atlantis* 26, 1 (2001): 45–54;
    Helen Smith and Pamela Wakewich, "Beauty and the Helldivers: Representing
    Women's Work and Identities in a War Plant Newspaper," *Labour / Le Travail*
    44 (Fall 1999): 71–107.

10 Cynthia Toman, *An Officer and a Lady: Canadian Military Nursing and the
    Second World War* (Vancouver: UBC Press, 2007); Jeff Keshen, *Saints, Sinners,
    and Soldiers: Canada's Second World War* (Vancouver: UBC Press, 2004),
    chapters 6–7, quotations from p. 177 and chapter 6 title.

11 Linda J. Quiney, "'Sharing the Halo': Social and Professional Tensions in the
    Work of World War I Volunteer Nurses," *Journal of the Canadian Historical
    Association* 9 (1998): 105–24.

12 Tarah Brookfield, "Divided by the Ballot Box: The Montreal Council of Women
    and the 1917 Election," *Canadian Historical Review* 89; 4 (December 2008):
    473–501.

13 Barbara Roberts, *"Why Do Women Do Nothing to End the War?": Canadian Feminist-Pacifists and the Great War* (Ottawa: CRIAW/ICREF, 1985).
14 Sarah Glassford and Amy Shaw, *A Sisterhood of Suffering and Service: Women and Girls of Canada and Newfoundland during the First World War* (Vancouver: UBC Press, 2012), 317.
15 Dionne Brand, "'We Weren't Allowed to Go into Factory Work until Hitler Started the War': The 1920s to 1940s," in *"We're Rooted Here and They Can't Pull Us Up": Essays in African Canadian Women's History*, ed. Peggy Bristow (Toronto: University of Toronto Press, 1994), 171–91.
16 See, for example, Pamela Sugiman, "Passing Time, Moving Memories: Interpreting Wartime Narratives of Japanese Canadian Women," *Histoire sociale / Social History* 37, 73 (2004): 51–79.
17 Alison Norman, "'In Defense of the Empire': The Six Nations of the Grand River and the Great War," in Glassford and Shaw, *A Sisterhood of Suffering and Service*, 29–50.
18 Ian Mosby, *Food Will Win the War: The Politics, Culture, and Science of Food on Canada's Home Front* (Vancouver: UBC Press, 2014).
19 Helene Moussa, "Violence against Refugee Women: Gender Oppression, Canadian Policy, and the International Struggle for Human Rights," *Resources for Feminist Research* 26, 3/4 (1998): n.p.
20 Janice Potter-MacKinnon, *While the Women Only Wept: Loyalist Refugee Women in Eastern Ontario* (Montreal: McGill-Queen's University Press, 1993).
21 James St G. Walker's *The Black Loyalists: The Search for a Promised Land in Nova Scotia and Sierra Leone, 1783–1870* (New York: Africana Publishing Co. and Dalhousie University Press, 1976) broadly explores Black Loyalist experiences but does not offer much of a gender analysis. See instead Debra L. Newman, "Black Women in the Era of the American Revolution in Pennsylvania," *Journal of Negro History* 61, 3 (July 1976): 276–89.
22 Elizabeth Elbourne, "Family Politics and Anglo-Mohawk Diplomacy: The Brant Family in Imperial Context," *Journal of Colonialism and Colonial History* 6, 3 (Winter 2005): 1–47.
23 See, for example, Franca Iacovetta, *Gatekeepers: Reshaping Immigrant Lives in Cold War Canada* (Toronto: Between the Lines, 2006); Frances Early, "Canadian Women and the International Arena in the Sixties: The Voice of Women / La Voix des femmes and the Opposition to the Vietnam War," in *The Sixties: Passion, Politics, and Style*, ed. Dimitry Anastakis (Montreal: McGill-Queen's University Press, 2004), 25–41; Tarah Brookfield, *Cold War Comforts: Canadian Women, Child Safety, and Global Insecurity* (Waterloo: Wilfrid Laurier University Press, 2012); Gary Kinsman and Patrizia Gentile, *The Canadian War on Queers: National Security as Sexual Regulation* (Vancouver: UBC Press, 2009).

24 Montreal Life Stories, http://www.lifestoriesmontreal.ca/, accessed 9 July 2015.

25 Elsbeth Heaman, "Constructing Innocence: Representations of Sexual Violence in Upper Canada's War of 1812," *Journal of the Canadian Historical Association* 24, 2 (2013): 115.

26 Barbara E. Austen, "Captured ... Never Came Back: Social Networks Among New England Female Captives in Canada, 1689–1763," *Dublin Seminar for New England Folklife Annual Proceedings* 14 (July 1989): 28–38; Marlene Epp, *Women without Men: Mennonite Refugees of the Second World War* (Toronto: University of Toronto Press, 2000).

27 Heaman, "Constructing Innocence," 148.

28 See Serge Patrice Thibodeau, *Journal de John Winslow à Grand-Pre* (Moncton: Perce-Neige, 2011), chapter 5. This translation and annotation of Winslow's journal provides new details of Acadian women's experiences with deportation, including their imprisonment as a ruse to draw out male kin and suggestions of sexual violence.

29 Useful starting ground for this work would be Cecilia Morgan, "'In Search of the Phantom Misnamed Honour': Duelling in Upper Canada," *Canadian Historical Review* 76, 4 (1995): 529–62; Rusty Bittermann, "Women and the Escheat Movement: The Politics of Everyday Life on Prince Edward Island," in *Separate Spheres: The World of Women in the 19th-Century Maritimes*, ed. Suzanne Morton and Janet Guildford (Fredericton, NB: Acadiensis Press, 1994), 23–38.

30 Tim Cook examines a significant portion of (non-gender-focused) Canadian military historiography in *Clio's Warriors: Canadian Historians and the Writing of the World Wars* (Vancouver: UBC Press, 2006).

31 Terry Copp and Bill McAndrew, *Battle Exhaustion: Soldiers and Psychiatrists in the Canadian Army, 1939–1945* (Montreal: McGill-Queen's University Press, 1990); Jonathan Vance, *Objects of Concern: Canadian Prisoners of War Through the Twentieth Century* (Vancouver: UBC Press, 1994).

32 Desmond Morton, *Fight or Pay: Soldiers' Families in the Great War* (Vancouver: UBC Press, 2004).

33 See, for example, Desmond Morton, *When Your Number's Up: The Canadian Soldier in the First World War* (Toronto: Random House, 1994).

34 For example, Cecilia Morgan, "Remembering the War of 1812: Gender and Local History in Niagara," *Canadian Issues* (Fall 2012): 6–9; Allan Greer, *The Patriots and the People: The Rebellion of 1837 in Rural Lower Canada* (Toronto: University of Toronto Press, 1993); Jarett Henderson, "Banishment to Bermuda: Gender, Race, Empire, Independence and the Struggle to Abolish Irresponsible Government in Lower Canada," *Histoire sociale / Social History* 46, 92 (November 2013): 321–48; Mary G. Chaktsiris, "'Our Boys with the Maple Leaf on Their Shoulders and Straps': Masculinity, the Toronto Press, and the

Outbreak of the South African War, 1899," *War and Society* 32, 1 (2013): 3–25;
Mark Moss, *Manliness and Militarism: Educating Young Boys in Ontario for War*
(Oxford: Oxford University Press, 2001).

35 James W. St. G. Walker, "Race and Recruitment in World War I: Enlistment of
Visible Minorities in the Canadian Expeditionary Force," *Canadian Historical
Review* 70, 1 (1989): 1.

36 Lara Campbell, "'We Who Have Wallowed in the Mud of Flanders': First World
War Veterans, Unemployment, and the Development of Social Welfare in Canada,
1929–1939," *Journal of the Canadian Historical Association* 11 (2000): 125–49.
The Laurier Centre for Military and Strategic Disarmament's study "Through
Veterans' Eyes: Digital Approaches to the Hidden Histories of Veterans, Families
and the State 1918–2000," directed by Mark Humphries, has digitized more than
203,000 files documenting the lives of Great War veterans, and promises to provide new insights into this question in years to come.

37 Paul Jackson, *One of the Boys: Homosexuality in the Military during World War II*
(Montreal: McGill-Queen's University Press, 2010).

38 Claire Cookson-Hills, "Confronting the Trauma of War: A Panel on the Past and
Present Experiences of Veterans," Tri-University History Conference, March
2018.

39 Sandra Whitworth, *Men, Militarism and UN Peacekeeping: A Gendered Analysis*
(London: Lynne Riemer Publishers, 2004), 3.

40 Much of what we know about the mixed-gender integration of the Canadian
armed forces at home and in NATO postings comes from histories written pre-
dominantly by servicewomen in the late 1970s and 1980s. See, for example,
Captain Suzanne Simpson, Major Doris Toole, and Cindy Player, "Women in the
Canadian Forces: Past, Present, and Future," *Atlantis* 4, 2 (1979): 267–83; Jean
E. Klick (US Air Force), "Utilization of Women in the NATO Alliance," *Armed
Forces and Society* 4, 4 (1978): 673–8.

41 Lara Campbell, Michael Dawson, and Catherine Gidney, eds, *Worth Fighting For:
Canada's Tradition of War Resistance from 1812 to the War on Terror* (Toronto:
Between the Lines, 2015).

SELECTED READINGS

Austen, Barbara E. "Captured … Never Came Back: Social Networks among New
England Female Captives in Canada, 1689–1763." *Dublin Seminar for New
England Folklife Annual Proceedings* 14 (July 1989): 28–38.

Brand, Dionne. "'We Weren't Allowed to Go into Factory Work until Hitler Started
the War': The 1920s to 1940s." In *"We're Rooted Here and They Can't Pull Us*

Up": Essays in African Canadian Women's History, edited by Peggy Bristow, 171–91. Toronto: University of Toronto Press, 1994.

Brookfield, Tarah. Cold War Comforts: Canadian Women, Child Safety, and Global Insecurity. Waterloo: Wilfrid Laurier University Press, 2012.

Campbell, Lara, Michael Dawson, and Catherine Gidney, eds. Worth Fighting for: Canada's Tradition of War Resistance from 1812 to the War on Terror. Toronto: Between the Lines, 2015.

Chaktsiris, Mary G. "'Our Boys with the Maple Leaf on Their Shoulders and Straps': Masculinity, the Toronto Press, and the Outbreak of the South African War, 1899." War and Society 32, 1 (2013): 3–25. https://doi.org/10.1179/07292473 12Z.00000000014

Coates, Colin, and Cecilia Morgan. Heroines and History: Representations of Madeleine de Verchères and Laura Secord. Toronto: University of Toronto Press, 2002.

Early, Frances. "Canadian Women and the International Arena in the Sixties: The Voice of Women / La Voix des femmes and the Opposition to the Vietnam War." In The Sixties: Passion, Politics, and Style, edited by Dimitry Anastakis, 25–41. Montreal: McGill-Queen's University Press, 2004.

Elbourne, Elizabeth. "Family Politics and Anglo-Mohawk Diplomacy: The Brant Family in Imperial Context." Journal of Colonialism and Colonial History 6, 3 (Winter 2005): 1–47. https://doi.org/10.1353/cch.2006.0004

Epp, Marlene. Women without Men: Mennonite Refugees of the Second World War. Toronto: University of Toronto Press, 2000.

Evans, Suzanne. Mothers of Heroes, Mothers of Martyrs: World War I and the Politics of Grief. Montreal: McGill-Queen's University Press, 2010.

Faragher, John Mack. "A Great and Noble Scheme: Thoughts on the Expulsion of the Acadians." Acadiensis 36, 1 (Autumn 2006).

Glassford, Sarah, and Amy Shaw. A Sisterhood of Suffering and Service: Women and Girls of Canada and Newfoundland during the First World War. Vancouver: UBC Press, 2012.

Heaman, Elsbeth. "Constructing Innocence: Representations of Sexual Violence in Upper Canada's War of 1812." Journal of the Canadian Historical Association 24, 2 (2013): 114–55. https://doi.org/10.7202/1025076ar

Iacovetta, Franca. Gatekeepers: Reshaping Immigrant Lives in Cold War Canada. Toronto: Between the Lines, 2006.

Kinsman, Gary, and Patrizia Gentile. The Canadian War on Queers: National Security as Sexual Regulation. Vancouver: UBC Press, 2009.

Magee, Kathryn. "'They Are the Life of the Nation': Women and War in Traditional Nadouek Society." In Rethinking Canada: The Promise of Women's History, 6th ed., edited by Mona Gleason, Tamara Myers, and Adele Perry, 12–22. Don Mills, ON: Oxford University Press, 2008.

Montreal Life Stories. http://www.lifestoriesmontreal.ca/, accessed 9 July 2015.

Morton, Desmond. *Fight or Pay: Soldiers' Families in the Great War*. Vancouver: UBC Press, 2004.

Mosby, Ian. *Food Will Win the War: The Politics, Culture, and Science of Food on Canada's Home Front*. Vancouver: UBC Press, 2014.

Moss, Mark. *Manliness and Militarism: Educating Young Boys in Ontario for War*. Oxford: Oxford University Press, 2001.

Pierson, Ruth Roach. *"They're Still Women after All": The Second World War and Canadian Womanhood*. Toronto: McClelland and Stewart, 1986.

Potter-MacKinnon, Janice. *While the Women Only Wept: Loyalist Refugee Women in Eastern Ontario*. Montreal: McGill-Queen's University Press, 1993.

Roberts, Barbara. *"Why Do Women Do Nothing to End the War?": Canadian Feminist-Pacifists and the Great War*. Ottawa: CRIAW/ICREF, 1985.

Simpson, Captain Suzanne, Major Doris Toole, and Ms Cindy Player. "Women in the Canadian Forces: Past, Present, and Future." *Atlantis* 4, 2 (1979): 267–83.

Stetz, Margaret. "'Woman as Mother in Headscarf': The Woman War Refugee and the North American Media." *Canadian Woman Studies* 19, 4 (2000): 66–70. *Canadian Periodicals Index Quarterly* (accessed October 24, 2018). http://link.galegroup.com.libproxy.mtroyal.ca/apps/doc/A63859100/CPI?u=mtroyalc&sid=CPI&xid=9d92ccee

Sugiman, Pamela. "Passing Time, Moving Memories: Interpreting Wartime Narratives of Japanese Canadian Women." *Histoire sociale / Social History* 37, 73 (2004): 51–79.

Toman, Cynthia. *An Officer and a Lady: Canadian Military Nursing and the Second World War*. Vancouver: UBC Press, 2007.

Whitworth, Sandra. *Men, Militarism, and UN Peacekeeping: A Gendered Analysis*. London: Lynne Riemer Publishers, 2004.

8 Historical Feminisms in Canada to 1940: Further Reflections on the So-Called First Wave

NANCY FORESTELL

In the midst of doing research for the second volume of *Documenting First Wave Feminisms*, I came across a 1910 letter from Catherine Hay, a domestic living in Toronto who had recently immigrated from Jamaica, to Lady Ishbel Aberdeen, the former president of the National Council of Women of Canada (NCWC) and ongoing president of the International Council of Women (ICW). In this letter, Hay protested the treatment she and other Jamaican domestics were receiving from the Young Women's Christian Association (YWCA) who, she posited, wanted "to dispose of us." As part of a self-described group of respectable, Christian women who were also British subjects, Hay questioned whether the YWCA afforded "protection" for all young women travelling abroad, or "is it for whites only?" She explained that she was appealing directly to Aberdeen after reading about a speech the ICW president had given in Toronto the previous year. Hay quoted Aberdeen as saying, "Woman must be protected, it makes no matter what the colour."[1] Coming across no further correspondence between Hay and Aberdeen, I hoped that the existing academic scholarship on the YWCA in Canada might provide a more detailed explanation of the Toronto YWCA's actions and the subsequent circumstances of these early twentieth-century Black Jamaican immigrants. This too proved unsuccessful.[2] A single photograph held by the Toronto Archives ended up being one of the few easily accessible clues about the fate of Catherine Hay and her contemporaries. This evocative black-and-white photograph taken circa 1912 depicts a small group of racialized women in front of a residence named "Ontario House," which the archival repository's explanatory note describes as YWCA accommodation "specifically for Black women." (See figure 1.) It would thus appear that the Toronto YWCA acceded, however reluctantly, to the demand by Black women for the provision of accommodation, although it would assume the form of segregated housing. Taken together, the letter and

1 Women in front of YWCA's Ontario House, ca. 1912. Photographer: William James. City of Toronto Archives Fonds 1244, Item 71.22

photograph in some respects provide only a fragmentary glimpse of a single episode in a long and complex history of feminist mobilization in this country. Yet it is also possible to see that they touch upon important and broader themes pertaining to historical feminisms in Canada.

These documents suggest how imperialism and colonialism operated as an organizing framework within which feminist engagement occurred from its very beginnings until well into the twentieth century, if not beyond. Moreover, they illustrate how the interconnected histories of colonialism and slavery continued to shape relations among and between feminist activists as they would still other histories of difficult border crossings and the formation and reformation of diasporic communities. One can also discern here the different and often contested meanings and practices related to feminism. Some women, most notably the middle-class Anglo-Celtic Protestant women who were prevalent among many of the mainstream women's organizations (including the YWCA), embraced a form of maternal feminism which constituted a powerful rationale for participation in a wide range of social reform and political campaigns. They could apply the knowledge and attributes they seemingly acquired as mothers to address various social ills and inequities, which, in some circumstances, included offering assistance to certain vulnerable female populations. For many other women, however, this specific iteration of feminism did not hold the same kind of appeal due to its often class elitism and discriminatory practices on the basis of race, ethnicity, religion, and colonial status. They pursued alternative avenues to achieving justice and equality, often drawing upon the strengths of women in their community, albeit in at least some instances in ways that foregrounded issues other than gender.

A final significant theme which the letter and photograph highlight is transnational cross-currents and collaborations. Numerous feminists, as Marilyn Lake has suggested, frequently breached the "border controls" of colony and nation in the nineteenth and twentieth centuries.[3] In Canada as elsewhere, large numbers became enmeshed in and greatly influenced by various international networks in which ideas and organizational initiatives constantly circulated. And at the same time, such border crossings, in either their intellectual or physical form, could be more challenging for some than for others. Further research may reveal whether any kind of allegiance, if only temporary, occurred between Hay and Aberdeen that might have allowed them to work across multiple and intersecting categories of social difference to effect change. Unfortunately, the photograph suggests that whether this occurred or not, the outcome was not necessarily the one Hay sought.

This chapter will explore some of the ways that these themes have been taken up or not in the existing scholarly literature on historical feminisms in Canada to 1940. After a brief explanation of terms and periodization, a broad overview of the historiography will be provided before addressing three main questions. First, what do we as yet know about the "untidy origins" of feminist activism in this region of North America, and how did these initial efforts continue to influence subsequent practices and priorities?[4] Second, to what extent has the historical scholarship adequately addressed the diverse range of feminisms which took shape over the course of the nineteenth century and into the twentieth? And third, how have questions raised about transnational influences and networks altered our understanding of Canadian feminist engagement, and what other lines of inquiry need to be pursued?

It is important to note here that the precise meaning of what actually constitutes "feminism" in previous historical eras has been widely debated by scholars over the past decades. Karen Offen has posited that historians have grappled with devising a definition which would "accommodate much diversity in strategies and tactics, but which in the final analysis rests on a single 'bottom line,' a common denominator – which boils down to challenging masculine domination."[5] Scholars have also been concerned about whether feminism can be applied to particular women's thoughts and actions prior to when the term first came into use in Europe in the 1880s. For the *Documenting First Wave Feminisms* series, Maureen Moynagh and I employed the term "to indicate an awareness on the part of women, that they are oppressed at least in part because of their sex, and to designate the analyses of oppression and struggles for liberation by and for women, whether or not the women in question used the term 'feminism.'"[6] We devised a definition, which will be employed in this chapter, meant to capture a range of beliefs and practices reflective of a critical, gendered consciousness prior to and after the late nineteenth century.

Some explanation is also required as to periodization. Until relatively recently much of the existing scholarship characterized feminist organizing as constituting three distinct waves, the first from the mid-nineteenth century to the 1920s, the second from the 1960s through the late 1970s, and the third from the 1980s onward. This formulation has come under increasing critique of late, most notably for the use of the wave metaphor and the time periods covered by each of the seemingly distinct and separate phases. Concerns have been raised about the wave metaphor and its association with water – that it reduces feminist activism to a cycle of accelerated momentum, climax, and inevitable decline. And that during such periods of decline there is the presumption that feminists wielded little influence and organizational efforts were minimal. Nancy Hewitt has also noted, "The script of feminist history – that each wave overwhelms and exceeds its predecessor, lends itself all too easily to whiggish interpretations of ever more radical, all-encompassing, and ideologically sophisticated movements."[7] Moreover, with specific regard to the so-called first wave, it has been observed that the standard narratives in various national contexts (but most notably those in Europe and North America) have tended to foreground the struggle for female suffrage and its most visible advocates, white middle-class women.[8] Such a narrow focus and chronology has resulted, furthermore, in downplaying or overlooking altogether other feminist initiatives and the involvement of less-privileged women. When scholars have turned their attention to feminist involvement in the North American labour movement in the twentieth century, for instance, they have uncovered rich histories of committed women achieving positive social change from the 1930s to the early 1960s, which had previously been considered a period of relative quiescence.[9]

Many scholars, including myself, have been unwilling to abandon the wave model altogether, despite its many shortcomings, and instead have called for a revision to its meaning and related chronology. One suggested reconceptualization of feminist movements has called for a shift in the concept of wave as a monolithic wall of water to promoting its association with sound waves that carry energy from one place to another. In other words, there is an emphasis on continuity, and thus not any abrupt end with a gap in between.[10] In addition, a much more expanded chronology has been advocated, most particularly for the initial phase(s) of feminist mobilization, as a means of decentring the suffrage narrative and its most visible adherents.[11] The term "first wave" will be employed in this chapter primarily to signal the beginnings of multiple conversations and practices which in many instances would continue well into the twentieth century. To some degree the decision to end the period covered at 1940 is arbitrary, although it is also meant to indicate that noticeable transformations occurred with the onset of the war and then in the postwar period.

Historiographical Overview

Perhaps one of the easiest observations to make about the scholarship pertaining to historical feminisms in Canada is that it remains underdeveloped. Why and how that is the case is more difficult to ascertain. As women's history emerged as a field within the discipline of history in Canada in the 1970s, the study of feminist thought and organizing was among the more prominent research topics. Such interest was linked in part to a younger generation of feminist scholars, many of whom saw themselves as social activists, being interested in exploring their political antecedents. This research was also initiated, as demonstrated by Joan Sangster in the next chapter in this volume, alongside widespread popular efforts among second wave feminists to uncover a diverse Canadian "herstory."[12] The academic scholarship on first wave feminism produced in the 1970s and 1980s raised important questions about national women's organizations, such as the National Council of Women of Canada (NCWC) and the Woman's Christian Temperance Union (WCTU), as well as provincially based nationalist organizations such as the Fédération Nationale Saint-Jean-Baptiste (FNSJB).[13] A wide range of topics were explored, including the study of working-class and farm women's attitudes towards suffrage, how Protestant women advocated on behalf of Chinese and Japanese immigrant women on the west coast, and the imperial context within which women's emigration from Britain to Canada was formulated.[14] The anthology produced in 1989 by Linda Kealey and Joan Sangster titled *Beyond the Vote: Canadian Women and Politics* marked a noteworthy departure from what had tended to be a historiographical concentration on Anglo-Celtic, Protestant, middle-class reformers (especially outside the context of Quebec), many of whom were liberal in their political orientation.[15] Further, it represented a move away from the time period which had been most closely studied up to that point, the 1870s to the 1920s. This volume explored the lives of female activists who were socialists and social democrats (including the francophone Thérèse Casgrain), Jewish homemakers, Finnish militants, and Ukrainian patriots, with particular attention paid to the interwar period.

In subsequent decades the study of historical feminisms was by no means abandoned, but there is little question that it garnered less scholarly attention. Of direct relevance here is the observation that even while the field of Canadian women's and gender history expanded significantly over this period, the number of its practitioners remained modest in comparison to the rest of the discipline. And thus, as some established academics shifted their attention to other research topics and many newly emerging scholars focused on new lines of inquiry, a practical result was that there were relatively few feminist historians who engaged with this topic.

The scholarly literature was also restricted in still other ways, with the debate which developed over the racial politics of first wave feminists being particularly illustrative. To briefly recount, a disagreement ensued among women's historians over the allegation first made by Carol Bacchi and later elaborated upon by Mariana Valverde that many first wave feminists were racist.[16] While some scholars agreed with this assessment, others strongly objected.[17] Subsequent scholarship attempted to avoid these polarized positions, especially as represented in the work of literary critic Janice Fiamengo, who cautioned against "the reductive conclusion that all first wave feminist writing promoted a monolithic racism" and argued that early feminists not be judged so harshly for being "a product of their age."[18] Useful insights were made in the midst of this debate about the dynamics of gender, race, and class; yet what is also striking about this discussion, with the advantage of hindsight (and further reflection), is that regardless of their specific position, each of these scholars continued "the preoccupation with articulate white, middle-class women."[19] The unstated assumption in the ongoing assessment of the degree of racial intolerance or tolerance among first wave feminists, which in at least some instances manifested itself in ambiguity and contradiction, is that most if not all were Euro-Canadian.[20] Acknowledgment of the presence and significance of Indigenous and other racialized women as feminists was largely bracketed out of this entire debate. For example, referring to one of the largest women's reform organizations at the turn of the century, the Woman's Christian Temperance Union (WCTU), Valverde has contended that "it was difficult if not impossible for Canada's women of colour to identify with the brand of feminism elaborated by the WCTU."[21] Yet she made this argument without any detailed interrogation of Black women's involvement, which in southwestern Ontario for a period of time appears to have been extensive. Moreover, the growing divergence between English-language and French-language scholarship in and about Canada and Quebec,[22] partially explains the virtual absence of any examination of the racial politics of francophone women (whether white, Indigenous, or women of colour) in the historical literature either at the time or subsequently.[23] Although Enakshi Dua argued forcefully for in-depth historical research on anti-racist feminisms in 1999, one could well contend that the field of Canadian women's and gender history has yet to adequately respond.[24]

In the past decade or so scholarly interest in historical feminisms in Canada in general and the first wave more specifically has noticeably increased. In addition to a number of documents projects,[25] there have been major studies produced on prominent early twentieth-century feminists such as Marie Gérin-Lajoie, Rose Henderson, and Ishbel Majoribanks (more commonly referred to as Lady Aberdeen).[26] Monographs have also been published on the feminist pursuit of justice in the criminal court system in Ontario, on their contributions to the reform of family law in British Columbia, and on their involvement in denominationally based organizations in Quebec.[27] This renewed interest, furthermore, has taken place amid growing evidence of the "transnational turn," with various scholars having situated their works within the broader context of transnational influences or networks, whether they be imperial, continental, or international in nature.[28] Certain aspects of feminist thought and action have by now been well researched, yet major gaps remain.

Untidy Origins

One of the least studied aspects of feminist organizing and beliefs in Canada remains its origins. Although the creation of the Toronto Women's Literary Club (TWLC) in 1876 was for a long time depicted as the semi-official date for the founding of the "woman's movement," there is growing recognition that a variety of different women and organizations were engaged in political endeavours pertaining to fair treatment and/or equal rights at least several decades earlier.[29] Scholars who have examined this topic in depth in other contexts have cautioned against the use of a precise date or a singular origin story given the untidy trajectory of feminism which they uncovered.[30] Far more research on the situation in British North America (BNA) is clearly called for, but that which has been completed thus far, although fragmentary, points to similarly uneven and complex origins.

These origins were profoundly influenced by the circumstances of British North America being part of a collection of disparate colonies and territories within the British Empire. As scholars Cecilia Morgan and Adele Perry have well demonstrated, gendered political debate and social action in the nineteenth century, whether in Upper Canada or in British Columbia, were fundamentally shaped by British imperial ties and ideology.[31] And of particular consequence, BNA was a white settler society in which clear distinctions were made between colonizer and colonized. Feminist historians of British settler societies elsewhere have drawn specific attention to the implications of the emergence of feminism alongside the displacement and oppression of Indigenous peoples.[32] Referring to feminists and their supporters in New Zealand and Australia, Patricia Grimshaw has noted that they "made their case for equity and justice for the female sex in societies immersed in negative constructions of Indigenous peoples of both sexes."[33]

These kinds of dynamics certainly became central in the genesis of women's organizing in British North America. But as a number of scholars have recently contended, is not one of the most important origin stories to be first considered how Indigenous women sought to question, if not resist, the consequences of colonialism, gendered and otherwise? Andrea Smith has posited that, "if we were to recognize the agency of Indigenous women in an account of feminist history, we might begin with 1492, when Native women collectively resisted colonization."[34] Jean Barman has raised a similar point with relation to Indigenous women on the west coast during what she refers to as the "cusp of contact."[35] Barman cites examples of Indigenous women in the eighteenth and nineteenth centuries acting "in ways consistent with the goals of feminism" *before* the full onset of the conditions of European patriarchy and colonialism. And thus one of the examples which she cites are the "uppity" Kwantlen women who inhabited Fort Langley in the 1820s, often refusing to be deferential to European fur traders and acting "in what they perceived to be their own best interests as women and as human beings."[36]

Such analysis and the histories on which they are based also have the potential to place the efforts of an individual such as Nahnebahwequa (Catherine Sutton) in a somewhat different light. The incisive critiques which Nahnebahwequa formulated in the 1850s about her own ill-treatment and that of Indigenous peoples more generally has been commented upon by various historians. Scholar Celia Haig-Brown has also called attention to her hybrid identity as the product of a mission education who converted to Christianity and later married an English immigrant, but who nonetheless defended her Indigenous heritage and the explicit discrimination she faced as an Indigenous woman.[37] However, to the degree that Nahnebahwequa has been recognized as making explicitly feminist arguments, and even adopting or adapting language being employed by Euro-Canadian women of the period, her accomplishments have often been treated as singular and somehow exceptional.[38] It might be more appropriate and more accurate to depict her eloquent interventions within a longer tradition of Indigenous feminism, which predated her birth and most definitely continued after her death.

Evidence provided primarily by American historians points to other aspects of the "Indigenous roots" of feminism on this continent. Sally Roesch Wagner and others have noted that at least from the 1830s onward Euro-American feminists such as Lydia Maria Child and Lucretia Mott were inspired by the cultural and political traditions of select Indigenous tribes that accorded women certain rights and political involvement.[39] The Haudenosaunee (Iroquois) garnered special notice due to their perceived matriarchal heritage and in particular the role granted to Haudenosaunee women as clan mothers to select or depose chiefs and to exercise other kinds of political authority in community meetings. Given that the Haudenosaunee occupied lands which crossed the international border, and that American reformers had regular contact with friends and family with a similar outlook in Upper Canada,[40] it is more than plausible that these Indigenous practices and beliefs had some degree of influence on feminists in British North America as well.

The ongoing legacy of slavery and participation in the international abolitionist movement were other key elements in the genesis of women's activism. While slaveholding was not as extensive in British North America as it was in the United States or the Caribbean, deeply entrenched asymmetries between white and Black colonists lived on even well after its official abolishment in the early 1830s. And hence as we'll see, this history of colonialism and slavery would continue to inform and delimit relations among and between groups of women activists in a variety of ways. Yet at least for a period of time in the early to mid-nineteenth century, the struggle to eliminate slavery elsewhere in the hemisphere and to assist Black refugees fleeing the United States created allegiances between Black and white abolitionists and, in time, support for "woman's rights." Research by Clare Midgely and Bonnie Anderson has indicated that female abolitionists in British North America were part of the "trans-Atlantic anti-slavery sisterhood" that developed in the early nineteenth century whose concerns over the condition of slaves became linked with an awareness of the inequitable condition of women.[41]

Prominent among this abolitionist network in BNA were free Blacks who came from the United States and white Quakers who Nancy Hewitt has described as "radical universalists."[42] These abolitionists employed a language of natural equal rights in seeking to redress the injustices of slavery, which they connected to another kind of bondage experienced by women. Mary Ann Shadd Cary, a free Black woman from a well-connected abolitionist family who arrived in Canada West from Delaware in the early 1850s and became

editor of the *Provincial Freeman*, was among the earliest and most public advocates of women's rights. Shirley Yee and Peggy Bristow, who have closely
studied Shadd Cary's writing and organizing, contend that she was part of a
larger community of Black women in the colony who endeavoured to improve
access to education, combat racism, and promote women's rights.[43] There is
some evidence that Black women in the colony of Nova Scotia were also engaged in similar activities.[44]

The degree to which Black and white activist women were able to easily
or consistently breach the racial divide remains unclear, and not surprisingly there is some indication of occasional conflict.[45] But there is also a
record of mixed-race attendance at lectures on anti-slavery and women's
rights, as well as support for integrated education. The precise connections
between organizations such as the Ladies Coloured Fugitive Association
(LCFA) and the all-white Toronto Ladies' Association for the Relief of
Destitute Fugitives (TLARDF)[46] – which were designed to aid Black refugees in Canada West in the wake of the 1850 Fugitive Slave Law in the
United States – have yet to be documented, but they did have common goals
and a shared outlook.

The equal rights ethos adopted by Black and white women in their abolitionist work was also evident in the literary societies they developed separately
beginning in the mid-nineteenth century. In the early 1850s, Black women in
Chatham and Windsor were among the first to form such groups, whose purpose was to enhance the education of its members.[47] Analogous groups among
white women did not begin appearing until several decades later. Heather Murray has maintained that a liberal education, which women sought through these
societies, served as a foundation for political activism and, in the specific case
of white women, created a forum from which they argued for access to higher
education.[48]

These endeavours existed alongside and sometimes interconnected with
ongoing efforts to improve married women's property rights in common-law
jurisdictions from the mid-nineteenth century onward, with the impetus in part
coming from female petitioners.[49] The tangible gains secured with each subsequent revision to married women's property legislation greatly enhanced the
"economic agency" of many women, as Peter Baskerville has contended, as it
served as a foundation in part for them securing equal political rights.[50] Additional clarification is required here, though, to specify that the women who
benefited the most from these changes were white, middle- and upper-class
women. Moreover, these gains took place at the same time that Indigenous
women who married non-Indigenous men lost possession of and access to an-
cestral lands.

Diverse Feminisms?

These strands of feminist advocacy coincided with other kinds of female organizing pertaining to temperance, religious charity, and missionary work, which all together laid the basis for women to play a much more significant role in public campaigns for equality, justice, and overall societal improvement. Many of these efforts were religiously inspired and denominationally based and only gradually and incompletely became more secular in orientation.[51] The international scholarly literature has increasingly emphasized the varied forms of historical feminisms which emerged in the nineteenth century or later in the twentieth century. In the American case, historians have challenged the myth, as Annalise Orelick has observed, "that activism around gender has been of interest only to a small slice of the overall population – white, middle-class women."[52] With regard to the situation in British North America and later the dominion of Canada, there is some indication of diverse expressions of feminism not only at the outset but thereafter. However, due in part to the early historiographical focus primarily on white, middle-class women, which was only partially revised in the modest volume of scholarship that followed, we have a far from complete understanding of the multiple cross-currents constituting women's activism in Canada during the first wave.

Without question the feminists who have been most extensively interrogated in the Canadian historiography are the Anglo-Celtic, Protestant, middle-class women who dominated in numbers and often in influence the suffrage groups and many of the social reform organizations which emerged in the late nineteenth century. An initial interpretive focus, which has been the subject of ongoing deliberation, is the significance and meaning of maternal feminism among these women. Early on in this discussion Carol Bacchi postulated that a clear demarcation be made between activists who she identified as employing equal rights arguments, which she depicted as "true feminists," and those who used maternalist arguments, which she characterized as "social reformers."[53] Part of Bacchi's formulation was soon refuted by the contention that pleas for social justice on the basis of equal rights were noticeably on the decline in Canada and elsewhere by the 1880s, but various scholars concurred with her assessment of maternal feminism as inherently conservative.[54] Veronica Strong-Boag's subsequent intervention was aimed at complicating the depiction of maternal feminists like Nellie McClung, who, she maintained, made claims strategically on the basis of maternal responsibility and/or equity against patriarchal privileges.[55]

The scholarly debate that ensued over the racial politics of first wave feminists focused primarily on this same population of Anglo-Celtic, Protestant, middle-class activists and their maternalism. These were the women, after all, who referred to themselves frequently as "mothers of the race." Having already referred to this discussion earlier in the chapter, I will raise just a couple of extra points here in light of subsequent published work. First, not only were the racial beliefs of these first wave feminists complex and varied, as Janice Fiamengo has argued, but so too was their maternalism, as other recent scholarship has demonstrated.[56] And thus, there is the well-documented example from the First World War period of pacifist and anti-imperialist Marion Francis Beynon appealing to women as mothers to protest against the imposition of military conscription, while Nellie McClung, who supported the war and was pro-imperialist, called on women in their capacity as mothers to do the opposite. Second, without denying the existence and persistence of such diversity, the maternal feminism formulated and practised by many Anglo-Celtic, Protestant, middle-class women often reaffirmed, as Amanda Glasbeek has claimed, "the authority of some women and the subordination of others" while further entrenching hierarchical race and class relations.[57] Third, historians need to be more consistent and exact in naming most of these activists and their politics liberal feminist as distinct from other expressions of maternalism. And finally, consideration needs to be given to the provocative point made by Margaret Jacobs with regard to maternalism and Indigenous peoples in the American context, which has potential applicability for Canada. Jacobs has noted that a core principle among many white maternalist feminists that mothers should be able to care for their children at home was not extended to American Indian women; instead many white women activists publicly promoted for the removal of Indigenous women's children to residential schools.[58] Canadian scholars have yet to adequately address what was advocated or not in this context. Even the "purposeful overlooking" which seems to have occurred among many white feminists regarding the plight of Indigenous women as mothers and Indigenous peoples more generally requires additional explanation.

Further interrogation and greater precision is also needed with regard to understanding the beliefs and practices of francophone Catholic women both inside and outside of Quebec. Much of the existing historiography focuses on the period after 1890 and almost exclusively on francophone Quebecois. Historians Yolande Pinard and Karine Hébert have examined the origins of francophone Catholic women's organizing in the wake of a papal call to social action in the 1890s. And both scholars point to the centrality of maternalist beliefs in the involvement of female Quebecois in the Montreal Local Council of Women (MLCW) and later in the separate umbrella organization, the FNSJB, formed in 1907.[59] Elizabeth Kirkland has posited that the anglophone

Protestant and Jewish women in MLCW and the francophone Catholic women in FNSJB, most of whom were middle-class or middle-upper-class, continued to work closely due to shared concerns over maternal and child mortality, moral reform, and even alcohol regulation.[60] They were able to bridge ethnic, linguistic, and religious differences due to shared class interests and liberal politics.[61] Yet there were clearly sources of tension as English Canadian nationalism among anglophone feminists became even more closely intertwined with British imperial aspirations in the early twentieth century and portrayed French Canadian nationalism in negative terms. Moreover, as in other jurisdictions under the Civil Code, improvements to women's legal status took precedence for francophone activists over the attainment of suffrage.[62] What were the exact points of convergence and divergence between francophone Catholic feminists and other populations in Quebec? How do we conceptualize the feminist aspirations of an ethnic and linguistic minority which continued to live with the consequences of British colonization but were of European origin? And what were their racial beliefs?

Feminist mobilization did not just involve particular populations of middle-class women though, as a number of Canadian historians have repeatedly argued. Indeed, considerable attention has been given to the involvement of working-class women in labour and community activism, with scholars examining how changing patterns of wage employment, the (non)involvement of women in the labour movement, and the economic status of working-class families garnered ongoing discussion and agitation over the course of the first wave. Christina Burr's research on female employment in the late nineteenth century explored some of the ways that working women battled against low wages and poor working conditions, including collective action through the union, the Knights of Labor (KoL), in the 1880s and 1890s.[63] However, as Linda Kealey's important national study covering the period from 1890 to 1920 has demonstrated, working women rarely had recourse to union organization due to ongoing resistance from the male-dominated labour movement and instead sought collective redress mainly through strikes.[64] Kealey's study reveals how working-class women attempted to oppose the inequities of industrial capitalism and on occasion inequities within the labour movement. Although the gender and class interests of labouring women in other industrialized countries received consistent support from middle-class feminists through organizations such as the Women's Trade Union League in the United States, these kinds of allegiances were far more sporadic in the Canadian context.[65] Scholarship on immigrant working women, most of whom were from continental Europe, shows a record of extensive intra-ethnic cooperation, although tensions persisted with relation to Jewish activists because of anti-Semitism.[66]

Working-class women also agitated as wives and as mothers. They organized in order to shore up the economic interests of the working class broadly and of their families individually, while at the same time legitimating a public role for themselves. Feminist historians have observed, for example, working-class women's participation in campaigns to promote the union label, to protest higher consumer prices, and to voice their approval for female suffrage.[67] Moreover, in numerous cases these endeavours simultaneously affirmed their socialist or, later in the interwar period, communist politics. As Joan Sangster has maintained, it represented a form of "militant mothering."[68] Involvement in union auxiliaries from early in the twentieth century onward represented yet another site for education and political action among working-class women.[69] In an examination of the Ladies Auxiliary of the Order of Sleeping Car Porters (OSCP) formed in the 1920s, Sarah-Jane Mathieu has argued convincingly that the auxiliary acted as a crucial organizational forum for Black women in urban centres across the country to advocate for their working-class husbands and to spearhead consumer and anti-racism efforts in their communities.[70]

Mathieu's study is of additional significance for addressing the still much understudied consequences of racism and other factors in shaping racialized women's activism. The de facto and de jure forms of segregation which became embedded in "Jim Crow" Canada at the turn of the twentieth century obviously delimited but did not eliminate the ability of Black and other racialized women to organize or advocate. Sylvia Hamilton and Dionne Brand have noted how involvement in African Canadian churches in the provinces of Nova Scotia and Ontario served as a strong foundation from which Black women pursued concerns related to temperance, education, and access to social services.[71] As Peggy Bristow has contended, although Black women lacked a national organization until after the Second World War, they were deeply enmeshed in their local communities. Her own study of the Windsor, Ontario, Hour-A-Day Study Club, which originated in the 1930s, has illustrated that its members were interested in issues related to not only child development but also citizen engagement in local government and the promotion of race pride.[72]

The ongoing pursuit of a white settler formation, which resulted in the selective and increasingly restrictive entry of immigrants from countries in Asia at the turn of the twentieth century, had specific implications for other groups of racialized women. Most importantly, diasporic communities were formed among Chinese, Japanese, and Indian immigrants, where women constituted a small minority. Immigration regulations varied somewhat between different Asian countries, but all restricted female migration in one way or another.[73] The dual impact of relatively small numbers and pervasive anti-Asian sentiments by Euro-Canadians thus created formidable challenges for female activism. However, emerging scholarship on Chinese women on the west coast indicates a shift at the dawn of the twentieth century from their being exclusively the objects of intervention by female missionaries to their participating in organizational efforts, which in time included concerns about women's equality.[74] Indeed, the Chinese Empire Ladies' Reform Association (CELRA) created in Victoria in the spring of 1903 has been credited as the first feminist group organized by and for Chinese women in either Canada or China. Research on Kang Tongbi, who spearheaded the formation of CELRA in Victoria and soon after in Vancouver, has shown that she was a vocal proponent of the emancipation of Chinese women.[75] Work on South Asian immigrant women has demonstrated a different pattern altogether. According to Enakshi Dua, Indian women became the topic of political mobilization but primarily as a "masculinist and racialized project" by Indian men, who portrayed them solely as mothers of racialized ethnic communities.[76]

And finally, the continued process of white settler formation, uneven and often regionally specific, had other consequences for Indigenous women, especially with regard to their ability to respond to and at times protest against the complex forces of colonialism. The historical scholarship that does exist has focused primarily on Kanyen'kehà:ka (Mohawk) women from southern Ontario. Feminist historians have been particularly interested in the written work and stage performances of E. Pauline Johnson, who was also known as Tekahionwake. Carole Gerson and Veronica Strong-Boag have observed that Johnson, who was of mixed Haudenosaunee-English ancestry, portrayed Indigenous women "as not only the equals of white women, but at times their superiors."[77] Other scholars have delved into the rich associational life among women which developed on the Six Nations Reserve, the product of extended contact with Euro-Canadians, some degree of acculturation, and relative economic prosperity.[78] One short-lived but noteworthy group was the Indian Moral Association (IMA), formed in 1907. And according to Alison Norman, although Indigenous women were often portrayed during this period as immoral, the IMA saw white society as a moral threat to women in the Six Nations community.[79]

Unfortunately, little research has yet been produced on Indigenous women's questioning of patriarchal and colonial practices from other nations. It is possible to surmise that as the settlement frontier moved west and further north in the latter decades of the nineteenth century and into the twentieth century, there were other incidents of "uppity women" on the "cusp of contact" referred to earlier in the chapter. Diane Payment has written about the actions of Métis women during and after the uprising of 1885, which offers a prominent example of collective female decision-making in the midst of an armed conflict and subsequent efforts aimed at financial redress and community rebuilding.[80] One wonders about other, less dramatic instances that nonetheless involved initiatives by women to advocate on behalf of themselves and their families. And while objections to the removal of children to residential schools at various times and in various locations have been well documented, historians might consider whether or how these actions represented a broader pattern of attempted decolonization and feminist activism.

Transnational Collaborations and Cross-Currents

This next section examines the impact of transnational collaborations and cross-currents as feminist internationalism greatly intensified in the latter decades of the nineteenth century and into the twentieth century. As already established earlier in the chapter, overlapping international and imperial ties were quite significant in the initial genesis of feminist organizing in British North America and then the new dominion of Canada. But what do we know about later developments? What patterns of engagement and forms of influence have been identified? How do they fit or not with those identified in the rapidly expanding international literature on formal organizational initiatives and informal connections?

While the Canadian historiography on transnational feminist connections is as yet relatively modest, the broad outlines of cross-border links have begun to emerge, with scholars able to build upon the extensive histories that have already been produced on international cooperation and conflict.[81] More specifically, it is possible to discern a number of "axes of influence" which evolved over time. The most significant remained Canadian involvement in transatlantic networks of mostly European and North American feminists who mobilized around issues of mutual interest, including temperance, suffrage, and labour rights. Many of these connections became both more extensive and more formal from the later decades of the nineteenth century with the creation of an ever-widening array of international women's organizations, most of whom had headquarters in Europe. British and American feminists continued to dominate, however, not only in number but also in shaping priorities and practices. As a result, Canadian activists and their endeavours were often accorded only a minor status. There were important exceptions, of course, with feminists from Canada initiating transnational connections and innovations as well as assuming leadership roles in key organizations and campaigns. For example, Lorna McLean has observed that the academic and staunch pacifist Julia Grace Wales, who attended the Women's Peace Conference held at The Hague in 1915, authored a key resolution which advocated the concept of continuous mediation without armistice.[82]

Within these transatlantic networks, British imperial concerns and allegiances continued to loom large as well. As Adele Perry has pointed out, particularly in the case of anglophone Protestant women, they "organized explicitly for and less often against British imperialism."[83] Many saw their efforts to secure certain civil rights and bring about what they considered positive social change in Canada as part of the larger "civilizing project" of imperialism. Such beliefs gained further expression with the creation of groups such as the Imperial Order Daughters of the Empire (IODE) in 1902, which went on to become the largest women's organization in the country by the time of the First World War.[84] Travel to and from the imperial metropole of London, which became ever more frequent during this time period, also greatly enhanced social and political connections.[85] Albeit less frequently, transatlantic links could at times be drawn upon to critique the ongoing consequences of imperialism and colonialism as occurred, for instance, in the 1920s over the imposition of an elected band council on the Six Nations Reserve by the Canadian federal government. This decision, which stripped Kanyen'kehà:ka women of the centuries-long tradition of choosing chiefs and participating in community decision-making as equal partners, was protested by at least some members of the reserve in conjunction with female members of the London-based British and Foreign Anti-Slavery Society and the Aborigines' Protection Society. And in turn a campaign was launched to mobilize members of various international women's organizations.[86]

Transpacific networks developed later, becoming identifiable in the final decades of the nineteenth century. Here too, international and imperial interests overlapped, as the earliest links appear to have been with feminists from the settler dominions of Australia and New Zealand. As Lisa Chilton's insightful study of the ongoing campaign to promote female British emigration to Canada and Australia between the 1880s and 1920s illustrates, this solidified connections between women reformers in these countries.[87] Although the role of Australian and New Zealand feminists has thus far been the primary focus in the scholarly literature, Canadian women also proved amenable to the initiative of their Antipodean peers to form the British Dominion Women's Suffrage Union (BDWSU) in 1914, which was intended to facilitate assistance from women in dominions with suffrage to those who were not.[88]

There were other kinds of transpacific contacts which developed outside of direct British imperial influences. Building upon relationships forged by Protestant missionaries, there is evidence of the Canadian YWCA sending a succession of young Anglo-Celtic women to work in Japan, as well as funding the provision of services and accommodation.[89] As a number of scholars have pointed out, however, many of the white, Western women who embarked on such careers in Asia often expressed in both word and deed a form of cultural imperialism.[90] Growing interest in creating improved cross-cultural understanding among women during the interwar period also led some Canadians to be part of the inauguration of the Pan-Pacific Women's Association (PPWA) in 1928. According to the Australian historian Fiona Paisley, who has written extensively on the PPWA, it was meant to represent a less "xenophobic" form of internationalism and facilitate closer East/West dialogue between feminists.[91] The increasing prominence of Canadian members within the organization in the 1930s was signalled with the election of Mary Bollert as its president and Vancouver as the site of its conference in 1937. Paisley makes the perceptive observation that Canadian conference organizers faced the glaring contradiction of "welcoming" women from countries throughout Asia at the same time as its own federal government retained immigration restrictions against these same populations.[92]

A prominent feature of transnational engagement during the first wave entailed participation in one of the explicitly defined international feminist organizations which originated from the 1880s onward. Among each of the largest international women's organizations prior to the Second World War – the International Council of Women (ICW), the International Alliance of Women (IAW), and the Women's International League for Peace and Freedom (WILPF) – Canada was one of its earliest national affiliates. Early affiliation in these primarily liberal feminist ventures signalled the degree to which select Canadian feminists and their organizations were deeply enmeshed in the networks of activist women who gave rise to these international groups and the perceived advantages that formal cross-border links could provide in terms of both inspirational ideas and practical support. Yet it did not necessarily translate into sustained engagement or influence in these organizations.

In many respects Canadian participation in the ICW was the most extensive, with representatives serving regularly in leadership positions as members of the executive and as conveners on standing committees well into the interwar period. The prominence of Canadians in the ICW signalled recognition of the organizational expertise they had acquired at a national and international level, as well as the continued close allegiance between the NCWC and the ICW's long-term president, Lady Aberdeen.[93] Involvement with the IAW was far more short-term and modest. When this organization's principal issue was the attainment of female suffrage, a number of well-known suffragists such as Augusta Stowe-Gullen and Flora MacDonald Denison were enthusiastic supporters and the Canadian Suffrage Association was a national affiliate. However, after some women attained the federal franchise in 1918 (as continued to be the case for some men) and the IAW broadened its agenda to more controversial topics such as birth control and women's employment rights in the 1920s, Canadian participation effectively lapsed.[94]

The situation which developed with WILPF was different yet again. While ICW and IAW members were primarily liberal feminists, most WILPF members in Canada and elsewhere identified as socialist or social democratic.[95] It also attracted a more diverse array of women in Canada. The largest and most active chapters were in larger cities such as Toronto, Winnipeg, and Vancouver, with members who were mostly middle-class and university educated, but working-class groups and farm women's organizations were also affiliated.[96] Furthermore, the organization's stated goals of promoting peace and intercultural dialogue resulted in one of the few instances we know about that involved Anglo-Celtic women working alongside rather than on behalf of racialized women, as occurred with the creation of an International Club in Vancouver.[97] Yet because WILPF members in Canada were less financially prosperous than their peers who were involved in ICW or IAW, their contributions to WILPF at the international level, which included conference attendance and filling positions on the executive board, were sporadic at best.

The extent to which francophone women in general and francophone Quebec women more specifically participated in these kinds of formal group initiatives remains unclear. Micheline Dumont and Louise Toupin have contended that francophone women in Quebec focused primarily on maintaining women's groups in the province, only shifting their attention elsewhere after attaining the vote in 1940. Certainly there is no indication of active participation in any of the large non-denominational international feminist organizations operating in the early twentieth century. Yolande Cohen has recently suggested, however, that Quebec francophone groups such as the Fédération Nationale Saint-Jean-Baptiste (FNSJB) were influenced by British and American networks and to some degree by the women's movement in France. Unfortunately, Cohen provides little in the way of evidence to back up these claims.[98] There is some suggestion of Quebec feminist involvement in the Union international des Ligues feminists catholiques (UILFC), first formed in 1910, with Anne-Marie Sicotte recounting at length Marie Gérin-Lajoie's attendance at this organization's conference in Rome in the spring of 1922.[99] However, Sicotte does not address the nature of Quebec feminist participation prior to or after this conference.

Less formal alliances are more difficult for feminist historians to trace, but they are no less important, especially in the case of working-class and rural women for whom "material resources were a crucial determinant of, and often an inhibition to, [their] political work."[100] Left-wing feminists in Canada, many of whom were working-class and immigrant, portrayed their struggle from the late nineteenth century onward as one which was against class exploitation and for female emancipation; just as importantly, they saw this struggle from the outset as international in scope. While the "woman question" remained a point of contention on the Canadian Left, most followed the directives of the Socialist International and later the Communist International, which at least in principle but not always in practice promoted women's equal rights.[101] Joan Sangster has well illustrated how advice, debate, and news circulated through newspapers, personal letters, and forms of "political tourism" among Canadian communist women from the 1920s to the 1940s expressly promoted internationalist sentiment.[102]

Border crossings in either their physical or intellectual form had particular and varied significance for successive generations of immigrants, as Marlene Epp and Franca Iacovetta so eloquently convey elsewhere in this volume. And in turn, these experiences shaped immigrant interest and engagement in women's issues and other political causes in Canada. Icelandic and Finnish immigrants, for example, brought with them to Canada knowledge of, if not experience in, widely supported women's movements in their home countries. Varpu Lindström-Best has maintained that Finnish women were also part of a North American activist network which was explicitly feminist.[103] With regard to Ukrainian women, many of whom were from peasant backgrounds, involvement in immigrant ethnic organizations such as the Women's Section of the Ukrainian Farmer Labour Temple Association (UFLTA) allowed them to gain literacy skills and a political education while pursuing local, national, and international concerns.[104] And for women such as Catherine Hay and the small number of her Jamaican contemporaries, the border controls were more formidable, their stay in Canada deemed contingent and temporary, and their treatment as immigrants overtly discriminatory. Nonetheless, as the documents discussed at the outset of this chapter illustrate, Hay was not lacking in the ability to formulate feminist arguments or challenge feminist practices.

Future Directions

In addition to the points already raised in this chapter, two further suggestions will be made by way of conclusion. First, in a region of North America with such a vast geography, uneven colonial and postcolonial development, and multifaceted populations of Indigenous peoples and settlers, the task of adequately capturing the nuances of historical feminisms in Canada will continue to be formidable. However, women's and gender historians will benefit from taking colonial/national specificity into account while at the same time pursuing larger interpretive questions related to imperialism, colonialism, nationalism, and transnationalism. Second, just as importantly, more careful analysis is required of the points of convergence and divergence with regard to gender, race, ethnicity, class, religion, and colonial status within the first wave in the transformation from colonies to nation(s). And on a related point, further interrogation is needed about when and how feminists were able to work across one or more categories of social difference and, just as importantly, when they were not.

NOTES

1 Nancy Forestell with Maureen Moynagh, eds, *Documenting First Wave Feminisms: Canada – National and Transnational Contexts*, vol. 2 (Toronto: University of Toronto Press, 2013), 44.

2 Diana Pedersen's scholarship on the YWCA in Canada, completed several decades ago, continues to offer the most comprehensive treatment of this organization. See, for example, Diana Pedersen, "Providing a Woman's Conscience: The YWCA, Female Evangelicalism, and the Girl in the City, 1870–1930," in Wendy Mitchinson et al., *Canadian Women: A Reader* (Toronto: Harcourt Brace, 1996), 194–211; Diana Pedersen, "'Keeping Our Good Girls Good': The YWCA and the 'Girl Problem,' 1870–1930," *Canadian Woman Studies* 7, 4 (Winter 1986): 20–4.

3 Marilyn Lake, "Nationalist Historiography, Feminist Scholarship, and the Promise and Problems of New Transnational Histories: The Australian Case," *Journal of Women's History* 19, 1 (Spring 2007): 180.

4 Lori Ginsberg uses the term "untidy origins" to characterize the origins of feminism in the United States, and it is also arguably applicable to the case of Canada. See Lori D. Ginsberg, *Untidy Origins: A Story of Woman's Rights in Antebellum New York* (Chapel Hill: University of North Carolina Press, 2005).

5 Karen Offen, "Introduction," in *Globalizing Feminisms: 1789–1945: Rewriting Histories*, ed. Karen Offen (New York: Routledge, 2010), xxxi.

6 Maureen Moynagh and Nancy Forestell, "Introduction," in *Documenting First Wave Feminisms: Transnational Collaborations and Cross-Currents*, vol. 1 (Toronto: University of Toronto Press, 2012), xxiv.

7 Nancy Hewitt, "Introduction," in *No Permanent Waves: Recasting Histories of US Feminism*, ed. Nancy Hewitt (New Brunswick, NJ: Rutgers University Press, 2010), 4. See also Kathleen Laughlin et al., "Is it Time to Jump Ship? Historians Rethink the Waves Metaphor," *Feminist Formations* 22, 1 (Spring 2010): 76–135.

8 Hewitt, "Introduction," 5.

9 See Dorothy Sue Cobble, *The Other Women's Movement: Workplace Justice and Social Rights in Modern America* (Princeton, NJ: Princeton University Press,

2005); Joan Sangster, *Transforming Labour: Women and Work in Post-War Canada* (Toronto: University of Toronto Press, 2010).

10 Nancy Hewitt, "Feminist Frequencies: Regenerating the Wave Metaphor," *Feminist Studies* 38, 3 (Fall 2012): 658–80.

11 Annalise Orelick, among others, has made this argument. See Annalise Orelick, *Rethinking American Women's Activism* (New York: Routledge, 2014). While the struggle to achieve the female franchise in Canada has not been as intensively interrogated as it has in other national contexts, it has long served as the unofficial bookends for the first wave. The most extensive coverage of female suffrage remains Catherine Cleverdon, *The Woman Suffrage Movement in Canada* (1950; rprt. Toronto: University of Toronto Press, 1974).

12 See Joan Sangster, *"Never Done*: Feminists Reinterpret Their Own History," in this collection.

13 See, for example, Veronica Strong-Boag, *The Parliament of Women: The National Council of Women of Canada, 1839–1929* (Ottawa: National Museums of Canada, 1977); Wendy Mitchinson, "The Woman's Christian Temperance Union: A Study in Organization," *International Journal of Women's Studies* 4, 2 (1981): 143–56; Marie Lavigne, Yolande Pinard, and Jennifer Stoddart, "The Fédération Nationale Saint-Jean-Baptiste and the Women's Movement in Quebec," in *A Not Unreasonable Claim: Women and Reform in Canada, 1880s–1920s*, ed. Linda Kealey (Toronto: Women's Press, 1979), 71–88.

14 Carol Lee Bacchi, *Liberation Deferred? The Ideas of English-Canadian Suffragists, 1877–1918* (Toronto: University of Toronto Press, 1983); Karen Van Dieren, "The Response of the WMS to the Immigration of Asian Women 1888–1942," in *Not Just Pin Money*, ed. Barbara K. Latham and Roberta J. Padro (Victoria: Comuson College, 1984), 79–97; Barbara Roberts, "'A Work of Empire': Canadian Reformers and British Female Emigration," in Kealey, *A Not Unreasonable Claim*, 185–202.

15 Linda Kealey and Joan Sangster, eds, *Beyond the Vote: Canadian Women and Politics* (Toronto: University of Toronto Press, 1989).

16 See Bacchi, *Liberation Deferred*; Mariana Valverde, "'When the Mother of the Race Is Free': Race, Reproduction, and Sexuality in First-Wave Feminism," in *Gender Conflicts: New Essays in Women's History*, ed. Franca Iacovetta and Mariana Valverde (Toronto: University of Toronto Press, 1992), 3–26.

17 Among those who refuted Valverde's contention, see Sharon Anne Cook, *"Through Sunshine and Shadow": The Woman's Christian Temperance Union, Evangelicalism, and Reform in Ontario, 1874–1930* (Montreal: McGill-Queen's University Press, 1995); and Randi Warne, *Literature as Pulpit: The Christian Social Activism of Nellie McClung* (Waterloo: Wilfrid Laurier University Press, 1993).

18 Janice Fiamengo, "A Legacy of Ambivalence: Response to Nellie McClung," in *Rethinking Canada: The Promise of Women's History*, 4th ed., ed. Veronica Strong-Boag, Mona Gleason, and Adele Perry (Toronto: Oxford University Press, 2002), 154.

19 Franca Iacovetta and Mariana Valverde, "Introduction," in Iacovetta and Valverde, *Gender Conflicts*, xiv.

20 Janice Fiamengo, *The Woman's Page: Journalism and Rhetoric in Early Canada* (Toronto: University of Toronto Press, 2008). All of the authors examined by Fiamengo are anglophone white women. See also Jennifer Henderson, *Settler Feminism and Race Making in Canada* (Toronto: University of Toronto Press, 2003).

21 Valverde, "When the Mother of the Race Is Free," 20.

22 Franca Iacovetta, among others, has made this contention. See Franca Iacovetta, "Gendering Trans/National Historiographies: Feminists Rewriting Canadian History," *Journal of Women's History* 19, 1 (2007): 211.

23 One of the very few exceptions is Andrée Levesque's examination of Eva Circe-Côté. See Andrée Levesque, "Social Relations in Quebec from 1900 to 1939 as Seen through the Eyes of a Woman of Letters: Eva Circe-Côté," *Zeitschrift für Kanada-Studien* 25, 2 (2005): 36–46. On the relative absence of academic discussions about the historical dimensions of race and racialization in Quebec, see Corrie Scott, "How French Canadians Became White Folks, or Doing Things with Race in Quebec," *Ethnic and Racial Studies* 39, 7 (June 2016): 1280–98.

24 Enakshi Dua, "Canadian Anti-Racist Feminism: Scratching the Surface of Racism," in *Scratching the Surface: Canadian Anti-Racist Feminist Thought*, ed. Enakshi Dua and Angela Robertson (Toronto: Women's Press, 1999), 7–31.

25 See, for example, Micheline Dumont and Louise Toupin, eds, *La pensée féministe au Québec: Anthologie; 1900–1985* (Montreal: Remue-ménage, 2003); Margaret Hobbs and Susan Wurtele, "The Woman's Pages of the *Western Producer, 1925–1939*: Violet McNaughton and Interwar Feminism in Canada," *Women and Social Movements in the US* 13, 2 (Sept. 2010). And see also Forestell with Moynagh, *Documenting First Wave Feminisms*, vols. 1 and 2.

26 Anne-Marie Sicotte, *Marie Gérin-Lajoie: Conquérante de la Liberté* (Montreal: Remue-ménage, 2005); Peter Campbell, *Rose Henderson: A Woman for the People* (Montreal: McGill-Queen's University Press, 2010); Veronica Strong-Boag, *Liberal Hearts and Coronets: The Lives and Times of Ishbel Majoribanks Gordon and John Campbell Gordon, the Aberdeens* (Toronto: University of Toronto Press, 2015).

27 Amanda Glasbeek, *Feminized Justice: Toronto Women's Court, 1913–1934* (Vancouver: UBC Press, 2009); Chris Clarkson, *Political Visions and Family Regulation in British Columbia, 1862–1940* (Vancouver: UBC Press, 2007);

Yolande Cohen, *Femmes Philanthropes: Catholiques, protestantes, et juives dans les organisations caritatives au Québec* (Montreal: Les Presses de l'Université du Québec, 2010).

28 See, for example, Linda Ambrose, *A Great Rural Sisterhood: Madge Robertson Watt and the ACWW* (Toronto: University of Toronto Press, 2015); Lorna McLean, "'The Necessity of Going': Julia Grace Wales' Transnational Life as Peace Activist and a Scholar," in *Feminist History: New Essays on Women, Gender, Work, and Nation*, ed. Catherine Carstairs and Nancy Janovicek (Vancouver: UBC Press, 2013), 77–95. For a historiographical discussion of the benefits of such an approach for first wave feminisms in Canada, see Nancy Forestell, "Mrs Canada Goes Global," *Atlantis* 30, 1 (2005): 7–20.

29 This shift in interpretation can be seen in editions of *Canadian Women: A History*. See Alison Prentice et al., *Canadian Women: A History*, 1st ed. (Toronto: Harcourt Brace, 1988), 174–5; Gail Cuthbert Brandt et al., *Canadian Women: A History*, 3rd ed. (Toronto: Nelson, 2011), 225–6.

30 See Nancy Hewitt, "Origin Stories: Remapping First Wave Feminism," in *Sisterhood and Slavery: Transatlantic Antislavery and Women's Rights*, Proceedings of the Third Annual Gilder Lehrman Center International Conference at Yale University, 25–8 October 2001; http://www.yale.edu/glc/conference/hewitt.pdf; see also Ginsberg, *Untidy Origins*.

31 This point is meant as a general observation made in both works, as neither focus at length on historical feminisms. See Cecilia Morgan, *Public Men and Virtuous Women: The Gendered Languages of Religion and Politics in Upper Canada, 1791–1850* (Toronto: University of Toronto Press, 1996); Adele Perry, *On the Edge of Empire: Gender, Race, and the Making of British Columbia, 1849–1971* (Toronto: University of Toronto Press, 2001).

32 See, for example, Patricia Grimshaw, "Settler Anxieties, Indigenous Peoples, and Women's Suffrage in the Colonies of Australia, New Zealand, and Hawai'i, 1888–1902," *Pacific History Review* 69, 4 (2000): 553–73.

33 Patricia Grimshaw, "Reading the Silences: Suffrage Activists and Race in Nineteenth-Century Settler Societies," in *Women's Rights and Human Rights: International Historical Perspectives*, ed. Patricia Grimshaw, Katie Holmes, and Marilyn Lake (London: Palgrave Macmillan, 2001), 33.

34 Andrea Smith, "Feminism without Apology," in *Unsettling Ourselves: Reflections and Resources for Deconstructing Colonial Mentality*, ed. Unsettling Minnesota Collective (2009), 158, https://unsettlingminnesota.files.wordpress.com/2009/11/um_sourcebook_jan10_revision.pdf.

35 Jean Barman, "Indigenous Women and Feminism on the Cusp of Contact," in *Indigenous Women and Feminism: Politics, Activism, Culture*, ed. Cheryl Zuzack et al. (Vancouver: UBC Press, 2010), 92–108.

36 Barman, "Indigenous Women," 93 and 99–100.
37 Celia Haig-Brown, "Seeking Honest Justice in a Land of Strangers: Nahne-bahwequa's Struggle for Land," *Journal of Canadian Studies* 36, 4 (2001/2): 143–70.
38 Haig-Brown, for example, depicts her as a "hero." "Seeking Honest Justice," 160. Although I did not use such laudatory language, I too think in retrospect that I treated Nahnebahwequa as exceptional. See Forestell with Moynagh, *Documenting First Wave Feminisms*, vol. 2.
39 Sally Roesch Wagner, "The Indigenous Roots of United States Feminism," in *Feminist Politics, Activism, and Vision: Local and Global Challenges*, ed. Lucianna Ricciutelli, Angela Miles, and Margaret McFadden (Toronto: Inanna Publications, 2004), 267–84; see also Gail Landsman, "The 'Other' as Political Symbol: Images of Indians in the Woman Suffrage Movement," *Ethnohistory* 39, 3 (Summer 1992): 247–84.
40 See Nancy Hewitt, "From Seneca Falls to Suffrage? Reimagining a 'Master' Narrative in US Women's History," in Hewitt, *No Permanent Waves*, 15–38.
41 This term is taken from Clare Midgely. See Clare Midgely, *Women against Slavery: The British Campaigns, 1780–1870* (New York: Routledge, 1992), 126–7; see also Bonnie Anderson, *Joyous Greetings: The First International Women's Movement, 1830–1860* (New York: Oxford University Press, 2000).
42 Nancy Hewitt has documented that female and male abolitionists in the United States regularly corresponded with and visited abolitionists in Upper Canada. See Hewitt, "Origin Stories."
43 Shirley J. Yee, "Gender Ideology and Black Women as Community Builders in Ontario, 1850–1870," *Canadian Historical Review* 75, 1 (March 1994): 53–73; and Peggy Bristow, "'Whatever You Raise in the Ground You Can Sell It in Chatham,' 1850–1865," in *"We're Rooted Here and They Can't Pull Us Up": Essays in African Canadian Women's History*, ed. Peggy Bristow (Toronto: University of Toronto Press, 1994), 69–142.
44 Allen Stouffer, conference paper cited in Brandt et al., *Canadian Women*.
45 I am referring here to criticism by Mary Ann Shadd Cary towards the TLARDF. See Mary Ann Shadd Cary, "Lectures" (1855), in *Documenting First Wave Feminisms*, vol. 2, 77–9.
46 Karen Leroux, "Making a Claim on the Public Sphere: Toronto Women's Anti-Slavery Activism, 1851–1854" (MA thesis, University of British Columbia, 1996), 79.
47 Bristow, "Whatever You Raise in the Ground," 122.
48 Heather Murray, "Great Works and Good Works: The Toronto Women's Literary Club, 1877–1883," in Strong-Boag, Gleason, and Perry, *Rethinking Canada*, 103–20.

49 Lori Chambers has argued that in the case of Canada West the initial legislation of 1859 "was more concerned with making men act in a responsible manner than with expanding 'woman's rights.'" At the same time, it was legislation which was sought and welcomed by women. See Lori Chambers, *Married Women and Property Law in Victorian Ontario* (Toronto: Osgoode Society for Canadian Legal History, 1997), 90–1.

50 ˙ Peter Baskerville, *A Silent Revolution? Gender and Wealth in English Canada, 1860–1930* (Montreal: McGill-Queen's University Press, 2008), 14.

51 For the most recent discussion of female efforts to systematize benevolence, see Carmen Nielson, *Private Women and the Public Good: Charity and State Formation in Hamilton, 1846–1893* (Vancouver: UBC Press, 2014).

52 Orelick, *Rethinking American Women's Activism*, 4.

53 See Bacchi, *Liberation Deferred.*

54 On the decline of equal rights feminism, see Linda Kealey, "Introduction," in Kealey, *A Not Unreasonable Claim*, 9. Among those who portrayed middle-class maternal feminists as conservative, see Wayne Roberts, "'Rocking the Cradle for the World': The New Woman and Maternal Feminism, 1877–1914," in Kealey, *A Not Unreasonable Claim*, 15–45.

55 Veronica Strong-Boag, "'Ever a Crusader': Nellie McClung, First-Wave Feminist," in *Rethinking Canada: The Promise of Women's History*, 2nd ed., ed. Veronica Strong-Boag and Anita Clair Fellman (Toronto: Copp, Clark Pitman, 1991), 308–21.

56 Janice Fiamengo, "Rediscovering Our Foremothers Again: The Racial Ideas of Canada's Early Feminists, 1885–1945," *Essays in Canadian Writing* 75 (Winter 2002): 85–118. On varied meanings of maternalism, see Ann Taylor Allen, *Feminism and Motherhood in Western Europe, 1890–1970: The Maternal Dilemma* (London: Palgrave Macmillan, 2005).

57 Glasbeek, *Feminized Justice*, 18.

58 Margaret Jacobs, "The Great White Mother: Maternalism and American Child Removal in the American West, 1880–1940," in *One Step over the Line: Toward a History of Women in the American West*, ed. Elizabeth Jameson and Sheila McManus (Edmonton: University of Alberta Press, 2008), 191–214.

59 Yolande Pinard, "Les débuts du movement des femmes à Montréal, 1893–1902," in *Travailleuses et féminists: Les femmes dans la société québecoise*, ed. Marie Lavigne and Yolande Pinard (Montreal: Boréal, 1983), 177–98; Karine Hébert, "A Maternalist Organization in Quebec: The Fédération Nationale Saint-Jean-Baptiste and the Struggle for Women's Suffrage," in *Quebec Since 1800: Selected Readings*, ed. Michael Behiels (Toronto: Irwin, 2002), 461–91.

60 Elizabeth Kirkland, "Mothering Citizens: Elite Women in Montreal, 1890–1914" (PhD diss., McGill University, 2011), 130–7.

61 Kirkland, "Mothering Citizens," 155. The point regarding shared liberal politics is my observation.

62 Andrée Levesque, "Social Relations," 45.

63 Christina Burr, *Spreading the Light: Work and Labour Reform in Late-Nineteenth-Century Toronto* (Toronto: University of Toronto Press, 1999).

64 Linda Kealey, *Enlisting Women for the Cause: Women, Labour, and the Left in Canada, 1890–1920* (Toronto: University of Toronto Press, 1998).

65 Ruth Frager, "Class and Ethnic Barriers to Feminist Perspectives in Toronto's Jewish Labour Movement, 1919–1939," *Studies in Political Economy* 30 (Autumn 1989): 153.

66 Frager, "Class and Ethnic Barriers," 153.

67 See Kealey, *Enlisting Women for the Cause*; for a recent piece on involvement in a campaign over milk pricing, see Julie Guard, "The Politics of Milk: Canadian Housewives Organize in the 1930s," in *Edible Histories, Cultural Politics: Towards a Canadian Food History*, ed. Franca Iacovetta, Valerie J. Korinek, and Marlene Epp (Toronto: University of Toronto Press, 2012), 271–85.

68 Joan Sangster, *Dreams of Equality: Women on the Canadian Left, 1920–1950* (Toronto: McClelland and Stewart, 1989).

69 See, for example, Sylvie Murray, "Quand les ménagères se font militantes: La Ligue auxiliaire de l'Association internationale des machinistes, 1905–1980," *Labour / Le Travail* 29, 1 (Spring 1992): 157–86.

70 Sarah-Jane Mathieu, *North of the Color Line: Migration and Black Resistance in Canada, 1870–1955* (Chapel Hill: University of North Carolina Press, 2010), 145–62.

71 Sylvia Hamilton, "The Women at the Well: African Baptist Women Organize," in *And Still We Rise: Feminist Political Mobilizing in Contemporary Canada*, ed. Linda Carty (Toronto: Women's Press, 1993), 173–88; Dionne Brand, *No Burden to Carry: Narratives of Black Working Women in Ontario, 1920s–1950s* (Toronto: Women's Press, 1991).

72 Peggy Bristow, "The Hour-A-Day Study Club," in Carty, *And Still We Rise*, 145–72.

73 Enakshi Dua, "The Hindu Woman's Question: Canadian Nation-Building and the Social Construction of Gender for South Asian Women," in *Anti-Racist Feminism: Critical Race and Gender Studies*, ed. George Dei and Agnes Calliste (Halifax: Fernwood, 2000), 55–72.

74 The "rescue home" established by the Methodist Women's Missionary Society in Victoria in 1887 was a key part of this work. At first it included only Chinese immigrants but in the 1900s housed Japanese immigrants as well. See, for example, Shelly Ikebuchi, "Marriage, Morals, and Men: Re/defining Victoria's Chinese Rescue Home," *BC Studies* 177 (Spring 2013): 65–84.

75 Jane Leung Larson, "The Kang Tongbi Collection of South Windsor, Connecticut," Paper given at Association of Asian Studies, 4 October 2014, https://drive.google.com/file/d/0By7Ajg4xYgVqUXFwbjlWNk0za0k/view.

76 Enakshi Dua, "Racializing Imperial Canada: Indian Women and the Making of Ethnic Communities," in *Sisters or Strangers? Immigrant, Ethnic, and Racialized Women in Canadian History*, ed. Marlene Epp, Franca Iacovetta, and Frances Swyripa (Toronto: University of Toronto Press, 2004), 83.

77 Carole Gerson and Veronica Strong-Boag, "Championing the Native: E. Pauline Johnson Rejects the Squaw," in *Contact Zones: Aboriginal and Settler Women in Canada's Colonial Past*, ed. Katie Pickles and Myra Rutherdale (Vancouver: UBC Press, 2005), 47; see also Cecilia Morgan, "'A Wigwam to Westminster': Performing Mohawk Identity in Imperial Britain, 1890s–1900s," *Gender and History* 25, 2 (2003): 319–41.

78 See, for example, Cecilia Morgan, "Performing for 'Imperial Eyes': Bernice Loft and Ethel Brant Monture, 1930–1960," in Pickles and Rutherdale, *Contact Zones*, 68–9; see also Alison Norman, "Race, Gender, and Colonialism: Public Life among the Six Nations of Grand River, 1899–1939" (PhD diss., University of Toronto, 2010), 251–90.

79 Norman, "Race, Gender, and Colonialism," 272.

80 Diane Payment, "'*La vie en rose*'? Métis Women at Batoche, 1870–1920," in *Women of the First Nations: Power, Wisdom, and Strength*, ed. Christine Miller and Patricia Chuchryk (Winnipeg: University of Manitoba Press, 1996), 18–37.

81 See, for example, Mrinalini Sinha, Donna Guy, and Angela Woollacott, eds, *Feminisms and Internationalism* (London: Blackwell, 1999); Ann Taylor Allen, Anna Cova, and Jane Purvis, "Introduction: International Feminisms," *Women's History Review* 19, 4 (September 2010): 493–501.

82 McLean, "The Necessity of Going," 77–95.

83 Adele Perry, "Women, Gender, and Empire," in *Canada and the British Empire*, ed. Philip Buckner (Toronto: Oxford University Press, 2008), 230–6.

84 For a more extended discussion of the IODE, see Katie Pickles, *Female Imperialism and National Identity: The Imperial Order Daughters of the Empire* (New York: Manchester University Press, 2002).

85 On travel to Britain, see Cecilia Morgan, *"A Happy Holiday": English Canadians and Transatlantic Tourism, 1870–1930* (Toronto: University of Toronto Press, 2008), 186–9.

86 Forestell with Moynagh, *Documenting First Wave Feminisms*, 2: 182–6.

87 Lisa Chilton, *Agents of Empire: British Female Migration to Canada and Australia* (Toronto: University of Toronto Press, 2007).

88 Angela Woollacott, "Australian Women's Metropolitan Activism: From Suffrage to Imperial Vanguard to Commonwealth Feminism," in *Women's Suffrage in*

the British Empire: Citizenship, Nation, and Race, ed. Ian Christopher Fletcher, Laura E. Nym Mayhall, and Philippa Levine (London: Routledge, 2000), 207–23.

89 See Margaret Prang, *A Heart at Leisure from Itself: Caroline MacDonald in Japan* (Vancouver: UBC Press, 1997).

90 See, for example, Ian Tyrell, *Woman's World, Woman's Empire: The Woman's Christian Temperance Union in International Perspective, 1880–1930* (Chapel Hill: University of North Carolina Press, 1991), 27–30.

91 Fiona Paisley, "Cultivating Modernity: Culture and Internationalism in Australian Feminism's Pacific Age," *Journal of Women's History* 14, 3 (2002): 105–32.

92 Fiona Paisley, *Cultural Internationalism and Race Politics in the Women's Pan-Pacific* (Honolulu: University of Hawaii Press, 2009), 138–41. This is not to suggest that local organizers supported such restrictions. More extensive research is required but at least a few were expressly critical.

93 Strong-Boag, *Liberal Hearts and Coronets*.

94 Nancy Forestell, "Transnational Citizenship in a Post-Suffrage Era? Canadian First Wave Feminism, 1919–1939," paper presented at the Annual Meeting of the Canadian Historical Association (CHA), University of Saskatchewan, June 2007.

95 Thomas Socknat, "For Peace and Freedom: Canadian Feminists and the Interwar Peace Campaign," in *Up and Doing: Canadian Women and Peace*, ed. Janice Williamson and Deborah Gorham (Toronto: Women's Press, 1989), 70.

96 Barbara Roberts, "Women's Peace Activism in Canada," in Kealey and Sangster, *Beyond the Vote*, 287–9.

97 Forestell, "Transnational Citizenship."

98 See Micheline Dumont and Louise Toupin, *Le pensée féministe au Québec*, 396; and Cohen, *Femmes Philanthropes*, 64–5.

99 Anne-Marie Sicotte, *Marie Gérin-Lajoie*, 365–83. Mention of the UIFLC is made in *Canadian Women: A History* but without any citation which documents Quebec participation. See Brandt et al., *Canadian Women*, 218, 270.

100 Joan Sangster, "Introduction," in *Crossing Boundaries: Women's Organizing in Europe and the Americas, 1880–1940s*, ed. Pernila Jonsson, Silke Neunsinger, and Joan Sangster (Uppsala: Uppsala University Press, 2007), 95–115.

101 On debates over the "woman question" among socialists, see Kealey, *Enlisting Women for the Cause*; and among communists, see Sangster, *Dreams of Equality*.

102 Joan Sangster, "Political Tourism, Writing, and Communication: Transnational Connections of Women on the Left, 1920s–1940s," in Jonsson, Neunsinger, and Sangster, *Crossing Boundaries*, 95–114.

103 Varpu Lindström-Best, "Finnish Socialist Women in Canada, 1890–1930," in Kealey and Sangster, *Beyond the Vote*, 196–216.

104 Frances Swyripa, *Wedded to the Cause: Ukrainian Women and Ethnic Identity to 1993* (Toronto: University of Toronto Press, 1993).

SELECTED READINGS

Bristow, Peggy. "'Whatever You Raise in the Ground You Can Sell It in Chatham': Black Women in Buxton and Chatham, 1850–1865." In *"We're Rooted Here and They Can't Pull Us Up": Essays in African Canadian Women's History*, edited by Peggy Bristow, 69–142. Toronto: University of Toronto Press, 1994.

Bacchi, Carol Lee. *Liberation Deferred? The Ideas of English-Canadian Suffragists, 1877–1918*. Toronto: University of Toronto Press, 1983.

Barman, Jean. "Indigenous Women and Feminism on the Cusp of Contact." In *Indigenous Women and Feminism: Politics, Activism, Culture*, edited by Cheryl Zuzack, Shari M. Huhndorf, Jeanne Perreault, and Jean Barman, 92–108. Vancouver: UBC Press, 2010.

Campbell, Peter. *Rose Henderson: A Woman for the People*. Montreal: McGill-Queen's University Press, 2010.

Cavanaugh, Catherine. "Irene Marryat Parlby: An 'Imperial Daughter' in the Canadian West, 1896–1934." In *Telling Tales: Essays in Western Women's History*, edited by Catherine Cavanaugh and Randi Warne, 100–22. Vancouver: UBC Press, 2000.

Cleverdon, Catherine. *The Woman Suffrage Movement in Canada*. 1950; rprt. Toronto: University of Toronto Press, 1974.

Cook, Sharon Anne. *"Through Sunshine and Shadow": The Woman's Christian Temperance Union, Evangelicalism, and Reform in Ontario, 1874–1930*. Montreal: McGill-Queen's University Press, 1995.

Devereaux, Cecily. "New Woman, New World: Maternal Feminism and the New Imperialism in the White Settler Colonies." *Women's Studies International Forum* 22, 2 (March–April 1999): 175–94.

Dua, Enakshi. "Racialising Imperial Canada: Indian Women and the Making of Ethnic Communities." In *Gender, Sexuality, and Colonial Modernities*, edited by Antoinette Burton, 119–33. New York: Routledge, 1999.

Duley, Margot. *Where Once Our Mothers Stood We Stand: Women's Suffrage in Newfoundland, 1890–1925*. Charlottetown, PEI: Gynergy, 1993.

Fiamengo, Janice. *The Woman's Page: Journalism and Rhetoric in Early Canada*. Toronto: University of Toronto Press, 2008.

Forbes, E.R. "Battles of Another War: Edith Archibald and the Halifax Feminist Movement." In *Challenging the Regional Stereotype: Essays on the 20th Century Maritimes*, edited by E.R. Forbes, 67–89. Fredericton, NB: Acadiensis Press, 1989.

Forestell, Nancy. "Mrs Canada Goes Global: First Wave Feminism Revisited." *Atlantis* 30, 1 (Fall 2005): 7–20.

Forestell, Nancy, with Maureen Moynagh, eds. *Documenting First Wave Feminisms: Canada – National and Transnational Contexts*, vol. 2. Toronto: University of Toronto Press, 2013.

Glasbeek, Amanda. *Feminized Justice: Toronto Women's Court, 1913–1934*. Vancouver: UBC Press, 2009.

Hébert, Karine. "A Maternalist Organization in Quebec: The Fédération Nationale Saint-Jean-Baptiste and the Struggle for Women's Suffrage." In *Quebec since 1800: Selected Readings*, edited by Michael Behiels, 469–91. Toronto: Irwin, 2002.

Kealey, Linda. *Enlisting Women for the Cause: Women, Labour, and the Left in Canada, 1890–1920*. Toronto: University of Toronto Press, 1998.

Kealey, Linda, and Joan Sangster, eds. *Beyond the Vote: Canadian Women and Politics*. Toronto: University of Toronto Press, 1989.

Kulba, Tracy, and Victoria Lamont. "The Periodical Press and Western Woman's Suffrage Movements in Canada and the United States: A Comparative Study." *Women's Studies International Forum* 29, 3 (May–June 2006): 265–78. https://doi.org/10.1016/j.wsif.2006.04.005

Levesque, Andrée. "Social Relations in Quebec from 1900 to 1939 as Seen through the Eyes of a Woman of Letters: Eva Circe-Côté." *Zeitschrift für Kanada-Studien* 25, 2 (2005): 36–46.

Murray, Heather. "Great Works and Good Works: The Toronto Women's Literary Club, 1877–1883." In *Rethinking Canada: The Promise of Women's History*, 4th ed., edited by Veronica Strong-Boag, Mona Gleason, and Adele Perry, 103–20. Toronto: Oxford University Press, 2002.

Pickles, Katie. *Female Imperialism and National Identity: The Imperial Order Daughters of the Empire*. New York: Manchester University Press, 2002.

Rhodes, Jane. *Mary Ann Shadd Cary: The Black Press and Protest in the Nineteenth Century*. Bloomington: Indiana University Press, 1998.

Roome, Patricia. "'From One Whose Home Is among the Indians': Henrietta Muir Edwards and Aboriginal Peoples." In *Unsettled Pasts: Reconceiving the West through Women's History*, edited by Sarah Carter, Lesley Erickson, Patricia Roome, and Char Smith, 47–78. Calgary: University of Calgary Press, 2005.

Sangster, Joan. *Dreams of Equality: Women on the Canadian Left, 1920–1950*. Toronto: McClelland and Stewart, 1989.

Sangster, Joan. "Political Tourism, Writing, and Communication: Transnational Connections of Women on the Left, 1920s–1940s." In *Crossing Boundaries: Women's Organizing in Europe and the Americas, 1880–1940s*, edited by Pernila Jonsson, Silke Neunsinger, and Joan Sangster, 95–114. Uppsala: Uppsala University Press, 2007.

Sicotte, Anne-Marie. *Marie Gérin-Lajoie: Conquérante de la Liberté*. Montreal: Remue-ménage, 2005.

Strong-Boag, Veronica. *Liberal Hearts and Coronets: The Lives and Times of Ishbel Majoribanks Gordon and John Campbell Gordon, the Aberdeens*. Toronto: University of Toronto Press, 2015.

– *The Parliament of Women: The National Council of Women of Canada, 1839–1929*. Ottawa: National Museums of Canada, 1977.

Thieme, Katja. "Uptake and Genre: The Canadian Reception of Suffrage Militancy." *Women's Studies International Forum* 29, 2 (May–June 2006): 279–88. https://doi. org/10.1016/j.wsif.2006.04.007

Valverde, Mariana. "'When the Mother of the Race Is Free': Race, Reproduction, and Sexuality in First-Wave Feminism." In *Gender Conflicts: New Essays in Women's History*, edited by Franca Iacovetta and Mariana Valverde, 3–26. Toronto: University of Toronto Press, 1992.

Yee, Shirley J. "Gender Ideology and Black Women as Community Builders in Ontario, 1850–1870." *Canadian Historical Review* 75, 1 (March 1994): 53–73. https://doi.org/10.3138/CHR-075-01-03

9 *Never Done*: Feminists Reinterpret Their Own History

JOAN SANGSTER

In *Lies My Teacher Told Me*, James Lowen describes a quiz he gives his university students on the social background of Americans opposed to the Vietnam War. While most students identified war resisters as elite and middle-class, wartime polling data said the opposite: elites were more likely to support the war; those with less education, including the working class and African Americans, did not. Why this construction of anti-war sentiment as white, educated, and privileged has been so historically resilient (and what the ideological consequences of this mythology are) is the question he and other American scholars are asking.[1]

If I were to poll university classes on the nature of "second wave" feminism in the 1960s and 1970s, it is likely they would check off two boxes: white and middle-class. "Liberal" might follow. Their conclusions are understandable, since this image is reinforced in both popular culture and academic writing. "Second wave" feminism, argues Janine Brodie, began as a "group of urban, white middle-class women."[2] Vanaja Dhruvarajan and Jill Vickers describe early feminist writing as steeped in the assumption that "sex/gender was central to all dimensions of human life everywhere." Until recently, feminists did not consider "racism, nationalism, class conflict, homophobia and ableism."[3] The historical writing emanating from second wave feminism was characterized by a preoccupation with "reform organizations and political struggles," other scholars tell us, particularly those of "articulate, white, middle-class women."[4] Even those sympathetic to the novel energy and insights of the "second wave" women's movement and aware of internal differences in theory/praxis note that women's issues were often "narrowly defined" as "white and middle class."[5]

There are two questions which emanate from this historiographical characterization of a white, middle-class feminism: How did it evolve, and has it been reinforced or challenged with our increasing distance from the 1970s, as new research comes to light? Perhaps it is time to revisit this taken-for-granted narrative of a white, middle-class feminism and also assess its ideological impact. Have we jumped to historiographical conclusions before thoroughly sifting through the historical evidence: the oral, textual, and visual sources of the time? This chapter is a partial contribution to this rethinking. After reviewing the historiography, I sample three 1970s popular feminist publications dealing with women's history: two newspapers from English and French Canada; a graphic novel on the history of Canada; and a popular, educational book on the history of women's work. What might their approach to women's history tell us about the politics of Canadian feminism in this period?

Second Wave Historiography

Academic writing examining working-class feminism or cross-class coalitions between feminists and labour has been more likely to challenge or complicate the dominant narrative of middle-class feminism.[6] Some authors have also shifted the political focus away from liberal feminism; Nancy Adamson locates the origins of the "women's liberation movement" (though defined as short-lived, from 1968 to 1971) in New Left and student politics, while Naomi Black argues that the "white, heterosexual" majority of the (second wave) movement, the "middle-class liberationists," nonetheless had a "class analysis" of women's oppression.[7] Recent discussions of anti-colonial struggles have also unsettled the narrative; Quebec historians have uncovered a revolutionary feminist point of view influenced by Third World liberation writing,[8] while historians of Indigenous struggles have traced Aboriginal women's organizing as they challenged a long-standing patriarchal state which had denied them basic rights.[9] Revisionist work in the United States has also challenged historical amnesia about anti-racist, working-class, and coalition feminist political work.

However, as long as we see these as "other" or alternative streams to the dominant "white middle-class feminism," the tendency to congeal second wave feminist politics into a white, middle-class, and liberal category will persist. Certainly, popular media reports of the women's movement in the 1970s often implied it was a revolt of the more privileged, concerned with upward mobility or trivial issues (such as beauty contests). US news, watched heavily in Canada, gave more space to white feminist leaders, less to parallel women's movements of poor, Latina, and Black women. As Barbara Freeman notes for Canada, and Bonnie Dow for the United States, sexist coverage, which minimized, simplified, and stereotyped feminist issues was extremely common.[10] Media characterizations, however, should be read as constructed stories, not objective evidence.

Press coverage raises the issue of not only the American saturation of Canadian air waves but also the inordinate influence of American feminism on Canadian political perceptions. Although feminism's transnational, global history has facilitated productive political dialogue across borders, we cannot automatically assume the common experience of feminists across borders, nor the presumed intellectual dominance of American feminism (Canadian feminists bemoaned a similar issue *within* the country as well, criticizing the presumed dominance of large centres like Toronto over outlying regions).

Renditions of Canadian feminism were thus refracted through American feminist experience and reflection, shaped by very different historical conditions. In US histories, for example, civil rights plays a more important role, the emergence of "second wave" feminism is often explained by only two political currents – "liberal and radical" (no mention of socialism) – and the story of feminists "Leaving the Left" (often referencing the same conference moment in 1969, as if they all exited the room, en masse, for good) has become a taken-for-granted turning point for feminists.[11] Yet the Canadian movement evolved in the context of different historical, social, and cultural conditions.

Of course, during the 1970s, some feminists did confess to their middle-class, white status – profusely so. In a collection of student writing from one of the first women's studies courses in Montreal, the editor apologies so often for being "a middle-class woman living in a middle-class environment" that the value of the book – capturing a "discovery" moment in women's studies in which multiple voices are all over the place – might be lost on us.[12] Memoirs of the women's movement like *Waking Up in the Men's Room* (though there are few in Canada compared to the United States) also repeat the notion that 1970s feminist movement was predominantly middle-class, although this author was not, and other memory collections offer a more diverse picture of backgrounds, also across English and French Canada.[13]

Moreover, feminist statements at the time often stressed their political *positions*, not just their social origins.[14] The question asked by US historian Ruth Rosen about second wave feminism may be relevant here: How do we account for the fluidity of class position and ethnic identity? In the United States, she contends, many second wave feminists came from working-class and ethnic backgrounds, the latter newly "whitened" European immigrant families whose upward mobility was built on college education. In Canada, the postwar "Fordist" period provided some limited hope of class mobility, and by the early 1970s, multiculturalist rhetoric had created somewhat more positive images of previously denigrated white, ethnic immigrants, though the legacy of Canada's racist immigration policy was still highly visible, both demographically and in racist discourse. The partial democratization of university education and enhanced economic security for a layer of the working class allowed their children to attend college and "become" middle-class (or, in my own case, GI benefits, unimagined during the Depression, allowed my working-class parents to secure an education and thus "become" middle-class after the war). Designating social origins, therefore, must wrestle with the fact that whoever we begin as, we may become someone else.

Perhaps most concerning is the way in which multiple categories, such as white and middle-class, are inevitably congealed, made into a unitary designation. As Radha Jhappan points out, collapsing class, race, and culture together risks creating a homogenized essentialism that may limit rather than complicate our understanding of human experience.[15] Can we assume that the social *origins* and *identities* of feminists – their class, race, sexuality, ethnicity, and so on – can be directly extrapolated to their feminist politics, or are the two related in more complicated ways, as experience and consciousness interact dialectically in changing historical contexts? In a reflection on the women's movement published at the end of the 1970s, Dorothy Smith argued that an emerging problem was the conflation of identity and politics: class should not be analysed as an "individual possession" but rather as a structural and social relationship, and one's political writing should not be simply equated with one's social "background."[16]

The history of feminist theory is implicated in this question. Until the Second World War, argues Vijay Agnew, feminist theory was predominantly about women's struggles to "gain equal rights," and only recently have theorists moved away from "locating a single factor" in women's oppression (i.e., gender).[17] Although somewhat ahistorical, this statement reflects 1980s–1990s feminist retrospective critiques of what was termed second wave "essentialism" with regard to race, class, and sexuality. Attempts to recast theory to more effectively address "race" tended to harden into an assumption that 1970s feminism was fuelled by naive white, middle-class "universalist" politics which collapsed under the weight of its irrelevance, despite the fact that second wave feminists claimed writing on race and interconnected oppressions was key to their politicization. Critiques of universalism were linked to the increasingly influential post-structuralist aversion to "grand narratives" like Marxism and radical feminism (which, true enough, had shaped the second wave). Post-structuralist theory, claim Lise Vogel and others, contributed to "amnesia" about the range of second wave theories, particularly those dealing with race, class, and imperialism.[18] "Third wave" writing, which strives for political analyses distinct from the second wave's countless problems (too numerous to mention), has reinforced an image of a 1970s white, middle-class liberal feminism, which was "rigid, judgmental, and essentialist," ignoring differences between women and positing instead a false notion of sisterhood. In contrast, third wave theorizing asserts its commitment to "multivocality" and attention to the complexity of difference.[19] Third wave political statements like these also serve *as* history by presenting an earlier generation of thinkers as naive and narrow and the subsequent third wave more progressive and inclusive than the previous generation.[20]

How historians have positioned the women's movement in the larger context of the social movements of the "long sixties" is also important. Not only initial press coverage but later histories interpret feminism through the prism of postwar affluence and generational rebellion: it was the product of "rising expectations," especially of middle-class, university-educated women. While Doug Owram acknowledges another, parallel stream of "older" feminists, such as those in Voice of Women, the "women's movement" is nonetheless portrayed as an extension of youth culture, the "mood of the 60s," and generational revolt: "a natural expression" of the baby boom.[21] Rising but stymied expectations were undoubtedly one factor behind feminism, but this does not necessarily mean a universalized liberal, middle-class feminist politics.

Research which locates the origins of the women's movement in the fertile environment of student politics may also give the impression of political homogeneity, but if one drills down into case studies on "women's liberation," complexity abounds: Simon Fraser University feminist students soon turned their attention to building a city-wide Women's Caucus which organized around non-student issues, and in small cities like Thunder Bay, the lonely existence of one feminist group necessitated cross-class alliances of old and young, student and worker.[22] Our understandable interest in the Royal Commission on the Status of Women (RCSW) may have also curtailed our vision of second wave feminism. Critiques of the RCSW have stressed its limited, liberal vision; it is often seen as a reflection of a middle-class, white feminism of the time.[23] While the women behind the RCSW were white, and the report predominantly liberal, actual testimony reveals a much more diverse female rebellion simmering – some women came to testify *against* liberal feminism (and imperialism). Partial pictures, in other words, need to be better connected to a diverse and complex whole.

Is it possible that our historiographical characterization of 1970s feminism has become prematurely constricted by a combined "whig/wave" paradigm of inevitable generational irrelevance and political improvement before we have really plumbed all the evidence? Have historians succumbed to Whiggish assumptions of a more complex, "inclusive" feminism over time: the women's movement becomes more theoretically sophisticated, more politically advanced, as it better grapples with questions of race, class, sexuality, and identity in "intersectional" ways – intersectionality being taken for granted as a superior approach? Whig progress also rides on waves: the second wave is more enlightened about difference than the first, the third more than the second, and the fourth will denounce us all!

The wave metaphor is itself a fraught issue. While I use the term, I feel hopelessly entrapped in a category I fundamentally question. The three wave metaphor has been hard to banish from our writing, but it should be challenged. It ignores feminist activity and theorizing in the so-called "trough" times between waves, and thus ongoing "streams" of feminist organizing over the nineteenth and twentieth centuries, which often connected feminism to other political ideals, including socialism, liberalism, anarchism, conservatism, pacifism, nationalism, anti-racism, and communism. It implicitly reinforces a narrative of a dominating, white, middle-class feminism, with first and second wave feminists cast rather singularly in this mould, and other feminist organizing based on class, race, and sexuality silenced and sidelined.[24] The wave paradigm masks intense debate within feminist cohorts, conflates the generational and political, and assumes a peer-driven movement.

On the other hand, I admit that social and political conditions may create periodic paradigm shifts, upsurges, fresh ideas and activities, as women stake out novel claims, ideals, and demands, pushing feminism in new directions. In the 1970s, new analyses of work, sexuality, and oppression were articulated, and countless forms of feminist cultural-political expression joyfully, angrily, and passionately laid claim to a "new" movement. Newspapers, magazines, comics, calendars, documentaries, posters, visual art, comedy, theatre, and more: all were part of a textual and visual project of politicization that spoke to new feminist energies and ideas. The three examples presented below were nestled within this larger feminist project of alternative publishing and visual display. Feminist and left-wing publishing houses founded in the 1970s nurtured both academic and popular publications: Women's Press, initially Women's Educational Press, produced fiction, scholarly works, children's books, and popular anthologies, and just over a decade later, Sister Vision Press, committed to publishing Black women and women of colour, was founded. Feminist and left-wing publishers resurrected the tradition of political pamphleteering, creating short but path-breaking discussions of feminist theory that crossed the academic-activist spectrum,[25] and more than one publishing house produced an annual women's calendar featuring "Herstory" vignettes to counter "mainstream" male history.

By the mid-1980s, approximately forty new feminist periodicals had been created: the median year of inception was 1979, the average run only seven years, a consequence of operating on shoestring budgets and primarily volunteer labour.[26] New feminist print media offered both an external, revitalized "public sphere" for debate and an internal space within the movement for political dialogue over contested issues.[27] Feminist newspapers in particular aimed to create a feminist community, validate new forms of cultural production, offer forums for organizing and discussion, and also provide new versions of women's history. This was evident in two of the very first newspapers of this era: the *Pedestal* and *Québécoise deboutte!*

Disrupting the Narrative I: The *Pedestal* and *Québécoise deboutte!*

The *Pedestal* (Vancouver) and *Québécoise deboutte!* (Montreal) both used articles on women's history to resurrect a forgotten past and contribute to a contemporary understanding of feminist politics and theory. Both were shaped by feminist, Marxist, New Left, and anti-colonial writing, though they were also the products of different political milieus: the *Pedestal* was originally founded in 1969 by the Vancouver Women's Caucus and *Québécoise deboutte!* was initiated by the Front de Libérations des Femmes (FLF) in 1971, with ties to Quebec nationalist and socialist politics. Yet both exhibited a historical consciousness deeply informed by an analysis of class and colonialism as they interacted with women's oppression; both saw historical knowledge as one key to unlocking the *raison d'être* of women's oppression.

The *Pedestal*'s first article in its Women in History series was a positive rendition of pioneer doctor Emily Stowe's achievements; it seemed to reinforce an emphasis on women notables, and white, professional ones at that.[28] Yet it was an anomaly. The *Pedestal* was little interested in women's history that focused on middle-class women, liberal reforms, and individual achievement and far more concerned with the revolutionary past associated with working-class women and socialist politics. In 1972, the history of International Women's Day (IWD) was tied together by a dizzying array of struggles: the British match girls strike of 1888, wives supporting striking miners in British Columbia in 1913, women joining relief strikes in the 1930s, and wartime women workers demanding day care as well as equal pay.[29] Suffrage was only "part of the struggle," and it emerged because of the development of large-scale capitalism and the employment of women in industry.[30]

Most of the *Pedestal*'s historical biographies were women on the Left. Rosa Luxemburg's revolutionary ideas were explored,[31] and subsequent profiles featured socialist Helena Gutteridge, communist Bella Hall Gauld, anarchist Emma Goldman, and guerrilla fighter and Palestine Liberation Organization (PLO) supporter Leila Khaled.[32] Goldman's anarchist-feminist critique of marriage and her work for the birth control movement were discussed, while Gutteridge's working-class organizing for suffrage – soapboxing and meetings at the Labour Council at night – were contrasted to the "afternoon parlour" meetings of middle-class suffragists. Nellie McClung appeared in this list of biographical luminaries but was dwarfed by more unconventional heroines, including Ethel Rosenberg (wrongly convicted), Constance Markiewitz (jailed for the Irish Republican cause), Hannah Mitchell (British Labour Party), and nurse Florence Nightingale.

The historical events profiled stressed women's role organizing against capital and the state. A reprinted article focused on British suffragettes, such as Sylvia Pankhurst, who opposed the First World War; other pieces explored the Industrial Workers of the World (celebrated for its rejection of race and gender membership restrictions), women's anti-capitalist organizing of the Depression, and women communards' heroic role in the Paris Commune. Not all these narratives celebrated victories; a piece on the Dirty Thirties admitted that women mobilized effectively against the relief camps, but they did not win their efforts to organize free birth control clinics in Vancouver. Grassroots educational tactics were part of the *Pedestal*'s efforts to redraw women's historical consciousness; workshops were organized so women could learn about the history they had missed in their schooling and that was still absent from mainstream culture.

Nor was workplace exploitation the only historical theme pursued. "Women of the Blues" traced the origins of blues to the poverty, oppression, and migrations of African Americans, with women's musical creations linked to their "proud tradition" of resistance, their expressions of "anger and frustration" at the oppressive economic and race structures of American life.[33] Women's roles in anti-imperialist struggles were also discussed, both abroad and at home. In "Double Oppression," Ellen Woodsworth traced the history of Aboriginal women's legal and social marginalization in the Indian Act, and the different historical constructions of white femininity as opposed to Indian womanhood: the former exalted, the latter denigrated. The pervasiveness of racism in a class society had led to divisions between white and Indian, she concluded, and to the "dehumanization and oppression" of Indian women, who were "fighting a double battle" against social indignities and economic exploitation. White feminists needed to "speak up" in solidarity.[34] What made her piece rather unusual for the time was her analytical effort to intertwine race and gender oppression, rather than locating – as many authors did – the struggles of Aboriginal and non-Aboriginal women in parallel narratives.

The FLF, which sponsored *Québécoise deboutte!*, Véronique O'Leary and Louise Toupin remember, drew together a coalition of working-class and middle-class women: workers from the theatre, trade unionists from the Confédération des syndicats nationaux (CSN), nurses, students, housewives, artists, researchers, and artists, most of whom had been touched by the vibrant socialist and nationalist agitations of 1960s Quebec.[35] *Québécoise debootte!* (*QD*) was *shaped* by intertwined national and international influences: structural changes in women's education, work, and family lives in the postwar period; 1968 in France; global anti-colonial liberation struggles; the cultural revolution in China; and American Black liberation struggles. After all, O'Leary and Toupin point out, "a cette époque, nous nous considerons commes les nègres blanc d'Amérique" and "commes femmes, nous identifions le racism dont les Noirs sont l'objet au sexismme que nous subissons."[36] For feminists, Quebec's struggle for self-determination within Canada was vital to feminism, summed up in the famous slogan "No women's liberation without Quebec liberation; no Quebec liberation without women's liberation."

Québécoise debootte!'s interpretation of history revealed a militant feminist concern with oppression, fused with an anti-capitalist critique and some attention to colonial structures of power. In the series explaining "Histoire d'une oppression," the first instalment explored the colonial policy of pro-natalism and Catholic ideology that together relegated women to a reproductive role and insisted on their subordinate submissiveness.[37] The history of Native-newcomer contact was the focus of the second instalment, adding more layers of colonialism to the story: white colonizers, including Jesuits, attempted to remake Indigenous egalitarian cultures in their own patriarchal image, encouraging the sexual and social repression of Indigenous women, whose "liberté sexuelle" threatened the white colonial project. This was not only a story of sexual repression; it was also one of "genocidal" elimination of the Indigenous peoples.[38] In the last of the historical trilogy, detailing the Conquest and the 1837 rebellion, women's role as insurrectionists was recuperated to show the historical erasure and suppression of women's revolutionary past.[39]

Articles on the origins of IWD and an interview with Madeleine Parent about her union work stressed the centrality of women to the history of working-class struggle in Quebec. Yet *QD*'s definition of women's history ventured far beyond paid labour: connections were made between sexuality, the family, love, religion, and capitalism. In "l'histoire d'amour," it was argued that, in order to understand the history of sexual repression, one had to probe multiple facets of women's lives as they intersected with men's. The Church was one cause of sexual repression, but so too was a system of education and a social order characterized by private property and the exploitation of workers. Ideas of private property, it was argued, invaded the family, reinforcing the cult of women's chastity, heterosexual romance, and the institution of marriage.

The family evolved as a "petit état dans l'état," shoring up a patrimonial social order, women's subordination, their internalization of inferiority, and the existence of prostitution and pornography. Even the alienation of capitalist work contributed to repression, as the family was an ideological "haven" in a world of endless work and exhaustion.

Lessons for the present were clear: emancipatory political analyses must connect class, colonialism, and gender in order to liberate women in both the external world of work and the internal world of desire.[40] Yet by the 1980s, O'Leary and Toupin argue, this innovative "second wave" feminist politics was forgotten and obscured, its revolutionary and radical moorings distorted or downplayed in feminist memory and by "amnésie des historiens."[41]

Disrupting the Narrative II: *She Named It Canada Because That Is What It Was Called*

Humour, comedy, and irony are valuable tools of any oppositional movement challenging the status quo. Second wave feminism used humour to consolidate itself as an alternative community and to lampoon mainstream society as well as its own politics, through theatre, impromptu performance, cartoons, and comics. *She Named It Canada* (*SNC*) was one example: a droll retelling of Canadian history in graphic novel (comic) form. The book was produced by the "Corrective Collective" (CC), feminists associated with the Vancouver Women's Caucus and the *Pedestal*, as a popular teaching tool for visiting US delegates to the 1971 Vancouver American-Indochinese peace conference.[42] Since Americans knew little or nothing of Canada's history, the CC resolved to offer delegates an accessible, illustrated comic that would recount Canada's "separate history," with an emphasis on its own social "struggles." As Barbara Todd, a CC member, recalls, "what we detected from our American sisters was a lack of awareness that Canada was an independent nation with its own history/colonial experience."[43] The intent behind *SNC* mirrored some of the political tensions underlying the conference; some Canadians felt that they were being "used" without much recognition, as Vancouver was merely a convenient staging ground for an American-dominated political project. This perception was shaped by the prevailing critique of American imperialism and an incipient "left nationalism," though the American historian of the conference concurs that American-Canadian tensions, along with other racial, national, sexual, and Third World issues, created an explosive conference.[44]

She Named It Canada was picked up by Toronto's James Lewis and Samuel Publishers for distribution, though the CC, unhappy with them, also did its own promotion. *SNC* went through three editions (largely without changes), circulated through radical circles, was used in some high schools, and spurred the CC on to other projects, including *Never Done*. What is remarkable is how quickly the CC produced an engaging book: from conception to finish it took a few months, accomplished with volunteer labour doing research, writing, and finally collating the book in Todd's basement. Four women took the lead in doing the writing, and illustrations were created by Colette French, an artist educated at Toronto's Central Tech's art program, who then taught art, managed art stores, and produced her own work. The CC taught themselves the book production process, though some of the final printing was done at Press Gang, a cooperative, left-wing press. While the "energizers" behind the project "were Andrea Lebowitz and Pat Hoffer," the book was a collective project, reflecting a commitment to a cooperative work ethic; even those CC members less directly involved felt they were providing "sisterly support."[45] The women met every few days at Pat Hoffer's apartment, not so much to thrash out a "theoretical perspective" but to push along the production, first laying out the chronology, then discussing how to interpret the key episodes, with French providing suggestions on illustrations.[46] Todd, later a historian of early modern Britain, had a history degree and research experience, so she played a major part in assembling the research, though she discovered how little was written on Canadian women; the researchers relied on Marxist and radical books by Stanley Ryerson, Charles Lipton, and Gustav Myers but devoured most anything they could find, from Harold Innis to Margaret Ormsby.[47]

Politically, *She Named It Canada* did not offer a "gender first" analysis, nor did it focus on middle-class women or trace an optimistic, Whig path of liberal progress. The CC did attempt to include women where they found enticing research leads; for example, sections on *les filles du roi* and women immigrants emphasized their "importation" as valuable workers and reproducers of labour. Women also appear as political actors in their own right: as Quebec *Patriotes*, suffragists, war workers, anti-war protesters, even the "girl" workers at Fortier's "black hole" cigar factory in Montreal, mentioned in the 1889 Royal Commission on Capital and Labour.[48] The creators also "consciously integrated" women into illustrations wherever possible; French used recurring images of women's domestic labour as a reminder that women's unpaid labour underwrote the construction of Canadian well-being and wealth.[49] Sometimes women's double day is referenced: First World War munitions workers, for instance, protested the "increase of their shift from 13 to 14 hours, since it gave them one less hour on the home shift."[50] However, a gendered analysis is not "the" defining theme of *SNC*, and it was not only the lack of source material but the CC's brand of feminist politics as well which shaped the comic. Although it did not embrace any one platform, the Caucus included Marxist, feminist, and socialist perspectives: "There was no one who would not have considered themselves socialists," remembers another participant. Producing an anti-colonial and left-wing version of peoples' history from below was the key goal.

From our perspective, their obvious omission was "race" and Indigenous history. The book opens with an apology, noting "the history of native peoples was omitted at their request. This omission in no way suggests that we are unaware of the crucial importance of their history on this continent." There was a conversation which determined the CC decision; it is possible those consulted were doubtful about the CC's ability to write Native history without extensive engagement with Native peoples, who had so often been misrepresented in Canadian history.[51] Yet *SNC* did not entirely ignore colonialism, or imperialism, as it was termed at the time; it was incorporated into the analysis of English-French relations and appeared in sections on Aboriginal peoples covering the fur trade, the Métis scrip issue, Louis Riel, and the 1885 Rebellion. The message about white settlement was clear: Europeans assumed the land was theirs to conquer so "explorers and HBC bigwigs" had those who actually *knew* the land (Aboriginal peoples) guide them through it: "following the wily beaver … 'explorers' 'discovered' the Northwest passage by hiring indigenous people who already knew the way."[52] Dispossession, therefore, was referenced but left underdeveloped.

Two intertwined themes dominated *SNC*: first, it traces the changing forces of economic development and political rule from above, including the empires shaping Canada (from France to Britain to the United States); ruling elites, from "compact families" and the Château Clique to the military industrial complex; the connections between political and economic power; the entrenched (and male) power of the Church, especially in Quebec; and the military and wars. On the other hand, the daily survival of working people and the oppositional forces from below – habitant, *coureur de bois*, working-class, poor, and farm peoples – are documented. Collective protest and unions are prominent, from the earliest protests by voyageurs (whose strike provided the iconic beaver, a recurring visual motif in *SNC*, a welcome reprieve from pursuit) to craft unions, the Nine Hours movement, the Winnipeg General strike, Depression relief protests, anti-war efforts, and contemporary struggles for self-determination in Quebec. Not surprisingly, the book ends with an explanation (for the American sisters) of American economic domination of the Canadian "hinterland" economy. This is a left-wing story of power and struggle, structure and agency, with a "nationalist" touch: its radical edge, including descriptions of the Front de libération du Québec (FLQ) without hysterical denunciation or a portrayal of the First World War as an "imperialist" war, were venturesome – and remain so in our times.

The CC attempted to inject humour into *SNC* with ironic editorializing, plays on historical terminology, and illustrations that gently mocked historical events or personalities. Britain's abolition of slavery, they note, was not just "humanitarian" but also motivated by "hard cold business sense"; it was discovered "one could continue to use 'slave labour' but abolish one's responsibility for its upkeep by substituting 'free' wage factory labour."[53] There was never any doubt where the benefits of immigrant labour power ended up: "other [early colonial] workers were called sailors who mostly caught cod, and sometimes cold (from vitamin C deficiency). The owners took 2/3 of the cod, but the workers got to keep the colds."[54] Liberal and Conservative leaders are lampooned equally: both Sir John A. Macdonald, with his penchant for patronage (the fathers of Confederation are hitched to a "gravy train"), and William Lyon Mackenzie King, Rockefeller's right-hand man, a "paragon of indecision" and "inheritor of a proud revolutionary name which he seemed intent on living down."[55] Female heroines like Laura Secord and Madeleine de Verchères are covered, but with tongue-in-cheek references: if Laura Secord had not crawled through the bush to warn British troops, we "would all be eating Martha Washington's chocolates now."[56] Not all events were potential for irony: the hanging of 1837 rebels and *Patriotes* or the state repression of strikers, for example, were not, and it was rather difficult to make the Rowell Sirois Report funny. Still, the comic book template allowed for many small panels, asides, and vignettes with short, caustic, satirical comments: it was smart, sassy, and amusing. Everyone should read it.

Disrupting the Narrative III: *Never Done: Three Centuries of Women's Work in Canada*

The Corrective Collective learned one key lesson from *She Named It Canada*: there was almost no Canadian women's history written. Shocked and upset at how marginal women were considered, they resolved to rectify this with a popular book looking at Canadian history through the lens of women's work. Originally titled "an embroidered history," to emphasize the multiple, intersecting threads of women's lives, *Never Done* was a pastiche-style publication that included historical narrative; short excerpts from primary sources; oral histories and biographies; a few imaginary reconstructions; and Colette French's lively illustrations. Pastiche was a creative choice to make the book accessible; it was also dictated by the frustratingly "fragmentary" sources they encountered.[57]

Never Done used less humour and irony than *SNC*'s comic book form, and instead of *SNC*'s emphasis on political chronology, there was more attention paid to material and social history, particularly the day-to-day survival of farm and working-class families. Like *SNC*, it was shaped by both a marxisant class and feminist analysis, and its strong focus on work reflected the feminist politics of the era; moreover, women's work included unpaid and paid labour, political organizing, and "the work nobody talks about" – i.e., prostitution.[58] One continuing, thematic thread of *Never Done* was women's "unchanging" and never-ending domestic labour: we "must begin with the home, for the work women did formed the core of their lives ... and the country would never have existed without" women's domestic work.[59] Traces of Maggie Benston's path-breaking theoretical work on domestic labour seem implicit in the book's priorities.

While short biographical sketches were used to humanize and enliven the story, the book's aim was far from liberal: Our intent is not to celebrate "those few women who achieved fame and recognition, though they are important. The crucial women are the millions who never became famous, for in those millions rests the history of women in Canada."[60] Like *SNC*, *Never Done* also referenced the original dispossession of Native peoples but did not develop this consistently; its focus was on white settlers, immigrants, and wage earners from pioneer times to the First World War. Published before Sylvia Van Kirk's pioneering writing on the work of fur trade women, the introduction described white settlers who laboured in some manner – as opposed to absentee landlords like Lord Selkirk – as "profit making commodities," but women were especially "valuable, for it was they who would establish a white population and transmit 'proper' social and religious values to the new colony."[61]

Facing a "desperate financial situation" and near bankruptcy, the CC looked for monetary aid to help with production: they "chased a government" grant, submitting a "Canadian Horizons" application to the federal government, and had notable endorsements from Margaret Laurence, Doris Shadbolt, and Dorothy Smith. They encountered disappointing rejection: "We were considered 'Marxist, radical, politically embarrassing etc.,'" they noted.[62] Their volunteer research was nonetheless thorough: they both combed through secondary material and incorporated an impressive range of snippets from original sources, ranging from Ella Sykes's "Home Help in Canada" to a City of Toronto welfare report on a poor widow to testimony from the 1895 Royal Commission on Sweating.

A more in-depth analysis of the political assumptions shaping their history is warranted, but I want to turn instead to their methods and reasons for promoting *this* kind of women's history. The CC felt existing historical writing was very "academic" and focused on singular woman achievers; instead, they would document the lives of "ordinary" women and their labour. *Never*

Done was to be an alternative, popular book for general readers and students, a consciousness-raising book about women's past. Their bibliography and list of archival references were supposed to be a useful resource for budding historians whose interest was sparked by the book, and they imagined this project as just the beginning, as they wanted to follow up with more in-depth popular regional versions, starting with western Canada. The CC did not want to use James Lewis Publishers again because the publisher had raised the price on *SNC* to cover distribution: this conflicted with the CC's aim of popular education and engagement – hence they moved to a more compatible political publisher, Women's Press.

By keeping the cost of a book below $1 –through their volunteer labour – the CC hoped the "everywoman" would read it. Their promotion of *Never Done* reached out to radical popular publications, teachers associations, and high schools, and they had some success at a time when there was more leeway for school text ordering: high school students in BC and a few farther afield studied it in class. A review in the *Vancouver Province* resulted in many letters from women who thought it sounded "interesting," but some academic responses were less generous. Women's Press sent the CC a review by Anne Roche, from the University of Toronto, in *Books in Canada*, which trashed the book with unbridled condescension: "One needn't take seriously *Never Done* as history ... which rarely rises above the level of high school satire ... and is a feminist polemic of mediocre nature." A "pissy" review from a journal that likes little "left of fascism," Women's Press reassured their sisters in the CC.[63] Roche, however, misconstrued the *raison d'être* of *Never Done*: it was *meant* to be a satirical history for high school students. Nor was it "bad" history, unsupported by research and evidence. Rather, *Never Done* was an attempt to shift the existing and implicitly *political* "malestream" version of Canadian history to a fundamentally different one stressing women's work and power relations of class and gender. Its failure to explore issues such as dispossession and its celebration of white pioneer women are certainly problematic from our point of view; however, in its context, it was a refreshing effort to both reinvent and popularize a radical version of Canadian history.

Conclusion

Asking how women's history was imagined and promoted by 1970s feminist activists in popular publications offers insights into their political goals and visions, their understanding of oppression, and how it should be challenged. In the brief run of the *Pedestal*, women fumbled towards a radical feminist politics shaped by anti-capitalist and anti-imperialist thinking, often focusing on the history of working-class women in revolt. Similar influences were apparent in *Québécoise deboutte!*, though it reflected a commitment to Quebec nationalism and independence and innovative theoretical efforts to understand the connections between religion, the family, and capitalism. Popular "peoples" histories, *She Named It Canada* and *Never Done* also represented efforts to connect gender and class analysis, to question imperialism, and to introduce readers – not academics – to a socialist-feminist perspective.

All three examples suggest the need to revisit a preconceived narrative of 1970s feminism as white, middle-class, and often liberal in political orientation – with those categories congealed rather than interrogated in their complexity. Intellectual "matricide" is almost inevitable in the feminist telling of history through "waves," warn American feminists rather pessimistically; our feminist "origins stories" are always "interested stories."[64] The latter has an element of truth, but feminist historians should think of our own work as "Never Done" and be wary of compressing our research into a predefined "whig/wave" paradigm. Second wave sources have barely been scratched; stories are still untold; and the relationship between experience and consciousness in changing historical contexts needs further explication. Our social experience and identities, including generational ones, shape how we understand the world, past and present, but do they necessarily determine it? Most feminists constructing these alternative historical alternatives came from working- and middle-class backgrounds, though who they were becoming mattered too; most were white, reflected in the stories told, though they also identified other forms of discriminatory "difference" based on language and culture as needing a historical makeover.

Finally, we need to ask: What are the ideological, political effects of this homogenization of "second wave" feminist history? It situates feminism as a liberal, bourgeois project rather than recognizing that many feminists saw gender as only one factor among a constellation of power relations shaping oppression and inequality, and it reinforces a history of feminism as relevant only for the privileged, rather than the product of both periodic coalitions and the struggles of middle-class, working-class, poor, and racialized women. If we see feminism flowing in streams, rather than cresting in congealed troughs and waves, we can better trace more diverse currents and equality-seeking efforts, as they ebb and flow over the twentieth century. While there is no doubt that liberal feminism, as managed and absorbed by mainstream institutions, has benefited affluent, educated, white women far more than others, this is not necessarily what feminism has to be, or should be, or even was. If we challenge the existing historiography, perhaps we can also complicate dismissive messages about feminism in our times. After all, linking the past and present to create a better future was a goal of second wave feminists worth remembering.

NOTES

1 James Loewen, *Lies My Teacher Told Me: Everything Your American History Textbook Got Wrong* (New York: New Press, 1995), 298–9.

2 Janine Brodie, *Politics on the Margins: Restructuring the Women's Movement* (Halifax: Fernwood Publishing, 1995), 10.

3 Vanaja Dhruvarajan and Jill Vickers, *Gender, Race, and Nation: A Global Perspective* (Toronto: University of Toronto Press, 2002), 60, 7.

4 Franca Iacovetta and Mariana Valverde, eds, *Gender Conflicts: New Essays in Women's History* (Toronto: University of Toronto Press, 1992), xiii, xiv, xv. Note the authors initially note a "diversity" of feminist ideas but later contradict this.

5 Nancy Adamson, Linda Briskin, and Margaret McPhail, *Feminists Organizing for Change: The Contemporary Women's Movement in Canada* (Toronto: Oxford University Press, 1988), 60.

6 Jill Vickers, Pauline Rankin, and Christine Appelle, *Politics as if Women Mattered: A Political Analysis of the National Action Committee on the Status of Women* (Toronto: University of Toronto Press, 1993). Meg Luxton, "Feminism as a Class Act: Working-Class Feminism and the Women's Movement in Canada," *Labour / Le Travail* 48 (2001): 63–88. John Cleveland, "New Left, Not New Liberal: 1960s Movements in English Canada and Quebec," *Canadian Review of Sociology and Anthropology* 41, 1 (2004): 67–84.

7 Nancy Adamson, "Feminist Libbers, Lefties, and Radicals: The Emergence of the Woman's Liberation Movement," in *A Diversity of Women: Ontario, 1945–1980*, ed. Joy Parr (Toronto: University of Toronto Press, 1995), 253–80; Naomi Black, "The Canadian Women's Movement: The Second Wave," in *Changing Patterns: Women in Canada*, ed. Sandra Burt, Lorraine Code, and Lindsay Dorney (Toronto: McClelland and Stewart, 1993), 155, 164.

8 Sean Mills, *The Empire within: Postcolonial Thought and Political Activism in Sixties Montreal* (Montreal: McGill-Queen's University Press, 2010).

9 Sharon Donna McIvor, "Self-Government and Aboriginal Women," in *Scratching the Surface: Canadian Anti-Racist Feminist Thought*, ed. Enakshi Dua and Angela Robertson (Toronto: Women's Press, 1999), 167–86.

10 Barbara Freeman, *The Satellite Sex: The Media and Women's Issues in English Canada, 1966–71* (Waterloo: Wilfrid Laurier University Press, 2001); Bonnie Dow, *Watching Women's Liberation, 1970: Feminism's Pivotal Year in Network News* (Urbana: University of Illinois Press, 2014).

11 Ruth Rosen, *The World Split Open: How the Modern Women's Movement Changed America* (New York: Viking, 2000), ch. 4; Estelle Freedman, *No Turning Back: The History of Feminism and the Future of Women* (New York: Random House, 2002), 85.

12 Margaret Anderson, ed., *Mother Was Not a Person* (Montreal: Black Rose Books, 1972), 2.
13 Catherine Macleod, *Waking Up in the Men's Room: A Memoir* (Toronto: Between the Lines, 1998); Judy Rebick, *Ten Thousand Roses: The Making of a Feminist Revolution* (Toronto: Penguin, 2005).
14 Judy Bernstein, Peggy Morton, Linda Seese, and Myrna Wood, "Sisters, Brothers, Lovers Listen," in *Women Unite! An Anthology of the Canadian Women's Movement* (Toronto: Women's Press, 1972), 31–40.
15 Radha Jhappan, "Post-Modern Race and Gender Essentialism or a Post-Mortem of Scholarship," *Studies in Political Economy* 51 (1996): 38.
16 Dorothy Smith, "Where There Is Oppression, There Is Resistance," *Branching Out* 6, 1 (1979): 15.
17 Vijay Agnew, *Resisting Discrimination: Women from Asia, Africa, and the Caribbean and the Women's Movement in Canada* (Toronto: University of Toronto Press, 1996), 13. The implication that liberal feminism prevailed until the 1940s obscures generations of left-wing feminists who grappled, in theory and practice, with the connections between gender, ethnicity, and class.
18 Lise Vogel, "Telling Tales: Historians of Our Own Lives," *Journal of Women's History* 2 (Winter 1991): 89–101.
19 R. Claire, "What Is Third-Wave Feminism?," *Signs* 34, 1 (Autumn 2008): 1; Natasha Pinterics, "Riding the Feminist Waves: In with the Third," *Canadian Women's Studies* 20/21, 4/1 (2009): 1–7.
20 Astrid Henry, *Not My Mother's Sister: Generational Conflict and Third Wave Feminism* (Bloomington: University of Indiana Press, 2004). These are American sources which again have dominated much of the conversation.
21 Doug Owram, *Born at the Right Time: A History of the Baby Boom Generation* (Toronto: University of Toronto Press, 1996), 250, 278.
22 Adamson, "Feminist Libbers, Lefties, and Radicals"; Roberta Lexier, "How Did the Canadian Women's Liberation Movement Emerge from the Sixties Student Movements? The Case of Simon Fraser University," *Women and Social Movements in the United States, 1600–2000* (Alexandria, VA: Alexander Street Press, 2009), http://womhist.alexanderstreet.com/.
23 Toni Williams, "Re-Forming 'Women's' Truth: A Critique of the Report of the Royal Commission on the Status of Women," *Ottawa Law Review* 22, 3 (1990): 725–59.
24 For American critiques of the wave metaphor, see Nancy Hewitt, ed., *No Permanent Waves: Recasting Histories of US Feminism* (New Brunswick, NJ: Rutgers University Press, 2010); Dorothy Sue Cobble, *The Other Women's Movement: Workplace Justice and Social Rights in America* (Princeton, NJ: Princeton University Press, 2004). For Canadian ones: Tarah Brookfield, *Cold*

War Comforts: Canadian Women, Child Safety, and Global Insecurity (Waterloo: Wilfrid Laurier University Press, 2012); Joan Sangster, "Radical Ruptures: Feminism, Labor, and the Left in the Long Sixties in Canada," *American Review of Canadian Studies* 40, 1 (2010): 1–21.

25 Charnie Guettel, *Marxism and Feminism* (Toronto: Women's Press, 1974); Dorothy Smith, *Feminism and Marxism: A Place to Begin, A Way to Go* (Vancouver: New Star Books, 1977).

26 Eleanor Wachtel, *Feminist Print Media* (Ottawa: Secretary of State, 1982), 23; and Eleanor Wachtel, *Update on Feminist Periodicals* (Ottawa: Secretary of State, 1985), 13.

27 Barbara Marshall, "Communications as Politics: Feminist Print Media in English Canada," *Women's Studies International Forum* 18, 4 (1995): 463–74.

28 "Women in History: Canada's First Woman Doctor," *Pedestal*, Feb. 1970, 2.

29 Barbara Hicks, "Women in the Thirties," *Pedestal*, June 1970, 2.

30 "International Women's Day," *Pedestal*, Mar. 1970, 1.

31 Sylvia Kitching, "Women in History: Rosa Luxemburg," *Pedestal*, Mar. 1970, 2.

32 Dodie Weppler, "Helena Gutteridge," May 1970, 2; Pat Hoffer, "Women in History: Bella Hall Gauld," July 1970, 2; Mary Borsky, "Emma: Women in History," Sept. 1970, 2; Pat Hoffer, "Leila Khaled: Women in Contemporary History," Oct. 1970, 2. All articles from the *Pedestal*.

33 Carol Phillips and Pat Hoffer, "Women of the Blues," *Pedestal*, Oct. 1970, 15.

34 Ellen Woodsworth, "Indian Women: Double Oppression," *Pedestal*, Mar. 1970, 7.

35 Véronique O'Leary and Louise Toupin, eds, "Pourquoi Ne Pas Toujours Repartir à Zéro," in *Québécoise deboutte! Une anthologie de textes du Front de libération des femmes (1969–1971) et du Centre des femmes (1972–1975)*, tome 1, 22–3.

36 O'Leary and Toupin, "Pourquoi Ne Pas Toujours Repartir à Zéro," 25.

37 "Histoire d'une oppression," *Québécoise deboutte! (QD)*, Nov. 1972, 12–15.

38 "Histoire d'une oppression: Les Amerindiens-nes," *QD*, Dec. 1972, 8.

39 "Histoire d'une oppression: La conquete et l'insurrection," *QD*, Feb. 1973, 5–9.

40 "Sexe et politique: La répression sexuelle: ça sert à qui?," *QD*, Mar. 1973, 5–12.

41 O'Leary and Toupin, "Pourquoi Ne Pas Toujours Repartir à Zéro," tome 1, 9.

42 The CC members were Karen Cameron, Andrea Lebowitz, Colette French, Barbara Todd, Pat Hoffer, Cathy Walker, Marge Hollibaugh, and Dodie Weppler.

43 Email from Barbara Todd to Joan Sangster, 4 August 2015.

44 Judy Tzu-Chun Wu, *Radicals on the Road: Internationalism, Orientalism, and Feminism during the Vietnam Era* (Ithaca, NY: Cornell University Press, 2013), ch. 8. She claims *SNC* was not ready in time for the conference but was distributed afterwards.

45 Email from Cathy Walker to Joan Sangster, 15 July 2015.

46 Todd email.

47 Todd email.
48 Corrective Collective, *She Named It Canada Because That's What It Was Called* (Toronto: James Lewis and Samuel Publishers, 1971), 46 (hereafter *SNC*).
49 Todd email.
50 *SNC*, 51.
51 Both participants remember this, but their memories differ on who the conversation was with.
52 *SNC*, 32.
53 *SNC*, 38.
54 *SNC*, 3.
55 *SNC*, 65.
56 *SNC*, 14.
57 SFU Archives, Andrea Lebowitz Collection, F 164-2-0-0-2, "outline."
58 Corrective Collective, *Never Done: Three Centuries of Women's Work in Canada* (Toronto: Canadian Women's Educational Press, 1974), 135.
59 *Never Done*, 2.
60 *Never Done*, 3.
61 *Never Done*, 4.
62 SFU, Lebowitz, F 164-2-0-0-2.
63 SFU, Lebowitz, F 164-2-0-0-5, Women's Press to CC Friends, 6 Jan. 1975.
64 Henry, *Not My Mother's Sister*, 9, 12.

SELECTED READINGS

Adamson, Nancy. "Feminist Libbers, Lefties, and Radicals: The Emergence of the Woman's Liberation Movement." In *A Diversity of Women: Ontario, 1945–1980*, edited by Joy Parr, 253–80. Toronto: University of Toronto Press, 1996.
Adamson, Nancy, Linda Briskin, and Margaret McPhail. *Feminists Organizing for Change: The Contemporary Women's Movement in Canada*. Toronto: Oxford University Press, 1988.
Agnew, Vijay. *Resisting Discrimination: Women from Asia, Africa, and the Caribbean and the Women's Movement in Canada*. Toronto: University of Toronto Press, 1996.
Anderson, Margaret. *Mother Was Not a Person*. Montreal: Black Rose Books, 1972.
Bernstein, Judy, Peggy Morton, Linda Seese, and Myrna Wood. "Sisters, Brothers, Lovers Listen." In *Women Unite! An Anthology of the Canadian Women's Movement*, 31–40. Toronto: Women's Press, 1972.
Black, Naomi. "The Canadian Women's Movement: The Second Wave." In *Changing Patterns: Women in Canada*, edited by Sandra Burt, Lorraine Code, and Lindsay Dorney, 151–76. Toronto: McClelland and Stewart, 1993.

Brodie, Janine. *Politics on the Margins: Restructuring the Women's Movement.* Halifax: Fernwood Publishing, 1995.

Brookfield, Tarah. *Cold War Comforts: Canadian Women, Child Safety, and Global Insecurity.* Waterloo: Wilfrid Laurier University Press, 2012.

Cleveland, John. "New Left, Not New Liberal: 1960s Movements in English Canada and Quebec." *Canadian Review of Sociology and Anthropology* 41, 1 (2004): 67–84. https://doi.org/10.1111/j.1755-618X.2004.tb02170.x

Cobble, Dorothy Sue. *The Other Women's Movement: Workplace Justice and Social Rights in America.* Princeton, NJ: Princeton University Press, 2004.

Corrective Collective. *Never Done: Three Centuries of Women's Work in Canada.* Toronto: Canadian Women's Educational Press, 1974.

Dhruvarajan, Vanaja, and Jill Vickers. *Gender, Race, and Nation: A Global Perspective.* Toronto: University of Toronto Press, 2002.

Dow, Bonnie. *Watching Women's Liberation, 1970: Feminism's Pivotal Year in Network News.* Urbana: University of Illinois Press, 2014.

Freedman, Estelle. *No Turning Back: The History of Feminism and the Future of Women.* New York: Random House, 2002.

– *The Satellite Sex: The Media and Women's Issues in English Canada, 1966–71.* Waterloo: Wilfrid Laurier University Press, 2001.

Guettel, Charnie. *Marxism and Feminism.* Toronto: Women's Press, 1974.

Henry, Astrid. *Not My Mother's Sister: Generational Conflict and Third Wave Feminism.* Bloomington: University of Indiana Press, 2004.

Hewitt, Nancy, ed. *No Permanent Waves: Recasting Histories of US Feminism.* New Brunswick, NJ: Rutgers University Press, 2010.

Iacovetta, Franca, and Mariana Valverde, eds. *Gender Conflicts: New Essays in Women's History.* Toronto: University of Toronto Press, 1992.

Jhappan, Radha. "Post-Modern Race and Gender Essentialism or a Post-Mortem of Scholarship." *Studies in Political Economy* 51 (1996): 15–63. https://doi.org/10.1080/19187033.1996.11675328

Lexier, Roberta. "How Did the Canadian Women's Liberation Movement Emerge from the Sixties Student Movements? The Case of Simon Fraser University." In *Women and Social Movements in the United States, 1600–2000.* Alexandria, VA: Alexander Street Press, 2009, http://womhist.alexanderstreet.com/.

Loewen, James. *Lies My Teacher Told Me: Everything Your American History Textbook Got Wrong.* New York: New Press, 1995.

Luxton, Meg. "Feminism as a Class Act: Working-Class Feminism and the Women's Movement in Canada." *Labour / Le Travail* 48 (2001): 63–88.

Macleod, Catherine. *Waking Up in the Men's Room: A Memoir.* Toronto: Between the Lines, 1998.

Marshall, Barbara. "Communications as Politics: Feminist Print Media in English Canada." *Women's Studies International Forum* 18, 4 (1995): 463–74. https://doi.org/10.1016/0277-5395(95)00045-E

McIvor, Sharon Donna. "Self-Government and Aboriginal Women." In *Scratching the Surface: Canadian Anti-Racist Feminist Thought*, edited by Enakshi Dua and Angela Robertson, 167–86. Toronto: Women's Press, 1999.

Mills, Sean. *The Empire within: Postcolonial Thought and Political Activism in Sixties Montreal.* Montreal: McGill-Queen's University Press, 2010.

Owram, Doug. *Born at the Right Time: A History of the Baby Boom Generation.* Toronto: University of Toronto Press, 1996.

Pinterics, Natasha. "Riding the Feminist Waves: In with the Third." *Canadian Women's Studies* 20/21, 4/1 (2009): 15–21.

Rebick, Judy. *Ten Thousand Roses: The Making of a Feminist Revolution.* Toronto: Penguin, 2005.

Rosen, Ruth. *The World Split Open: How the Modern Women's Movement Changed America.* New York: Viking, 2000.

Sangster, Joan. "Radical Ruptures: Feminism, Labor, and the Left in the Long Sixties in Canada." *American Review of Canadian Studies* 40, 1 (2010): 1–21. https://doi.org/10.1080/02722010903536920

Smith, Dorothy. *Feminism and Marxism: A Place to Begin, A Way to Go.* Vancouver: New Star Books, 1977.

– "Where There Is Oppression, There Is Resistance." *Branching Out* 6, 1 (1979): 10–15.

Snyder, R. Claire. "What Is Third-Wave Feminism?" *Signs* 34, 1 (Autumn 2008): 175–96.

Vickers, Jill, Pauline Rankin, and Christine Appelle. *Politics as if Women Mattered: A Political Analysis of the National Action Committee on the Status of Women.* Toronto: University of Toronto Press, 1993.

Vogel, Lisa. "Telling Tales: Historians of Our Own Lives." *Journal of Women's History* 2 (Winter 1991): 89–101. https://doi.org/10.1353/jowh.2010.0097

Wachtel, Eleanor. *Feminist Print Media.* Ottawa: Secretary of State, 1982.

– *Update on Feminist Periodicals.* Ottawa: Secretary of State, 1985.

Williams, Toni. "Re-Forming 'Women's' Truth: A Critique of the Report of the Royal Commission on the Status of Women." *Ottawa Law Review* 22, 3 (1990): 725–59.

Wu, Judy Tzu-Chun. *Radicals on the Road: Internationalism, Orientalism, and Feminism during the Vietnam Era.* Ithaca, NY: Cornell University Press, 2013.

10 Beyond Sisters or Strangers: Feminist Immigrant Women's History and Rewriting Canadian History

MARLENE EPP AND FRANCA IACOVETTA

In February 2015, then prime minister Stephen Harper announced that he would appeal a federal court ruling that declared unlawful his government's ban on the wearing of a niqab by women when taking the oath of Canadian citizenship. The controversy had erupted when Zunera Ishaq, an immigrant woman from Pakistan, refused to remove her face veiling during her public citizenship ceremony in 2013, in defiance of a 2011 policy which banned the practice. In explaining her action, Ishaq said, "I am not looking for Mr. Harper to approve my life choices or dress. I am certainly not looking for him to speak on my behalf and 'save' me from oppression, without even ever having bothered to reach out to me and speak with me … While I recognize that [the wearing of the niqab is] not for everyone, it is for me. To me, the most important Canadian value is the freedom to be the person of my own choosing. To me, that's more indicative of what it means to be Canadian than what I wear."[1]

The "history" of this particular event has yet to be written, but it reveals a great deal about the writing of what is now commonly referred to as Canadian immigrant women's history – the theme of this chapter. First of all, the event involving Ishaq is a sharp reminder, if such is required, of the connections between past and present, as patterns of behaviour repeat themselves (if not in identical ways) over time. It illustrates the manner in which contemporary Canada is a product of past attitudes, practices, and policies as well as a site of continually contested imaginings, including gendered ones. The debates over Muslim women's dress point to a long-running historical theme whereby lawmakers and law-enforcers attempt to impose white, Eurocentric, and male notions of nation-building on the bodies and lives of immigrant women – and to the ways in which, historically and in the present, dress can act as a powerful marker of racial or "in-between" racial status. Ishaq's response illustrates that immigrant women are not, nor have they been in the past, passive or silent in the face of gender and culture-based discrimination, even if many of them have had neither the formal language skills nor media opportunity to so directly disagree with a prime minister. Historically, some of the most marginalized of women – including immigrants – have talked back to hostile and exploitative elites through collective protest. Today, we are able to hear and record Ishaq's words almost immediately, and thus know her ideas and choices and also her resistance – what women's historians have referred to as her "agency."

Undoubtedly, Ishaq has many "sisters" in her chosen country of residency and citizenship – women who are empathetic and embracing of who she is as university educated, an immigrant, a Muslim, a mother, and a community volunteer. It is certainly true that there are others who consider her a "stranger" because of her ethnicity and religion; and she may feel equally adamant in her view of them as strangers. It is the dichotomy – perhaps better understood as a dialectic – of immigrant, ethnic, and racialized women as "sisters" or "strangers," and of how we might engage the complex dynamics involved, that frames the discussion which follows.

Published in 1986, the essay collection *Looking into My Sister's Eyes: An Exploration in Women's History* represented something of a watershed. Its timing reflected and reinforced a then emerging literature on immigrant women that, for different reasons, regions, and eras, was positioning them as important actors in Canadian history.[2] Close to twenty years later, another anthology on immigrant, racialized, and ethnic women – *Sisters or Strangers?* (2004) – drew on feminist anti-racist theories and postcolonial approaches to more critically probe the relationship of immigrant women with each other across race and ethnicity and class, with the Canadian state and its citizens, and within their own families and communities. Just over a decade after *Sisters or Strangers?* initially appeared, the increased activity in the field, including among new scholars, and the rise or intensification of interest in new paradigms or in re-interrogating the still important "older" questions and sources led to a new, revised, and expanded version of *Sisters or Strangers?* (2016).[3] Our contribution to *Reading Canadian Women's and Gender History* addresses the historical scholarship on immigrant women through an examination of these three key volumes, with an emphasis on the scholarship produced from the late 1980s to the early twenty-first century that was included in and/or influenced the two editions of *Sisters or Strangers?*

This chapter highlights Canadian feminist engagements with national and international debates and developments that over the last three decades have not only enriched the field but also contributed significantly to the rewriting of Canadian history. We consider the shifts in subject or approach, the rise of new or modified theoretical frameworks, and the efforts at methodological innovation or reflection. Yet rejecting a simplistic "new is better" doctrine, we also address, for twenty-first-century readers, the "older" insights that remain important. For instance, that new histories of immigrant women are being made on a daily basis warrants methodological approaches which "discover" and "uncover" women's lived experience – like that of Ishaq. In addressing the broader intellectual and political contexts in which this scholarship has been produced, and the relevant interdisciplinary and international literatures, our historiographical essay moves well beyond Canada and these texts. Still, we appreciate that many noteworthy publications on immigrant women will not be acknowledged.

We begin with a few generalizations. Over the past four decades, historical writing about immigrant women has moved from "the shadows" of the Canadian past to occupy a more public position within Canadian history and historiography.[4] We have witnessed an increased diversification in the Canadian scholarship, most evident perhaps in the discernible shift from an earlier focus on "white" British and European women to a more recent focus on "not-white" women from non-Western origins. This changing focus reflects in part the shifting ethnic and racial character of immigration itself over more than 500 years but also the influence of feminist critical race scholarship.[5] Furthermore, studies informed by feminist, materialist, postcolonial, and diasporic perspectives, and oral history methods, have sought in similar but also quite different ways to disrupt essentialized constructs of womanhood as well as normalized understandings of the nation state.

The labour- and left-focused histories informed by socialist feminism drew attention to immigrant and ethnic women's myriad labours and enriched understandings of working-class life,[6] union organizing, and radical ethnic cultures; the latter also went "beyond the nation" by charting their subjects' involvement with feminist and/or workers' internationalist movements.[7] The much larger body of scholarship on immigrant women which has emerged over the past forty years has dealt with such themes as ethnic resilience, religious identities, domestic violence, generational transmission, material culture, emotional attachment, and food, and these have also explicitly and implicitly critiqued nation-bound histories.[8] Cross-border and international collaborations have contributed to the decentring of nation-bound histories within North America and beyond.[9] Finally, although neither transnational migration nor diasporic identity are new phenomena, but instead have lengthy histories, scholarly engagements with these concepts have shaped recent writing on immigrant women, especially contemporary migrants, and also attracted new feminist scholars, including historians, to the field. Below, we discuss this work in light of late twentieth- and early twenty-first-century migration patterns, globally and in Canada, and with reference to the divergent theoretical approaches and debates. We also explain the appeal of the transnational turn – also a theme in chapters by Flynn and Aladejebi and by Forestell in this volume – to feminist historians of migration and the very compelling historical reasons for rewriting Canadian history as transnational history.

Recovery: *Looking into My Sister's Eyes*

Described as a "pioneering enterprise" in the larger field of women's history, the thirteen essays on immigrant and ethnic women in Canada that composed the 1986 *Looking into My Sister's Eyes: An Exploration in Women's History* followed a stimulating conference organized by the Multicultural History Society of Ontario (MHSO), which included scholars, community historians, and students of women's history. This award-winning volume reflected the growing trend to "rewrite" the Canadian past from a social history perspective. As contributors to that original project, we agreed with the MHSO's position that this recuperative project was an important "beginning" and that "much remains to be done." With an emphasis on recovering the voices of women (whether by reading archival documents against the grain or by conducting oral interviews) and on telling the stories of individual women and groups of women marginalized even in Canadian women's history, *Looking into My Sister's Eyes* focused attention on women's contributions to their families and ethnic communities in a Canadian, mainly Ontario, setting. Hence, the repeated references to "contributing to ethnic cohesion," "creating and sustaining an ethnocultural heritage," and helping to form "community consciousness." This "contributive" approach was evident in the many chapters that illuminated women's charitable and religious work within the Jewish and Armenian communities, and women's activity in Polish, Greek, Macedonian, Ukrainian, and Mennonite ethnic organizations. Some of the essays highlighted the labouring identities of immigrant women, including Finnish and British domestics, a Chinese restaurant and laundry owner, and Italian factory workers. Many of the essays also explored female immigrant roles and experiences within patriarchal family structures.

The essays reflected, in many cases, the personal identities of their authors, who chose to write about the communities to which they themselves belonged or identified with. The recuperative act of historical research and writing, which remains important today as attested to by other chapters in this volume, was thus both political and personal, even if the authors did not share a common political or intellectual mandate with each other or with their subject matter.

Indeed, many of them referenced the "insider-outsider" dilemma (or opportunity) – the relative merits and pitfalls of researching and writing from within or outside of a group or culture – but they were not especially self-reflective about the tensions, creative or otherwise, about it.[10] A close connection to their subjects enabled many of the authors to conduct their own or utilize existing oral histories, but, again, they were not explicit about the matter. Nor did they reflect particularly critically on the status or character of the oral history material itself. Already by the late 1970s, feminist theorists of oral history and women's narratives were debating the nature of memory, but the "reflexive turn" that emphasized meaning and subjectivity became prominent in later studies.

Significantly, a few of the essays in *Looking into My Sister's Eyes* waged perspectives that later gained greater traction within the field and evolved into books that became core readings on the history of female migration and in Canadian women's history more broadly. Already known among labour and left feminist historians for her rich sources on radical Finns, Varpu Lindström's *Defiant Sisters: A Social History of Finnish Immigrant Women in Canada* (1988) became widely cited by women's historians for its use of oral history as a central methodology, and also for so robustly refuting stereotypes about women immigrants and domestic labourers as compliant, passive, and family-focused.[11] Historian Marilyn Barber's essay on young British women who came to Ontario between 1900 and 1930 to work as domestic servants was an early contribution to understanding the importance and prevalence of female immigrant domestic labour in early twentieth-century Canada, and her research still holds a singular place in the literature.[12] The three editors of *Sisters or Strangers?* (2004) contributed essays to the volume that were part of their graduate student research and went on to publish books that became core readings in Canadian immigration history.[13]

Although there was a certain "sisterly" feeling that participants in the *Looking into My Sister's Eyes* project were embarking on something new and important in the study of Canadian history, the concept of sisterhood as a construct for thinking about the history of immigrant women was limited. Many of the essays acknowledged differences or tensions, particularly those related to class, but the diverse groups of women examined in the collection were viewed largely as "sisters" – if not in relation to each other, then certainly with respect to the emphasis that the authors placed on the commonalities they shared, especially with regard to their marginal positions *vis-à-vis* the anglophone or francophone majority. Also present, and equally unarticulated, was the notion that they were "sisters" by virtue of their shared sex and socially prescribed gender roles, whose combined impact cut across any differences rising from ethnicity or race. The most glaring omission was the absence of racialized subjects;

the one exception, Dora Nipp's essay on Chinese women in the interwar era, provided a corrective to the prevailing stereotype of the male-only character of early twentieth-century Chinese migration to Canada.

Interrogation: *Sisters or Strangers?*

A second phase, for the purposes of this survey, in the writing of immigrant women's history in Canada, coalesced around a workshop and the edited collection of essays that resulted in *Sisters or Strangers? Immigrant, Ethnic, and Racialized Women in Canadian History*, published by the University of Toronto Press in 2004. Most scholars of immigrant and refugee women, including left feminist scholars like ourselves and other participants, remained committed to writing about still neglected female subjects and to "mainstreaming" the history of such women into both women's and gender history and Canadian history generally. The volume thus encompassed a greater number and diversity of ethnic, immigrant, and racialized identities within which the specificity of gendered experience was being recovered and analysed.

In part, the scholarship which went into the 2004 project represented the growth and legitimation of new social histories that (notwithstanding a conservative backlash) recognized regionalism, gender, class, race, ethnicity, and sexuality, for instance, as important analytical categories as well as markers of identity in shaping the Canadian experience. Vibrant scholarship emerged that illuminated historical actors with multiple identities – as workers, as wives and mothers, as physical bodies, as religious believers, and as political activists, for instance. If the possibility of writing "a" Canadian history became increasingly unfeasible, greater complexity made for a richer and deeper collection of histories that challenged a nation-bound frame. If such a thing as the evolution of a national story existed, we said in 2004, it revolved around the interaction between and negotiations over privilege and power among people with varied backgrounds, histories, and experiences based on group identification. Despite the challenge of writing histories of a nation that emphasized multiple intersectional identities, feminist anti-racist historians increasingly called for a "national" history that recognized the necessity of human mobility and analysed migration within complex frameworks in which women act with multidimensional interests.

Scholars working within other subject areas of social history, and in related social science disciplines, took this interrogation further by not only investigating the history of racialized women from different vantage points but also challenging the boundaries defining the field, introducing new theoretical insights and paradigms, and re-articulating often taken-for-granted categories such as nation, nation-building, and borders.[14] For example, feminist race critiques of Canada and its liberal myths were probed in a 2000 special theme issue of the woman's studies journal *Atlantis*, which adopted the deliberately provocative title, "Whose Canada Is It?" Suggesting that dominant definitions of Canada and Canadian are "class-based, racist, sexist, and heterosexist," the editors emphasized the need to question and explore the extent to which immigrant and racialized women share in projects of nation-building, and they questioned liberal notions of Canada as a place where everyone can be both different and equal.[15]

Also important was the scholarly work on immigrant women in Canada being done by political scientists, sociologists, and historians who were exploring the relationship between Canada's status as a white settler nation and its imagined self-identity as a liberal "nation of immigrants," combined with its disreputable history as a colonizer of Indigenous peoples. The burgeoning field of postcolonial theory, and especially its application in gendered ways by influential feminist scholars, presented new frameworks for re-evaluating the subjectivities of white women colonizers and their complicit roles as oppressors of Indigenous and other non-white women. A contact zones frame that treated the subjects in a site of encounter not in terms of their separateness but rather "in terms of interlocking understandings and practises, often within radically asymmetrical relations of power," also gained traction.[16] In Canadian applications of postcolonial insights to the study of colonialism, past and ongoing, we saw continuing efforts to recouple the intertwined but too-long-separated histories of Indigenous and immigrant policies and peoples in Canada, a subject of growing interest.[17]

Such efforts were also accompanied by close scrutiny of official policies and practices of Canadian multiculturalism. Anti-racist scholars, among them leading left feminists like Himani Bannerji, critiqued the policies for masking racism and an ethnic "vertical mosaic" that perpetuated exclusionary attitudes and behaviour towards individuals and groups who exist outside an essentialist image of a Canadian as not only white but also of English or French background.[18] A multicultural policy meant to show some accommodation for white ethnic groups, they argued, could not even begin to accommodate people of colour, including migrant women and those from not-white countries. Critiques of multiculturalism remain important,[19] though Bannerji's reconsideration of the policy in light of today's "dark times" is noteworthy.[20]

The main interrogation in the *Sisters or Strangers?* project – prompting the question mark in the title – that informed the introduction and all of the essays either implicitly or explicitly was whether notions of sisterhood could justifiably be applied between women whose dominant racial or class experiences are antithetical. Were immigrant women – or women who were othered by virtue of race, ethnicity, and minority status – truly sisters? Or did their historic experience make them feel more like strangers – with each other, within the nation, within their communities, and sometimes even within their own homes?

We inserted the question mark in *Sisters or Strangers?* partly to underscore that historical experience is often characterized by dichotomies – that cohesion could be offset by alienation, that common gender can exist alongside oppression, that women could be simultaneously attracted and repelled by their ethnicity, that women's contributions might be undermined by their exclusion or marginalization, and that victimization and agency are never mutually exclusive, and also that neither life experiences nor scholarly analysis can be fully comprehended by opposing dualisms. It also revealed our agreement with feminist critiques of a women's history that stressed the commonalities among women while neglecting or downplaying the divisions among them, with some of the most pointed critiques at the time coming out of African American women's history and feminist critical race studies.[21]

All of the chapters of *Sisters or Strangers?* (2004) interrogate the encounter between immigrant, ethnic, and racialized women and the nation in which they settled. Some of the authors addressed the theme through the more traditional, and yet still important, focus on the contributions immigrant women made to their families and communities, both in acculturation to Canadian society and in the preservation of ethnic distinctiveness in hostile contexts. Midge Ayukawa, for instance, describes the role of Japanese Canadian mothers, many of them the pioneering picture brides who joined husbands they had never met in Canada, in preserving Japanese cultural traditions among their children as a way of developing a sense of self-esteem and even superiority in the face of vile racial discrimination.[22] The passing on of cultural traditions across generations is also the theme of Isabel Kaprielian-Churchill's study of intermarriage among Armenians in Canada and the United States. She notes the high rate of exogamy among Armenians, suggesting that so-called mixed marriage did not necessarily lead to a complete loss of ethnic distinctiveness. Also important is her willingness to document the unflattering, indeed stigmatizing, ways in which "full-blooded" Armenians have labelled, and othered, the non-Armenian spouses of family members ("odars") and the products of those unions ("halfbreed").[23]

The chapters informed by postcolonial approaches interrogated not only the "sisters" construct but also the notions of "whiteness" in the work of colonizer-immigrants. Cecilia Morgan examines the discourse of colonial missionaries working among Indigenous women and men in Upper Canada during the period of the 1820s–1850s; the efforts to Christianize First Nations women included making them into "good housewives" and "fit mothers" modelled on the gender, race, and class identities of British white women. Building on the work of feminist scholars who persuasively documented the patriarchal character of Christian conversion, she suggests that the colonization project involved both a transformation of gender identities among Indigenous people and a reinforcement of those identities among the colonizers themselves.[24]

Bringing together histories of immigration and Indigenous peoples – also part of a postcolonial gaze – Adele Perry's chapter on the immigration to British Columbia of white women in the mid-nineteenth century shows how the women's arrival both confirmed and challenged the racial mission of reinforcing "whiteness" in colonial British Columbia. Perry points out the centrality of immigration to an imperialist agenda that was both racialized and gendered, demonstrating that the importation of white women immigrants served particular nation-building interests.[25] Using a similar approach applied to women migrants from India at the beginning of the twentieth century, Enakshi Dua analyses how the racialization of the idea and practice of Canadian citizenship developed as a way of excluding certain racialized groups of potential immigrants. As Dua observes, the erroneously labelled Hindu Woman's Question also illuminates the gendered and racialized manner in which ethnic communities developed. Her attention to the lobbying by white middle-class feminists in support of admitting women they considered racially inferior on the grounds of the latter's "civilizing" influence over the men of a "bachelor" (hence dangerous) foreign community, and in enabling the creation of a separate community with households headed by petty patriarchs, references an ongoing debate in women's history – the racial politics of first wave feminism, addressed more thoroughly in this volume by Nancy Forestell.[26]

Feminist critiques of the family and feminist family histories that have exposed the gendered power relations between unequal members inform the arguments made by authors about immigrant families being not just cohesive bulwarks against "Canadian" society but also sites for marital discord and generational conflict. The chapters documenting such conflicts challenge earlier disaggregated models of family cooperation and represent significant shifts in the historiography on immigrant and racialized women. In their respective legal-oriented chapters on spousal murder and alleged domestic violence, Lisa Mar and Barrington Walker not only emphasize the racialization of non-white women, doing so largely through a focus on discourse rather than experience, but show a willingness to make "public" topics formerly too "private" for exposure. It is demonstrated in Mar's study of a 1919 anti-Chinese riot in Lindsay, Ontario, that erupted in response to alleged domestic violence within a Chinese Canadian family. It is also acutely evident in Walker's study of spousal murder within Black households in late nineteenth-century Ontario; moreover, his concept of Black men's "residual patriarchy" challenges the work of African American feminists who have critiqued white feminists for not appreciating that Black families provide a refuge from white racist society.[27] Flynn and Aladejebi also address these issues in this volume. Gender relations within the household are explored as well by Gertrude Mianda in her essay about Black African francophone women in post-1970 Montreal and Toronto. Her study illustrates how the cultural patterns – in this case regarding male-female conjugal roles – of an immigrant group can be at serious odds with those of the host society.[28]

Even as approaches to understanding immigrant women within their ethnic households reflected an evolving scholarship in women's history generally, original research simultaneously rejected the image of the immigrant woman relegated mainly to the private sphere of home. Several chapters in the 2004 project also feature working immigrant women, although most of them are not workplace studies per se. Lorna McLean and Marilyn Barber's discussion of Irish domestics in nineteenth-century Ontario and their encounters with courts of law (over incidents of drunkenness and criminality) and rates of imprisonment and institutionalization reflects an engagement with feminist legal and moral regulation studies. It also touches on the vulnerability of foreign (Irish Catholic) working-class women to diagnoses of "madness."[29] Drawing on her archive of oral histories, Karen Flynn's chapter on the middle-class and professionally trained Black Caribbean immigrant nurses who worked in Canadian hospitals after the Second World War focuses less on work (and labour recruitment policies) and more on how this understudied Caribbean group interpreted their experiences, including with racism. It, too, breaks down race-, class-, and gender-based assumptions about Black women immigrants.[30]

A contribution to new feminist scholarship on the Cold War and the established historiography on left women's (consumer) activism, Julie Guard delineates the significant presence of "ethnic" women in the Housewives Consumers Association, which organized protests against postwar price hikes in consumer goods. These women – from multiple immigrant backgrounds but sharing leftist politics – were suppressed by a Cold War national security state that stereotyped both their femininity as "sisters" and their ethnicity as "strangers."[31] The importance of ethnic women's radical politics, as well as the gender constraints they faced, is also illustrated in Ester Reiter's chapter on the summer camps for children established by leftist Jewish women.[32]

Together, the chapters in *Sisters or Strangers?* adopted what were then current theoretical frameworks – such as feminist anti-racist and postcolonial thinking, as well as more familiar material-feminist ones – and utilized the methods and sources popularized by social and women's historians. Transnationalism was also emerging as an important analytical tool in migration studies in the 1990s, and this too can be seen in a number of the chapters in *Sisters or Strangers?*, even if authors do not explicitly identify their work in this way. It was also evident in the work on feminist and leftist labour movements that crossed and transcended borders and on refugee and diaspora migrations that maintained homeland ties in many ways. The transnational "turn" did, however, gain even greater traction in scholarship of the new millennium and is thus a key analytical framework in the second edition of *Sisters or Strangers?* Given its currency, it is also a key theme in various chapters in this volume.

Twists, Turns, and Returns: *Sisters or Strangers?* "Revisited"

In the early 1990s, the term "transnationalism" became part of the scholarly agenda of the social sciences. Some of the influential analyses observed that the social practices of many migrants' lives occurred almost simultaneously on the territories of more than one national state, and they defined this way of life as transnationalism. They suggested that transnationalism was a new development: whereas immigrants from the past had broken with their home countries in order to migrate and had sought and quickly achieved assimilation, contemporary "trans-migrants" used new technologies of air travel, telephones, satellites, and digital communications to maintain ties to their homeland. Some viewed the concept as not "across" or "crossing" a national boundary but instead "beyond" the territory or power of a single nation state, leading some theorists of globalization to view the rising international migrations of the last decade of the twentieth century as indicators of the declining importance of national states. To others it suggested that national states were threatened in their sovereignty not only by multinational corporations and border-crossing flows of capital but by twenty-first-century transnational migrants too.[33]

In response, immigrant historians already attuned to questions of the nation state and border-crossing subjects, including the feminists among them, and who knew that earlier immigrants had maintained ties to their real or imagined homelands and that their identities and cultural practices were shaped in part by such ties, did not think of this as a new phenomenon.[34] When historians have tracked transnational migrations, they have usually meant migrations that cross an international border, whether into (immigration) or out of (emigration) the territory of a particular nation state. Studies of nineteenth- and twentieth-century mass migrations of European groups revealed that many of the main features of contemporary globalization – economic inequality, massive circulation of capital and labour, free trade ideologies, new cheaper and speedier technologies of transportation and commerce – were important factors shaping the lives of earlier men and women, who were equally mobile, albeit in different ways.[35] These immigrants also displayed characteristics of transnational identities.[36]

The transnational approach imbedded in the new immigrant history was evident in *Sisters or Strangers?* (2004). The focus of much of this literature, including that on women, had been on the transition from rural peasants to urban workers through the migration experience, and on questions of cultural transfer in associational life and material culture, as well as how relationships with a "homeland" and a past lived elsewhere influence individuals, families, and communities well into the post-migration generations. Such formations were viewed not in a one-directional way but, rather, as the complex and evolving product of multiple adaptations of migrants who modified pre-migration strategies and rituals to meet new world contexts and also initiated new ones while maintaining links with kin back home. Some of the chapters in the first edition of *Sisters or Strangers?* acknowledged the importance of this dynamic in the economic, emotional, and social lives of immigrant women. For example, in her examination of newspaper images, Varpu Lindström demonstrated the way in which media propaganda created an idealized Finnish Canadian woman based on the activities of women in Finland during the Winter War against Russia in 1939–40. In this analysis, which tackles the transnational in another way, events in the "homeland" had a significant impact on how a hitherto marginalized ethnic group was perceived by Anglo-Canadians and how Finnish Canadian women were temporarily transformed into familiar "sisters." Paula Draper's study of Jewish Holocaust survivors in Canada demonstrates in very poignant ways how successful post-migration lives can belie ongoing struggles with the pre-migration tragedy experienced by their families and community. Using Edmonton as her setting, Frances Swyripa links both the pre- and post-migration experiences in analysing the role gendered images play in the sacred space of Canadian ethnic churches.[37]

While rejecting the view that transnational migrations and identities are new, we recognize that the past twenty years have seen "the emergence of quantitatively more and qualitatively different kinds of transnational linkages," prompting increased scholarly interest in studying the many facets of transnationalism, including transnational identities, local networks, and family relationships, as well as the transnationalism within politics, social movements, religion, media, and other spheres of activity.[38] Feminist historians of immigrant women have explored women's ongoing emotional attachments (or not) to their homeland, and noted their articulations of what were often hybrid identities. But, again, to avoid essentializing female identities, one must recognize the transnational political activism and attitudes of women as well as the intense loyalty or hatred they maintain towards the politics of their homelands. In addition to the chapters in the original *Sisters or Strangers?* that situated individual topics in multiple territories, with subjects that crossed borders mentally and/or physically, the new essays in the second edition, including but not limited to those dealing with more recent or contemporary immigrant women in Canada, reflect the "transnational turn" – indeed, its twists and turns – in a more intentional manner.

Thus, they document the various transnational social practices, networks, and mindsets that typically linked individuals to many different foreign places – which takes us to the term "diaspora." Some critics have argued that the increasing tendency among scholars today to use diaspora, or diasporic consciousness, to refer to "practically any population which is considered 'deterritorialised' or 'transnational' – that is, which has originated in a land other than which it currently resides, and whose social, economic, and political networks cross the borders of nation-states or, indeed, span the globe,"[39] means that the categories can lose their analytical power. There is value in this critique, and scholars studying "first-generation immigrants" should consider it. Still, the elasticity of the term "diaspora" has enabled different applications. Some scholars have made compelling arguments for why it is helpful to use a diasporic approach to study non-forced migrations, the term having once applied strictly to forced migrations, such as the Jewish and African (slavery) diasporas.[40] Others have applied the concept of diasporic consciousness (attachments to more than one place) to the life of a border-crossing subject in order to better understand that subject's multifaceted identity. Afua Cooper offers such a case for viewing the enslaved Marie-Joseph Angélique not simply as a slave woman who was part of a forced diaspora but as a complex female subject who embodied "double or triple diasporic" identities – to Africa through ancestry, to Portugal and Europe, where she lived for years as a free woman, and to the Americas, to which she migrated and lived as an enslaved woman. In doing so, she draws on W.E.B. Du Bois's concept of Black "double consciousness" and seeks to write Canada into the concept and history of the Black Atlantic that its leading theorist, Paul Gilroy, left out.[41]

The case for a diasporic frame is also being made by feminist scholars using oral interviews to study contemporary refugee women, whose multiple border crossings have become increasingly common. This multidisciplinary, and often theoretical and self-reflexive, oral history scholarship has produced much evidence in support of the thesis that the intensification of women's movements across multiple borders and temporary settlement in multiple nation states is giving rise to highly complex identities that can be described as multidirectional and multilayered, hence the use of the term "diasporic." This scholarship asserts, too, that for female immigrants, diaspora, like notions of nationalism, may have particular gendered implications.

Feminist applications of diaspora theory deeply inform the work on contemporary and recent "non-Western" refugee women, where analyses of women's hybridity and diasporic identities are stressed, including in oral histories. Of particular appeal to Nadia Jones-Gailani in her analysis of oral interviews with recent Iraqi refugee women in Amman, Toronto, and Detroit is the notion of a "third space." A theory of "cultural difference" strongly associated with Homi K. Bhabha, third space theory emphasizes the uniqueness of each person as a "hybrid," in some sense "caught between two worlds" but whose emotional and psychological state of being occurs within a symbolic space outside both home- and host-land.[42] Jones-Gailani uses the concept of "a third space" as "a safe space" of trust created within the interview wherein refugee women can feel empowered to be candid about opinions they normally keep silent out of fear of repercussion.[43]

The notion that diaspora is as much an emotional and psychological entity as an actual border-crossing informs the new chapter by Grace L. Sanders Johnson. She applies diaspora to a shared social space where young Haitian women migrants in Montreal created, cultivated, and negotiated their woman-centred consciousness and transnational feminism. This study of the transnational feminist identities of Haitian women in 1960s, 1970s, and 1980s Quebec, especially Montreal, documents the women's changing diasporic ties to families in Haiti, especially Port-au-Prince, and how their politicization as left feminists was informed by and negotiated through both homeland and Quebec political and social movements.[44]

Even while academics were introducing new theoretical frameworks to think about migration broadly, the diversity in ethnicity and country of origin for immigrants to Canada increased significantly over the last decades of the twentieth century and into the twenty-first, making "diversity" more and more Canada's reality. The first edition of *Sisters or Strangers?* included research on Japanese, Chinese, Black, African, Aboriginal, Irish, Finnish, Ukrainian, Italian, Jewish, Mennonite, Armenian, and South Asian Hindu women. The second is more inclusive, with new chapters on Arabic, Greek, Portuguese, Doukhobor, Swedish, Haitian, Filipino, Icelandic, and Iraqi women. While still not claiming to be comprehensive in subject or period coverage, and also acknowledging the limitations of this exercise, the new edition sought to resemble something closer to the classic *Unequal Sisters: A Inclusive Reader in U.S. Women's History*, now in its current fourth edition – a huge volume with thirty-six articles covering a wide range of topics, spanning several hundred years, and embracing numerous categories of immigrant, ethnic, and racialized women in US history. Far more than just size, however, we wanted to emulate *Unequal Sisters'* efforts to "incorporate the lessons of an intersectional feminism, in which identity incorporates multiple dimensions so that one is not merely gendered or raced or classed or abled but all of these factors combine and refract upon each other in a *mezcla* (mixture) of self and society."[45]

While not as inclusive as the US reader, *Sisters or Strangers?* "revisited" captures an even greater cross-section of the women and female groups who migrated to Canada across a longer historical period – nearly 300 years. This meant moving back in time, to early eighteenth-century New France and to Cooper's study on the enslaved Angélique, as well as moving forward to the recent migration of Iraqi refugee women studied by Jones-Gailani. The adoption of Lesley Erickson's 1995 work on Swedish prairie homesteaders increased the volume's regional, rural, and ethnic-group as well as chronological coverage, as did Willeen Keough's recent article on Irish women in eighteenth- and nineteenth-century Newfoundland.[46] Moreover, the inclusion of new works on "British" immigrants demonstrates how historians using "newer" (to them) sources and approaches to examine what was earlier critiqued as prioritizing white women migrants are producing new insights. Juxtaposing the discourse on Irish immigrant women in Newfoundland that came from the British authorities, the Catholic Church, and through oral tradition, Keough's close attention to oral sources, in particular recorded "folk" oral traditions, shows how women developed their own identities in between the imposed discourse and the lived realities of their lives. In so doing, she also challenges the polarized debates on "discourse" versus "experience" that engaged women's historians during the 1990s. Lisa Chilton's chapter on British female migration to Canada in the late nineteenth and early twentieth centuries offers a fresh perspective on this massive managed migration by analysing the correspondence written by female settlers that, in particular, sheds light on the relationship between the emigrants and the emigrators – the individuals who organized the process. It is also a contribution to the "new imperialism."[47]

Once again, migration and settlement are in some way part of each chapter's story, but immigration or migration or transnational migration is conceptualized from a number of different angles. In some cases, female immigrants are the active subjects; in others, they are the targets of external social, political, or legal agendas. In some of the essays, immigration is a recent personal experience, while in others migration – whether forced, voluntary, or assisted – is a phenomenon felt in the lives of second- and third-generation Canadians. The second edition offers greater insight into the differences between voluntary immigrants and involuntary refugees, slaves or political exiles, between

Indigenous peoples and recent newcomers, and between ethnic or racial identities that individuals and groups willingly adopt and those that are imposed on them. The implications are great for how we understand the role of ethnicity and race in Canadian history and society. Within these parameters, the essays show immigrant, ethnic, and racialized women interacting in one way or another with Canadian (or pre-Canadian) society. These interactions take the form of encounters with state institutions, such as the courts, and government immigration and settlement officials; for instance, Laura Madokoro's revisionist assessment of Canadian immigration practices in the post–Second World War period reveals how, despite a historiography which suggests a more "open door" policy, the state's attitudes towards Chinese refugees and gendered assumptions about their family structures led to racialized and exclusionary practices.[48] Moving much closer to the present, Glenda Bonifacio's chapter on temporary migrant workers from the Philippines, who are numerically dominant in Canada's Live-in Caregiver Program, analyses women's responses to the settlement services provided by government and civil society in both sending and receiving nations. While the term itself is not used in this example of her research, transnational identities are central to the lives of Filipino women who provide "care" across opposite sides of the globe.[49]

Immigrant women's spaces of contact also include relations with employers, charitable and religious organizations, neighbourhoods, and resident Canadians. In addition, the essays show women acting within the context and priorities of their own particular ethnic or racial groups, as members of communities and families that are self-defined and inward-looking and who often maintain ties with "their people" outside Canada. Or as members who protest, in different ways, the injustices of society, in some cases acting with defiant communities or springing into action out of great disagreement with imposed inequalities; for instance, Susana Miranda probes the "ethnic" elements of women's labour activism in her study of Portuguese cleaning women who became militant political subjects in the early 1980s.[50] All of these subjects, we still argue, legitimately form part of a transnational Canadian history.

Growth in other interdisciplinary fields of study has also influenced recent scholarship. Once dismissed by elitist academics as the stuff of domestic science, then women's studies programs and historical museums – or of self-serving "foodies" – food studies has become a lively area of inquiry in almost all disciplines.[51] Two essays in the 2004 edition of *Sisters or Strangers?* reflected this direction. Franca Iacovetta and Valerie Korinek's analysis of food practices in the context of reception work and social service activities among immigrant and refugee women in the post–Second World War era reveals that even while the "peculiar" eating customs of immigrants were celebrated as part of postwar pluralism, immigrant women were encouraged by experts to shop, cook, and eat "Canadian." Food, then, acted as a signifier of difference between cultures, but eating and the gendered functions surrounding it also were a site of power negotiation and encounter in which "immigrant" and "host" cultures were both transformed. Marlene Epp's examination of the food shortages and later abundance experienced by Mennonite refugees prior to and following their immigration to Canada after the Second World War sheds light on the place of food in their post-migration memories and lives. Mindful of the need to resist essentializing women by highlighting the meaning of food in their lives while also actively involved in "growing" an emerging Canadian food history, we also needed to both widen and shift the focus of analysis. Helen Vallianatos and Kim Raine's study of contemporary Arab and South Asian food consumption patterns in Calgary and women's identity formation in immigrant households enhances the new volume's racial and regional diversity and chronological coverage while reinforcing its feminist mandate.[52] Food-related migration studies are almost inevitably transnational, given the interest in tracing the hybridity of foodways in between homeland and host-land, but there is nothing inevitably feminist (or anti-capitalist) about food history unless we make it so.

One of the main methodologies utilized in the 1986 *Looking into My Sister's Eyes* was oral history, and it remains central to the new literature in immigrant women's history, even while becoming more sophisticated and problematized by debates within the field of oral history itself. Oral interviews have long been recognized as one of the best – and sometimes the only – methods for gaining entry into the past lives of immigrant women.[53] They continue to be a crucial source for obtaining the first-person experiences of little-studied groups, like the 10,000 Greek immigrant women recruited to work as domestics, studied by Noula Mina, who makes familiar use of her narrative sources but within a racially informed feminist framework of analyses. She also does not use her oral history material in isolation but assesses it against different types of sources – something Italian historian Luisa Passerini urged scholars to do during the heady years of oral history resurgence in the 1970s.[54]

The ongoing use of oral sources has also reflected the shift to memory studies. Thus, recent studies do not just use (and sometimes in fact reject) oral interviews to supply "information" or anecdote, but rather analyse the manner and meaning in women's oral narratives, drawing on concepts of "social" and "collective" memory, as well as subjectivity, and on the interpretive material that emerges from the relationship between interviewer/historian and interviewee/subject. In many ways prompted by feminist debates, discussions of "shared authority" or the meaning of silences, or the role of intersubjectivity and reflexivity, are now as central to oral-interview-based studies as the subject matter itself.[55] Many oral interviews, along with other autobiographical sources such as memories, diaries, and letters, are also being interpreted with respect to theories of memory and trauma.[56] This is especially salient for studies of immigrant women who, like the different ethno-religious groups of Iraqi women that Jones-Gailani interviewed, arrived in Canada from contexts of war, hunger, displacement, and persecution. The interviews are analysed for counter-narratives that undermine the state-defined masculine national myth of a unified Iraq. Dealing with a racialized Canadian group, Pamela Sugiman's essay on Japanese Canadian women who were interned by the Canadian state during the Second World War similarly utilizes the concept of memory to break down the dichotomy of past and present and demonstrates that women's oral narratives revealed how much their past trauma was still very "present" in their lives.[57] The richness of theoretical and methodological development in the field is evident in many of the new chapters in the second edition of *Sisters or Strangers?*

The immigrant letter is also a familiar source to migration historians, but proactive researchers are building new archives – both physical and digital, both private and public – of letters entrusted to them by their "informants" in order to analyse women's lives in transnational and cross-border settings. Such first-person and, in most cases, private sources, allow historians to analyse past experience for what letters reveal about "affect" – now a concept central to the history of emotions – in the lives of immigrant women. In analysing love letters between Canada and Italy in the post-1945 era, Sonia Cancian demonstrates the importance of transnational relationships in the lives of immigrants and non-migrants alike. By documenting women's romantic ideals and desires, she also challenges stereotypes of immigrant women as "sexless subjects."[58]

The applications of material history approaches involving the use of artefacts also inform new work on immigrant women. Turning to a supposedly long-assimilated white and northern Scandinavian group, Icelanders in western Canada and the United States, Laurie Bertram's transnational study of the women in Icelandic communities from 1874 to 1933 uses hair, clothing, and other artefacts to explore the rise, ebbs, flows, and resurgence of a hybrid ethnic culture that responded to Anglo North American demands for both assimilation and the public performance of difference (as in participation in male-led multi-ethnic parades). She also uncovers the alternative and less public female commemorations of infant deaths and the preserved artefacts (hair, clothing, photos) by which women remember loss. In her "fibre-focused" chapter on Icelandic immigrant women, she shows how hair and clothing styles became a site of conflict between women and male leaders in the midst of negotiating transnational identities that emerged in relation to late nineteenth- and early twentieth-century Icelandic nationalist movements.[59]

Bertram's chapter touches as well on questions related to the history of body – another field of study that has witnessed considerable theoretical debate as well as much recent historical research, but the body is the central focus of Ashleigh Androsoff's new chapter on Doukhobor women. The body, it has been argued, can act as a signifier or metaphor of the nation and, like the other ideological aspects of nation-building, can exclude as much as it includes. In her analysis of the media portrayals of and public attitudes towards Doukhobor women who disrobed in protest over government treatment of their ethno-religious community, Androsoff documents how the image of the naked Doukhobor woman standing before her flame-engulfed home was used repeatedly to embody the Doukhobors' "stranger" status within Canadian society in the mid-twentieth century. She also shows that the intense public scrutiny of these women's bodies began much earlier, with the group's arrival on the prairies in 1899, and that among the different portrayals that emerged (some of them positive enough to make them "distant cousins" to Canadians), it was the preoccupation with the women's supposedly "unusually large ... and powerful frame," and their capacity for heavy (even beastly) labour so antithetical to dominant ideals of femininity, that heavily shaped public opinion of them as ill-adjusted strangers who could never become sisters to Canadian women.[60]

Future Directions and Suggestions

As editors of *Sisters or Strangers?* "revisited," we acknowledge that many groups are still under-represented, or even absent, especially those that were part of immigrant arrivals in the latter years of the twentieth and early decades of the twenty-first centuries. Chapters in this book on Black women by Flynn and Aladejebi and on religion by Robertson address and point to ongoing gaps in the literature. There is social science literature on numerous recently arrived groups, but historical work on significant migrations from the 1970s and on is still waiting to be done.

The historiography reveals a continuing interest in women's roles as workers and activists and their roles within their families and ethnic communities but a lack of comparative and/or thematic approaches.[61] Explorations of women's activism and involvement in public-sphere politics continues, but apart from focused studies on women within ethno-religious groups such as Doukhobors, Mennonites, and Jews, feminist historians have neglected the role of religion in immigrant women's lives. Given the growth of the Muslim, Hindu, and Buddhist population in Canada, and the use of women's bodies and lives as a site of debate, more historical inquiry about their presence within Canada is needed. Furthermore, we know almost nothing about queer immigrant women or those with disabilities, although, thanks to the social scientists and creative writers, there is a crack opening in that door. More studies are needed that differentiate the immigrant experience as voluntary migration and the refugee experience as forced migration. The vast increase in the numbers of people displaced from their homes by war and other forms of violence, persecution, and environmental disaster should be reflected in more studies of the gendered nature of refugee migrations – including women's vulnerability and strength within those movements. The "No One Is Illegal" movement also points to another topic requiring attention, as does the growing number of female-dominated temporary worker migrations. Thus, we end with the same cautiously optimistic tone that accompanied the publication of *Looking into My Sister's Eyes*: new beginnings have been made but much has yet to be done.

NOTES

1 Zunera Ishaq, "Why I Intend to Wear a Niqab at My Citizenship Ceremony," *Toronto Star*, 16 March 2015, 3, https://www.thestar.com/opinion/commentary/2015/03/16/why-i-intend-to-wear-a-niqab-at-my-citizenship-ceremony.html, accessed 6 April 2015.
2 *Looking into My Sister's Eyes* was edited by sociologist Jean Burnet and published by the Multicultural History Society of Ontario. The literature published before or at the same time included work on domestics, the ethnic left, and homesteading, group, and community studies that featured women. A sample includes Linda Rasmussen, *A Harvest yet to Reap: A History of Prairie Women* (Toronto: Women's Press, 1976); Helen Potrebenko, *No Streets of Gold: A Social History of Ukrainians in Alberta* (Vancouver: New Star, 1977); Marilyn Barber, "The Women Ontario Welcomed: Immigrant Domestics for Ontario Homes, 1870–1930," *Ontario History* 72, 3 (September 1980): 148–72; Joy Parr, *Labouring Children: British Immigrant Apprentices to Canada, 1869–1924* (London: Croom Helm, 1980); Joan Sangster, "Finnish Women in Ontario, 1890–1930," *Polyphony* 3, 2 (Fall 1981): 46–54; Ruth Frager, "Sewing Solidarity: The Eaton's Strike of 1912," *Canadian Woman Studies* 7, 3 (Fall 1986): 96–8; Franca Iacovetta, "Primitive Villagers and Uneducated Girls: Canada Recruits Domestics from Italy," *Canadian Woman Studies* 7, 8 (Winter 1986): 14–18. See also Jason H. Silverman, "Mary Ann Shadd and the Search for Equality," in *Black Leaders of the Nineteenth Century*, ed. Leon Litwack and August Meier (Urbana: University of Illinois Press, 1988), 87–102; and literature noted in the chapter by Karen Flynn and Funké Aladejebi in this volume.

3 Both editions of *Sisters or Strangers? Immigrant, Ethnic, and Racialized Women in Canadian History* were published by University of Toronto Press. Editors of the 2004 edition were Marlene Epp, Franca Iacovetta, and Frances Swyripa. Epp and Iacovetta edited the 2016 edition.

4 A similar pattern exists for the United States. As examples, see Donna Gabaccia, *From the Other Side: Women, Gender, and Immigrant Life in the US, 1820–1990* (Bloomington: Indiana University Press, 1994); Donna Gabaccia and Vicky Ruiz, eds, *American Dreaming, Global Realities: Rethinking US Immigration History* (Urbana: University of Illinois Press, 2006).

5 Important exceptions include the Caribbean domestics who came to Canada in the interwar period; see Agnes Calliste, "Canada's Immigration Policy and Domestics from the Caribbean: The Second Domestic Scheme," in *Race, Class, and Gender: Bonds and Barriers*, ed. Jessie Vorst (Toronto: Between the Lines, 1989), 136–68.

6 For example, Bettina Bradbury, "Pigs, Cows, and Boarders: Non-wage Forms of Survival among Montreal Families, 1861–1891," *Labour / Le Travail* 14 (1984): 9–46, and other articles that culminated in her *Working Families: Age, Gender, and Daily Survival in Industrializing Montreal* (Toronto: McClelland and Stewart, 1993).

7 For example, the articles published in the 1980s (and early 1990s) that culminated in the following monographs: Joan Sangster, *Dreams of Equality: Women on the Canadian Left, 1920–1950* (Toronto: McClelland and Stewart, 1989); Ruth A. Frager, *Sweatshop Strife: Class, Ethnicity, and Gender in the Jewish Labour Movement of Toronto, 1900–1939* (Toronto: University of Toronto Press, 1992); Linda Kealey, *Enlisting Women for the Cause: Women, Labour, and the Left in Canada, 1890–1920* (Toronto: University of Toronto Press, 1998). For an analysis of the similarities and differences between such works, see Franca Iacovetta, "Manly Militants, Defiant Domestics, and Cohesive Communities: Writing about Immigrants in English Canada," *Labour / Le Travail* 36 (1995): 217–52.

8 Besides the many works cited here, recent contributions include Vijay Agnew, ed., *Diaspora, Memory, and Identity: A Search for Home* (Toronto: University of Toronto Press, 2005); Marlene Epp, *Mennonite Women in Canada: A History* (Winnipeg: University of Manitoba Press, 2008); and essays in Franca Iacovetta, Valerie Korinek, and Marlene Epp, eds, *Edible Histories, Cultural Politics: Towards a Canadian Food History* (Toronto: University of Toronto Press, 2012).

9 Studies of labouring and left immigrant women that adopt an explicitly transnational frame include Donna R. Gabaccia and Franca Iacovetta, eds, *Women, Gender, and Transnational Lives: Italian Workers of the World* (Toronto: University of Toronto Press, 2002); Evangelia Tastsoglou, ed., *Women, Gender, and Diasporic Lives: Labor, Community, and Identity in Greek Migrations* (Lanham, MD: Lexington Books, 2009).

10 See Hasia R. Diner, "Insights and Blind Spots: Writing History from Inside and Outside," in *Strangers at Home: Amish and Mennonite Women in History*, ed. Kimberly D. Schmidt, Diane Zimmerman Umble, and Steven D. Reschly (Baltimore: Johns Hopkins University Press, 2002), 21–38. See also Marlene Epp, *Women without Men: Mennonite Refugees of the Second World War* (Toronto: University of Toronto Press, 2000).

11 Published by the Multicultural History Society of Ontario. The author or editor of many volumes on Finns, Lindström reprinted her articles on women in Varpu Lindström, ed., *I Won't Be a Slave! Selected Articles in Finnish Canadian Women's History* (Beaverton, ON: Aspasia Books, 2010).

12 A good summary is in Marilyn Barber, *Immigrant Domestic Servants in Canada* (Ottawa: Canadian Historical Association, 1991).

13 Franca Iacovetta, *Such Hardworking People: Italian Immigrants in Postwar Toronto* (Toronto: University of Toronto Press, 1992); Epp, *Women without Men*; Frances Swyripa, *Wedded to the Cause: Ukrainian-Canadian Women and Ethnic Identity, 1891–1991* (Toronto: University of Toronto Press, 1993).

14 For example, Nira Yuval-Davis, *Gender and Nation* (London: Sage Publications, 1997); Cynthia Cockburn, *The Space between Us: Negotiating Gender and National Identities in Conflict* (London: Zed Books, 1998); special issues of *Canadian Woman Studies*, "Immigrant and Refugee Women," 19, 3 (Fall 1999), and "National Identity and Gender Politics," 20, 2 (Summer 2000).

15 Tania Das Gupta and Franca Iacovetta, "Whose Canada Is It? Immigrant Women, Women of Colour and Feminist Critiques of 'Multiculturalism,'" *Atlantis* 24, 2 (Spring 2000): 1–4.

16 Mary Louise Pratt, *Imperial Eyes: Travel Writing and Transculturation* (London: Routledge, 1992). Also, Antoinette Burton, *Burdens of History: British Feminists, Indian Women, and Imperial Culture, 1865–1915* (Chapel Hill: University of North Carolina Press, 1994); Frederick Cooper and Ann Laura Stoler, eds, *Tensions of Empire: Colonial Cultures in a Bourgeois World* (Berkeley: University of California Press, 1997); Inderpal Grewal and Caren Kaplan, eds, *Home and Harem: Nation, Gender, Empire, and the Cultures of Travel* (Durham, NC: Duke University Press, 1996); Ruth Roach Pierson and Nupur Chaudhuri, eds, *Nation, Empire, Colony: Historicizing Gender and Race* (Bloomington: Indiana University Press, 1998).

17 Adele Perry, *On the Edge of Empire: Gender, Race, and the Making of British Columbia, 1849–1871* (Toronto: University of Toronto Press, 2001); Corey Snelgrove, Rita Dhamoon, and Jeff Corntassel, "Unsettling Settler Colonialism: The Discourse and Politics of Settlers, and Solidarity with Indigenous Nations," *Decolonization: Indigeneity, Education, and Society* 3, 2 (2014): 1–32; see the debate: Bonita Lawrence and Enakshi Dua, "Decolonizing Antiracism," *Social*

Justice 32, 4 (2005): 120–43; and response: Nandita Sharma and Cynthia Wright, "Decolonizing Resistance, Challenging Colonial States," *Social Justice* 35, 3 (2008): 120–38.

18 Himani Bannerji, "On the Dark Side of the Nation: Politics of Multiculturalism and the State of 'Canada,'" *Journal of Canadian Studies* 31, 3 (Fall 1996): 103–30; her *The Dark Side of the Nation: Essays on Multiculturalism, Nationalism, and Gender* (Toronto: Canadian Scholars Press, 2000); Vic Satzewich, ed., *Deconstructing a Nation: Immigration, Multiculturalism, and Racism in 90s Canada* (Halifax: Fernwood Publishing, 1992); Veronica Strong-Boag et al., *Painting the Maple: Essays on Race, Gender, and the Construction of Canada* (Vancouver: UBC Press, 1998).

19 Sheyfali Saujani, "Empathy and Authority in Oral Testimony: Feminist Debates, Multicultural Mandates, and Reassessing the Interviewer and Her 'Disagreeable' Subjects," *Histoire sociale / Social History* 45, 90 (November 2012): 361–91; Eve Haque, *Multiculturalism within a Bilingual Framework: Language, Race, and Belonging in Canada* (Toronto: University of Toronto Press, 2012).

20 Himani Bannerji, "Multiple Multiculturalisms and Charles Taylor's Politics of Recognition," in *Whither Multiculturalism? A Politics of Dissensus*, ed. Barbara Saunders and David Haljan Leuven (Belgium: Leuven University Press, 2003), 35–45.

21 For example, Patricia J. Williams, *Alchemy of Race and Rights* (Cambridge, MA: Harvard University Press, 1991); Ruth Frankenberg, *White Women, Race Matters: The Social Construction of Whiteness* (Minneapolis: University of Minnesota Press, 1993); Evelyn Brooks Higginbotham, "African-American Women's History and the Metalanguage of Race," *Signs* 17, 2 (1992): 251–74.

22 Midge Ayukawa, "Japanese Pioneer Women: Fighting Racism and Rearing the Next Generation," in *Sisters or Strangers?* (1st ed.), 233–47. See also her book, *Hiroshima Immigrants in Canada, 1891–1941* (Vancouver: UBC Press, 2008).

23 Isabel Kaprielian-Churchill, "Odars and 'Others': Intermarriage and the Retention of Armenian Ethnic Identity," in *Sisters or Strangers?* (1st ed.), 248–65. See also her book *Like Our Mountains: A History of Armenians in Canada* (Montreal: McGill-Queen's University Press, 2005).

24 Cecilia Morgan, "Turning Strangers into Sisters: Missionaries and Colonization in Upper Canada," in *Sisters or Strangers?* (1st ed.), 23–48.

25 Adele Perry, "Whose Sisters and What Eyes? White Women, Race, and Immigration to British Columbia, 1849–1871," in *Sisters or Strangers?* (1st ed.), 49–70.

26 Most Indian migrants were Sikhs from Punjab. Enakshi Dua, "Racializing Imperial Canada: Indian Women and the Making of Ethnic Communities," in *Sisters or Strangers?* (1st ed.), 71–85.

27 Lisa R. Mar, "The Tale of Lin Tee: Madness, Family Violence, and Lindsay's Anti-Chinese Riot of 1919," 108–29; and Barrington Walker, "Killing the Black Female Body: Black Womanhood, Black Patriarchy, and Spousal Murder in Two Ontario Criminal Trials, 1892–1894," 89–107, both in *Sisters or Strangers?* (1st ed.). Walker's edited *The History of Immigration and Racism in Canada: Essential Readings* (Toronto: Canadian Scholars Press, 2008) includes important articles on women immigrants.

28 Gertrude Mianda, "Sisterhood versus Discrimination: Being a Black African Francophone Immigrant Woman in Montreal and Toronto," in *Sisters or Strangers?* (1st ed.), 266–84.

29 Lorna R. McLean and Marilyn Barber, "In Search of Comfort and Independence: Irish Immigrant Domestic Servants Encounter the Courts, Jails, and Asylums in Nineteenth-Century Ontario," in *Sisters or Strangers?* (1st ed.), 133–60.

30 Karen Flynn, "Experience and Identity: Black Immigrant Nurses to Canada, 1950–1980," in *Sisters or Strangers?* (1st ed.), 381–98. See also her *Moving beyond Borders: A History of Black Canadian and Caribbean Women in the Diaspora* (Toronto: University of Toronto Press, 2011).

31 Julie Guard, "Canadian Citizens or Dangerous Foreign Women? Canada's Radical Consumer Movement, 1947–1950," in *Sisters or Strangers?* (1st ed.), 161–89.

32 Ester Reiter, "Camp Naivelt and the Daughters of the Jewish Left," in *Sisters or Strangers?* (1st ed.), 365–80.

33 This summary draws on Donna R. Gabaccia's "Juggling Jargons: Transnationalism," *Traverse* 1 (2005): 49–64; and Gabaccia and Iacovetta, "Introduction," in Gabaccia and Iacovetta, *Women, Gender, and Transnational Lives*. The referenced works are Nina Glick-Schiller, Linda Basch, and Cristina Blanc-Szanton, eds, *Towards a Transnational Perspective on Migration: Race, Class, Ethnicity, and Nationalism Reconsidered* (New York: New York Academy of Sciences, 1992); Arjun Appadurai, *Modernity at Large: Cultural Dimensions of Globalization* (Minneapolis: University of Minnesota Press, 1996); Saskia Sassen, *Losing Control? Sovereignty in an Age of Globalization* (New York: Columbia University Press, 1996).

34 For example, Donna Gabaccia and Franca Iacovetta, "Women, Work, and Protest in the Italian Diaspora: An International Research Agenda," *Labour / Le Travail* 42 (1998): 161–81.

35 On the transnational proletarian migrations studied before the ascendancy of the term "transnationalism," see, for example, Donna Gabaccia, Franca Iacovetta, and Fraser Ottanelli, "Laboring across National Borders: Class, Gender, and Militancy in the Proletarian Mass Migrations," special issue on transnational labour history, *International Labor and Working-Class History* (ILWCH) 66 (Fall 2004): 57–77.

36 Social scientists have since modestly historicized their views and talk of collapsing nations is over. Nina Glick-Schiller and Georges Fouron, *Georges Woke Up Laughing: Long-Distance Nationalism and the Search for Home* (Durham, NC: Duke University Press, 2001); see also Gilberto Fernandes, "Of Outcasts and Ambassadors: The Making of Portuguese Diaspora in Postwar North America" (PhD diss., York University, 2014).

37 Varpu Lindström, "Propaganda and Identity Construction: Media Representation in Canada of Finnish and Finnish-Canadian Women during the Winter War of 1939–1940," 287–313; Paula Draper, "Surviving Their Survival: Women, Memory, and the Holocaust," 399–414; and Frances Swyripa, "The Mother of God Wears a Maple Leaf: History, Gender, and Ethnic Identity in Sacred Space," 341–61, all in *Sisters or Strangers?* (1st ed.).

38 Vic Satzewich and Lloyd Wong, eds, *Transnational Identities and Practices in Canada* (Vancouver: UBC Press, 2006), preface. See also several essays in Tastsoglou, *Women, Gender, and Diasporic Lives*.

39 Steven Vertovec, "Three Meanings of 'Diaspora' Exemplified among South Asian Religions," *Diaspora* 7, 2 (1999): 277.

40 Examples of compelling diasporic approaches to non-forced migration include Donna Gabaccia, *Italy's Many Diasporas* (London: Routledge, 2000); Marlene Epp, "Pioneers, Refugees, Exiles, and Transnationals: Gendering Diaspora in an Ethno-Religious Context," *Journal of the Canadian Historical Association* 12 (2001): 137–53; Tastsoglou, *Women, Gender, and Diasporic Lives*; and recent dissertations such as Grace L. Sanders Johnson, *La Voix des Femmes: Haitian Women's Rights, National Politics, and Black Activism in Port-au-Prince and Montreal, 1935–1986* (PhD diss., University of Michigan, 2013); Laurie Bertram, "New Icelandic Ethnoscapes: Material, Visual, and Oral Terrains of Cultural Expression in Icelandic Canadian History, 1875–Present" (PhD diss., University of Toronto, 2010); Nadia Jones-Gailani, "Iraqi Women in Diaspora: Resettlement, Religion, and Remembrance in the Iraqi Diaspora in Toronto and Detroit" (PhD diss., University of Toronto, 2013); and Noula Mina, "Homeland Activism, Public Performance, and the Construction of Identity: An Examination of Greek Canadian Transnationalism, 1900–1990s" (PhD diss., University of Toronto, 2014).

41 Afua Cooper, "A New Biography of the African Diaspora: The Life and Death of Marie-Joseph Angélique, Black Portuguese Slave Women in New France, 1725–1734," in *Global Conversations: New Scholarship on the History of Black Peoples*, ed. Darlene Clark Hine (Chicago: University of Illinois Press, 2009), 46–73, shortened and reprinted in *Sisters of Strangers?* (2nd ed.), 23–43; Paul Gilroy, *The Black Atlantic: Modernity and Double Consciousness* (Cambridge, MA: Harvard University Press, 1993).

42 Homi K. Bhabha, *The Location of Culture* (Abingdon: Routledge, 1994). The feminist scholarship includes Parin Dossa, *Racialized Bodies, Disabling Worlds: Storied Lives of Immigrant Muslim Women* (Toronto: University of Toronto Press, 2009); Chandra Talpady Mohanty, "Under Western Eyes: Feminist Scholarship and Colonial Discourses," in *Third World Women and the Politics of Feminism*, ed. Chandra Mohanty, Ann Russo, and Lourdes Torres (Bloomington: Indiana University Press, 1991), 51–80; Lila Abu-Lughod, "Do Muslim Women Really Need Saving? Anthropological Reflections on Cultural Relativism and Its Others," *American Anthropologist* 104, 3 (2002): 783–90.

43 Nadia Jones-Gailani, "Feminist Oral History and Assessing the Dueling Narratives of Iraqi Women in Diaspora," in *Sisters or Strangers?* (2nd ed.), 584–602.

44 Grace L. Sanders Johnson, "Haitian Feminist Diasporic Lakou: Haitian Women's Community Organizing in Montreal, 1960–1980," in *Sisters and Strangers?* (2nd ed.), 372–92.

45 Vicki L. Ruiz and Ellen Carol DuBois, eds, *Unequal Sisters: An Inclusive Reader in US Women's History*, 4th ed. (New York: Routledge, 2008).

46 Lesley Erickson, "The Interplay of Ethnicity and Gender: Swedish Women in Southeastern Saskatchewan," in *"Other" Voices: Historical Essays on Saskatchewan Women*, ed. Dave De Brou and Aileen Moffatt (Regina: Canadian Plains Research Centre, 1995), reprinted in *Sisters or Strangers?* (2nd ed.), 172–90; Willeen G. Keough, "Unpacking the Discursive Irish Woman Immigrant in Eighteenth- and Nineteenth-Century Newfoundland," *Irish Studies Review* 21, 1 (2013): 55–70, shortened and reprinted in *Sisters or Strangers?* (2nd ed.), 44–63.

47 As in re-examining the connections between Britain and Canada through the categories of gender and race: Lisa Chilton, "Letters 'Home' from Canada: British Female Emigrants and the Imperial Family of Women," excerpted and revised from *Agents of Empire: British Female Migration to Canada and Australia, 1860s–1930* (Toronto: University of Toronto Press, 2007), in *Sisters or Strangers?* (2nd ed.), 153–71.

48 Laura Madokoro, "'Slotting' Chinese Families and Refugees, 1947–1967," *Canadian Historical Review* 93, 1 (March 2012): 25–56, shortened and reprinted in *Sisters or Strangers?* (2nd ed.), 479–99.

49 Glenda Tibe Bonifacio, "I Care for You, Who Cares for Me? Transitional Services of Filipino Live-in Caregivers in Canada,"*Asian Women* 24, 1 (2008): 24–50, shortened and reprinted in *Sisters or Strangers?* (2nd ed.), 252–70. See also her book, *Pinay on the Prairies: Filipino Women and Transnational Identities* (Vancouver: UBC Press, 2014).

50 Susana Miranda, "'An Unlikely Collection of Union Militants': Portuguese Immigrant Cleaning Women Become Political Subjects in Postwar Toronto,"

Atlantis 32, 1 (2007): 111–21, reprinted in *Sisters or Strangers?* (2nd ed.), 393–408.

51 See, for instance, Franca Iacovetta, Valerie Korinek, and Marlene Epp, eds, *Edible Histories, Cultural Politics: Towards a Canadian Food History* (Toronto: University of Toronto Press, 2012).

52 Helen Vallianatos and Kim Raine, "Consuming Food and Constructing Identities among Arabic and South Asian Immigrant Women," *Food, Culture, and Society* 11, 3 (September 2008): 356–73, shortened and reprinted in *Sisters or Strangers?* (2nd ed.), 455–73.

53 Several of the *Looking into My Sister's Eyes* authors drew on the large oral history collection created by the MHSO in the 1970s and 1980s.

54 Noula Mina, "Taming and Training Greek 'Peasant Girls' and the Gendered Politics of Whiteness in Postwar Canada: Canadian Bureaucrats and Immigrant Domestics, 1950s–1960s," *Canadian Historical Review* 94, 4 (December 2013): 514–39, shortened and reprinted in *Sisters or Strangers?* (2nd ed.), 231–51. On Passerini and oral history before and after the self-reflexive turn, see Donna Gabaccia and Franca Iacovetta, eds, "Borders, Conflict Zones, and Memory: Scholarly Engagements with Luisa Passerini," special theme issue, *Women's History Review* 25, 3 (May 2016).

55 There is a rich literature on oral history methodology. For some sense of the trajectories in feminist scholarship, see, for example, Personal Narratives Group, *Interpreting Women's Lives: Feminist Theory and Personal Narratives* (Bloomington: Indiana University Press, 1989); Daphne Patai and Sherna Berger Gluck, eds, *Women's Words: The Feminist Practice of Oral History* (New York: Routledge, 1991); and, most recently, Katrina Srigley, Stacey Zembrzycki, and Franca Iacovetta, eds, *Beyond Women's Words: Feminisms and the Practices of Oral History in the Twenty-First Century* (New York: Routledge, 2018). Recent Canadian work includes Stacey Zembrzycki, *According to Baba: A Collaborative Oral History of Sudbury's Ukrainian Community* (Vancouver: UBC Press, 2014); Alexander Freund, *Oral History and Ethnic History* (Ottawa: Canadian Historical Association, 2014); and Kristina R. Llewellyn et al., *The Canadian Oral History Reader* (Montreal: McGill-Queen's University Press, 2015).

56 The literature in memory studies is also extensive. Feminist contributions include Luisa Passerini, ed., *Memory and Totalitarianism: International Yearbook of Oral History and Life Stories*, vol. 1 (Oxford: Oxford University Press, 1992); Marlene Epp, "The Memory of Violence: Soviet and East European Mennonite Refugees and Rape in the Second World War," *Journal of Women's History* 9, 1 (1997): 58–87; Hasia R. Diner, *Hungering for America: Italian, Irish, and Jewish Foodways in the Age of Migration* (Cambridge, MA: Harvard University Press, 2001).

57 Pamela Sugiman, "'Days You Remember': Japanese Canadian Women and the
    Violence of Internment," in *Not Born a Refugee Woman: How Refugee Women
    Reclaim Their Identities in Research, Education, Policy, and Creativity*, ed.
    Maroussia Hajdukowski-Ahmed and Nazilla Khanlo (New York: Berghahn Books,
    2008), 113–34; shortened and reprinted in *Sisters or Strangers?* (2nd ed.), 566–83.

58 Sonia Cancian, "From Montreal and Venice with Love: Migrant Letters and
    Romantic Intimacy in Italian Migration to Postwar Canada," excerpted and
    revised from ch. 4 of her *Families, Lovers, and Their Letters: Italian Postwar
    Migration to Canada* (Winnipeg: University of Manitoba Press, 2010), in *Sisters
    or Strangers?* (2nd ed.), 191–203. On the history of emotions, see, for example,
    Nicole Eustace et al., "*AHR* Conversation: The Historical Study of Emotions,"
    American Historical Review 117, 5 (2012): 1487–531; on the immigrant letter,
    Bruce S. Elliott, David A. Gerber, Suzanne M. Sinke, eds, *Letters across Borders:
    The Epistolary Practices of International Migrants* (New York: Palgrave Macmillan, 2006).

59 Laurie K. Bertram, "Fashioning Conflicts: Gender, Power, and Icelandic
    Immigrant Hair and Clothing in North America, 1874–1933," in *Sisters or
    Strangers?* (2nd ed.), 275–97.

60 Ashleigh Androsoff, "A Larger Frame: 'Redressing' the Image of
    Doukhobor-Canadian Women in the Twentieth Century," *Journal of the Canadian
    Historical Association* 18, 1 (2007): 81–105, shortened and reprinted in *Sisters
    or Strangers?* (2nd ed.), 298–316; Patrizia Gentile and Jane Nicholas, eds,
    Contesting Bodies and Nation in Canadian History (Toronto: University of
    Toronto Press, 2013).

61 Rhonda Hinther, *Perogies and Politics: Canada's Ukrainian Left, 1891–1991*
    (Toronto: University of Toronto Press, 2018); Julie Guard, *Radical Housewives:
    Price Wars and Food Politics in Mid-Twentieth-Century Canada* (Toronto:
    University of Toronto Press, 2018).

SELECTED READINGS

Agnew, Vijay, ed. *Diaspora, Memory, and Identity: A Search for Home.* Toronto:
    University of Toronto Press, 2005.
Bannerji, Himani. *Demography and Democracy: Essays on Nationalism, Gender, and
    Ideology.* Toronto: Canadian Scholars Press, 2011.
Bohaker, Heidi, and Franca Iacovetta. "Making Aboriginal People 'Immigrants Too':
    A Comparison of Citizenship Programs for Newcomers and Indigenous Peoples in
    Postwar Canada, 1940s–1960s." *Canadian Historical Review* 90, 3 (2009): 427–62.
    https://doi.org/10.3138/chr.90.3.427

Bristow, Peggy, ed. *"We're Rooted Here and They Can't Pull Us Up"*: Essays in *African Canadian Women's History*. Toronto: University of Toronto Press, 1994.

Burnet, Jean. *Looking into My Sister's Eyes: An Exploration in Women's History*. Toronto: Multicultural History Society of Ontario, 1986.

Caroli, Betty Boyd, and Robert F. Harney, eds. *The Italian Immigrant Woman in North America*. Toronto: Multicultural History Society of Ontario, 1978.

Dossa, Parin. *Racialized Bodies, Disabling Worlds: Storied Lives of Immigrant Muslim Women*. Toronto: University of Toronto Press, 2009.

Dubinsky, Karen, Adele Perry, and Henry Yu. *Within and without the Nation: Canadian History as Transnational History*. Toronto: University of Toronto Press, 2015.

Epp, Marlene.*Women without Men: Mennonite Refugees of the Second World War*. Toronto: University of Toronto Press, 2000.

Epp, Marlene, and Franca Iacovetta, eds. *Sisters or Strangers? Immigrant, Ethnic, and Racialized Women in Canadian History*, 2nd ed. Toronto: University of Toronto Press, 2016.

Flynn, Karen. *Moving beyond Borders: A History of Black Canadian and Caribbean Women in the Diaspora*. Toronto: University of Toronto Press, 2011.

Frager, Ruth A. *Sweatshop Strife: Class, Ethnicity, and Gender in the Jewish Labour Movement of Toronto, 1900–1939*. Toronto: University of Toronto Press, 1992.

Freund, Alexander, ed. *Beyond the Nation? Immigrants' Local Lives in Transnational Cultures*. Toronto: University of Toronto Press, 2012.

Gabaccia, Donna R., and Franca Iacovetta, eds. *Women, Gender, and Transnational Lives: Italian Workers of the World*. Toronto: University of Toronto Press, 2002.

Grewal, Inderpal, and Caren Kaplan. *Scattered Hegemonies: Postmodernity and Transnational Feminist Practices*. Minneapolis: University of Minnesota Press, 1994.

Iacovetta, Franca. "Gendering Trans/National Historiographies: Feminists Rewriting Canadian History." *Journal of Women's History* 19, 1 (2007): 206–13. https://doi.org/10.1353/jowh.2007.0016

– "Post-Modern Ethnography, Historical Materialism, and Decentring the (Male) Authorial Voice: A Feminist Conversation." *Histoire sociale / Social History* 32, 64 (November 1999): 275–94.

– *Such Hardworking People: Italian Immigrants in Postwar Toronto*. Toronto: University of Toronto Press, 1992.

Lindström, Varpu, ed. *I Won't Be a Slave! Selected Articles in Finnish Canadian Women's History*. Beaverton, ON: Aspasia Books, 2010.

Man, Guida, and Rina Cohen, eds. *Engendering Transnational Voices: Studies in Family, Work, and Identity*. Waterloo: Wilfrid Laurier University Press, 2015.

Mayer, Tamar, ed. *Gender Ironies of Nationalism: Sexing the Nation*. London: Routledge, 2000.

Oikawa, Mona. *Cartographies of Violence: Japanese Canadian Women, Memory, and the Subjects of the Internment*. Toronto: University of Toronto Press, 2012.

Sangster, Joan. "Telling Our Stories: Feminist Debates and the Use of Oral History." *Women's History Review* 1, 5 (1994): 5–28. https://doi.org/10.1080/09612029400200046

Silvera, Makeda. *Silenced: Talks with Working Class Caribbean Women about Their Lives and Struggles as Domestic Workers in Canada*, rev. ed. Toronto: Sister Vision Press, 1992.

Silverman, Eliane Leslau. *The Last Best West: Women on the Alberta Frontier, 1880–1930*. Montreal: Eden Press, 1984.

Swyripa, Frances. *Wedded to the Cause: Ukrainian-Canadian Women and Ethnic Identity, 1891–1991*. Toronto: University of Toronto Press, 1993.

Tastsoglou, Evangelia, and Peruvemba S. Jaya. *Immigrant Women in Atlantic Canada: Challenges, Negotiations, Re-constructions*. Toronto: Canadian Scholars Press, 2011.

11 Primal Urge/National Force: Sex, Sexuality, and National History

HEATHER STANLEY

Sex and sexuality are relative newcomers to Canadian historiography. The children of feminist and LGTTBQ activist-scholar parents, social historians published the field's first works in the 1980s. They viewed their nation's historiographical landscape, populated with economic theories of great rivers, political biographies of founding fathers, and discussions of staple trades, but bereft of people such as themselves: women, the working class, people of colour, and peoples whose sexuality did not comply with a rigid heterosexual eroticism. Foundational social history narratives, and sexuality histories in particular, extended Canada's historiography and pushed sexuality stories from the margins into the centre. Politically, historical existence became modern resistance. As the field widened during post-structuralism's rise, many scholars adopted tools such as discourse analysis, deconstructing the historical roots of categories previously understood as universal and fixed. Women's histories became more than telling the stories of females: they interrogated how concepts such as "woman" had shifted across time and space. LGTTBQ scholars, while still bringing the hidden history of LGTTBQ Canadians to the forefront, historicized the heterosexual-homosexual binary and grappled with questions such as whether sexual object choice equalled (or equals) identity.

In making these historical additions, sex and sexuality historians (along with their other social history counterparts) did not simply broaden Canadian historiography, they reformed it, often challenging the legitimacy of conclusions made by earlier historians. Unsurprisingly, this historiography also found itself embattled; many dominant scholars pushed back against what they saw as investigations into frivolous topic areas motivated by personal interest. Other than Jack Granatstein's *Who Killed Canadian History?*[1] the most (in)famous of these attacks was Michael Bliss's "Privatizing the Mind: The Sundering of Canadian History, the Sundering of Canada."[2] Bliss, in an homage to his mentor

Donald Creighton, bemoaned the lack of historians focused on "national" topics. While he noted that the historians of Creighton's era wore nationalist blinders which narrowed the focus of their work, he also alleged that as social history became an increasingly popular specialization, average Canadians no longer looked to the university historian to tell them "where we came from, who we are, and where we might be going."[3] Bliss connected what he viewed as a nationwide political malaise to a lack of Canadian self-identity. Unlike Americans, whose national sense of self was of mythic quality and quantity, Canadians were "hungry" for a sense of themselves and their nation that "could be subscribed to from St. John's through the Baie Comeau, Montreal, Winnipeg, Regina and Calgary, to Vancouver, Victoria, Whitehorse, and Inuvik."[4]

Bliss's article sparked, and continues to spark, "spirited" debate. Fourteen years later, Steven Maynard wrote a provocative response, "The Maple Leaf (Gardens) Forever: Sex, Canadian Historians and National History," in which he argued that sexuality and Canada's national sense of itself were inherently intertwined. A deliberately polemical think piece, Maynard used the 1999 under aged same-sex scandal at the iconic Maple Leaf Gardens arena, the civil service purges of gays and lesbians, and the treatment of Indigenous children in residential schools to discuss how nationalism, nationality, and sexuality are consistently intertwined.[5]

This chapter is inspired by the space created between Bliss's and Maynard's very different views of sexual history and the relationship of history to nationalism and nation-building, and it seeks to push this history further by incorporating both gender and corporeality into the wider discussion. Countries (re) create their national self-identities in myriad ways: unique geographies, shared customs, and occasions of national importance. Yet these common identifiers must be enacted by individual citizen bodies. Real people maintain common customs by their continued performance, and their bodies are used to demark events participated in by "nations," such as wars. The citizen body is the base material of which a nation and national identity is formed. Citizen bodies are never neutral; they are sorted into positive categories such as useful and normal, and negative categories of inadequate, abnormal, and grotesque.

This chapter uses the writing produced by sexuality and gender historians over the last twenty-five years to trace the transformations of the idealized citizen body throughout Canadian history. I focus on three time periods: the fur trade and (re)settlement era, the Victorian era, and the Second World War and postwar rebuilding era. Long treated as national and political touchstones, each of these periods clearly demonstrate the formation of a Canadian national identity on the foundation of an idealized citizen body that was white, middle-class, heterosexual, and gender-role-conforming. However, as such categories of difference are historically intersectional, these categories were often policed through the discipline of other elements of the citizen body, particularly sexuality. Thus, a body deemed unworthy of citizenship rights, by, for example, being Indigenous and "unfeminine," was policed sexually via surveillance, containment, and sexualized violence. Sex and sexuality were a lever used by elite Canadians to shift discourses of normality in their favour. However, as the pre-eminent sexual theorist Michel Foucault demonstrates, sex and sexuality as discourses are naturally productive.[6] As the political and social elites of Canadian society continuously tried to build their nation via their narrative of the fitness and normality of the white, middle-class, heterosexual, gender-conforming body, they simultaneously had to resist and helped to define the boundaries of the "others," who, in turn, simultaneously subverted and redefined the boundaries of the ideal. Therefore, this chapter produces parallel narratives of both the ideal citizen bodies, which were supposed to create a national uniformity in its citizens, and the actual bodies whose experiences continuously problematized those attempts with their tenacious difference.[7]

Any discussion of understandings of "nation" in Canada sparks questions about Quebec, particularly how Quebecois bodies fit within Canada's contested multinational history. There is evidence that during certain times elites viewed the ideal citizen body as primarily English and Protestant. Quebecois bodies were often viewed as problematically excessive due to both their assumed Gallic temperament and their Catholic spirituality.[8] However, the way that francophone citizen bodies interacted with the larger sociopolitical relationship between Quebec and Canada – including, for example, francophone understandings of the role of mothers and motherhood, feminism in the Catholic Church and within the Quebec nationalist movement, and perception of the role of sexuality in resisting cultural assimilation – makes the topic too complex to be examined within the limits of this chapter. Rather than providing a token surface examination, this chapter instead is intended as a starting point from which examinations of the intersections of sex, sexuality, and nation throughout Canada can, and should be, undertaken.

The Fur Trade and Early Settlement

Sex was a featured concern of the earliest Canadian policy.[9] Both colonial and missionary officials were initially shocked by what they saw as the excessive sexual permissibility of local Indigenous persons. New France officials, fed by lurid accounts of explorers, placed Indigenous bodies within a long-standing scientific tradition of hypersexualized colonized "others."[10] French colonials viewed the elaborate networks and social-sexual mores of the nearest Indigenous groups and, instead of seeing the complexity of that system, assumed no such system existed. Yet New France officials also felt that Indigenous sexual potential could be harnessed for the colonial good and that the intermarriage of Indigenous women and colonial men solved a number of complications, not the least of which was the problematic ratio of six white men to every white woman. Local Jesuit priests encouraged intermarriage as a gateway to the conversion of Indigenous peoples and as way to the curb the practice of more illicit and short-term liaisons between First Nations women and white men, which were thought to threaten the long-term stability of the colony. Marriage within a proper Catholic ceremony was deemed a key component in keeping colonizer men, in particular the *coureurs de bois*, from "going native."[11]

As the colony became established, the French state brought in more white women, and officials began to discredit racial intermarriage as undesirable and unnecessary. However, the *coureurs de bois* refused to give up their relationships with Indigenous women, as these had become crucial to their fur trade successes; indeed, it was social-sexual encounters and the economic benefits which accompanied them that gave the North West Company (NWC) a chance of surviving and thriving against the rival British Hudson's Bay Company (HBC), which had the benefit of Royal Charter and eventual conquest.[12]

The HBC organized their colonial presence along sexual lines, choosing a same-sex monastic, military model that forbade sexual liaisons with the local peoples in the hopes it would avoid potentially dangerous conflicts. However, as Jennifer Brown notes, the London officials had little control over the faraway actions of their men, and "the geographical gulf between London and the Bay would become a social one as well, as the traders formed common values and ways of coping with fur trade life."[13] HBC men soon learned what the NWC had long known: maintaining a long-term connection with an Indigenous woman provided fur traders with much more than sexual and emotional release.[14] Such a relationship was a gateway for European men into the complex network of kinship ties within Indigenous societies, often securing him first pick of the prime furs from his wife's relations. In addition to serving as fur trade brokers, Indigenous women also filled crucial roles as linguistic and cultural interpreters. Despite the initial misgivings of HBC officials, HBC men were soon competing with NWC men for the most influential unions. When the two companies merged in 1821, almost all of the fur trade officials within Canada and most of the lower-ranking officers had engaged in a long-term relationship with an Indigenous woman, termed "marriages in the custom of the country" or "*à la façon du pays.*"[15]

While Canada remained as sojourner society for European men, such sexual power for Indigenous women was deemed acceptable, even exciting. Because Canada was still defined as a space of the exotic "other," Indigenous female sexuality was seen as contained within the larger colonial context. However, as more and more traders spent increasingly long periods of time in (what would become) Canada, it became increasingly conceptualized as "home," and the patriarchal and sexual standards of Europe were increasingly applied to the sexual landscape. "[European men] were particularly anxious to estrange their daughters from Indian influence. It was believed that the free manner in which Indian mothers discussed sexual matters made it impossible for fathers to inculcate in their daughters proper feminine virtues, especially chastity."[16]

As Canada shifted to being a colony rather than a trade outpost, Métis women became sought after as the most desirable fur trade brides. They were viewed as the best of both worlds, their assumed Indigenous physical and sexual exoticness tempered by a European upbringing. However, Sylvia Van Kirk argues that the increasing Europeanization of sexual values proved a dramatic turning point for Indigenous women, stripping them of much of the agency and power they had enjoyed as "women in between." When white women arrived and Canada was fully transformed into a settler colony, Indigenous bodies were redefined as only fit for fulfilling sexual needs on a short-term basis. Many scholars and activists have argued that this historical devaluation of female Indigenous bodies continues to be felt in the sexualized violence against Indigenous women and girls and in the unwillingness or inability of governments and law enforcement to address these issues.[17]

Van Kirk's work has been both lauded as a crucial turning point in Canadian women's and Indigenous history and also critiqued – often simultaneously. Though Van Kirk's interpretation remains the dominant framework for understanding this period, there is no denying that her understanding of the sexual interrelationships between Indigenous women and newcomer men is, at times, naive and overly romantic, as she often skims over the inherent racial inequalities present in each union.[18] Due to her focus on heterosexual marriage, Van Kirk is also able to omit many less savoury details of colonial sexual interaction, including rape and incest, and there is almost no discussion of sex work as labour – both paid and unpaid. Further, Van Kirk's division of colonial erotics into three distinct periods has been viewed as too rigid and uncomplicated. Adele Perry, in her in-depth examination of the colonial social-sexual relationships between James Douglas and his Métis wife Amelia Connolly in *Colonial Relations*, complicates Van Kirk's narrative. Perry both demonstrates that North American social-sexual relationships were part of a larger colonial kinship network and explores how, for mixed-race colonial elite families such as the Douglas-Connollys, maintaining a colonial position was a complicated dance on the axes of race, class, and power.[19] Finally, as with all cases where elite white women write the history of Indigenous women, there are questions of power within the realm of academics itself and who has the right and the opportunity to speak for whom.

Yet Van Kirk and her contemporaries, though limited in many ways by their 1970s liberal feminism, did make an enormous contribution in the destabilization of some of the core myths dominating North American history. First, by asking the seemingly simple question "where were all the women?" Van Kirk and Brown countered dominant histories of the fur trade as solely an economic process. What had essentially been a history of "stuff" being moved from one place to another by great white men became a more nuanced history where Indigenous women (twice marginalized and thus hitherto ignored as irrelevant) served as primary movers within the system. Secondly, works such as *Many Tender Ties* helped to demythologize "the West" as a place empty of people yet rich in staple resources, to be conquered by strong white pioneer families so beloved in nation-building heritage remembrances. Van Kirk opened a door to demonstrations that not only was the ideal of both the Canadian and American West as "virgin land" ripe for the taking false, but that virgin land was a sexualized, colonial trope used to reframe and contain Indigenous title, discursively making way for the "right" kind of settlers.

Other scholars have continued to protest the erasure or containment of Indigenous bodies within settler histories by demonstrating how "problematic" Indigenous bodies continued to influence the pattern of settlement. For example, Sarah Carter examines, in *The Importance of Being Monogamous*, how Indian agents were tasked to crack down on Indigenous polygamy in large part to police incoming Mormon polygamist colonists.[20]

Victoriana Regina: Women as Mothers and Mothers as Citizens

The open and fertile prairie regions being tamed by the hands of strong young men of impeccable European descent, aided by their pretty pink-cheeked wives and abundant children, was a powerful image in selling Canada as a new Eden. However, as time passed, Canadian reformers became increasingly concerned about the presence of "snakes" in their paradise. They feared the pollution of Canada's potential by unsuitable immigrants, the poor, Indigenous persons, and those deemed "feebleminded," who threatened to overwhelm the Anglo-Saxon minority. Such bodies were deemed out of control due to excessive drinking, immorality, and the production of excessive numbers of children. As Mariana Valverde, in *The Age of Light, Soap, and Water*, argues, the ability to control one's body, especially sexual urges, was intimately tied to the project of nation-building:

> The rhetoric of national decline and "weakening of moral fiber" through excessive sexuality is so familiar ... that few writers have taken the time to analyse its roots. It is important, however, to treat such statements not as vacuous rhetorical flourishes but as highly meaningful indicators signalling a belief in the nation's need for specifically *moral* subjects. The nation (as distinct from the state) is, in the discourse of national degeneration, seen as rather fragile and as subject to a quasi-physical process of decay that can only be halted if the individuals, the cells of the body politic, take control over their innermost essence or self.[21]

Even though it was assumed that the undesirable bodies of Canada would never be able to fully conform to elite standards, it was expected they could at least mimic those traits to a certain degree. This response was not unique in Canada – both Britain and the United States experienced variations of the Victorian social purity movement. Canada made the movement its own, however, by the use of metaphors that referenced Canadian national symbols, such as mountains and prairies. Elites even laid claim over the purity of the colour white as particularly appropriate to Canada's snowy winter landscape.[22]

Canadian social purists grounded their mission in Victorian understandings of sex and gender. According to Wendy Mitchinson, within Victorian medical science a woman's biology was not only her destiny, it was her whole being: social, sexual, emotional, and intellectual. Women's sole physical and social reason for being was to be a mother. Encoded in this ideal were both the medical and scientific support of women's subordination to men and the ideology of separate spheres. However, allowing women only to be competent within the private sphere reinforced their idealized lack of agency. Only (white) men, doctors claimed, had the constitution to deal with the rigours and strains of public life, and women who transgressed the sphere of the private domestic home risked their femininity and potentially their fertility overall.[23] In contrast, women within the domestic sphere were thought to be biologically superior to men: inherently more moral, more emotionally intuitive, and better at dealing with issues that involved other women or children. Crucially, because women were only allowed competencies within the private sphere, "the characteristics attributed to women were those which made them dependent on others and responsive to others. Tact, adaptability, and intuition were traits necessary for individuals who did not have power."[24] At the same time, sexuality continued to be classed and raced as the working classes and non-white women were seen as being either environmentally or biologically unable to control their passions, making them excellent targets for white, Anglo-Saxon, Protestant reformers.[25]

Safeguarding women as mothers became one way that many middle-class reformers expressed their citizenship; they classified themselves as "mothers of the race" or protectors of women's ability to reproduce the race. Valverde notes that "race" was a deliberately slippery term, sometimes encompassing the human race and other times referring to the fears that the "right" race – white, Anglo-Saxon Protestants – was not producing as fast as others. The concept of being a mother to the race also had two other important discursive factors. First, middle-class women who eschewed biological motherhood or were unable to reproduce were able to claim many of the benefits of biological motherhood by working in social reform. Helen MacMurchy, one of Canada's first female medical doctors, was able to use the rhetoric of protective motherhood to gain a position as chief of the newly created Federal Division of Child Welfare in 1919 despite remaining childless her entire life.[26] Second, women who claimed that title inherently infantilized those they helped. If the reformer was the mother, the entire working-class and non-white populations were children. Consequently, elite white, Anglo-Saxon, Protestant women increased their social citizenship capital by presenting themselves as mothers of the nation while simultaneously increasing their power through the sexual surveillance and control of other women.

The connection between motherhood and citizenship rights is aptly demonstrated by the strong links between the social purity movement and the push for female suffrage in Canada. As Carol Lee Bacchi notes, the Canadian suffrage movement, in direct contrast to the more equality-focused American and British suffrage movements, was dominated by members who viewed the goal of suffrage as ensuring "good Christian womanhood [had] a political voice."[27] The combination of the social purity movement and suffrage meant that a woman's citizen rights and her right to political participation were contingent on her performance of the proper social-sexual role of wife and mother. In accordance with separate sphere ideology, women needed to vote to protect their sphere, the home, from the incursions of the outside world, including crime, disease, and especially alcohol. In turn, many suffragists argued women would serve their nation by bringing their domestic prowess to clean up and re-moralize the political world by rooting out corruption in the same way they banished dirt from their households.[28] This dominant discourse of the roles of women in nation-building is not without its critics. As Nancy Forestell demonstrates in her chapter, both regional feminist groups (in particular, Indigenous feminist groups) and African Canadian activists problematized the dominance that authors such as Bacchi give to elite white feminists. However, when it came to crafting a narrative that brought together concepts of nationhood and women's participation in the nation through the official channels of suffrage, elite white feminists were extremely successful in crafting a maternal feminist political platform that overwhelming privileged their concerns and reflected their perspectives on what the ideal female citizen of Canada would be.

The links between motherhood and citizenship also affected the ways that reformers viewed the bodies that they deemed in need of restructuring. Women in the working classes were not seen as economically productive bodies but as future mothers. The main concern was that with Canada's industrialization, women working in both factories and the newly created department stores were taxing themselves in ways that could threaten their ability to conceive when they inevitably took up their proper roles as wives and mothers. Backed by medical horror stories of barren shop girls, reformers focused their efforts on improving working conditions for future mothers rather than for women as workers. This meant that the morality of the workplace and the biological "safety" of the workplace – manifest in reforms such as ensuring well-ventilated and gender-segregated washroom facilities – were the main features of their platforms rather than economic issues such as a living wage.[29]

There was also great concern about the fact that working-class women's bodies were also public bodies. Previously, the bodies of young working-class women were controlled either by the patriarchal surveillance of their fathers or, more commonly, under the supervision imposed on women working in domestic service. When reformers became aware that some working-class women engaged in the public system of "treating" – trading sexual encounters for admission into the newly developed working-class entertainments such as fairs and nickelodeons – they conceptualized it as moral weakness that could potentially lead to full-time prostitution.[30] The fact that women's relative poverty meant that economic exchanges were naturally made part of their social-sexual organization, or the potential that some working-class women thought the transactions were fair, was not discussed.

The circle connecting problematic working-class sexuality to public spaces, and safe working-class sexuality to domestic service, was made even more complete by the fact that social reformers tried to redeem prostitutes by placing them in Magdalen homes to retrain them as domestic servants. Though the conditions of such homes might have been preferable to jails, almost no Victorian woman would hire a former sex worker as a domestic even if the woman in question wanted to give up a much more secure income for work which was largely considered the worst of all female occupations. Furthermore, as Constance Backhouse has demonstrated, domestic service, far from being a sexual saviour, was a position of high sexual danger, with many young women falling victim to the upper-class husbands and sons of the house-hold.[31] Moral reformers also tended to focus on redeeming white prostitutes despite the fact that many sex workers were women of colour, with Indige-nous women, then as now, being over-represented both in the profession and in police action against it. This deliberately racist myopia was epitomized in the white slavery scares perpetuated in part by prominent suffragist Emily Murphy. In *The Black Candle*, Murphy falsely informed readers that there was an underground trade in prostitution and opium run by Chinese immigrants. Murphy and others swapped urban legends of pure, young, white women drugged and forced into prostitution; despite the lack of a single documented case within Canada, the phenomenon soon became a "moral panic." According to Valverde, moral panics are crucial historical moments, as they illuminate the social uncertainties of a particular time period. In this case the narrative of white slavery demonstrates elite Canada's fears about uncontrolled female bodies in urban environments, a perceived decrease in sexual morality, and non-white immigration.[32]

Though some historians dismiss the social purity and social reform activ-ists of the Victorian era, their concerns over undesirable bodies would have long-term consequences with the advent of eugenics. As historians Erika Dyck and Angus McLaren show, fears that working-class, immigrant, and Indigenous reproduction would swamp the desirable production of white, Anglo-Saxon Canadians led to the isolation and sterilization of hundreds of Canadians.[33] In Alberta, eugenics had its perfect storm. Female political leaders, including Emily Murphy and the rest of the Famous Five, who had learned important political strategies during the successful push for suffrage, were able to use the West's image as a Garden of Eden to argue for "weeding" the population, in part to counteract the effects of what they viewed as overly liberal immigration policies. Eugenics leaders denied the rights of many Albertan women and men to reproduction based on their definition of "feeble mindedness," which was elastic enough to cover a multitude of situations and which they also used to deny those citizen bodies the right of consent, meaning many were sterilized without permission or even without their knowledge.[34]

One group of women who largely escaped the public eyes of reformers dur-ing the Victorian era were lesbians. Though gay male sex had been known, feared, and policed since the earliest settlements, the segregation of the private sphere actually meant that women could live together with other women quite openly and without fear of censure.[35] Indeed, the idealization of the Victorian woman as largely passionless also served to protect lesbian women, as affec-tions expressed between females were seen as normal and essentially asexual. As long as the more obviously sexual elements of lesbian relationships were kept private, women could maintain a loving relationship with fairly little issue. However, the doctrine of separate spheres also limited lesbian expression. While two women living together was socially acceptable, it was only economically viable to a few with secure work or independent means because the separate sphere ideology was dependent on passing a woman from a breadwinner father to a breadwinner husband. Some women did manage to make such an arrangement work, though perhaps only other lesbian couples recognized it. Cameron Duder, in *Awfully Devoted Women*, presents a portion of a letter from Bud Williams to her partner Frieda Fraser about her suspicions that her aunt's cook and housemaid were "devoted women."

> [My aunt] told me that her cook and housemaid – who were by way of being ladies – had never had jobs before, but that their families had been rather disagreeable about their being awfully devoted and so they had up and left, and this was the only thing they could do. However, they love it as it meant living together. So there seems to be a fair amount of it about.[36]

Segregation within the private sphere may have afforded some lesbians protection, especially when compared with the persecution of gay men; it has proven incredibly problematic for historians. As male homosexual sexual intercourse was historically illegal and deemed a threat to national stability due to its often public nature as well as its non-procreative and presumed counter-masculine effects, gay men show up in the historical record a great deal more than lesbian women. While such sources, notably court records and police reports, must be read carefully due to their clear homophobia, it has been much easier for historians to prove homosexual men's historical existence and fill in some of the details of their lives. This is further aided by the fact that publicity of gay male sex, though discriminatory, allowed some gay men to understand the scope of their community much sooner than lesbian females. Further, a conviction of sodomy or buggery leaves the nature of an encounter largely sexually unambiguous, meaning gay historians are able to assert the presence of historical homosexual acts, though authors such as Paul Jackson caution against conflating a homosexual act with a homosexual identity.[37] Whether two women who express devotion for each other should be viewed as "bosom friends" or an intimate couple has long plagued lesbian historians within Canada and beyond. The concerns expressed about potential solutions to the question of whether they "did it" in the past also clearly demonstrate the ongoing activist participation in this history.[38] Many international authors writing in the 1980s, such as Adrienne Rich, Judith Bennett, and Martha Vicinus, used terms such as "lesbian continuum," "lesbian-like," and "intimate friends" respectively, to avoid assigning a lesbian identity to historical figures or even assuming a female same-sex act occurred without an archival declaration.[39] This was interpreted by many next-generation authors as an unwillingness to place what in 1980s society was still deemed a shameful identity on historical figures, and early scholars were subject to accusations of cowardice. Others have argued that it is inappropriate to put the modern label "homosexual" on historical acts, as the meaning of such a label is in itself a historical artefact.[40]

Still other scholars, including Duder, challenge historians who posit that proof of genital contact is required to prove a lesbian act. He correctly notes that historians have consistently assumed the heterosexuality of almost all persons in the past without requiring a sexual declaration.[41] However, the question of how to "correctly" write the historical erotics of the human body remains contested and will only become more so as contemporary understandings of the plurality of sexual expression and identity becomes increasingly recognized. Questions of how to write the history of transgendered persons, asexuality, and bisexuality are currently pushing the bounds of the discipline as well as challenging the traditional sources base.

The Second World War and the Nuclear Family Rebuilds

Many conservative historians view the Second World War as a watershed moment for Canada; it was the first major international event that Canada participated in as a country in its own right rather than as a British possession.[42] For many contemporary Canadian elites, however, it was also a time to renegotiate gender and sexual roles that had been disrupted by the four decades of change and flux due to the Great War and Great Depression. This has caused historians such as Ruth Roach Pierson to argue that Canadian women's involvement in war service work was not an uncomplicated first step towards second wave feminism, as is commonly believed.[43] The gendered and sexual discourses of the Second World War demonstrate both a fear about women's changing role in the past and attempts to reassert women's separate spheres in the present – postwar rebuilding, in fact, started while the war was still on.

Women war workers had their femininity and their sexuality rigidly policed both to protect Canada's rebuilding phase and because it soon became clear that concerns over femininity were at the crux of recruitment difficulties. Great pains were taken to demonstrate the continued normality of war service workers often by linking dress and grooming habits to feminine character traits. Women serving the military auxiliaries were particularly targeted, as the Second World War marked the first time that women served in uniform in great numbers, crossing one of the major gender lines for the first time.[44] Pierson points to a series of publicity photos taken of the women in the Canadian Women's Army Corps as providing a visual narrative of femininity and heterosexual desirability by portraying a "narcissism," which demonstrated that women were only fit for military service in the short term, as well as reassurance that being in the military during an emergency would not compromise a women's natural feminine impulses to be sexually desirable.[45]

One of the reasons that military officials and Canadian elites focused so heavily on femininity and heterosexuality was that Canadians had become increasingly aware of the existence of female homosexuals throughout the twentieth century, and it was during the war period that they first became constructed as threats to Canadian nationhood. Particular attention was paid to the figure of the butch lesbian, whose deviancy was multiplied by her seeming gender inversion. Butch-femme bar culture, in which lesbians, mainly of the working class, created an erotic community for themselves, came later to Canada than in the United States. Yet by the middle of the Second World War lesbians were becoming increasingly visible, and the butch in particular was constructed as a danger to young heterosexual women.[46]

Military service was regarded as an attractive option for many lesbian women. It provided an excellent place to meet other women and an economic solution that allowed women to live independently within an economic system that viewed women as short-term workers.[47] Unfortunately, it is impossible to get an accurate sense of how many lesbians served within the armed forces. In direct contrast to the way that homosexual men were treated by official military policy, any woman dismissed for committing a homosexual act was categorized as suffering a psychological impairment rather than a specific sexual offence.[48]

While the military attempted to avoid accusations that women in the military were homosexual by focusing attention on their heterosexual normality, they did open themselves to concerns about military women's heterosexual morality. As such, the military ran a parallel propaganda campaign portraying military women as extremely chaste.[49] This perpetuated a long-running sexual double standard for male and female soldiers. Only male soldiers were provided with training and prophylactics to prevent the spread of venereal disease, which was characterized as being primarily spread by women – both sex workers and "loose" girls.[50] Canadian women war workers, and especially women military workers, were sexually constrained to preserve their value as symbols of national womanhood – sexually normal but also chaste and therefore perfect future wives for returning soldiers.

The rise in public awareness about female homosexuality was facilitated by the rise of psychoanalysis in the wartime and postwar era, particularly the works of Freud. Psychoanalysis gained prominence in the postwar era in part because of the growing social rejection of eugenics due to its association with Nazi Germany.[51] Nonetheless, psychoanalysis, like eugenics, provided a "scientific" framework that addressed the social anxieties about the bodies of the nation and was a powerful tool to maintain the status quo. Notably, it legitimized the Victorian ideal of the "companionate marriage" in which a couple were equal but provided very different and strictly defined gendered actions within the union. Sex between married persons was also no longer deemed a necessary sin but became celebrated as the glue that held postwar marriages together and, through that couple, the nuclear family and nation. Heterosexuality continued to be normalized, with the new idea that sex was a positive force as long as it was between a man and a woman and contained within a monogamous marriage. Psychoanalytic principles, some of them quite far divorced from the original theory, permeated every aspect of postwar life, magazines, the churches, the family doctor, and especially the school system and youth organizations that used the discourse of Freud to define normality for postwar Canadians. Heteronormativity and strict adherence to gender roles were the only ways to be a normal, healthy, and good citizen.[52] Mona Gleason, in *Normalizing the Ideal*, demonstrates how the postwar period collapsed the diversity of families to create the illusion of a homogeneous state. Teachers and other youth workers were recruited to report on problematic families so they could be given expert advice on how to bring their bodies into compliance with what was ultimately an unattainable idealization.[53]

A main target of this normalization process were the many immigrant families coming to Canada from Eastern Europe. Like the Mormon dissenters before them, these families were seen as problematic and undesirable due to their assumed inability to assimilate to Canadian social standards. As Franca Iacovetta has argued, they were most often targeted for not conforming to the Canadian nuclear family ideal both in the gender relationships between husband and wife and because they did not view the nuclear family as a self-contained unit. Being an immigrant automatically placed certain bodies in the category as problematic and, like the working-class and immigrant bodies of the Victorian age, Cold War immigrant bodies were thought to be prone to excess. Thus, when "June A.," a young girl with Ukrainian parents, was brought before the family courts for being overly promiscuous, her body was pathologized as inherently oversexualized, characterized by the early onset of physical puberty thought common to some immigrant groups. However, her personal responsibility for her actions was mitigated due to her supposed ethnic disadvantages and assumed poor upbringing. It was assumed June had a poor understanding of Canadian social-sexual mores because her mother, who was viewed as mannish due to her habit of wearing slacks, and her supposedly ineffectual, emasculated father did not conform to them.[54]

Psychoanalysis also medicalized homosexuality. No longer was it only a sin; any deviance from a heterosexual norm was taken as evidence of a deep psychological issue likely rooted in childhood. In these cases, too, mothers were usually blamed for the maladjustment of their children. In particular, overbearing, non-feminine mothers were accused of causing homosexuality in their sons. Though less codified than male homosexuals, lesbians were also deemed to be sick and were publicly persecuted in the postwar era at levels not yet seen in Canada.[55] At this time there was almost no separation of the ideas of gender (socially defined) and sex (visually defined). A person with female genitalia was "naturally" feminine/female. As a result of the conflation of gender and sex, butch lesbians were defined as even more abnormal and persecuted not only because they were more visible in their transgressions but also because they were viewed as not quite women. Working-class butch lesbians also frequently found themselves the targets of homophobic police violence. Gary Kinsman and Patrizia Gentile, in *The Canadian War on Queers*, recount the heartbreaking narrative of Arlene, a Toronto lesbian, who identified as butch. Arlene noted it was quite common for women such as herself to be picked up by the Toronto police, beaten up, and stripped naked before having to find their way home. Arlene also recounts that when she was picked up at age seventeen, the cops raped her and that the rape of lesbian women was a common fear tactic used to police women's actions and their ability to conduct their erotic life in public.[56] Lesbians of colour were also targeted disproportionality by the legal system.[57]

Lesbian social worlds were heavily divided by class at this time, and though middle-class "respectable" lesbians had less to fear in terms of physical attack, they faced serious social consequences for coming out of the closet. Many postwar lesbian women remained closeted because they feared losing their children, who were usually conceived in a heterosexual relationship that they had entered into in order to participate in "normal society." Coming out or being outed as a lesbian and then losing custody of one's children was such a common experience that in 1978, the feminist lesbian group Wages Due set up the Lesbian Mothers Defense Fund to provide financial, legal, and social support for lesbian mothers seeking to keep their kids.[58] Stories such as these echo the calls made by Shannon Stettner, Kristin Burnett, and Lori Chambers in their chapter, to expand the historiography of reproductive rights beyond the mainly white, middle-class, and heteronormative definition which focuses on the right to limit fertility and access abortion. Future historians need to, as they do, reimagine the historical citizen body to include stories of women fighting to keep the children they want to have and to raise them in a safe and healthy environment within the larger reproductive narrative.

In the postwar era, lesbian civil servants and RCMP employees were also made vulnerable by the largely imagined threat of Cold War Communist infiltration, which was also used to persecute and purge homosexual federal employees. However, Kinsman and Gentile note that it was gay men rather than lesbians who were most commonly targeted. All homosexuals in "sensitive" roles after the war were thought to be potential security risks because their sexuality made them liable to blackmail. The reasons for gay men's increased persecution were twofold. Gay men's erotic networks were largely public, often based around cruising spots in parks, public bathrooms, and bathhouses. This greater visibility made gay men seem more of a threat to social stability and made their networks more easily watched. Lesbians, with the exception of working-class butch-femme bar culture, tended to meet in private homes, and authorities found it difficult to infiltrate their communities. During the postwar era, gay men were also equated with sex perversion and were viewed nationwide as a threat to children. This moral panic further demonized homosexual men and was used to justify their greater surveillance and punishment.[59]

The fact that lesbians tended to be persecuted less than their gay male counterparts does not mean they were safe or that they enjoyed sexual freedom. The narrators in Duder's work remind us that in addition to dealing with all these external factors, lesbian couples still faced the problems common to all couples: separation due to working situations, jealousy, infidelity, and substance abuse and physical violence.[60] Heterosexual couples could seek the help of outside services to deal with such issues; lesbian bodies were not welcome to participate in a society that was rooted in a celebration of the heterosexual nuclear family ideal. As Karen Dubinsky notes, "to the normal go considerable spoils," of which the most often overlooked is the ability to participate fully in public life.[61]

Postwar attempts to maintain a Canadian identity that was built on the white, heterosexual, middle-class, and gender-conforming ideal citizen body was like putting a lid on a pot about to boil over; it provided temporary containment at best. In the 1960s and 1970s the persistent existence of bodies not conforming to the ideal increasingly asserted their presence within Canada, demanding their rights as citizens and proving the ideal body as tyrannical myth. It is not surprising then that many of those same persons also challenged the ideal of a unified Canadian historical identity as nothing more than a national myth.

Yet, as this chapter demonstrates, there are ways we can talk about a Canada-wide history beyond the repressive and restrictive nationalist histories of the previous era. Though the history of Canada's constant search for the conformity of its peoples is not particularly edifying, and its complexity is difficult to contain within the bounds of a heritage plaque, documenting the attempts to create an elitist-imagined unity is more interesting and historically honest than perpetuating that myth. Further, and in recognition of the power contained in the act of writing history, the constancy of disenfranchised bodies in protesting their disenfranchisement is something to celebrate, albeit without creating a triumphant positivist history. Bodies can change the national narrative.

Much work remains for sex and sexuality historians. Canada's sexuality history is only beginning to become truly national, moving beyond the dominance of central Canada and outside major urban centres. Works such as Korinek's examination of gay and lesbian lives in the prairie regions demonstrate this diversification.[62] As sexual identities continue to be claimed, there will be increasing need for those histories to be explored, and lesbian lives, especially prior to the oral history era, remain largely undocumented. There is also a great need to continue to explore the intersections of race, gender, and sexuality in Canadian history. The theoretical scope of new works could be expanded by drawing attention to how actual corporeal bodies interacted with concepts of the body to create a national "body politic." Continued collaboration with disciplines focused on embodiment, such as the recently emergent disability studies, will likely provide fruitful new understandings of the way the physical body interacts with society.

Current events have made it clear that such historical examinations are both personally and politically relevant. The recent challenges to the Charter of Rights and Freedoms by sex workers, the persistent issue of sexualized violence against Indigenous women and the continued devaluation of their bodies by political and social elites, the increased surveillance of citizens under the auspices of counterterrorism, and the emergence of an increasingly complex and fluid schema of sexual identities are national political issues that can benefit from historical context and analysis. Furthermore, these historical narratives represent more inclusive, and therefore more authentically national, answers to the current questions of "where we came from, who we are, and where we might be going" than previous debates on Canadian identity solely centred on great rivers, the minutiae of Second World War battles, or the intricacies of Confederation can claim to do.

NOTES

1 J.L. Granatstein, *Who Killed Canadian History?* (Toronto: Harper Collins, 1998).
2 Michael Bliss, "Privatizing the Mind: The Sundering of Canadian History, the Sundering of Canada," *Journal of Canadian Studies* 26, 4 (Winter 1991): 5–17.

3 Bliss, "Privatizing the Mind," 15.

4 Bliss, "Privatizing the Mind," 12.

5 Steven Maynard, "The Maple Leaf (Gardens) Forever: Sex, Canadian Historians, and National History," *Journal of Canadian Studies* 36, 2 (Summer 2001): 70–105.

6 Michel Foucault, *The History of Sexuality* (New York: Pantheon Books, 1978), 19–20.

7 The ensuing narrative focuses primarily on women. However, given the fact that male and female and masculine and feminine were created throughout the time period in question as binary opposites, the essay also addresses male citizen bodies.

8 Mariana Valverde, *The Age of Light, Soap, and Water: Moral Reform in English Canada, 1885–1925* (Toronto: University of Toronto Press, 2008).

9 I realize that "Canada" did not exist during this time. However, for the sake of clarity I have chosen to use the modern designation to refer to the lands that are currently part of this nation.

10 Jennifer S.H. Brown, *Strangers in Blood: Fur Trade Company Families in Indian Country* (Vancouver: UBC Press, 1980), 4.

11 Brown, *Strangers in Blood*, 3, 4–5.

12 Brown, *Strangers in Blood*, 5.

13 Brown, *Strangers in Blood*, 17.

14 Sylvia Van Kirk, *Many Tender Ties: Women in Fur-Trade Society, 1670–1870* (Winnipeg: Watson and Dwyer, 1980).

15 Brown, *Strangers in Blood*, 51; Van Kirk, *Many Tender Ties*, 36–40.

16 Van Kirk, *Many Tender Ties*, 103.

17 Jean Barman, "Aboriginal Women on the Streets of Victoria," in *Contact Zones: Aboriginal and Settler Women in Canada's Colonial Past*, ed. Katie Pickles and Myra Rutherdale (Vancouver: UBC Press, 2005), 205–6.

18 Adele Perry, "Historiography That Breaks Your Heart: Van Kirk and the Writing of Feminist History," in *Finding a Way to the Heart: Feminist Writings on Aboriginal and Women's History*, ed. Robin Jarvis Brownlie and Valerie J. Korinek (Winnipeg: University of Manitoba Press, 2012), 81–97.

19 Adele Perry, *Colonial Relations: The Douglas-Connolly Family and the Nineteenth-Century Imperial World* (Cambridge: Cambridge University Press, 2015).

20 Sarah Carter, *The Importance of Being Monogamous: Marriage and Nation-Building in Western Canada to 1915* (Edmonton: Athabasca University Press, 2008), 75, 194–229.

21 Valverde, *The Age of Light, Soap, and Water*, 28.

22 Valverde, *The Age of Light, Soap, and Water*, 15–17.

23 Wendy Mitchinson, *The Nature of Their Bodies: Women and Their Doctors in Victorian Canada* (Toronto: University of Toronto Press, 1991), 17–18, 40.

24 Mitchinson, *The Nature of Their Bodies*, 38.

25 Valverde, *The Age of Light, Soap, and Water*, 60.

26 Veronica Strong-Boag, "Canada's Women Doctors: Feminism Constrained," in *A Not Unreasonable Claim: Women and Reform in Canada, 1880–1920s*, ed. Linda Kealey (Toronto: Women's Press, 1979), 124.

27 Carol Lee Bacchi, *Liberation Deferred? The Ideas of the English-Canadian Suffragists, 1877–1918* (Toronto: University of Toronto Press, 1983), 24.

28 Bacchi, *Liberation Deferred*, 33.

29 Constance Backhouse, *Petticoats and Prejudice: Women and the Law in Nineteenth-Century Canada* (Toronto: Women's Press, 1991), 260–92; Valverde, *The Age of Light, Soap, and Water*, 97–102.

30 Carolyn Strange, *Toronto's Girl Problem: The Perils and Pleasures of the City, 1880–1930* (Toronto: University of Toronto Press, 1995), 116–20.

31 Backhouse, *Petticoats and Prejudice*, 55–69.

32 Valverde, *The Age of Light, Soap, and Water*, 95–103.

33 Erika Dyck, *Facing Eugenics: Reproduction, Sterilization, and the Politics of Choice* (Toronto: University of Toronto Press, 2013); Angus McLaren, *Our Own Master Race: Eugenics in Canada, 1885–1945* (Oxford: Oxford University Press, 1997).

34 Dyck, *Facing Eugenics*, 6, 12.

35 Gary Kinsman, *The Regulation of Desire: Homo and Heterosexualities*, 2nd ed. (Montreal: Black Rose Books, 1996), 100–36.

36 Cameron Duder, *Awfully Devoted Women: Lesbian Lives in Canada, 1900–65* (Vancouver: UBC Press, 2010), 64. It is likely that the families of the women realized the relationship had become sexual.

37 Paul Jackson, *One of the Boys: Homosexuality in the Military during World War II* (Montreal: McGill-Queen's University Press, 2004), 11–23.

38 This is, of course, how Anne of Green Gables describes her relationship with her best friend Diana. For an interesting article about the language of devotion, sexuality, and Lucy Maud Montgomery, see Laura M. Robinson, "'Sex Matters': L.M. Montgomery, Friendship, and Sexuality," *Children's Literature* 40 (2012): 167–90.

39 Adrienne Rich, *Blood, Bread, and Poetry: Selected Prose, 1979–1985* (New York: W.W. Norton, 1994); Judith M. Bennett, "'Lesbian-Like' and the Social History of Lesbianism," *Journal of the History of Sexuality* 9, 1/2 (2000): 1–24; Martha Vicinus, "Lesbian History: All Theory and No Facts or All Facts and No Theory?" *Radical History Review* 60 (1994): 24–42.

40 Jackson, *One of the Boys*.

41 Karen Duder, "Public Acts and Private Languages: Bisexuality and the Multiple Discourses of Constance Grey Swartz," *BC Studies* 136 (Winter 2002/3): 3–6.

42 J.L. Granatstein and Desmond Morton, *Canada and the Two World Wars* (Toronto: Key Porter Books, 2003).

43 Ruth Roach Pierson, *"They're Still Women after All": The Second World War and Canadian Womanhood* (Toronto: McClelland and Stewart, 1986).

44 Pierson, *"They're Still Women after All,"* 129–68.

45 Pierson, *"They're Still Women after All,"* 145; Gary Kinsman and Patrizia Gentile, *The Canadian War on Queers: National Security as Sexual Regulation* (Vancouver: UBC Press, 2010), 63.

46 Duder, *Awfully Devoted Women*, 206; Kinsman and Gentile, *The Canadian War on Queers*, 63–5.

47 Kinsman and Gentile, *The Canadian War on Queers*, 65.

48 Duder, *Awfully Devoted Women*, 206; Kinsman and Gentile, *The Canadian War on Queers*, 65; Jackson, *One of the Boys*, 63–5, 84–6, 91–2. Jackson does note that in practice many military commanders protected homosexual men in their units.

49 Pierson, *"They're Still Women after All,"* 169–87.

50 Pierson, *"They're Still Women after All,"* 208.

51 This does not mean the ideas behind eugenics were also discarded. In many cases they were repackaged using the language of psychoanalysis to give them continued legitimacy. Furthermore, Alberta's sterilization policy remained on the books until the 1970s. Dyck, *Facing Eugenics*, 8.

52 Mary Louise Adams, *The Trouble with Normal: Postwar Youth and the Making of Heterosexuality* (Toronto: University of Toronto Press, 1997).

53 Gleason, *Normalizing the Ideal*, 4.

54 Franca Iacovetta, "Parents, Daughters, and Family Court Intrusions into Working-Class Life," in *On the Case: Explorations in Social History*, ed. Franca Iacovetta and Wendy Mitchinson (Toronto: University of Toronto Press, 1998), 312–37.

55 Duder, *Awfully Devoted Women*, 47.

56 Kinsman and Gentile, *The Canadian War on Queers*, 214.

57 Constance Backhouse, *Carnal Crimes: Sexual Assault Law in Canada, 1900–1975* (Toronto: Osgoode Society for Canadian Legal History, 2008), 193–226.

58 Kinsman and Gentile, *The Canadian War on Queers*, 291.

59 Kinsman and Gentile, *The Canadian War on Queers*, 53–114.

60 Duder, *Awfully Devoted Women*, 208–13.

61 Karen Dubinsky, *The Second Greatest Disappointment: Honeymooning and Tourism at Niagara Falls* (Toronto: Between the Lines, 1999), 228.

62 Valerie J. Korinek, "'We're the Girls of the Pansy Parade': Historicizing Winnipeg's Queer Subcultures, 1930s–1970," *Histoire sociale / Social History* 45, 89 (2012): 117–55. See also, Valerie J. Korinek, *Prairie Fairies: A History of Queer Communities and People in Western Canada, 1930–1985* (Toronto: University of Toronto Press, 2018).

SELECTED READINGS

Adams, Mary Louise. *The Trouble with Normal: Postwar Youth and the Making of Heterosexuality*. Toronto: University of Toronto Press, 1997.

Bacchi, Carol Lee. *Liberation Deferred? The Ideas of the English-Canadian Suffragists, 1877–1918*. Toronto: University of Toronto Press, 1983.

Backhouse, Constance. *Carnal Crimes: Sexual Assault Law in Canada, 1900–1975*. Toronto: Osgoode Society for Canadian Legal History, 2008.

– *Petticoats and Prejudice: Women and the Law in Nineteenth-Century Canada*. Toronto: Women's Press, 1991.

Barman, Jean. *French Canadians, Furs, and Indigenous Women in the Making of the Pacific Northwest*. Vancouver: UBC Press, 2014.

Brown, Jennifer H.S. *Strangers in Blood: Fur Trade Company Families in Indian Country*. Vancouver: UBC Press, 1980.

Brownlie, Robin Jarvis, and Valerie J. Korinek, eds. *Finding a Way to the Heart: Feminist Writings on Aboriginal and Women's History in Canada*. Winnipeg: University of Manitoba Press, 2012.

Carter, Sarah. *The Importance of Being Monogamous: Marriage and Nation Building in Western Canada*. Edmonton: Athabasca University Press, 2008.

Chenier, Elise. "Hidden from Historians: Preserving Lesbian Oral History in Canada." *Archivaria* 68 (Fall 2009): 247–69.

– *Strangers in Our Midst: Sexual Deviancy in Postwar Ontario*. Toronto: University of Toronto Press, 2008.

Dubinsky, Karen. *Improper Advances: Rape and Heterosexual Conflict in Ontario, 1880–1929*. Chicago: University of Chicago Press, 1993.

Duder, Cameron. *Awfully Devoted Women: Lesbian Lives in Canada, 1900–65*. Vancouver: UBC Press, 2010.

Dyck, Erika. *Facing Eugenics: Reproduction, Sterilization, and the Politics of Choice*. Toronto: University of Toronto Press, 2013.

Gentile, Patrizia, and Jane Nicholas, eds. *Contesting Bodies and Nation in Canadian History*. Toronto: University of Toronto Press, 2013.

Gleason, Mona. *Normalizing the Ideal: Psychology, Schooling, and the Family in Postwar Canada*. Toronto: University of Toronto Press, 1999.

Jackson, Paul. *One of the Boys: Homosexuality in the Military during World War II*. Montreal: McGill-Queen's University Press, 2004.

Kinsman, Gary. *The Regulation of Desire: Homo and Heterosexualities*, 2nd ed. Montreal: Black Rose Books, 1996.

Kinsman, Gary, and Patrizia Gentile. *The Canadian War on Queers: National Security as Sexual Regulation*. Vancouver: UBC Press, 2010.

Korinek, Valerie J. *Roughing It in the Suburbs: Reading Chatelaine Magazine in the Fifties and Sixties*. Toronto: University of Toronto Press, 2000.

– "'We're the Girls of the Pansy Parade': Historicizing Winnipeg's Queer Subcultures, 1930s–1970." *Histoire sociale / Social History* 45, 89 (2012): 117–55. https://doi.org/10.1353/his2012.0002

Maynard, Steven. "Through a Hole in the Lavatory Wall: Homosexual Subcultures, Police Surveillance, and the Dialectics of Discovery, Toronto, 1890–1930." *Journal of the History of Sexuality* 5, 2 (1994): 207–42.

McLaren, Angus, and Arlene Tigar McLaren. *The Bedroom and the State: The Changing Practices and Politics of Contraception and Abortion in Canada, 1880–1980*. Toronto: McClelland and Stewart, 1986.

Mitchinson, Wendy. *The Nature of Their Bodies: Women and Their Doctors in Victorian Canada*. Toronto: University of Toronto Press, 1991.

Morgan, Cecilia. *Public Men and Virtuous Women: The Gendered Languages of Religion and Politics in Upper Canada*. Toronto: University of Toronto Press, 1996.

Nicholas, Jane. *The Modern Girl: Feminine Modernities, the Body, and Commodities in the 1920s*. Toronto: University of Toronto Press, 2015.

Perry, Adele. *Colonial Relations: The Douglas-Connolly Family and the Nineteenth-Century Imperial World*. Cambridge, MA: Cambridge University Press, 2015.

– *On the Edge of Empire: Gender and the Making of British Columbia, 1849–1871*. Toronto: University of Toronto Press, 2001.

Pickles, Katie, and Myra Rutherdale, eds. *Contact Zones: Aboriginal and Settler Women in Canada's Colonial Past*. Vancouver: UBC Press, 2005.

Pierson, Ruth Roach. *"They're Still Women after All": The Second World War and Canadian Womanhood*. Toronto: McClelland and Stewart, 1986.

Ross, Becki L. *The House That Jill Built: A Lesbian Nation in Formation*. Toronto: University of Toronto Press, 1995.

– *Burlesque West: Showgirls, Sex, and Sin in Postwar Vancouver*. Toronto: University of Toronto Press, 2009.

Sangster, Joan. *Regulating Girls and Women: Sexuality, Family, and the Law in Ontario, 1920–1960*. Oxford: Oxford University Press, 2001.

Sethna, Christabelle. "The Evolution of the Birth Control Handbook: From Student Peer-Education Manual to Feminist Self-Empowerment Text, 1968–1975." *Canadian Bulletin of Medical History* 23, 1 (Spring 2006): 89–118. https://doi.org/10.3138/cbmh.23.1.89

Strange, Carolyn. *Toronto's Girl Problem: The Perils and Pleasures of the City, 1880–1930*. Toronto: University of Toronto Press, 1995.

Strong-Boag, Veronica. *The New Day Recalled: Lives of Girls and Women in English Canada, 1919–1939*. Toronto: Penguin, 1988.

Vacante, Jeffrey. "Writing the History of Sexuality and 'National' History in Quebec." *Journal of Canadian Studies* 39, 2 (Spring 2005): 31–55. https://doi.org/10.3138/jcs.39.2.31

Valverde, Mariana. *The Age of Light, Soap, and Water: Moral Reform in English Canada, 1885–1925.* Toronto: University of Toronto Press, 2008.

Van Kirk, Sylvia. *Many Tender Ties: Women in Fur-Trade Society, 1670–1870.* Winnipeg: Watson and Dwyer, 1980.

12 Challenging Work: Feminist Scholarship on Women, Gender, and Work in Canadian History

LISA PASOLLI AND JULIA SMITH

Introduction: Understanding the Complexity of Women's Labouring Lives

On a rainy morning in March 1976, about 150 day care workers gathered in front of the Vancouver courthouse for a day of leafletting, picketing, and speeches. Many of these day care workers were members of the Service, Office, and Retail Workers' Union of Canada (SORWUC). In concert with other childcare workers and supporters, SORWUC members had initiated a one-day strike to protest their low wages, long hours, and lack of benefits, and they linked their labour struggles to the "over-all problems of day care" stemming from a lack of government support.[1] Moreover, as members of a feminist union, they argued that a commitment to good, publicly funded day care services was the right of every child and family in British Columbia. Without affordable and accessible childcare, SORWUC members contended, the women who made up 40 per cent of the provincial workforce were unable to participate fully and equally in public life. The striking childcare workers thus objected to the notion that they were "just babysitters" selfishly demanding more money; they insisted that fairly treated employees were essential to a high-quality childcare system for all.[2] In short, the strikers demonstrated that they considered the private work of caregiving to be a matter of public importance.

The SORWUC childcare workers are the focus of a research project that we began a few years ago. In telling their story, we intended to draw attention to the history of childcare labour – an area of scholarship that remains sorely unexplored in Canada. Our investigations, however, challenged us on another level to think about how historians have categorized women's work. In particular, we were prompted to think about what Allison Tom calls the "messiness" of childcare labour, in that it represents a tangled overlap of public and private, paid and unpaid, skilled and unskilled labour.[3] Childcare workers perform the traditionally private labour of caregiving for pay in a public setting. In their demands for better wages and working conditions, the unionized childcare workers that we studied emphasized an "ethic of care," connecting their status, skills, and value as paid employees to motherhood and caregiving, long considered "labours of love."[4] In conceptualizing the importance of their work, they did not distinguish between "love and money."[5] Furthermore, SORWUC childcare workers recognized that their labour was embedded in a larger discussion about childcare policy and about how society and the state value caregiving labour in relation to wage labour. SORWUC members insisted that the quality of their working lives was inseparable from a broader public commitment to universal childcare, a linchpin for gender equality. In sum, the SORWUC story complicated many of our preconceived notions of women's public and private labouring lives and how such categories have been constructed.

The "messiness" of the SORWUC story is the impetus for this chapter, which offers a broad overview of forty years of feminist historiography on women, gender, and work.[6] Women's work has always defied easy explanation and simple categorization. Over the past several decades, feminist scholars have shed light on the many dimensions of women's work by analysing women's relationship to the paid labour force and the union movement, the taken-for-grantedness of their assignment to the domestic sphere, and the way that state policies shape their relationship to the public and private worlds of work. Early interdisciplinary scholarship that emphasized the interconnectedness of women's public and private labour and demonstrated women's vital contribution to social reproduction under capitalism served as a crucial catalyst for the study of women's work. Since then, the field has moved in new directions that include analyses of gender, race, and ethnicity and of how wage-earning and caregiving are inscribed in social policies. At the same time, historians of work have benefited from the insights of other fields of history, including immigrant and Indigenous history. In this chapter, we discuss several of these historiographical threads. We conclude by returning to the story of the SORWUC members and paid caregiving work that sparked our analysis and by offering some reflections on how embracing the messiness of childcare work offers new avenues for historical inquiry into women's labouring lives.

The Early Years

The development of feminist scholarship on the history of women and work in Canada parallels the growth of women's history and labour and working-class history. As feminists were developing the field of women's history in the

1970s, labour history underwent a period of transformation. Developments in international historiography and theories of class – particularly studies of working-class formation, culture, and control – led to a shift in the trajectory of labour historiography in Canada.[7] They breathed new life into Marxist understandings of class as a relationship rooted in workers' lived experience, and they inspired a new generation of scholars to undertake analyses of class experience, formation, and culture. Feminist scholars made significant contributions to the new field of working-class history. To address the dearth of studies and sources on working women, they collected statistics, documented women's stories and experiences, and reinserted women workers into the historical narrative. Activists and scholars also produced research and resource guides meant to spur further analysis into the history of women's work.[8]

Early studies led to important insights about the worlds of women's paid work. By poring through census data and other archival reports, scholars demonstrated that women have always composed a significant part of the paid labour force and that they worked in a variety of sectors, from domestic service and nursing to teaching and manufacturing. They also revealed the systemic inequalities experienced by women workers, arguing that many earned less than their male counterparts, struggled to find full-time work, and remained confined to "pink-collar" jobs. In addition, their analyses of the "feminization" of particular jobs, such as teaching and clerical work, and the decline of women from other industries, such as dairying, highlighted the gendered dimensions of work and the labour process.[9]

Feminist historians also produced valuable analyses of women's involvement in workers' movements, including unions and left politics. Such studies demonstrated the significant contributions women made to a variety of groups, including several political parties and countless trade unions and women's auxiliaries. At the same time, historians revealed the gendered dynamics of unions and the Left, and they highlighted the many barriers that limited working women's opportunities and efforts to organize, including their precarious employment, irregular working hours, and isolated working conditions, factors compounded by the burden of the double day and the sexism of many male trade unionists.[10] Feminist scholars have also examined the unique circumstances shaping women's work and labour activism in Quebec, including the Catholic Church, powerful social norms, and the distinct history of trade union development in the province.[11] Studies of women's labour and left activism thus challenged claims that women workers have always had lower rates of unionization because they are not interested in unionization and have proven difficult to organize. As Ruth Frager explains in her study on women workers and the Canadian labour movement in the late nineteenth and early twentieth centuries, "For male workers, active participation in the labour movement required time, energy, and dedication that was often extraordinary. For female workers, it was often impossible."[12]

Feminist dialogues with Marxist theory in the 1960s and 1970s led to important insights about the interconnectedness of women's paid and unpaid labour. Like their colleagues in political economy, sociology, and other disciplines, feminist historians sought to understand women's inequality in the wage labour force and under capitalism more broadly, and in doing so launched the "domestic labour debates." These debates led to the crucial insight that women's oppression in modern society is rooted in the invisible, undervalued "labours of love" that women perform in the home. Capitalist production, these theorists argued, required women's private labour "as a condition of its existence," but it assigned no economic or social value to women's work feeding, clothing, and sustaining waged workers' home lives, as well as reproducing and caring for the next generation of workers.[13] Canadian scholars made important contributions to this international and interdisciplinary literature, including such collections as *Hidden in the Household: Women's Domestic Labour under Capitalism* and *The Politics of Diversity: Feminism, Marxism, and Nationalism*.[14] These debates also generated significant discussions about strategies and policies to advance women's liberation, such as "Wages for Housework."[15]

Though criticized for dissolving into "in-house" conflicts about the technical aspects of Marxism, the scholarship generated as part of the domestic labour debates provided a number of theoretical insights that proved crucial for the historical study of women's work.[16] The focus on the domestic sphere in particular contributed to a deeper understanding of the secondary status of women's paid labour, since their assignment to the home underpinned the belief that women worked only for "pin money" and "led to a justification of the lower wages and limited employment opportunities to which women themselves have often been resigned."[17] More broadly, to understand all of the ways that women's unpaid work contributed to their inequality, scholars recognized a need to understand women's domestic labour "more precisely" and in "greater empirical and historical detail."[18] A touchstone for these careful studies of women's domestic lives was Meg Luxton's *More Than a Labour of Love: Three Generations of Women's Work in the Home*, in which she documents all of the physical, economic, social, and emotional labours that Manitoban women performed in the home throughout the twentieth century.[19] Luxton and others helped to reverse the "invisibility" of housework and to treat women's domestic labour with the "same seriousness and respect as labour in public settings."[20]

Scholars whose work was ostensibly outside the boundaries of labour and working-class history also generated rich portraits of women's working lives;

they made important contributions to our understanding of the fluidity of women's paid and unpaid work, as well as the importance of that work to society more broadly. Sylvia Van Kirk's and Jennifer Brown's groundbreaking work on Indigenous women's domestic labour between the seventeenth and nineteenth centuries, for example, led to new interpretations of the social and economic underpinnings of the fur trade and analysed colonialism as a gendered project.[21] Similarly, Dionne Brand's work on Black Canadian women in the twentieth century revealed the importance of their paid domestic work to their families' material well-being and acknowledged that their private and voluntary work as mothers, caregivers, community workers, and auxiliaries to Black men's unions was just as crucial for sustaining family and cultural life.[22]

Meanwhile, studies of immigrant and working-class households revealed the multifaceted nature of women's labour. In doing so, they contributed to a more robust working-class history, moving away from "formal labour institutions" to the everyday lives of working people.[23] Bettina Bradbury's *Working Families: Age, Gender, and Daily Survival in Industrializing Montreal* and Suzanne Morton's *Ideal Surroundings: Domestic Life in a Working-Class Suburb in the 1920s* were typical of this kind of history. Both studies centre their analysis on women's and children's paid and unpaid labour, viewing it as the key to working-class family survival – just as important as, if not more important than, men's wages.[24] In the same vein, the Italian immigrant women studied by Franca Iacovetta moved in and out of paid and unpaid labour as family needs demanded.[25] By showing that women's labour in working-class, immigrant, and racialized families was not always "hidden in the household," these kinds of studies allowed for a deeper understanding of gender, class, and race relations in Canada.

By the mid-1990s, massive strides had been made in understanding the complexity of women's labouring lives and how their experiences of public and private work were shaped by gender, class, race, and ethnicity. Yet when it came to the field of working-class and labour history, studies like Bradbury's, Morton's, and Iacovetta's were somewhat exceptional. Feminist labour historians pointed out that a sizable gulf continued to exist between working-class and women's history and that the history of women's work and a "gendered history of class formation" were never entirely integrated into working-class history.[26] This was partly explained by a move away from the theoretical perspectives – namely Marxist-feminism – that informed so much of the early analysis of women's public and private working lives.[27] As Joan Sangster commented at the turn of the millennium, the full incorporation of the "complex combinations" of women's unpaid, domestic, private, and informal work into the world of formal, public, and waged labour remained and remains a "perennial dilemma" for historians.[28]

Expanded Understandings of Women's Working Lives

Building on several decades of research and activism, in the 1990s shifts in theory and analysis pushed the field of women's labour and working-class history in important new directions. The increasing popularity of post-structuralist theory and the accompanying – and contested – development of gender as a "useful category of historical analysis" influenced the historical scholarship on women, gender, and work; many of the studies produced during this period focused on gender, discourse, and identity.[29] Feminist scholars analysed how gender shaped women's *and* men's experiences of work, and they continued to highlight the gendered dynamics of the labour process and the workplace, as well as unions and left political parties.[30] In some cases, historians used post-structuralist theories of gender to examine the construction of male and female working-class identities, or "the processes by which their meanings have been made."[31] Studies such as Joy Parr's *The Gender of Breadwinners: Women, Men, and Change in Two Industrial Towns, 1880–1950* demonstrated that the meanings of such things as work, gender, and household roles vary with time and place and are subject to change in response to other elements of daily life. Thus, they emphasized the fluidity of gender roles, particularly regarding work, and how they are constructed in relation to one another and to a variety of other factors. At the same time, older approaches did not disappear entirely. Other historians continued to view class as a social relationship rather than an identity, using materialist-feminist theory and political economy to examine how gender and class intersected to shape working-class experiences.[32] As in previous decades, interdisciplinary feminist scholars also generated important analyses, particularly around women's involvement in the labour movement. In *Labour's Dilemma: The Gender Politics of Auto Workers in Canada, 1937–1979*, for example, Pamela Sugiman showed how women workers responded to inequality by adopting "gendered strategies" in their struggle to achieve "dignity, respect, and rights" in the workplace and in unions.[33]

Concomitantly, studies of immigrant and racialized women traced the contours of inequality among and between paid labourers. A particularly important subject for this kind of analysis has been the history of immigrant domestic workers. As Sedef Arat-Koç explains, gender subordination is a "universal condition" for all domestic workers in industrial capitalism, but scholars also need to go beyond gender analysis to consider how the domestic labour relationship reinforces hierarchies of race and ethnicity.[34] Such scholarship shows how the employment of immigrant domestic workers in private households structured "asymmetrical race and class relations *among* women."[35] That is, immigrant women and especially women of colour – which throughout the twentieth century included women recruited from central and Eastern Europe, the Caribbean, and the Philippines – were viewed as "cheap, temporary, and expendable labour," whereas white British domestics were viewed as potential "nation-builders and civilizers."[36] Race and ethnicity thus led to more severely circumscribed rights and opportunities; however, as many scholars point out, this dynamic did not preclude a history of organizing and resistance on the part of those workers.[37]

Building on Van Kirk's and Brown's influential studies about women's fur trade labour, a new generation of scholars continued to probe the changing worlds of Indigenous women's work, often through their analyses of colonialism's gendered dynamics. Historians examined changing patterns of Indigenous women's paid work across the nineteenth and twentieth centuries, which depended on the needs of their families, their "ambitions, values, and abilities," and their obligations and desires to support community and kinship networks.[38] Like working-class and immigrant women, strict notions of "public" and "private" labour did not make sense in the context of Indigenous women's working lives. Moreover, this body of scholarship complicated the notion of colonialism as a simplistic or one-way process. John Lutz's work on Lekwammen women on Vancouver Island, for example, showed that industrialization changed gender relations in perhaps unexpected ways: in some instances, women actually gained economic power in their families because of new opportunities for paid work in fish canneries. Studies by Lutz and others reminded historians of women's work that "gender only makes sense as an analytical category when linked to race, age, and social position."[39]

Advancements in the field of social welfare history offered new possibilities for historians interested in women, gender, and work as well. In what was long a "gender-blind" field, in the 1980s scholars interested in the welfare state began to consider how social policies were inscribed with – and reinforced – gendered ideas about work.[40] Certainly, the state's role in shaping gendered labour structures had always been part of women's labour history; some of the first studies of women's paid labour analysed the often-contradictory nature of working women's relationship to the state through minimum wage laws, government mobilization of wartime workers, and intervention in labour disputes.[41] Like these early labour histories, feminist scholars of social policy showed that the welfare state represented a "paradox in gender terms." On the one hand, women were excluded from welfare benefits designed for male-coded work, and they were "regulated" by welfare administrators entrusted with upholding standards of morality and domesticity.[42] On the other hand, the state could be an ally, as in the case of women seeking financial independence after a marriage breakup.[43]

Feminist scholarship on social policy was particularly important for what it revealed about the societal value ascribed to women's domestic labour. A key insight was that the model of a male breadwinner family shaped welfare rights and labour policy. Correspondingly, the value of women's caregiving and motherwork was only secondarily and uneasily encoded into social policies, if at all.[44] Studies that traced maternalist ideology and the state provided crucial fodder for thinking about the worth of women's private labours. Margaret Little's work on British Columbia mothers' pensions, for example, revealed that policymakers and the public recognized motherwork as a "service to the state" in raising the future citizenry and thus considered women entitled to pensions as their right.[45] But not all women: the caregiving and mothering of poor, immigrant, and racialized women was not considered essential to nation-building. Instead, these marginalized women were denied supports like mothers' pensions and funnelled into the labour force, where their second-class and poorly compensated paid work was considered a defence against dependency – a strategy that by the late twentieth century would be called "workforce activation," in many cases sustained by targeted and still-inadequate childcare subsidies.[46] Over the course of the twentieth century, though, maternalist-based social policy even for white women declined, as governments at all levels preferred to leave motherwork and carework in the realm of private responsibility. That ideological position explains, for example, the consistent unwillingness to support childcare programs.[47] Of course, not all jurisdictions in Canada were identical. Scholars have shown that the history of Quebec childcare and family policy deviated from trends in English Canada. While Ontario embraced federally funded day care centres during the Second World War, working mothers in Quebec were, like many of their compatriots, "war[y] of state involvement" and preferred to make private childcare arrangements.[48] Fifty years later, however, the introduction of the $5-a-day universal day care program in Quebec was unique in Canada. Besides rationales that include "social solidarity," historians have pointed out that the $5-a-day strategy was based on a belief that women were valuable members of the paid labour force.[49] Taken together, these studies reveal the state's ambivalence about women's public and private working lives. Feminist scholars thus developed yet another angle from which to analyse the intersectional nature of women's inequality.

Considering Future Directions

Feminist historians in the twenty-first century continue to document, revise, and challenge our interpretations of women's labouring lives. Important new contributions build on the field's strong tradition of chronicling women's work.

Studies of women's wage labour in the Great Depression and in the decades immediately following the Second World War demonstrate, for example, that although their experiences of paid work during these periods were more complex than previously assumed, women continued to be constrained by an overwhelmingly conservative gender and social order.[50] Other recent scholarship continues to highlight the connections between women's feminist and working-class activism, examining working-class women's contributions to the feminist and labour movements in the post–Second World War period.[51] Still others recover as-yet-untold stories about marginalized women workers. Karen Flynn's *Moving beyond Borders: A History of Black Canadian and Caribbean Women in the Diaspora*, for example, considers the complex lives of Black women who worked as nurses while also managing private labour in their communities and families.[52] Indigenous women who worked as domestics, nurses, hairdressers, and labour activists in the twentieth century are featured in Mary Jane Logan McCallum's study.[53] Considered together, current scholarship on the history of women, gender, and work speaks to the important legacy of feminist historiography and, at the same time, reminds us that many women's experiences of work remain obscured and marginalized. Thus, it is vital that scholars continue to engage in the type of recovery histories that were so crucial to the early years of women's history.

Much work remains to be done. The integration of scholarship on Quebec and English Canada and by francophones and anglophones remains an ongoing problem, as it does in Canadian history more broadly. Historians of Quebec have shown that "the ideological influence of the Church created different sets of domestic, familial, and sexual expectations for working-class women ... to negotiate," but scholars have produced limited comparative work that takes these differences into consideration.[54] Beyond the perennial problem of Quebec-English Canada integration, other factors have contributed to the need for a renewed commitment to a robust and comprehensive women's labour history. Shifts in theory, politics, and research interests have meant that in recent years, fewer scholars teach and study the history of workers and working-class issues. The decline in Canadian labour and working-class history as a field of study reflects the erosion of workers' power in Canadian society, as unionization rates continue to fall and the labour movement becomes increasingly impotent and ineffective. In light of these developments, it is critical that scholars continue to teach labour and working-class history so as to provide students with much-needed critical analyses of working people and the issues that shape their lives and to foster the development of future generations of labour and working-class historians.

In thinking about future directions for the field of women, gender, and labour history, we want to conclude by returning to the SORWUC childcare workers. In researching their story, we turned to the historiography of women and work to make sense of their experiences. The intersecting currents of feminist scholarship that we have briefly surveyed in this chapter challenged us to think about the "messiness" of their public and private labours, and how the values of their waged and caregiving work were built into the architecture of the state in the ongoing context of capitalist accumulation. It helped us to understand why SORWUC workers were underpaid and undervalued, despite their efforts to dislodge notions of "car[ing] for love" and "earn[ing] for money."[55] It allowed us to see that poorly treated childcare workers are a symptom of a much broader neglect of social policies designed for gender equality, including childcare. At the same time, the historiography prompted questions we were unable to answer but that, if we could, would undoubtedly enrich our analysis: What were the racial and class identities of the union members and how did that contribute to their relationship to the state and their own understandings of public and private work? In other words, the SORWUC story reminded us of the value of long historiographical traditions beginning with interdisciplinary Marxist-feminist analysis, particularly with regard to social reproduction and the integration of public and private. It also points to the importance of questions raised by a new generation of histories on gender, class, race, ethnicity, and labour.

In moving the field forward, it is important for historians to draw on past trends, revisit old debates, and embrace the intersectional and interdisciplinary approaches that continue to develop. In the spirit of the feminist historians of the 1960s and 1970s who drew so heavily on political economy, we, too, looked across disciplinary boundaries for an analytical framework for the SORWUC childcare workers' story. In doing so, we encountered a body of scholarship examining how societies are responding to a "crisis of care" that has resulted from the decline of male breadwinner families, an aging population, and the neoliberal retrenchment of welfare states.[56] Scholars in this field have done important work on the transnational networks and migrations of caregivers, and in the Canadian context, the Live-in Caregiver Program (LCP) has come under particular scrutiny.[57] The federal government touts migrant women as an innovative solution to the country's childcare crisis, but feminist scholars have pointed out that the program relies on their exploitation. Filipina caregivers, for example, face onerous and even abusive working conditions, stigmatization in the labour market, and "graduated and uneven" rights.[58] The result is that some women – namely, white professional women – see gains in their citizenship rights through workplace advancement at the "expense of ... migrant women of color."[59] Understanding the complex encounter of women's "public" and "private" working lives, as scholars have illustrated, requires analysis of gender, class, race, ethnicity, patterns of migration, immigration policy, and the politics of caregiving. The sharp contrast between liberation for some women workers and the continued marginalization of others should be a question that feminist historians continue to probe by drawing on existing threads of historiography (among others, that of immigrant domestic workers) and asking new questions: What were the networks of "private" caregiving work that sustained some women's entry into the "public" sphere of waged work? Who were the women providing the caregiving work that allowed other women to be "liberated" by wage work? How did caregiving workers understand the relationship between "love and money"? How was the invisibility and, likely, the class and race of caregivers linked to the undervaluing of caregiving work, especially as reflected in social policies around childcare? What was the relationship between the women who sought childcare and those who provided it?

The messiness of public and private also needs to be considered more closely from women's own perspectives. Again, we look to contemporary studies across disciplinary boundaries to suggest directions for historical research. In their work on Indigenous caregiving politics, for example, Tammy Harkey and Paul Kershaw argue that mothers' and families' "right to care" is an integral part of "self-defined cultural revitalization" in Indigenous communities because of the legacy of racist child welfare practices like residential schools and the "Sixties Scoop."[60] Women in these communities, in other words, consider their private work of caregiving to have public value, not just in an economic sense but in a cultural and social sense as well. Historians should draw from these contemporary insights for questions about the past: What did a "woman-friendly" state look like for Indigenous mothers working as domestic servants in the middle of the century? How do we understand the process of "diverted mothering" for Indigenous women and how it undermined their work of cultural reproduction?[61] Incorporating the "voices of women marginalized by class, race, and indigeneity," as Lynne Marks et al. argue, will necessarily complicate the "mainstream feminist discourse" that equated liberation with paid employment. In their work on welfare rights feminism within the second wave, Marks et al. show that poor and racialized women in the 1970s and 1980s fought for state support to stay home with their children, which often put them in conflict with more established groups like the National Action Committee on the Status of Women (NAC). More historical work along these lines will no doubt reveal even more "fault line[s]" in feminism's history and necessarily complicate the constructed boundaries between women's public and private labouring lives.[62]

Feminist historians must remain committed to researching and teaching women's messy and intersectional labouring lives in the past, not just for the sake of better history but for a better analysis of women's working lives in the present.

Many women continue to work in precarious positions and under exploitative conditions. Understanding the dimensions of their inequality requires consideration of how their private, domestic, and caregiving work shapes their opportunities in the public, waged sphere – and vice versa – and how the value of their work has historically been entrenched in the structures of states, markets, and families. Documenting and analysing the history of workers' struggles and successes, the complexity of their lives, and the gendered dynamics of the working-class experience remains vitally important to understanding our current situation and mounting effective challenges to the status quo.

NOTES

1 "Day-Care Staff Back 24-Hour Strike," *Vancouver Sun*, 29 March 1976. For more information on SORWUC, see Julia Smith, "An 'Entirely Different' Kind of Union: The Service, Office, and Retail Workers' Union of Canada (SORWUC), 1972–1986," *Labour / Le Travail* 73 (Spring 2014): 23–65.

2 University of British Columbia Library Rare Books and Special Collections, SORWUC fonds, box 6, file 1, "Background to Day Care Strike," n.d.; Dee Korman, "West End Daycare Dilemma," *West End Courier (Vancouver)*, 24 March 1976.

3 Allison Tom, "The Messy Work of Child Care: Addressing Feminists' Neglect of Child Care Workers," *Atlantis* 18, 1 & 2 (1992): 77.

4 Ellen Reese, "But Who Will Care for the Children? Organizing Child Care Providers in the Wake of Welfare Reform," in *Intimate Labors: Cultures, Technologies, and the Politics of Care*, ed. Eileen Boris and Rhacel Salazar Parreñas (Stanford, CA: Stanford University Press, 2010), 232.

5 Allison Tom, "Good Work in Canadian Childcare: Complicating the Love/Money Divide," *Atlantis* 29, 1 (Fall/Winter 2004): 35.

6 Our analysis is mostly limited to works published in English due to our limited abilities to read French. Unfortunately, many disciplines, including history, suffer from a "lack of dialogue" between francophone and anglophone scholars in Canada. For a useful discussion of the issue in regard to history, see Dominique Clément, "Generational Change and Writing Canadian History: Obstacles to an Inclusive National History," *Canadian Issues: Faire comprendre la réalité francophone canadienne: Le defi de renforcer l'identité par l'enseignement de l'histoire* (Summer 2011): 75–8, https://historyofrights.ca/wp-content/uploads/pubs/article_ACS_generation.pdf (accessed 19 October 2018).

7 E.P. Thompson, *The Making of the English Working Class* (New York: Vintage Books, 1966); Herbert Gutman, *Work, Culture, and Society in Industrializing America: Essays in American Working-Class and Social History* (New York: Knopf, 1976);

David Montgomery, *Workers' Control in America: Studies in the History of Work, Technology, and Labor Struggles* (New York: Cambridge University Press, 1979).

8 Corrective Collective, *Never Done: Three Centuries of Women's Work in Canada* (Toronto: Canadian Women's Educational Press, 1974), 141–50; Kathryn McPherson, *A "Round the Clock Job": A Selected Bibliography on Women's Work at Home in Canada* (Ottawa: Minister of Supply and Services Canada, 1983).

9 See the chapters by D. Suzanne Cross, Alison Prentice, and Marjorie Griffin Cohen in *The Neglected Majority: Essays in Canadian Women's History*, vol. 1, ed. Susan Mann Trofimenkoff and Alison Prentice (Toronto: McClelland and Stewart, 1977), and vol. 2 (Toronto: McClelland and Stewart, 1985). See also Pat Armstrong and Hugh Armstrong, *The Double Ghetto: Canadian Women and Their Segregated Work* (Toronto: McClelland and Stewart, 1978); Veronica Strong-Boag, "The Girl of the New Day: Canadian Working Women in the 1920s," *Labour / Le Travail* 4 (1979): 131–64; Marie Lavigne and Jennifer Stoddart, "Women's Work in Montreal at the Beginning of the Century," in *Women in Canada*, rev. ed., ed. Marylee Stephenson (Don Mills, ON: General Publishing Co., 1977), 129–47; Janice Acton, Penny Goldsmith, Bonnie Shepard, eds, *Women at Work: Ontario, 1850–1930* (Toronto: Canadian Women's Education Press, 1974); Francine Barry, *Le travail de la femme au Québec: L'évolution de 1940 à 1970* (Montreal: Les presses de l'Université du Québec, 1977).

10 Star Rosenthal, "Union Maids: Organized Women Workers in Vancouver, 1900–1915," *BC Studies* 41 (Spring 1979): 36–55; Sara Diamond, "A Union Man's Wife: The Ladies' Auxiliary Movement in the IWA, the Lake Cowichan Experience," in *Not Just Pin Money: Selected Essays on the History of Women's Work in British Columbia*, ed. Barbara K. Latham and Roberta J. Pazdro (Victoria, BC: Camosun College, 1984), 287–96; Linda Kealey and Joan Sangster, eds, *Beyond the Vote: Canadian Women and Politics* (Toronto: University of Toronto Press, 1989).

11 Marie Lavigne and Yolande Pinard, eds, *Les femmes dans la société québécoise: Aspects historiques* (Montreal: Boréal Express, 1977); Marie Lavigne and Yolande Pinard, eds, *Travailleuses et feminists: Les femmes dans la société Québécoise* (Montreal: Boréal Express, 1983); Andrée Lévesque, *Making and Breaking the Rules: Women in Quebec, 1919–1939*, trans. Yvonne M. Klein (Toronto: McClelland and Stewart, 1994), originally published in French in 1989 as *La norme et les déviantes: Des femmes au Québec pendant l'entre-deux-guerres*.

12 Ruth Frager, "No Proper Deal: Women Workers and the Canadian Labour Movement, 1870–1940," in *Union Sisters: Women in the Labour Movement*, ed. Linda Briskin and Lynda Yanz (Toronto: Women's Educational Press, 1983), 47.

13 Michèle Barrett and Roberta Hamilton, "Introduction," in *The Politics of Diversity: Feminism, Marxism, and Nationalism*, ed. Roberta Hamilton and Michèle Barrett (London: Verso, 1986), 16.

14 Bonnie Fox, ed., *Hidden in the Household: Women's Domestic Labour under Capitalism* (Toronto: Women's Press, 1980); Barrett and Hamilton, *Politics of Diversity*; Heather Jon Maroney and Meg Luxton, "From Feminism and Political Economy to Feminist Political Economy," in *Feminism and Political Economy: Women's Work, Women's Struggles*, ed. Heather Jon Maroney and Meg Luxton (Agincourt, ON: Methuen Publications, 1987); Margaret Benston, "The Political Economy of Women's Liberation," *Monthly Review* 21 (September 1969): 13–27. See also the articles in *Atlantis* (Fall 1981).

15 Ruth Roach Pierson, "The Politics of the Domestic Sphere," in *Canadian Women's Issues*, vol. 2, *Bold Visions*, ed. Ruth Roach Pierson and Marjorie Griffin Cohen (Halifax: James Lorimer and Co., 1993), 10.

16 Emily M. Nett, review of *Hidden in the Household*, ed. Bonnie Fox, *Canadian Journal of Sociology* 6, 4 (Autumn 1981): 528.

17 Linda Kealey, "Introduction," in Acton, Goldsmith, and Shepard, *Women at Work*, 7.

18 Veronica Strong-Boag, "Discovering the Home: The Last 150 Years of Domestic Work in Canada," in *Women's Paid and Unpaid Work: Historical and Contemporary Perspectives*, ed. Paula Bourne (Toronto: New Hogtown Press, 1985), 40; Barrett and Hamilton, "Introduction," 16.

19 Meg Luxton, *More Than a Labour of Love: Three Generations of Women's Work in the Home* (Toronto: Women's Educational Press, 1980).

20 Penny Kome, *Somebody Has to Do It: Whose Work Is Housework?* (Toronto: McClelland and Stewart, 1982); Strong-Boag, "Discovering the Home," 55; Ruth Roach Pierson, *"They're Still Women after All": The Second World War and Canadian Womanhood* (Toronto: McClelland and Stewart, 1986).

21 Sylvia Van Kirk, *Many Tender Ties: Women in Fur-Trade Society, 1670–1870* (Winnipeg: Watson and Dwyer, 1980); Jennifer Brown, *Strangers in Blood: Fur Trade Company Families in Indian Country* (Vancouver: UBC Press, 1980).

22 Dionne Brand, ed., with the assistance of Lois De Shield and the Immigrant Women's Job Placement Centre, *No Burden to Carry: Narratives of Black Working Women in Ontario, 1920s to 1950s* (Toronto: Women's Press, 1991); Dionne Brand, "'We Weren't Allowed to Go into Factory Work until Hitler Started the War': The 1920s to the 1940s," in *"We're Rooted Here and They Can't Pull Us Up": Essays in African Canadian Women's History*, ed. Peggy Bristow (Toronto: University of Toronto Press, 1994), 171–92.

23 Joan Sangster, "Women and Work: Assessing Canadian Women's Labour History at the Millennium," *Atlantis* 25, 1 (Fall/Winter 2000): 53.

24 Bettina Bradbury, *Working Families: Age, Gender, and Daily Survival in Industrializing Montreal* (Toronto: McClelland and Stewart, 1993); Suzanne Morton, *Ideal Surroundings: Domestic Life in a Working-Class Suburb in the 1920s* (Toronto: University of Toronto Press, 1995).

25 Franca Iacovetta, *Such Hardworking People: Italian Immigrants in Postwar Toronto* (Montreal: McGill-Queen's University Press, 1992).

26 Joan Sangster, "Feminism and the Making of Canadian Working-Class History: Exploring the Past, Present, and Future," *Labour / Le Travail* 46 (Fall 2000): 139; Bettina Bradbury, "Women's History and Working-Class History," *Labour / Le Travail* 19 (Spring 1987): 23–43; Joanne Burgess, "Exploring the Limited Identities of Canadian Labour: Recent Trends in English-Canada and Quebec," *International Journal of Canadian Studies* 1–2 (1990): 149–73.

27 Lydia Sargent, ed., *Women and Revolution: A Discussion of the Unhappy Marriage of Marxism and Feminism* (Montreal: Black Rose Books, 1981).

28 Sangster, "Feminism and the Making of Canadian Working-Class History," 147.

29 See, for example, the debate between Joan Sangster, Karen Dubinsky, Lynne Marks, Franca Iacovetta, and Linda Kealey that appeared in *Left History* 3, 1 (1995): 109–21, and 3, 2 (1995): 205–48.

30 Julie Guard, "Fair Play or Fair Pay? Gender Relations, Class Consciousness, and Union Solidarity in the Canadian UE, 1949 to 1955," *Labour / Le Travail* 37 (Spring 1996): 149–77; Linda Kealey, *Enlisting Women for the Cause: Women, Labour, and the Left in Canada, 1890–1920* (Toronto: University of Toronto Press, 1998); Gillian Creese, *Contracting Masculinity: Gender, Class, and Race in a White-Collar Union, 1944–1994* (Don Mills, ON: Oxford University Press Canada, 1999).

31 Joy Parr, *The Gender of Breadwinners: Women, Men, and Change in Two Industrial Towns, 1880–1950* (Toronto: University of Toronto Press, 1990), 9.

32 Joan Sangster, *Earning Respect: The Lives of Working Women in Small-Town Ontario, 1920–1960* (Toronto: University of Toronto Press, 1995); Mercedes Steedman, *Angels of the Workplace: Women and the Construction of Gender Relations in the Canadian Clothing Industry, 1890–1940* (Toronto: Oxford University Press, 1997).

33 Pamela Sugiman, *Labour's Dilemma: The Gender Politics of Auto Workers in Canada, 1937–1979* (Toronto: University of Toronto Press, 1994), 8–9.

34 Sedef Arat-Koç, "From 'Mothers of the Nation' to Migrant Workers," in *Not One of the Family: Foreign Domestic Workers in Canada*, ed. Abigail B. Bakan and Daiva Stasiulis (Toronto: University of Toronto Press, 1997), 54–80.

35 Abigail B. Bakan and Daiva K. Stasiulis, "Making the Match: Domestic Placement Agencies and the Racialization of Women's Household Work," *Signs* 20, 2 (Winter 1995): 303, emphasis added. See also Makeda Silvera, *Silenced: Talks with Working Class Caribbean Women about Their Lives and Struggles as Domestic Workers in Canada* (Toronto: Sister Vision Press, 1989); Marilyn Barber, *Immigrant Domestic Servants in Canada* (Ottawa: Canadian Historical Association, 1991).

36 Arat-Koç, "From 'Mothers of the Nation,'" 54; Lisa Chilton, *Agents of Empire: British Female Migration to Canada and Australia, 1860–1930* (Toronto: University of Toronto Press, 2007).

37 See the articles by Judy Fudge, Miriam Elvir, and Pura M. Velasco in Bakan and Stasiulis, *Not One of the Family*; Ruth Frager, *Sweatshop Strife: Class, Ethnicity, and Gender in the Jewish Labour Movement of Toronto, 1900–1939* (Toronto: University of Toronto Press, 1992).

38 Jennifer Blythe and Peggy Martin McGuire, "The Changing Employment of Cree Women in Moosonee and Moose Factory," in *Women of the First Nations: Power, Wisdom, and Strength*, ed. Christine Miller and Patricia Chuchryk (Winnipeg: University of Manitoba Press, 1996), 131.

39 John Lutz, "Gender and Work in Lekwammen Families," in *In the Days of Our Grandmothers: A Reader in Aboriginal Women's History in Canada*, ed. Mary-Ellen Kelm and Lorna Townsend (Toronto: University of Toronto Press, 2006), 241.

40 Alvin Finkel, *Social Policy and Practice in Canada: A History* (Waterloo: Wilfrid Laurier University Press, 2006), 7; James Struthers, *The Limits of Affluence: Welfare in Ontario* (Toronto: University of Toronto Press and Ontario Historical Studies Series, 1994), 3–18.

41 Ruth Pierson, "Women's Emancipation and the Recruitment of Women into the Labour Force in World War II," in *The Neglected Majority*, vol. 2, 125–45; Joan Sangster, "The 1907 Bell Telephone Strike: Organizing Women Workers," *Labour / Le Travail* 3 (1978): 109–30; Marilyn Barber, "The Women Ontario Welcomed: Immigrant Domestics for Ontario Homes, 1870–1930," in *The Neglected Majority*, vol. 2, 102–21; Margaret E. McCallum, "Keeping Women in Their Place: The Minimum Wage in Canada, 1910–25," *Labour / Le Travail* 17 (Spring 1986): 29–56.

42 Ann Porter, *Gendered States: Women, Unemployment Insurance, and the Political Economy of the Welfare State in Canada, 1945–1997* (Toronto: University of Toronto Press, 2003); Ruth Roach Pierson, "Gender and the Unemployment Insurance Debates in Canada, 1934–40," *Labour / Le Travail* 25 (Spring 1990): 77–103; Margaret Jane Hillyard Little, *No Car, No Radio, No Liquor Permit: The Moral Regulation of Single Mothers in Ontario, 1920–1997* (Toronto: Oxford University Press, 1998).

43 Suzanne Morton, *Wisdom, Justice, and Charity: Canadian Social Welfare through the Life of Jane B. Wisdom* (Toronto: University of Toronto Press, 2014).

44 Alvin Finkel, "Changing the Story: Gender Enters the History of the Welfare State," *Tijdschrift voor Sociale Geschiedenis* 22, 1 (1996): 67–81; Nancy Christie, *Engendering the State: Family, Work, and Welfare in Canada* (Toronto: University of Toronto Press, 2000); Lara Campbell, *Respectable Citizens: Gender, Family, and Unemployment in Ontario's Great Depression* (Toronto: University of

Toronto Press, 2009); Anne Forrest, "Securing the Male Breadwinner: A Feminist Interpretation of PC 1003," in *Labour Gains, Labour Pains: 50 Years of PC 1003*, ed. Cy Gonick, Paul Phillips, and Jesse Vorst (Winnipeg: Society for Socialist Studies; Halifax: Fernwood Publishing, 1995), 139–62.

45 Margaret Hillyard Little, "Claiming a Unique Place: The Introduction of Mothers' Pensions in BC," *BC Studies* 105–6 (Spring/Summer 1995): 80–102.

46 Jeanne Fay, "The 'Right Kind' of Single Mothers: Nova Scotia's Regulation of Women on Social Assistance, 1956–77," in *Mothers of the Municipality: Women, Work, and Social Policy in Post-1945 Halifax*, ed. Judith Fingard and Janet Guildford (Toronto: University of Toronto Press, 2005), 141–68; Lisa Pasolli, *Working Mothers and the Child Care Dilemma: A History of British Columbia's Social Policy* (Vancouver: UBC Press, 2015).

47 Annis May Timpson, *Driven Apart: Women's Employment Equality and Child Care in Canadian Public Policy* (Vancouver: UBC Press, 2001); Rianne Mahon, "The Never-Ending Story: The Struggle for Universal Child Care Policy in the 1970s," *Canadian Historical Review* 81, 4 (December 2000): 582–622.

48 Magda Fahrni, *Household Politics: Montreal Families and Postwar Reconstruction* (Toronto: University of Toronto Press, 2005), 58.

49 Jane Jenson, "Against the Current: Child Care and Family Policy in Quebec," in *Child Care Policy at the Crossroads: Gender and Welfare State Restructuring*, ed. Sonya Michel and Rianne Mahon (New York: Routledge, 2002): 310–11.

50 Joan Sangster, *Transforming Labour: Women and Work in Post-War Canada* (Toronto: University of Toronto Press, 2010); Katrina Srigley, *Breadwinning Daughters: Young Working Women in a Depression-Era City, 1929–1939* (Toronto: University of Toronto Press, 2010).

51 Meg Luxton, "Feminism as a Class Act: Working-Class Feminism and the Women's Movement in Canada," *Labour / Le Travail* 48 (Fall 2001): 63–88; Andrée Lévesque, ed., *Madeleine Parent: Activist* (Toronto: Sumach Press, 2005); Smith, "An 'Entirely Different' Kind of Union."

52 Karen C. Flynn, *Moving beyond Borders: A History of Black Canadian and Caribbean Women in the Diaspora* (Toronto: University of Toronto Press, 2011).

53 Mary Jane Logan McCallum, *Indigenous Women, Work, and History, 1940–1980* (Winnipeg: University of Manitoba Press, 2014).

54 Sangster, "Feminism and the Making of Working-Class History," 146–7.

55 Tom, "The Messy Work of Child Care," 77.

56 Ann Shola Orloff, "From Maternalism to 'Employment for All': State Policies to Promote Women's Employment across the Affluent Democracies," in *The State After Statism: New State Activities in the Age of Liberalization*, ed. Jonah D. Levy (Boston: Harvard University Press, 2006), 230–68; Margaret Little and Lynne Marks, "Ontario and British Columbia Welfare Policy: Variants on a

Neoliberal Theme," *Comparative Studies of South Asia, Africa, and the Middle East* 30, 2 (2010): 192–203.

57 In 2014, the federal government introduced a series of reforms to the LCP. The LCP is now one of three pathways to permanent residency under the Caregiver Program; the other two are the Caring for Children Pathway and the Caring for People with High Medical Needs Pathway. The latter two have no live-in requirement.

58 Ethel Tungohan et al., "After the Live-in Caregiver Program: Filipina Caregivers' Experiences of Graduated and Uneven Citizenship," *Canadian Ethnic Studies* 47, 1 (2015): 87–105; Geraldine Pratt, *Families Apart: Migrant Mothers and the Conflicts of Labor and Love* (Minneapolis: University of Minnesota Press, 2012).

59 Bakan and Stasiulis, "Making the Match," 331.

60 Paul Kershaw and Tammy Harkey, "The Politics and Power in Caregiving for Identity: Insights for Indian Residential School Truth and Reconciliation," *Social Politics* 18, 4 (2011): 590.

61 Margaret D. Jacobs, "Diverted Mothering among American Indian Domestic Servants, 1920–1940," in *Indigenous Women and Work: From Labor to Activism*, ed. Carol Williams (Chicago: University of Illinois Press, 2012), 179–80.

62 Lynne Marks et al., "'A Job That Should Be Respected': Contested Visions of Motherhood and English Canada's Second Wave Women's Movements, 1970–1990," *Women's History Review* 25, 5 (2016): 771–90. See also Lynne Marks, "Feminism and Stay-at-Home-Motherhood: Some Critical Reflections and Implications for Mothers on Social Assistance," *Atlantis* 28, 2 (Spring/Summer 2004): 73–83.

SELECTED READINGS

Acton, Janice, Penny Goldsmith, and Bonnie Shepard, eds. *Women at Work: Ontario, 1850–1930*. Toronto: Canadian Women's Educational Press, 1974.

Bakan, Abigail B., and Daiva Stasiulis, eds. *Not One of the Family: Foreign Domestic Workers in Canada*. Toronto: University of Toronto Press, 1997.

Barry, Francine. *Le travail de la femme au Québec: L'évolution de 1940 à 1970*. Montreal: Les presses de l'Université du Québec, 1977.

Bourne, Paula, ed. *Women's Paid and Unpaid Work: Historical and Contemporary Perspectives*. Toronto: New Hogtown Press, 1985.

Bradbury, Bettina. *Working Families: Age, Gender, and Daily Survival in Industrializing Montreal*. Toronto: McClelland and Stewart, 1993.

Brand, Dionne, ed., with the assistance of Lois De Shield and the Immigrant Women's Job Placement Centre. *No Burden to Carry: Narratives of Black Working Women in Ontario, 1920s to 1950s*. Toronto: Women's Press, 1991.

Bristow, Peggy, ed. *"We're Rooted Here and They Can't Pull Us Up": Essays in African Canadian Women's History*. Toronto: University of Toronto Press, 1994.

Campbell, Lara. *Respectable Citizens: Gender, Family, and Unemployment in Ontario's Great Depression*. Toronto: University of Toronto Press, 2009.

Christie, Nancy. *Engendering the State: Family, Work, and Welfare in Canada*. Toronto: University of Toronto Press, 2000.

Creese, Gillian. *Contracting Masculinity: Gender, Class, and Race in a White-Collar Union, 1944–1994*. Don Mills, ON: Oxford University Press Canada, 1999.

Flynn, Karen C. *Moving beyond Borders: A History of Black Canadian and Caribbean Women in the Diaspora*. Toronto: University of Toronto Press, 2011.

Fox, Bonnie, ed. *Hidden in the Household: Women's Domestic Labour under Capitalism*. Toronto: Women's Press, 1980.

Frager, Ruth. *Sweatshop Strife: Class, Ethnicity, and Gender in the Jewish Labour Movement of Toronto, 1900–1939*. Toronto: University of Toronto Press, 1992.

Iacovetta, Franca. *Such Hardworking People: Italian Immigrants in Postwar Toronto*. Montreal: McGill-Queen's University Press, 1992.

Kealey, Linda. *Enlisting Women for the Cause: Women, Labour, and the Left in Canada, 1890–1920*. Toronto: University of Toronto Press, 1998.

Kome, Penny. *Somebody Has to Do It: Whose Work Is Housework?* Toronto: McClelland and Stewart, 1982.

Latham, Barbara K., and Roberta J. Pazdro, eds. *Not Just Pin Money: Selected Essays on the History of Women's Work in British Columbia*. Victoria, BC: Camosun College, 1984.

Luxton, Meg. *More Than a Labour of Love: Three Generations of Women's Work in the Home*. Toronto: Women's Educational Press, 1980.

Maroney, Heather Jon, and Meg Luxton, eds. *Feminism and Political Economy: Women's Work, Women's Struggles*. Agincourt, ON: Methuen Publications, 1987.

McCallum, Mary Jane Logan. *Indigenous Women, Work, and History, 1940–1980*. Winnipeg: University of Manitoba Press, 2014.

Morton, Suzanne. *Ideal Surroundings: Domestic Life in a Working-Class Suburb in the 1920s*. Toronto: University of Toronto Press, 1995.

Parr, Joy. *The Gender of Breadwinners: Women, Men, and Change in Two Industrial Towns, 1880–1950*. Toronto: University of Toronto Press, 1990.

Pasolli, Lisa. *Working Mothers and the Child Care Dilemma: A History of British Columbia's Social Policy*. Vancouver: UBC Press, 2015.

Pierson, Ruth Roach. *"They're Still Women after All": The Second World War and Canadian Womanhood*. Toronto: McClelland and Stewart, 1986.

Porter, Ann. *Gendered States: Women, Unemployment Insurance, and the Political Economy of the Welfare State in Canada, 1945–1997*. Toronto: University of Toronto Press, 2003.

Sangster, Joan. *Earning Respect: The Lives of Working Women in Small-Town Ontario, 1920–1960*. Toronto: University of Toronto Press, 1995.

– *Transforming Labour: Women and Work in Post-War Canada*. Toronto: University of Toronto Press, 2010.

Steedman, Mercedes. *Angels of the Workplace: Women and the Construction of Gender Relations in the Canadian Clothing Industry, 1890–1940*. Toronto: Oxford University Press, 1997.

Sugiman, Pamela. *Labour's Dilemma: The Gender Politics of Auto Workers in Canada, 1937–1979*. Toronto: University of Toronto Press, 1994.

Timpson, Annis May. *Driven Apart: Women's Employment Equality and Child Care in Canadian Public Policy*. Vancouver: UBC Press, 2001.

13 Realizing Reproductive Justice in Canadian History

SHANNON STETTNER, KRISTIN BURNETT, AND
LORI CHAMBERS

Overwhelmingly the historical literature on women's reproductive health experiences in Canada has focused on a few narrow but important issues: how women have had children, specifically the circumstances surrounding pregnancy and childbirth, and the legalities surrounding women's ability not to have children, such as the availability of birth control, sterilization, and abortion. The literature tends to examine these issues individually, instead of in concert or as part of the spectrum of women's reproductive health experiences. Consequently, we are left with compartmentalized depictions of women's reproductive lives. Our chapter suggests that the historiography on abortion, birth control, pregnancy, and childbirth needs to more fully incorporate an intersectional approach, which is central to understanding how multiple and sometimes conflicting identities shape reproductive health and rights. Our analysis illuminates how embracing a reproductive justice framework complicates understandings of people's lives and helps to elucidate not only the institutional and social oppressions that affect reproduction, but also how those oppressions have shaped the (re)telling of reproductive histories. We examine the changing historiography of women's reproductive health, noting important parallels with the Canadian feminist movement and larger trends in Canadian history. We argue for shifting the focus away from concentrating primarily on the legality of various reproductive health practices to looking at the broader social, economic, and political conditions that determine who has the right to reproduce or not and under what conditions these events take place. Drawing on a reproductive justice framework would force scholars to push the boundaries of the questions we ask, not only of our research subjects but also of ourselves.

Defining Reproductive Justice and Embodying Intersectionality

In 1997 sixteen women of colour organizations in the United States came together to found SisterSong: Women of Color Reproductive Health Collective in order to build a coalition interested in moving beyond what they perceived as the polarizing and inadequate language used by both pro-choice and pro-life organizations.[1] SisterSong revived the term "reproductive justice" (originally coined in 1994) because it captured the structural and social changes that are required to bring about the transformation of a society that would truly place women in control of their reproductive lives. Loretta Ross, one of the founders and a long-time national coordinator of SisterSong, defines "reproductive justice" as the "complete physical, mental, spiritual, political, social and economic well-being of women and girls, based on the full achievement and protection of women's human rights."[2] Reproductive justice speaks to "the right to have children, not have children, and to parent the children we have in safe and healthy environments" and insists that it is the obligation of the state and the broader society to ensure that the social, political, economic, and cultural conditions necessary to exercise one's decisions exist for everyone.

Reproductive justice draws from epistemological interventions made by Black American feminists and legal scholars like Kimberlé Crenshaw.[3] In her influential 1989 work "Demarginalizing the Intersection of Race and Sex: A Black Feminist Critique of Antidiscrimination Doctrine, Feminist Theory and Antiracist Politics," Crenshaw made evident the limitations of regarding race and gender as "mutually exclusive categories of experience and analysis."[4] In other words, if we only see Black women as women, or as Black, we are ignoring how "one's location in multiple socially constructed categories affects one's lived experiences, social roles, and relative privilege or disadvantage."[5] We need, as Crenshaw urges, to see that the "elision of difference in identity politics is problematic, fundamentally because the violence that many women experience is often shaped by other dimensions of their identities, such as race and class."[6]

Intersectionality is at the heart of reproductive justice, but conversations about the adoption of "reproductive justice" in Canada are more recent than in the United States. In 2011, activist Jessica (Yee) Danforth, the founder and executive director of the Native Youth Sexual Health Network, argued that reproductive justice has been unevenly accepted by the "pro-choice" movement here. She observed a "deeply-entrenched reluctance to adopt reproductive justice at all" as well as a more nominal adoption of the term, arguing that reproductive justice "appears to be this 'add-on' of 'it looks good to have it' so even if it's included in an organization's mandate, their policies, procedures, and practices don't change."[7] While some improvement is evident since 2011 on the activist front, academics in Canada have similarly been slow to adopt a reproductive justice approach in studies of reproductive health issues, and thus a framework that truly considers or makes visible women's intersecting and sometimes competing/conflicting categories of identity.

The Contours of Women's Reproductive Health Historiography

Several parallels can be drawn between the growth of women's reproductive health historiography and the rise of the modern Canadian feminist movement. The writing of women's history has gone through several stages. Women's history emerged as a crucial component of social history, a branch of history that focuses on investigating the lives of "ordinary" people, especially marginalized groups whose stories had largely been absent from dominant historical narratives.[8] Despite efforts to focus on everyday people inherent in social history, initially many historians of women's history conducted what has been identified by Gerda Lerner as a kind of "compensatory history";[9] that is, early efforts to incorporate women and reproductive issues into the historical narrative focused on telling stories about "great women." In the reproductive health context, such works tended to look at figures like Emily Stowe and Helen MacMurchy.[10] Although more recent scholarship continues to include these women, greater attention is now directed to assessing their historical legacy within a complex story that includes their pro-eugenics and forced-sterilization politics as significant elements of their feminist practice.[11] A reproductive justice approach demands that complexity be acknowledged and that multiple voices be heard. The histories of childbirth and midwifery, and of the legal regulation of reproduction, have only just begun to adopt this approach.

In considering the conditions under which women give birth, women's experiences frequently have been reduced to singular and essentialized notions of what defines/determines womanhood and what stands for the "average" experience. Such interpretations do not allow for understandings of race, class, sexuality, ethnicity, gender identity, and space. The inclusion of settler colonialism as an essential point of analysis within all women's reproductive histories has been limited, for instance. Indeed, colonization, as it is studied within Canada, is read almost solely as the problem of the colonized and not as it pertains to the colonizers as well. The history of midwifery illustrates why a reproductive justice framework is necessary (but too often still has not been adopted). Until very recently, conventional examinations of midwifery in Canada outlined a very narrow history wherein the demise of midwifery was located at the turn of the nineteenth century with the allopathic assault in concert with the rise of specialities in obstetrics and a growing desire of medical doctors to assert their authority over women's bodies and broaden their fee schedule to include childbirth (a guaranteed income).[12] Most accounts of midwifery do not consider the continued use of midwives by ethnic communities, who also drew on these women's expertise when their European Canadian and urban counterparts were largely having hospital births.[13] However, recent historiography has complicated this monolithic narrative to suggest that space (and race) played enormous roles in determining the decline of midwifery and the nature of the relationship between doctors and midwives. Works like *Reconceiving Midwifery* and *Push!* have offered a broader evaluation of midwifery in terms of geography, suggesting that midwifery practices persisted in rural and northern regions far longer than in urban and southern locales.[14] Still, very little has been written on the reproductive experiences of Black and other racialized women in Canada. As Karen Flynn and Funké Aladejebi discuss in their chapter in this collection, the "writing of Black Canadian women's history is still in its recovery stages."

An examination of the work of midwives also opens up the category of "midwife" to individuals who are concerned with more than just the "catching of babies."[15] A recent work on Mennonite midwives' reproductive practice and knowledge was not limited to childbirth but also included a broad range of healing work that formed a core part of social, and community, relationships.[16] For instance, many women who practised as midwives also served as undertakers and general healers. Similarly, Indigenous women provided an enormous range of curative and caregiving practices in their communities and to newcomers in western Canada.[17] Nor did the relationships of Indigenous midwives begin and end with childbirth; instead they "maintained long-term relationships with the children they helped bring into the world," forming a complex web of social networks through informal systems of health and caregiving.[18] Work by activist-academic Jessica Shaw, while not historical, also illustrates the connections between abortion and midwifery as basic equity issues that need to be examined within a reproductive justice framework.[19] Clearly, there is a growing and healthy literature on midwifery, pregnancy, and childbirth, including new works published in a 2014 special issue of the *Canadian Bulletin of Medical History* on reproductive health history in Canada. Although these articles continue to be largely dominated by the middle-class, white experience, gender, age, and class have been more conscientiously examined.[20] Indeed, a recent consideration of underage or teen pregnancy has made a significant addition to the literature that complicates when and how women or girls experience reproduction and the roles played by allied health care professions.[21]

The bulk of reproductive historiography in Canada, however, still examines the struggle to gain access to effective birth control and the decriminalization of abortion. This makes sense when we consider that many of the academics writing those histories were engaged with second wave feminism, and decriminalizing abortion was one of the major issues such feminists sought to address. These works trace the contours of Canada's abortion laws after Confederation, underscoring the enduring impact of the first Criminal Code of Canada in 1892, which established abortion as a crime and made the sale, distribution, or advertisement of contraception or abortifacients illegal. In 1969 a series of revisions were made to the code that included the decriminalization of homosexuality, birth control, and therapeutic abortions.[22] Within these studies, the efforts of physicians, clergy, and politicians, among others, to criminalize and decriminalize (and recriminalize) contraception and abortion have been dominant themes.[23] This focus on legality, however, obscures the lived experiences of marginalized groups, for whom legal rights too often remain abstract and unattainable.

Multiple historians have illustrated that birth control gained broader public support largely in the context of the Great Depression and was increasingly seen as another solution to widespread and intractable poverty.[24] In this environment, governments, churches, political groups, and social organizations were concerned with the purported over-reproduction of those deemed undesirable – racialized, Indigenous, poor, immigrant, and ethnic women – in other words, those women who strayed from the white, Anglo-Saxon, Protestant, middle-class ideal.[25] Birth control clinics were established in most major cities in North America, and although clinics faced legal challenges they were eventually tolerated.[26] However, services were reserved for those married women who had their husbands' permission and had already borne a couple of children or those women deemed unfit to procreate.[27] Access to birth control was not about the right of women to control their own bodies but rather about the perceptions of the dominant society regarding who should have children.

Before the Second World War, birth control advocates sought to limit the fecundity of those women perceived to be "unfit." Of particular concern to many social reformers were individuals characterized as mentally or physically disabled. Such individuals were disproportionately targeted under Alberta's Eugenics Laws (and eugenics laws and underground abortion practice, in other provinces).[28] Work on the eugenics movement in Canada illustrates the deeply conservative nature of the birth control lobby and draws explicit connections between birth control, sterilization, and nation-building.[29] Indeed, making women and their reproductive capabilities responsible for the perceived "racial degeneration" of Canadian society firmly situated women's reproductive choices within the public domain and therefore rendered women subject to increasing scrutiny and regulation.[30] Significant works in the field have shown how sterilization, fuelled by fears about growing urbanization, immigration, racial impurity, and disability, was a mechanism employed by the state to control how marginalized populations reproduced, raised their children, and determined the contours of their lives and communities.[31]

Comparatively there has been a relative dearth of works that examine the history of abortion and birth control in Canada from the 1930s to the 1960s, aside from the aforementioned state-sponsored eugenics and sterilization programs. This focus has a great deal to do with the historiographical tendency that has characterized women's struggles for equality as a series of movements or waves and the greater visibility of the abortion rights movement during the 1960s and onward. In focusing primarily on law, and on questions that have been central to their own activism, such histories, inadvertently, have narrowed the field of study with regard to reproduction to regularly exclude the conditions under which women rear their children, as well as the impact of race, class, and ethnicity on the experiences of reproduction. In a context in which social supports for poor, racialized minorities and single (particularly unwed) mothers were very limited,[32] marginalized peoples faced, and continue to face, very different challenges than those most often considered by birth control and abortion activists and scholars.

In addition to confronting disproportionate surveillance, racialized and marginalized communities also struggled to feed their families and to raise their children under situations in which parenting practices and traditional knowledges were regarded as inferior by the dominant society. While middle-class white women fought for the ability to limit their fertility (and to enjoy their sexuality), Indigenous and racialized women fought to keep and raise their children. Indigenous communities and families were under assault.[33] The assimilative efforts of the federal and provincial governments criminalized Indigenous motherhood, which became embodied in the forced removal of children, first through residential schools and later through provincial child welfare policies infamously referred to as the "Sixties Scoop." It is troubling to note that such practices continue in modern guise today: Indigenous peoples in Canada make up only 3 per cent of the population yet make up more than 40 per cent of the children currently in foster care.[34] The federal government and churches and their missionary organizations have worked very hard to force Indigenous peoples to adopt European Canadian childrearing practices. The stereotype of Indigenous women "as unfit parents in need of state observation, guidance, and intervention" has a long and powerful history in Canada,[35] and there is an enormous body of literature on these topics, yet the experiences of Indigenous women are not included in accounts of reproductive history if we focus exclusively on law and abortion.[36]

Indigenous women face the simultaneous constraints of settler colonialism and sexism: in other words, the embodied violence faced by Indigenous women has everything to do with their identities as Indigenous people and as women. For instance, the state's use of sterilization against Indigenous women functioned simultaneously as a cost-saving public measure and to serve the interests of capital, facilitate the expropriation of Indigenous lands, undermine Indigenous sovereignty, and impair the ability of communities to be healthy and to have healthy children.[37] A recent work notes that even though there was no formal sterilization legislation that existed in northern Canada (broadly defined to include the provincial North and the Arctic), unlike in Alberta and British Columbia, there is evidence that Inuit, Métis, and First Nations women were sterilized with the knowledge of Indian Health Services.[38] Sterilization (as used against Indigenous peoples) can be viewed as part of a larger process "to separate Aboriginal peoples from their lands and resources while reducing the numbers of those to whom the federal government has obligations."[39] Therefore, we need to be cognizant of not only the significance of land as sitting at the heart of how settler colonialism is operationalized but also how land as sacred is intimately tied to Indigenous concepts of reproductive justice and community well-being. Scholars exploring the impact of industrial pollution on the Aamjiwnaang First Nation argue that assaults on Indigenous bodies need to be read as a total embodied assault on culture and community. Accordingly, "policy geared toward decolonization and social equity must move away from the singularity of the female body involved in birth and reproduction to think more broadly about the contextually embedded reproducing body."[40] This means that reproductive history cannot focus primarily on abortion and birth control when some women were explicitly denied the right to have children and for their communities to continue to exist as vibrant healthy entities.

The literature on abortion and reproductive rights in Canada, however, does not generally include work on sterilization, or broader questions of reproductive autonomy beyond the right not to have children. In part, this was fuelled by ideological and activist concerns in the 1990s when Canadian women faced assaults on the right to abort; attempts by the anti-choice movement to have the fetus declared a person dominated the abortion landscape in the 1980s and 1990s. Many works in this era originated from within the discipline of political science instead of history, and their focus on political discourse meant that their attention was on dominant meanings and the process of meaning making, not on the lived experiences of women contending with reproductive health issues and confronting the laws governing women's bodies.[41] Since the legal status of abortion has been formally settled (despite occasional challenges to the status quo), in recent studies the focus has shifted away from legal battles, and historians have begun to explore the personal and intimate reproductive experiences and challenges of average women in Canada (although this continues to be a largely white and middle-class project). Here such works have focused on the development of the birth control pill;[42] grassroots organizing around birth control information at Canadian universities in the 1960s and 1970s;[43] surveillance of birth control and abortion activists by the RCMP;[44] links between abortion activism and the anti-war movement in the early 1970s;[45] ongoing problems women face in regard to abortion access and the subsequent emergence of abortion "tourism" within Canada;[46] and women's discussions of birth control and abortion within the Royal Commission on the Status of Women.[47]

Responding to a re-evaluation of the uneven availability of abortion on request in Canada are recent and growing critiques of the roles provincial governments have played in denying women access to abortion – in spite of the 1988 Supreme Court *Morgentaler* decision. Some provincial governments continue to refuse to integrate abortion into the "publicly funded health care system," and access remains difficult or impossible in rural and northern regions across the country.[48] Such scholarship has also included an exploration of anti-abortion organizations, especially historical (and ongoing) opposition to abortion in the Maritimes.[49] These works outline the political and legal struggles women and their allies faced and continue to face, and they illustrate how access remains an illusion for many women. As a result, academics have also begun to explore what women do in the absence of access, although this avenue of inquiry remains a nascent one. Nonetheless, while extremely important, many of these studies continue to examine abortion in relative isolation – that is, as a decision, action, or procedure in response to a reproductive moment or episode – but one divorced from a woman's familial or community life and the larger structures that in many ways predetermine her choice(s).

The voices captured in these studies are overwhelmingly those of privileged white, middle-class women who could speak and act publicly in ways that many marginalized women could not and cannot. For instance, while the rise of abortion tourism is troubling, the financial and social resources required to undertake such trips lie beyond the reach of many women. Although these works are critical of limited visions of reproductive autonomy, they generally do not explore the experiences of marginalized and racialized women. To some extent, this myopia reflects the largely white, middle-class nature of both the mainstream women's movement in Canada and the composition of women academics at Canadian universities more generally. Many of the concerns that affect poor and racialized women are not caught up within the purview of the abortion rights movement and are better situated within a reproductive justice framework. This oversight reveals how far certain colonized, racialized, marginalized, and disadvantaged groups in Canada are from even entering into discussions about birth control and abortion as relevant to their lives. Instead, they continue to have to fight for their very right to exist as distinct cultures and peoples. Sterilization is an obvious example of this paradox. While primarily white, middle-class women advocated for the right to access sterilization as a form of permanent birth control, Indigenous and other racialized and marginalized women were struggling to resist forced or coerced sterilization.[50] Reproductive oppression looks very different for white, middle-class women seeking to overcome criminalization or medicalization and to win the right not to reproduce than it does for racialized women who are seeking the rights and the means to reproduce, raise the children they have, and keep their families and communities safe and intact.[51] Similarly, historical scholarship in Canada is largely silent when it comes to issues of transgender, genderqueer, and non-binary (gender-non-conforming) people, and reproductive health history is no exception. This is an area in which scholars need to do better in future studies; we regret having failed to do so in this piece. Reproductive histories that include a reproductive justice analysis must consider how "reproductive bodies are used as mechanisms of oppression against whole communities."[52] Thus, the incorporation of reproductive justice more firmly into historical inquiry necessitates a shift away from a legalistic, rights-based framework of choice that emphasizes the protection of individuals to a framework that includes broader social and political contexts and communities, as well as an understanding of collective rights and obligations.

Applying a Reproductive Justice Framework

Women's reproductive choices are not simply reflective of isolated moments or episodes frozen in time; rather they are cumulative decisions located within the social, political, economic, cultural, and legal structures and contours of their lives. As Audre Lorde points out, "we do not live single-issue lives."[53] Expanding on this idea, Loretta Ross maintains that the "ability of any woman to determine her own reproductive destiny is directly linked to the conditions in her community and these conditions are not just a matter of individual choice and access."[54] Therefore, we suggest that scholars who work within the historical frames of labour, family, child welfare, health and health care, domestic violence, state oppression, and control must consider many of the structural barriers and issues that are faced by racialized and marginalized women.

Incorporating these intersectional approaches within women's reproductive health histories requires us to better situate women's reproductive experiences as reflective of a "full spectrum" of social, economic, and political considerations. Part of the answer lies in writing narratives that incorporate a diversity of experiences.[55] Social history moved us away from grand narratives, but we still have a tendency to apply local findings to the national level. There is no one history but, as Lesley Biggs has argued, multiple, ongoing, and concurrent histories.[56] The structural barriers that prevent women (and entire communities) from accessing necessary resources are where we should shift our focus.

The inclusion of systems of power as an essential point of analysis within women's reproductive histories has also been limited. There are numerous intersecting power systems affecting reproductive health choices, including settler colonialism, capitalism, patriarchy, globalization, racism/white supremacy, heterosexism, transphobia, and so forth. As space constraints do not allow for an assessment of all, we will briefly explore white supremacy and colonialism as structures that privilege particular groups over others and allow people with a particular skin colour (white) to accrue unearned privilege. White supremacy is employed to describe the structural inequalities that result from and reinforce the continued supremacy of whites over non-whites. Typically when academics examine the impact of racism and colonialism on Indigenous and racialized communities and women, they address them in isolation, firmly locating these issues within the bodies of the colonized and not the colonizer. We need to broaden this discussion to recognize these systems of power as fundamentally rooted within the very structures of a white settler society and not just those communities most obviously and negatively affected. SisterSong believes that liberation is possible only when those who are the most vulnerable are able to exercise all of their human rights without fear, discrimination, or retaliation. The most marginalized communities must have access to the resources and power necessary to live self-determined lives; only then can we call our society "free."

In terms of reproductive justice, greater attention to white supremacy pushes us to examine the voices and perspectives that are missing in the pieces we write. Most of the reproductive health histories that have been written have told the story of white, middle-class women. More often than not, this focus is addressed with a statement that explains the inherent biases in sources (e.g., that written sources are often left by women who both are literate and have leisure time) and left there. We contend that we need to do a better job of asking ourselves some hard questions, such as why are we okay stopping where we do, why is it acceptable that some voices are left out of the histories we write, why is my focus white, middle-class women, and then how can I change that? Arundhati Roy observes, "There's really no such thing as the 'voiceless.' There are only the deliberately silenced, or the preferably unheard."[57] Sometimes finding marginalized voices is a matter of addressing the biases within ourselves, looking in new places, or reconsidering the definitions of what we call knowledge. To write more inclusive and representative histories, we need to be more concerned about *choosing* to listen to the voices and experiences of marginalized and racialized women – both historically and in the ways in which we carry out our work. By being aware of and questioning our complicity in power structures and systems from which we benefit, we begin to construct more inclusive histories. As scholars, centring the experiences of the most marginalized may mean that we have to work beyond or outside our expertise – by creating academic and community partnerships that provide an opening beyond the material directly, and comfortably, in front of us (and traditionally considered to be the subject matter of history). It also means that we cannot disconnect our academic work from our activist work. The scholarship we produce has real-life meaning and consequences; women's lives are impacted by our complicity in structures of power. We have to be answerable to the communities with whom we work and to make sure the research we undertake is driven by the needs of communities and action-oriented, particularly when working with Indigenous communities. Importantly, this needs to happen alongside a questioning of the whiteness of academe and its lack of racial and ethnic diversity. The structures of academe, which are embedded within the colonial and white supremacist system, need to be challenged as well.

Conclusion

A reproductive justice framework challenges us to explore the divergent reproductive experiences of women based on issues of class, ethnicity, race, language, ability, age, sexual identity, religion, and relationship status, among other factors. Examining structural inequalities – both historical and those that shape our current research – means not accepting imaginary "silences" in the historical narratives and going beyond the traditional limits of what historians have been taught to use as sources. Reproductive justice forces us to acknowledge greater disparity of experience across Canada and to see commonality of experiences across national boundaries. Moving beyond studies that address these issues only peripherally will result in telling a history that is more complicated and better reflects women's lives and the impact of reproductive policies on the "oppression [of] whole communities."[58] We must move away from a legalistic rights-based framework of choice and consider broader social and political contexts, collective rights, and obligations. And we must be committed to changing those contexts and realities. Ultimately, incorporating a reproductive justice framework within reproductive historiography will require not only that the scope of the histories we write be broadened, but also that the profession itself be transformed: marginalized peoples must be in academe to tell their own stories.

NOTES

1 On reproductive justice, see Loretta Ross, "What Is Reproductive Justice?" *The Pro-Choice Public Education Project*, available at http://www.protectchoice.org/section.php?id=28, accessed 18 October 2014; Kimberlé Crenshaw, "Mapping the Margins: Intersectionality, Identity Politics, and Violence against Women of Color," *Stanford Law Review* 43, 6 (1991): 1242; Kimberlé Crenshaw, "Demarginalizing the Intersection of Race and Sex: A Black Feminist Critique of Antidiscrimination Doctrine, Feminist Theory, and Antiracist Politics," *University of Chicago Legal Forum* 140 (1989): 139–67.

2 Loretta Ross, "Understanding Reproductive Justice: Transforming the Pro-Choice Movement," *Off Our Backs* 36, 4 (2006): 14.

3 Patricia Hill Collins, *Black Feminist Thought: Knowledge, Consciousness, and the Politics of Empowerment* (New York: Routledge, 2000). See also foundational theorists like Audre Lorde, *Sister Outsider: Essays and Speeches* (Freedom: Crossing Press, 1984); Deborah King, "Multiple Jeopardy, Multiple Consciousness: The Context of Black Feminist Ideology," *Signs: Journal of Women in Culture and Society* 14, 1 (1988): 42; Hortense Spillers, "Interstices: A Small Drama of Words," in *Pleasure and Danger: Exploring Female Sexuality*, ed. Carole S. Vance (Boston: Routledge and Kegan Paul, 1984), 73–100; Crenshaw, "Demarginalizing the Intersection of Race and Sex," 139.

4 Crenshaw, "Demarginalizing the Intersection of Race and Sex," 139.

5 Karen Jones, "Intersectionality and Ameliorative Analyses of Race and Gender," *Philosophy Studies* 171, 1 (2014): 100.

6 Crenshaw, "Mapping the Margins," 1242.

7 Jessica Yee, "Reproductive Justice – for Real, for Me, for You, for Now," in *Sister-Song: Women of Color Reproductive Justice Collective Anthology* (forthcoming). Yee's full essay is available online at http://jolocas.blogspot.ca/2011/11/reproductive-justice.html, accessed 20 January 2013.

8 For examples of such works see Franca Iacovetta, *Such Hardworking People: Italian Immigrants in Postwar Toronto* (Montreal: McGill-Queen's University Press, 1992); Franca Iacovetta and Wendy Mitchinson, eds, *On the Case: Explorations in Social History* (Toronto: University of Toronto Press, 1998).

9 Gerda Lerner, "Placing Women in History: Definitions and Challenges," *Feminist Studies* 3, 1 (1975): 5–14.

10 For a largely uncritical and laudatory history of Margaret Sanger in the United States, see Ellen Chesler, *Woman of Valor: Margaret Sanger and the Birth Control Movement in America* (New York: Simon and Schuster, 1976). For a similar account of Marie Stopes in Great Britain, see J. Rose, *Marie Stopes and the Sexual Revolution* (London: Faber and Faber, 1992). The movement was less developed in Canada and studies of its impact are limited. See Angus McLaren, "What Has This to Do with Working Class Women," *Histoire sociale / Social History* 14, 28 (1981): 435–54; Angus McLaren, "The First Campaign for Birth Control Clinics in British Columbia," *Journal of Canadian Studies* 19, 3 (1984): 50–64; and Angus McLaren, "Keep Your Seats and Face Facts: Western Canadian Women's Discussions of Birth Control in the 1920s," *Canadian Bulletin of Medical History* 8, 1 (1991): 187–201.

11 Mariana Valverde, "'When the Mother of the Race Is Free': Race, Reproduction, and Sexuality in First-Wave Feminism," in *Gender Conflicts: New Essays in Women's History*, ed. Franca Iacovetta and Mariana Valverde (Toronto: University of Toronto Press, 1992); Sheila Gibbons, "'Our Power to Remodel Civilization': The Development of Eugenic Feminism in Alberta, 1909–1921," *Canadian Bulletin of Medical History* 31, 1 (2014): 123–42.

12 Jo Oppenheimer, "Childbirth in Ontario: The Transition from Home to Hospital in the Early Twentieth Century," *Ontario History* 75 (1983): 36–60.

13 Marlene Epp, "Midwife-Healers in Canadian Mennonite Immigrant Communities: Women Who Made Things Right," *Histoire sociale / Social History* 60 (November 2007): 323–44; Lesley Biggs, "The Case of the Missing Midwives: A History of Midwifery in Ontario from 1795–1900," *Ontario History* 65, 1 (1983): 21–35; and Veronica Strong-Boag and Kathryn McPherson, "The Confinement of Women: Childbirth and Hospitalization in Vancouver, 1919–1939," *BC Studies* 69/70 (1986): 142–74.

14 Ivy Lynn Bourgeault, Cecilia Benoit, and Robbie Davis-Floyd, *Reconceiving Midwifery* (Montreal: McGill-Queen's University Press, 2004); Denyse Baillargeon, *Babies for the Nation: The Medicalization of Motherhood in Quebec, 1910–1970* (Waterloo: Wilfrid Laurier University Press, 2004).

15 Ivy Lynn Bourgeault, *Push! The Struggle for Midwifery in Ontario* (Montreal: McGill-Queen's University Press, 2006).

16 Marlene Epp, "Catching Babies and Delivering the Dead: Midwives and Undertakers in Mennonite Settlement Communities," in *Caregiving on the Periphery: Historical Perspectives on Nursing and Midwifery in Canada*, ed. Myra Rutherdale (Montreal: McGill-Queen's University Press, 2010), 61–83; Wendy Mitchinson, *The Nature of Their Bodies: Women and Their Doctors in Victorian Canada* (Toronto: University of Toronto Press, 1991).

17 Kristin Burnett, *Taking Medicine: Women's Healing Work and Colonial Contact in Southern Alberta, 1880–1930* (Vancouver: UBC Press, 2010).

18 Kristin Burnett, "Obscured Obstetrics: Indigenous Midwives in Western Canada," in *Recollecting: Lives of Aboriginal Women of the Canadian Northwest and Borderlands*, ed. Sarah Carter and Patricia McCormack (Edmonton: Athabasca University Press, 2012), 169.

19 Jessica Shaw, "Abortion as a Social Justice Issue in Contemporary Canada," *Critical Social Work* 14, 2 (2013): 2–17, http://www1.uwindsor.ca/criticalsocialwork/ abortion_in_canada, accessed 18 May 2015; Jessica Shaw, "The Medicalization of Birth and Midwifery as Resistance," *Health Care for Women International* 34, 6 (2013): 522–36. https://doi.org/10.1080/07399332.2012.736569.

20 Nevertheless, we acknowledge Joan Sangster's caution in this volume not to conflate "multiple categories, such as white and middle-class ... into a unitary designation."

21 Sharon Wall, "They're More Children Than Adults: Teens, Unmarried Pregnancy, and the Canadian Medical Profession," *Canadian Bulletin of Medical History* 31, 2 (2014): 49–69; Sharon Wall, "'Some Thought They Were 'in Love'": Sex, White Teenagehood, and Unmarried Pregnancy in Early Postwar Canada," *Journal of the Canadian Historical Association / Revue de la Société historique du Canada* 25, 1 (2014): 207–41.

22 See A. Anne McLellan, "Abortion Law in Canada," in *Abortion, Medicine, and the Law*, ed. J. Douglas Butler and David F. Walbert (New York: Facts on File, 1992), 334; Shelley A.M. Gavigan, "On 'Bringing on the Menses': The Criminal Liability of Women and the Therapeutic Exception in Canadian Abortion Law," *Canadian Journal of Women and the Law* 1, 2 (1986): 279–312; Constance Backhouse, "Involuntary Motherhood: Abortion, Birth Control, and the Law in Nineteenth-Century Canada," *Windsor Yearbook of Access to Justice* 3 (1983): 61–130.

23 Following Lord Ellenborough's Act was Lord Lansdowne's Act (1828), which criminalized instrumental abortions both before and after quickening (in addition to those abortions brought on by noxious substances). See John Keown, *Abortion, Doctors, and the Law: Some Aspects of the Legal Regulation of Abortion in England from 1803 to 1982* (Cambridge: Cambridge University Press, 1988): 26–48. Shannon Stettner's dissertation focused on recovering women's voices in the discussion of abortion reform that dominated the 1960s: Stettner, "Women and Abortion in English Canada: Public Debates and Political Participation, 1959–1970" (PhD diss., York University, 2011), 4–22.

24 Angus McLaren and Arlene Tigar McLaren, *The Bedroom and the State: The Changing Practices and Politics of Contraception and Abortion in Canada, 1880–1997* (Toronto: University of Toronto Press, 1997); Angus McLaren, "The First

Campaign for Birth Control Clinics in British Columbia," *Journal of Canadian Studies* 19, 3 (1984): 50–64; Linda Revie, "More Than Just Boots! The Eugenic and Commercial Concerns behind A.R. Kaufman's Birth Controlling Activities," *Canadian Bulletin of the History of Medicine* 23, 1 (2006): 119–43.

25 Jana Grekul, "Sterilization in Alberta, 1928–1972: Gender Matters," *Canadian Review of Sociology* 45, 3 (2008): 247–66; Jana Grekul, "A Well-Oiled Machine: Alberta's Eugenics Program, 1928–1972," *Alberta History* 59, 3 (2011): 16–24; Erika Dyck, *Facing Eugenics: Reproduction, Sterilization, and the Politics of Choice* (Toronto: University of Toronto Press, 2013).

26 Dianne Dodd, "The Canadian Birth Control Movement on Trial," *Histoire sociale / Social History* 16, 32 (1983): 411–28; Revie, "More Than Just Boots!"; and McLaren, *The Bedroom and the State.*

27 Dianne Dodd, "The Hamilton Birth Control Clinic of the 1930s," *Ontario History* 75, 1 (1983): 71–86.

28 Jana Grekul, Arvey Krahn, and Dave Odynak, "Sterilizing the Feeble-Minded: Eugenics in Alberta, Canada, 1929–1972," *Journal of Historical Sociology* 17, 4 (2004): 358–84; and Dyck, *Facing Eugenics.*

29 Valverde, "When the Mother of the Race Is Free."

30 Gerald Thomson, "A Baby Show Means Work in the Hardest Sense: The Better Baby Contests of the Vancouver and New Westminster Local Councils of Women," *BC Studies* 128 (2000): 12. The Alberta *Sexual Sterilization Act* – passed in 1928, revised in 1937 and 1942, and not repealed until 1972 – is the most studied example of such legislation in Canada, but British Columbia also passed sterilization laws, and sterilization bills were proposed and debated in other provinces: Timothy Caulfield and Gerald Robertson, "Eugenic Policies in Alberta: From Systematic to Systemic?" *Alberta Law Review* 35 (1996): 59–79; and Dyck, *Facing Eugenics.*

31 Valverde, "When the Mother of the Race Is Free"; Dyck, *Facing Eugenics;* Joan Sangster, *Regulating Girls and Women: Sexuality, Family, and the Law in Ontario, 1920–1960* (Don Mills, ON: Oxford University Press, 2001); Constance Backhouse, *Petticoats and Prejudice: Women and Law in Nineteenth-Century Canada* (Toronto: Women's Press, 1998); Mariana Valverde, *The Age of Light, Soap, and Water: Moral Reform in English Canada, 1885–1925* (Toronto: McClelland and Stewart, 1991).

32 Lori Chambers, *Misconceptions: Unmarried Motherhood and the Ontario Children of Unmarried Parents Act, 1921–1969* (Toronto: University of Toronto Press and the Osgoode Society for Legal History, 2008); Lori Chambers,"Unwed Mothers, the Children's Aid Society, Adoption, and the Rhetoric of Choice in Ontario, 1921–1969," *Ontario History* 97, 2 (2006), 161–82; and Lori Chambers, *A Legal History of Adoption in Ontario, 1921–2015* (Toronto: University of Toronto Press and the Osgoode Society for Legal History, 2016).

33 Nor can we overlook the experiences of recently arrived immigrants and state efforts to produce "new Canadians" through the denigration of cultural practices and the imposition of European Canadian domesticity like culinary practices. See, for example, Heidi Bohaker and Franca Iacovetta, "Citizenship Programs for Newcomers and Indigenous Peoples in Postwar Canada, 1940s–1960s," *Canadian Historical Review* 90, 3 (2009): 427–61; Franca Iacovetta, "Jell-O Salads, One-Stop Shopping, and Maria the Homemaker: The Gender Politics of Food," in *Sisters or Strangers? Immigrant, Ethnic, and Racialized Women in Canadian History*, ed. Marlene Epp, Franca Iacovetta, and Francis Swyripa (Toronto: University of Toronto Press, 2004), 190–232. With regard to Indigenous women, see D. Memmee Lavell-Harvard and Jeanette Corbiere Lavell, eds, *"Until Our Hearts Are on the Ground": Aboriginal Mothering, Oppression, Resistance, and Rebirth* (Toronto: Demeter Press, 2006).

34 Randi Cull, "Aboriginal Mothering under the State's Gaze," in Lavell-Harvard and Lavell, *Until Our Hearts Are on the Ground,* 149.

35 Cull, "Aboriginal Mothering," 141.

36 There is a wealth of literature on residential schooling in Canada. For example, see, Truth and Reconciliation Commission of Canada (TRC), *Honouring the Truth, Reconciling for the Future: Summary of the Final Report of the Truth and Reconciliation Commission of Canada*, 2015. The full report is available at http://www.trc.ca/websites/trcinstitution/index.php?p=890; TRC, *They Came for the Children: Canada, Aboriginal Peoples, and Residential Schools* (Winnipeg: Canadian Truth and Reconciliation Commission, 2012); John Milloy, *A National Crime: The Canadian Government and the Residential School System, 1879 to 1986* (Winnipeg: University of Manitoba Press, 1999); Roland Chrisjohn and Sherri Young, *The Circle Game: Shadows and Substance in the Indian Residential School Experience* (Penticton First Nation: Theytus Books, 1997). For examples of the Canadian child welfare system see Vandha Sinha and Anna Kozlowski, "The Structure of Aboriginal Child Welfare in Canada," *International Indigenous Policy Journal* 4, 2 (2013): 1–21; Brittany Baker, Gerald Taiaiake Alfred, and Thomas Kerr, "An Uncaring State? The Overrepresentation of First Nations Children in the Canadian Child Welfare System," *Canadian Medical Association Journal* 186, 14 (2014): E533–35; Lori Chambers, "Indigenous Children and Provincial Child Welfare: The 'Sixties Scoop,'" in *Aboriginal History in Canada*, 2nd ed., ed. Kristin Burnett and Geoff Read (Don Mills, ON: Oxford University Press, 2016); and Allyson Stevenson, "Vibrations across a Continent: The 1978 Indian Child Welfare Act and the Politicization of First Nations Leaders in Saskatchewan," *American Indian Quarterly* 37, 1 (2013): 218–36.

37 Karen Stote, "The Coercive Sterilization of Aboriginal Women in Canada," *American Indian Culture and Research Journal* 26, 3 (2012): 117–50; Grekul,

"Sterilization in Alberta"; Grekul, "A Well-Oiled Machine"; Jane Lawrence, "The Indian Health Service and the Sterilization of Native American Women," *American Indian Quarterly* 24, 3 (2000): 400–19; Sally Torpy, "Native American Women and Coerced Sterilization: On the Trail of Tears in the 1970s," *American Indian Culture and Research Journal* 24, 2 (2000): 1–23.

38 Stote, "Coercive Sterilization"; Karen Stote, *An Act of Genocide: Colonialism and the Sterilization of Aboriginal Women* (Halifax: Fernwood, 2015).

39 Stote, "Coercive Sterilization," 141.

40 Sarah Marie Wiebe and Erin Marie Konsmo, "Indigenous Body as Contaminated Site? Examining Struggles for Reproductive Justice in Aamjiwnaang," in *Fertile Ground: Exploring Reproduction Canada*, ed. Stephanie Paterson, Francesca Scala, and Marlene Sokolon (Montreal: McGill-Queen's University Press, 2014): 325–58. See also Winona LaDuke, "Akwesasne: Mohawk Mothers' Milk and PCBs," in *All Our Relations: Native Struggles for Land and Life* (Cambridge, MA: South End Press, 1999), 11–26.

41 See, for example, Janine Brodie, Shelley Gavigan, and Jane Jensen, *The Politics of Abortion* (Toronto: Oxford University Press, 1992); and Gail Kellough, *Aborting Law: An Exploration of the Politics of Motherhood and Medicine* (Toronto: University of Toronto Press, 1996).

42 Christabelle Sethna, "A Bitter Pill: Second Wave Feminist Critiques of Oral Contraception," in *Canada: Confederation to the Present*, ed. Bob Hesketh and Chris Hackett (Edmonton: Chinook Multimedia, 2001); Jessica Haynes, "The Great Emancipator? The Impact of the Birth Control Pill on Married Women in English Canada" (PhD diss., Carleton University, 2013).

43 Christabelle Sethna, "The University of Toronto Health Service, Oral Contraception, and Student Demand for Birth Control," *Historical Studies in Education* 17, 2 (2005): 265–92; Christabelle Sethna, "Chastity Outmoded: The Ubyssey: Sex and the Single Girl, 1960–1970," in *Creating Post-War Canada: Community, Diversity, and Dissent*, ed. Magda Fahrni and Robert Rutherdale (Vancouver: UBC Press, 2008), 289–314; and Christabelle Sethna, "The Evolution of the Birth Control Handbook," *Canadian Bulletin of Medical History* 23 (2006): 89–118.

44 Christabelle Sethna and Stephen Hewitt, "Clandestine Operations: The Vancouver Women's Caucus, the Abortion Caravan, and the RCMP," *Canadian Historical Review* 90, 3 (2009): 463–96.

45 Shannon Stettner, "We Are Forced to Declare War: Linkages between the 1970 Abortion Caravan and Women's Anti-Vietnam War Activism," *Histoire sociale / Social History* 46, 92 (November 2013): 423–41.

46 Christabelle Sethna and Marion Doull, "Far from Home? A Pilot Study Tracking Women's Journeys to a Canadian Abortion Clinic," *Journal of Obstetrics and Gynaecology Canada* 29, 8 (August 2007): 640–7; Beth Palmer, "Lonely, Tragic,

but Legally Necessary Pilgrimages: Transnational Abortion Travel in the 1970s," *Canadian Historical Review* 92, 4 (2011): 637–64; Christabelle Sethna, Beth Palmer, Katrina Ackerman, and Nancy Janovicek, "Choice Interrupted: Travel and Inequality of Access to Abortion Services since the 1960s," *Labour / Le Travail* 7 (2013): 29–48; Christabelle Sethna, "All Aboard: Canadian Women's Abortion Tourism, 1960–1980," in *Gender, Health, and Popular Culture*, ed. Cheryl Warsh (Waterloo: Wilfrid Laurier University Press, 2011): 89–108. On access, see also Nancy Janovicek, "Protecting Access to Abortion Services in Rural Canada: A Case Study of the West Kootenays, British Columbia," *Magazine of Women's History* 73, Special Issue on Abortion (2013): 19–28.

47 Shannon Stettner, "He Is Still Unwanted: Women's Assertions of Authority over Abortion in Letters to the Royal Commission on the Status of Women," *Canadian Bulletin of Medical History* 29, 1 (2012): 151–71.

48 Joanne Erdman, "In the Back Alleys of Health Care: Abortion, Equality, and Community in Canada," *Emory Law Journal* 56, 4 (2007): 1093–156. See also Howard A. Palley, "Canadian Abortion Policy: National Policy and the Impact of Federalism and Political Implementation on Access to Services," *Publius: The Journal of Federalism* 36, 4 (2006): 565–86.

49 Katrina Ackerman, "Not in the Atlantic Provinces: The Abortion Debate in New Brunswick, 1980–1987," *Acadiensis* 41, 1 (2012): 75–101; Katrina Ackerman, "In Defence of Reason: Religion, Science, and the Prince Edward Island Anti-Abortion Movement, 1969–1988," *Canadian Bulletin of Medical History* 31, 2 (2014): 117–38; Colleen MacQuarrie, Jo-Ann MacDonald, and Cathrine Chambers, *Trials and Trails of Accessing Abortion in PEI: Reporting on the Impact of PEI's Abortion Policies on Women*, January 2014, http://colleenmacquarrie.blogspot.com/2014/01/research-report-understanding-for.html.

50 Stettner, "He Is Still Unwanted," 160; Revie, "More Than Just Boots!," 135; McLaren and McLaren, *The Bedroom and the State*, 134; Stote, *An Act of Genocide*, 46–100.

51 For more on reproductive oppression, see Shaw, "Full-Spectrum Reproductive Justice," 143–59.

52 Barbara Gurr, *Reproductive Justice: The Politics of Health Care for Native American Women* (New Brunswick, NJ: Rutgers University Press, 2015), 26.

53 Audre Lorde, *Sister Outsider: Essays and Speeches* (Berkeley, CA: Crossing Press, 2012).

54 Loretta Ross, "Understanding Reproductive Justice," *Trust Black Women*, March 2011, http://www.trustblackwomen.org/our-work/what-is-reproductive-justice/9-what-is-reproductive-justice, accessed 31 January 2016.

55 We draw this phrasing from Shaw, "Full-Spectrum Reproductive Justice."

56 Biggs, "Rethinking the History of Midwifery in Canada," 17–45.

57 Arundhati Roy, "The 2004 Sydney Peace Prize Lecture: Peace and the New
Corporate Liberation Theology," *University of Sydney News Blog*, 4 November
2004, http://sydney.edu.au/news/84.html?newsstoryid=279, accessed 24 October
2014.
58 Gurr, *Reproductive Justice*, 26.

SELECTED READINGS

Reproductive Justice

Gurr, Barbara. *Reproductive Justice: The Politics of Health Care for Native American Women*. New Brunswick, NJ: Rutgers University Press, 2015.
Shaw, Jessica. "Abortion as a Social Justice Issue in Contemporary Canada." *Critical Social Work* 14, 2 (2013). http://www1.uwindsor.ca/criticalsocialwork/abortion_in_canada
– "Full-Spectrum Reproductive Justice: The Affinity of Abortion Rights and Birth Activism." *Studies in Social Justice* 7, 1 (2013): 143–59. https://doi.org/10.26522/ssj.v7i1.1059
Wiebe, Sarah Marie, and Erin Marie Konsmo. "Indigenous Body as Contaminated Site? Examining Struggles for Reproductive Justice in Aamjiwnaang." In *Fertile Ground: Exploring Reproduction in Canada*, edited by Stephanie Paterson, Francesca Scala, and Marlene Sokolon, 325–58. Montreal: McGill-Queen's University Press, 2014.
Yee, Jessica. "Reproductive Justice – for Real, for Me, for You, for Now." In *SisterSong: Women of Color Reproductive Justice Collective Anthology* (forthcoming). Found online at http://jolocas.blogspot.ca/2011/11/reproductive-justice.html, accessed 20 January 2013.

Intersectionality

Collins, Patricia Hill. *Black Feminist Thought: Knowledge, Consciousness, and the Politics of Empowerment*. New York: Routledge, 2000.
Crenshaw, Kimberlé. "Demarginalizing the Intersection of Race and Sex: A Black Feminist Critique of Antidiscrimination Doctrine, Feminist Theory, and Antiracist Politics." *University of Chicago Legal Forum* 140 (1989): 139–67.
– "Mapping the Margins: Intersectionality, Identity Politics, and Violence against Women of Color." *Stanford Law Review* 43, 6 (1991): 1241–99. https://doi.org/10.2307/1229039
Jones, Karen. "Intersectionality and Ameliorative Analyses of Race and Gender." *Philosophy Studies* 171, 1 (2014): 99–107.

King, Deborah. "Multiple Jeopardy, Multiple Consciousness: The Context of Black Feminist Ideology." *Signs: Journal of Women in Culture and Society* 14, 1 (1988): 42–72. https://doi.org/10.1086/494491

Lorde, Audre. *Sister Outsider: Essays and Speeches.* Berkeley, CA: Crossing Press, 1984.

Ross, Loretta. "Understanding Reproductive Justice: Transforming the Pro-Choice Movement." *Off Our Backs* 36, 4 (2006): 14–19.

Spillers, Hortense. "Interstices: A Small Drama of Words." In *Pleasure and Danger: Exploring Female Sexuality*, edited by Carole S. Vance, 73–100. Boston: Routledge and Kegan Paul, 1984.

Midwifery

Bourgeault, Ivy Lynn. *Push! The Struggle for Midwifery in Ontario.* Montreal: McGill-Queen's University Press, 2006.

Bourgeault, Ivy Lynn, Cecilia Benoit, and Robbie Davis-Floyd. *Reconceiving Midwifery.* Montreal: McGill-Queen's University Press, 2004.

Burnett, Kristin. "Obscured Obstetrics: Indigenous Midwives in Western Canada." In *Recollecting: Lives of Aboriginal Women of the Canadian Northwest and Borderlands*, edited by Sarah Carter and Patricia McCormack, 157–71. Edmonton: Athabasca University Press, 2012.

Epp, Marlene. "Catching Babies and Delivering the Dead: Midwives and Undertakers in Mennonite Settlement Communities." In *Caregiving on the Periphery: Historical Perspectives on Nursing and Midwifery in Canada*, edited by Myra Rutherdale, 61–88. Montreal: McGill-Queen's University Press, 2010.

– "Midwife-Healers in Canadian Mennonite Immigrant Communities: Women Who Made Things Right." *Histoire sociale / Social History* 80 (2007): 323–44.

Shaw, Jessica. "The Medicalization of Birth and Midwifery as Resistance." *Health Care for Women International* 34, 6 (2013): 522–36. https://doi.org/10.1080/07399 332.2012.736569

Motherhood

Baillargeon, Denyse. *Babies for the Nation: The Medicalization of Motherhood in Quebec, 1910–1970.* Waterloo: Wilfrid Laurier University Press, 2004.

Chambers, Lori. *A Legal History of Adoption in Ontario, 1921–2015.* Toronto: University of Toronto Press and the Osgoode Society for Legal History, 2016.

– *Misconceptions: Unmarried Motherhood and the Ontario Children of Unmarried Parents Act, 1921–1969.* Toronto: University of Toronto Press and the Osgoode Society for Legal History, 2008.

Comacchio, Cynthia. *Nations Are Built of Babies: Saving Ontario's Mothers and Children, 1900–1940*. Montreal: McGill-Queen's University Press, 1993.

Cull, Randi. "Aboriginal Mothering under the State's Gaze." In *"Until Our Hearts Are on the Ground": Aboriginal Mothering, Oppression, Resistance, and Rebirth*, edited by D. Memmee Lavell-Harvard and Jeanette Corbiere Lavell, 141–56. Toronto: Demeter Press, 2006.

Wall, Sharon. "They're More Children than Adults: Teens, Unmarried Pregnancy, and the Canadian Medical Profession." *Canadian Bulletin of Medical History* 31, 2 (2014): 49–69.

Birth Control

Dodd, Dianne. "The Canadian Birth Control Movement on Trial." *Histoire sociale / Social History* 16, 32 (1983): 411–28.

– "The Hamilton Birth Control Clinic of the 1930s." *Ontario History* 75, 1 (1983): 71–87.

Revie, Linda. "More Than Just Boots! The Eugenic and Commercial Concerns behind A.R. Kaufman's Birth Controlling Activities." *Canadian Bulletin of Medical History* 23, 1 (2006): 119–43. https://doi.org/10.3138/cbmh.23.1.119

Sethna, Christabelle. "A Bitter Pill: Second Wave Feminist Critiques of Oral Contraception." In *Canada: Confederation to the Present*, edited by Bob Hesketh and Chris Hackett. Edmonton: Chinook Multimedia, 2001.

– "Chastity Outmoded: The Ubyssey, Sex, and the Single Girl, 1960–1970." In *Creating Post-War Canada: Community, Diversity, and Dissent*, edited by Magda Fahrni and Robert Rutherdale, 289–314. Vancouver: UBC Press, 2008.

– "The Evolution of the Birth Control Handbook." *Canadian Bulletin of Medical History* 23 (2006): 89–118. https://doi.org/10.3138/cbmh.23.1.89

– "The University of Toronto Health Service, Oral Contraception, and Student Demand for Birth Control." *Historical Studies in Education* 17, 2 (2005): 265–92.

Abortion

Ackerman, Katrina. "In Defence of Reason: Religion, Science, and the Prince Edward Island Anti-Abortion Movement, 1969–1988." *Canadian Bulletin of Medical History* 31, 2 (2014): 117–38. https://doi.org/10.3138/cbmh.31.2.117

– "Not in the Atlantic Provinces: The Abortion Debate in New Brunswick, 1980–1987." *Acadiensis* 41, 1 (2012): 75–101.

Backhouse, Constance. "The Celebrated Abortion Trial of Dr Emily Stowe, Toronto, 1879." *Canadian Bulletin of Medical History* 8, 2 (1991): 159–87. https://doi.org/10.3138/cbmh.8.2.159

– "Involuntary Motherhood: Abortion, Birth Control, and the Law in Nineteenth-Century Canada." *Windsor Yearbook of Access to Justice* 3 (1983): 61–130.

– *Petticoats and Prejudice: Women and Law in Nineteenth-Century Canada*. Toronto: Women's Press, 1992.

– "Physicians, Abortions, and the Law in Early Twentieth-Century Ontario." *Canadian Bulletin of Medical History* 10 (1993): 229–49. https://doi.org/10.3138/cbmh.10.2.229

Brodie, Janine, Shelley Gavigan, and Jane Jensen. *The Politics of Abortion*. Toronto: Oxford University Press, 1992.

Erdman, Joanne. "In the Back Alleys of Health Care: Abortion, Equality, and Community in Canada." *Emory Law Journal* 56, 4 (2007): 1093–156.

Janovicek, Nancy. "Protecting Access to Abortion Services in Rural Canada: A Case Study of the West Kootenays, British Columbia." *Magazine of Women's History* 73, Special Issue on Abortion (Autumn 2013): 19–28.

MacQuarrie, Colleen, Jo-Ann MacDonald, and Cathrine Chambers. *Trials and Trails of Accessing Abortion in PEI: Reporting on the Impact of PEI's Abortion Policies on Women*, January 2014. http://colleenmacquarrie.blogspot.com/2014/01/research-report-understanding-for.html

McLaren, Angus. "Illegal Operations: Women, Doctors, and Abortion, 1886–1939." *Journal of Social History* 26, 4 (1993): 797–816. https://doi.org/10.1353/jsh/26.4.797

McLaren, Angus, and Arlene Tigar McLaren. *The Bedroom and the State: The Changing Practices and Politics of Contraception and Abortion in Canada, 1880–1997*. 1986; rprt. Toronto: Oxford University Press, 1997.

Palley, Howard A. "Canadian Abortion Policy: National Policy and the Impact of Federalism and Political Implementation on Access to Services." *Publius: The Journal of Federalism* 36, 4 (2006): 565–86. https://doi.org/10.1093/publius/pjl002

Palmer, Beth. "Lonely, Tragic, but Legally Necessary Pilgrimages: Transnational Abortion Travel in the 1970s." *Canadian Historical Review* 92, 4 (2011): 637–64. https://doi.org/10.3138/chr.92.4.637

Sethna, Christabelle. "All Aboard: Canadian Women's Abortion Tourism, 1960–1980." In *Gender, Health, and Popular Culture*, edited by Cheryl Warsh, 89–108. Waterloo: Wilfrid Laurier University Press, 2011.

Sethna, Christabelle, and Marion Doull. "Far from Home? A Pilot Study Tracking Women's Journeys to a Canadian Abortion Clinic." *Journal of Obstetrics and Gynaecology Canada* 29, 8 (August 2007): 640–7. https://doi.org/10.1016/S1701-2163(16)32560-9

Sethna, Christabelle, and Stephen Hewitt. "Clandestine Operations: The Vancouver Women's Caucus, the Abortion Caravan, and the RCMP." *Canadian Historical Review* 90, 3 (2009): 463–96. https://doi.org/10.3138/chr.90.3.463

Sethna, Christabelle, Beth Palmer, Katrina Ackerman, and Nancy Janovicek. "Choice Interrupted: Travel and Inequality of Access to Abortion Services since the 1960s." *Labour / Le Travail* 7 (2013): 29–48.

Stettner, Shannon. "We Are Forced to Declare War: Linkages between the 1970 Abortion Caravan and Women's Anti-Vietnam War Activism." *Histoire sociale / Social History* 46, 92 (2013): 423–41.

– "He Is Still Unwanted: Women's Assertions of Authority over Abortion in Letters to the Royal Commission on the Status of Women." *Canadian Bulletin of Medical History* 29, 1 (2012): 151–71. https://doi.org/10.3138/cbmh.29.1.151

Sterilization

Caulfield, Timothy, and Gerald Robertson. "Eugenic Policies in Alberta: From Systematic to Systemic?" *Alberta Law Review* 35 (1996): 59–79.

Dyck, Erika. *Facing Eugenics: Reproduction, Sterilization, and the Politics of Choice*. Toronto: University of Toronto Press, 2013.

Grekul, Jana. "Sterilization in Alberta, 1928–1972: Gender Matters." *Canadian Review of Sociology* 45, 3 (2008): 247–66. https://doi.org/10.1111/j.1755-618X.2008.00014.x

– "A Well-Oiled Machine: Alberta's Eugenics Program, 1928–1972." *Alberta History* 59, 3 (2011): 16–24.

Lawrence, Jane. "The Indian Health Service and the Sterilization of Native American Women." *American Indian Quarterly* 24, 3 (2000): 400–19. https://doi.org/10.1353/aiq.2000.0008

Stote, Karen. *An Act of Genocide: Colonialism and the Sterilization of Aboriginal Women*. Halifax: Fernwood, 2015.

– "The Coercive Sterilization of Aboriginal Women in Canada." *American Indian Culture and Research Journal* 26, 3 (2012): 117–50.

Torpy, Sally. "Native American Women and Coerced Sterilization: On the Trail of Tears in the 1970s." *American Indian Culture and Research Journal* 24, 2 (2000): 1–22. https://doi.org/10.17953/aicr.24.2.7646013460646042

Law/Morality

Backhouse, Constance. *Petticoats and Prejudice: Women and Law in Nineteenth-Century Canada*. Toronto: Women's Press of Canada, 1999.

Sangster, Joan. *Regulating Girls and Women: Sexuality, Family, and the Law in Ontario, 1920–1960*. Don Mills, ON: Oxford University Press, 2001.

Valverde, Mariana. *The Age of Light, Soap, and Water: Moral Reform in English Canada, 1885–1925*. Toronto: McClelland and Stewart, 1991.

Contributors

Funké Aladejebi is an assistant professor of history and gender and women's studies at the University of New Brunswick. She is currently working on a manuscript titled "'Girl You Better Apply to Teachers' College': The History of Black Women Educators in Ontario, 1940s–1980s," which explores the importance of Black Canadian women in sustaining their communities and preserving a distinct Black identity within restrictive gender and racial barriers. She has published articles in *Ontario History* and *Education Matters*. Her research interests are in oral history, the history of education in Canada, Black feminist thought, and transnationalism.

Denyse Baillargeon is a professor of history at the University of Montreal. A specialist in the history of women, children, and health, she is the author of many scholarly works on these subjects. Her book *Un Québec en mal d'enfants: La médicalisation de la maternité, 1910–1970* (Remue-ménage, 2004) – translated in 2009 as *Babies for the Nation: The Medicalization of Maternity in Quebec, 1910–1970* (Wilfrid Laurier University Press) – won the Clio-Québec Prize from the Canadian Historical Association, the Lionel-Groulx – Yves Saint-Germain prize from the Institut d'histoire de l'Amérique française, and the Jean-Charles-Falardeau awarded by the Canadian Federation of the Humanities and Social Sciences. She is also the author of *Brève histoire des femmes au Québec* (Boréal, 2012), translated as *A Brief History of Women in Quebec* (Wilfrid Laurier University Press, 2014). Her current research examines public financing campaigns for Sainte-Justine Hospital from the 1920s to the 1960s; advertising for over-the-counter drugs in Quebec from 1920 to 1970; and, with Josette Brun and Estelle Lebelle, the *Femmes d'Aujourd'hui* television program broadcast by Radio-Canada from 1966 to 1982.

Tarah Brookfield is an associate professor in history and youth and children's studies at Wilfrid Laurier University. She is the author of *Cold War Comforts: Canadian Women, Child Safety, and Global Insecurity* (Wilfrid Laurier University Press, 2012) and *Our Voices Must Be Heard: Women and the Vote in Ontario* (UBC Press, 2018).

Kristin Burnett is an associate professor in the Department of Indigenous Learning and the coordinator of the graduate program in social justice studies at Lakehead University. She is the author of *Taking Medicine: Women's Healing Work and Colonial Contact in Southern Alberta, 1880–1930*. Her current research project looks at the relationships between health, food sovereignty, and colonialism in northern First Nations communities.

Lori Chambers is a professor in the Department of Women's Studies at Lakehead University, where she teaches courses in feminist theory, women's legal history, reproductive justice, and queer studies.

Marlene Epp is a professor of history and peace and conflict studies at Conrad Grebel University College at the University of Waterloo. Her teaching and research interests include the history of immigrants and refugees in Canada, Mennonite studies, and food history. She is co-editor of *Sisters or Strangers? Immigrant, Ethnic, and Racialized Women in Canadian History* (University of Toronto Press, 2016) and author of *Refugees in Canada: A Brief History* (Canadian Historical Association, 2017).

Karen Flynn is an associate professor in the Departments of Gender and Women's Studies and African American Studies at the University of Illinois, Urbana-Champaign. Dr Flynn's book *Moving beyond Borders: Black Canadian and Caribbean Women in the African Canadian Diaspora* (University of Toronto Press, 2011) won the Lavinia L. Dock Award from the American Association of the History of Nursing.

Nancy Forestell is a professor jointly appointed to the Department of History and the Women's and Gender Studies Program at St Francis Xavier University. Her research has appeared in such journals as *Labour / Le Travail*, *Atlantis: Critical Studies in Gender, Culture, and Social Justice*, and *Labor: Studies in Working-Class History of the Americas*. Along with Maureen Moynagh she is co-editor of the two-volume *Documenting First Wave Feminisms* (vol. 1: *Transnational Collaborations and Crosscurrents*; vol. 2: *Canada: National and Transnational Contexts*).

Sarah Glassford is a social historian of twentieth-century Canada with a PhD from York University. She is the author of *Mobilizing Mercy: A History of the Canadian Red Cross* (McGill-Queen's University Press, 2017) and co-editor with Amy Shaw of *A Sisterhood of Suffering and Service: Women and Girls of Canada and Newfoundland during the First World War* (UBC Press, 2012).

Susan M. Hill is an associate professor of history and the director of the Centre for Indigenous Studies at the University of Toronto. She is a Haudenosaunee citizen from Six Nations of the Grand River Territory. Her areas of research include Haudenosaunee history, Indigenous research methodologies and ethics, and Indigenous territoriality. She is the author of *The Clay We Are Made Of: Haudenosaunee Land Tenure on the Grand River* (University of Manitoba Press, 2017).

Franca Iacovetta is a professor of history at University of Toronto, co-editor of the Studies in Gender and History series (University of Toronto Press), and past president of the Berkshire Conference of Women Historians. Co-editor of *Sisters or Strangers?* (University of Toronto Press, 2016) and the *Women's History Review* theme issue on Luisa Passerini (2016), Dr Iacovetta is completing a book on women's community-based pluralism.

Nancy Janovicek is an associate professor of history at the University of Calgary. She is the author of *No Place to Go: Local Histories of the Battered Women's Shelter Movement* (UBC Press, 2007) and co-edited with Catherine Carstairs *Writing Feminist History: New Essays on Women, Gender, Work, and Nation* (UBC Press, 2012). She is the 2016 winner of the Marion Dewar Prize in Canadian Women's History.

Mary Jane Logan McCallum is a professor of history at the University of Winnipeg. She is of Lunaape heritage and a member of the Munsee Delaware Nation. Her areas of interest include Indigenous-state relations, Indigenous women's history, and modern Indigenous history, especially in the fields of health, education, and labour. Her first book is *Indigenous Women, Work, and History, 1940–1980*, and she is currently studying modern Indigenous histories of tuberculosis.

Katherine M.J. McKenna is an associate professor in the Departments of History and Women's Studies and Feminist Research at the University of Western Ontario. Her research and publication has focused on women's and gender history in the late eighteenth to early twentieth centuries in a North Atlantic context, the life and work of Winnipeg journalist E. Cora Hind, violence against women and children, and more recently, colonial East African women's and gender history.

Carmen Nielson is an associate professor of history in the Department of Humanities at Mount Royal University, Calgary, and the author of *Private Women and the Public Good: Charity and State Formation in Hamilton, Ontario, 1846–93* (UBC Press, 2014). Her work has been published in *Gender and History*, *Women's History Review*, and *Canadian Historical Review*. Her article "Caricaturing Colonial Space: Indigenized, Feminized Bodies and Anglo-Canadian Identity, 1873–1894" (*CHR*, December 2015) won the 2015 Hilda Neatby prize for best English-language article published in Canada in women's and gender history.

Lisa Pasolli is an assistant professor of history at Queen's University. Her teaching and research interests include Canadian, women's and gender, and social policy history, and she is the author of several works on the history of childcare politics in Canada, including her award-winning book *Working Mothers and the Child Care Dilemma: A History of British Columbia's Social Policy*.

Beth A. Robertson is a historian of gender, sexuality, and the body. Her recently released book, *Science of the Séance: Transnational Networks and Gendered Bodies in the Study of Psychic Phenomena, 1918–1940* (UBC Press, 2016), utilizes the insights of queer theory and feminist technoscience to analyse a transnational network of interwar psychical researchers and mediums. Robertson is currently a sessional lecturer and research associate at Carleton University in Ottawa.

Joan Sangster is Vanier Chair and a member of the Department of Gender and Women's Studies at Trent University. She has published monographs and articles relating to feminist historiography; law and the criminalization of women; and women, work, and the labour movement. Her book *The Iconic North: Images of Aboriginal Life in Postwar Canada* (UBC Press, 2016) won the CHA/SHC Clio-North Prize from the Canadian Historical Association. Her latest book is *One Hundred Years of Struggle: The History of Women and the Vote in Canada* (UBC Press, 2018).

Julia Smith is a Banting Postdoctoral Fellow and Honorary Grant Notley Memorial Postdoctoral Fellow in the Department of Sociology at the University of Alberta. She has published articles on feminist union organizing and labour relations in the service sector.

Heather Stanley is an instructor at Vancouver Island University. A historian of gender and sexuality, she is in the last stages of completing a monograph on the sexual lives of Canadian women during the post–Second World War era. She is currently working on a social history of postpartum depression and maternal mental illness within Canada in the twentieth century.

Shannon Stettner teaches in the Women's Studies Department at the University of Waterloo. Her research examines abortion rights and reproductive justice activism in Canada. She has edited several collections, including *Without Apology: Writings on Abortion in Canada* (Athabasca University Press, 2016); *Transcending Borders: Abortion in the Past and Present* (Palgrave Macmillan, 2017); and *Abortion: History, Politics, and Reproductive Rights after Morgentaler* (UBC Press, 2018).

Index

Aberdeen, Lady, 171, 173, 188
abolitionism. *See* ex-slaves; slavery
abolitionists, 179–80, 195n42
Aborigines' Protection Society, 187
abortion, 302, 303–4, 311n23. *See also*
  reproductive justice
academe: and activism, 308; and
  feminist scholars, 12; and Indigenous
  peoples, 15, 28, 45–6; and
  power, 260; and racism, 14; and
  self-glorification, 41; and white
  supremacy, 307–8
academic histories vs. community
  histories, 11, 33–4, 41
Acadian expulsion, 151
account books, 111
activism: abortion, 303, 304–5;
  and academe, 308; and Best, 74;
  biographies, 73–4; Black women,
  74–5; and feminism wave metaphor,
  174; feminist history, 175–6;
  historians, 8; Indigenous women,
  32, 47–8 (*see also* Idle No More);
  modern, 16–17. *See also* grassroots
Adamson, Nancy, 204
African Americans. *See* Black people;
  Black women; Black women's history

The Age of Light, Soap, and Water
  (Valverde), 260–1
agency: and bodies, 146n24; and
  feminism, 137; and history, 32;
  history in feminism, 131–2; and
  interior sense of self/exterior social
  acts, 141–2; of Métis women, 259;
  and rationality, 140–1; rearticulation
  of, 143–4; and religion, 130–1,
  135–8, 225; and scholarship, 40; and
  spiritualism, 140, 142–4; women in
  war, 153–4
Agnew, Vijay, 206
Aladejebi, Funké, 63–89, 321
alcohol, 118, 120. *See also* taverns
Alexander, Nina Mae, 80
amateur vs. professional history/
  preservation: historians, 8, 11,
  26–7, 33–4, 37; Quebec history,
  94–5; women's and gender history, 8,
  26–7, 33–4
Ancestors in the Archives, 35
Anderson, Bonnie, 179
Androsoff, Ashleigh, 243
Angélique, Marie-Joseph, 77, 237
Anglicans, 119, 137
Anne of Green Gables, 273n38

Studies in Gender and History

General Editors: Franca Iacovetta and Karen Dubinsky